Tanja Reiffenrath
Memoirs of Well-Being

body cultures

Tanja Reiffenrath works in Student and Academic Services at the University of Goettingen, Germany. Her research interests include socially inclusive pedagogies and the internationalization of the curricula.

Tanja Reiffenrath
Memoirs of Well-Being
Rewriting Discourses of Illness and Disability

[transcript]

This thesis was accepted as a doctoral dissertation in fulfillment of the requirements for the degree »Doktor der Philosophie« by the Faculty of Arts and Humanities at the University of Paderborn in 2015.

Bibliographic information published by the Deutsche Nationalbibliothek
The Deutsche Nationalbibliothek lists this publication in the Deutsche Nationalbibliografie; detailed bibliographic data are available in the Internet at http://dnb.d-nb.de

© 2016 transcript Verlag, Bielefeld

All rights reserved. No part of this book may be reprinted or reproduced or utilized in any form or by any electronic, mechanical, or other means, now known or hereafter invented, including photocopying and recording, or in any information storage or retrieval system, without permission in writing from the publisher.

Cover layout: Kordula Röckenhaus, Bielefeld
Printed in Germany
Print-ISBN 978-3-8376-3546-1
PDF-ISBN 978-3-8394-3546-5

Contents

Acknowledgements | 7

1. Introduction | 9

CONTEXTUAL AND THEORETICAL FRAMEWORK

2. Illness and Disability in Contemporary Memoirs | 29
2.1 Illness and Disability on the Literary Market:
The Age of the Memoir | 29
2.2 The Personal and the Theoretical:
Memoirs of Well-Being as Academic Memoirs | 36
2.3 Narrating Illness and Disability:
Conventional Scripts and Their Revisions | 40

3. Approaching 'Well-Being' | 49
3.1 Health Problems and the Problem with 'Health' | 49
3.2 Rewriting Cure: The Remission Society | 60
3.3 Recovering the Body: Embodiment and the Remission Society | 68

THE 'CASE STUDIES'

4. Healing Beyond Reconstruction:
Ampu-Narration in Audre Lorde's *The Cancer Journals* | 75
4.1 Against Linearity, Certainty, and Closure:
Deconstructing the Triumph Narrative in *The Cancer Journals* | 83
4.2 Subverting the (Silent) War on Breast Cancer:
Lorde's Vision of the 'Warrior' | 93
4.3 Exposing the Post-Mastectomy Body:
Lorde's Rejection of (Narrative) Prosthesis | 103

5. Musical Cu[r]e:
Reconnection in Oliver Sacks's *A Leg to Stand On* | 119
5.1 "Bringing the Body Back In":
Embodiment in Sacks's Memoir | 125
5.2 Encountering the Doctor:
Sacks, Dr. Swan, and the Disappointment with the Biomedical Cure | 130
5.3 Recovery in Action: Sacks's "Muscle Music" | 142

5.4 Merging the Objective and the Subjective:
Sacks's 'Neurology of Identity' | 148

6. **"She Rides It Like an Untamed Pony":
The Politics of Well-Being in Simi Linton's
*My Body Politic*** | 157
6.1 *My Body Politic* and the 'New Disability Memoir' | 162
6.2 From Cure to Accommodation:
Introducing Disability Rights into the Progress Narrative | 167
6.3 Becoming Disabled:
Community, Sexuality, and the "Body Politic" | 177
6.4 Beholding (the Pleasures of) Disabled Bodies | 189

7. **Variation and Well-Being: Rethinking The Impaired Body
in Kenny Fries's *The History of My Shoes and the Evolution
of Darwin's Theory*** | 199
7.1 Rethinking Impairment beyond the
Medical and Social Model | 205
7.2 Rewriting the (Hi)Story of the Impaired Body
in Fries's Memoir | 214
7.3 Variation and Contingency:
Deconstructing Dis/Ability | 223
7.4 "Everything an Adaptation":
Alternative Ways of Coping with Impairment | 230

8. **Rewriting the Diagnostic Narrative:
Siri Hustvedt's *The Shaking Woman or
A History of My Nerves*** | 239
8.1 The Personal Meets the Scientific:
The 'Brain Memoir' | 244
8.2 Beyond Diagnosis:
The Case of The Shaking Woman | 251
8.3 "A Woman is Shaking:"
Hysteria and the Discourse of Disease | 257
8.4 *The Shaking Woman* as Therapeutic Narrative | 269

9. **Conclusion** | 281

Bibliography | 295

Acknowledgements

The work on this project – my dissertation in American Studies at the University of Paderborn – has not only been an academic but also an emotional venture and this book could not have been completed without the guidance and support of many people.

I would like to express my sincere gratitude to my advisor Prof. Dr. Miriam Strube for her continuous support in all academic questions, her inspiration, encouragement, and enthusiasm for the project, as well as for the time we shared when I was part of her team in the Department of English and American Studies at the University of Paderborn. I am very grateful to Prof. Dr. Christoph Ribbat who shared his immense knowledge and offered important advice, both with regard to the project and my future career. Moreover, I would also like to thank Prof. Dr. Merle Tönnies and Dr. Jarmila Mildorf for taking time out of their busy schedules to join my committee, where they provided insightful comments and thought-provoking questions.

Appreciation also goes to my former colleagues Dr. Daniela Babilon, Eric Erbacher, Markus Wierschem, and Alexandra Hartmann, who not only shared office space with me but also good times and offered valuable suggestions for many of the (sub)chapters published here, and to Petra Tegtmeier, who always had a reassuring answer to my questions and helped me with so many practical issues. A special note of thanks also goes out to Dr. Andrea Krause and Prof. Beth Goering for their assistance in accessing seemingly inaccessible texts and for the stimulating conversations we have had and will hopefully continue to have. Moreover, I am also indebted to Dr. Sara Strauß for productive discussions of the topic and my approach from the time I formulated early drafts to the preparation of my defense.

I would like to thank the DAAD for a scholarship that made research at Columbia University possible, as well as the Faculty of Arts and Humanities of the University of Paderborn for several travel grants, and the DGS-Stiftung for awarding the DGS-Forschungspreis to parts of this study in 2012.

I am deeply grateful for the friends I have made along the way, and I would like to acknowledge the strong friendships of those that have accompanied me through the years and lent their support in various ways. I would also like to take this opportunity to express my profound gratitude to my parents, without whom I would have never enjoyed so many opportunities, and my brother Tim for their moral support, trust, and love. A heartfelt thank you also goes out to Gudrun and Klaus, who have always taken a keen interest in my work. Finally, I will always remember and cherish the continuous support and encouragement of my partner Nils, and I am immensely grateful for his unwavering love.

1. Introduction

In recent years, the word "health" has become virtually ubiquitous. In the United States, "health care" and "health insurance" have long constituted critical and highly contested issues, not least since President Barack Obama signed the groundbreaking Patient Protection and Affordable Care Act into law in March 2010. Political matters cast aside, the very use of the word "health" in this context bespeaks America's contemporary preoccupation with health and, simultaneously, its collective fear of falling ill. While in many other languages, the health care system is termed not with reference to "health," but indeed to "illness," the case it aims to insure, the English term reflects the significance of health in U.S. society. Memoir and Disability Studies scholar Thomas Couser thus defines American society as at once disease and health conscious – an utterance not to be taken as a contradiction, but one that needs to be understood as society's mandate that individuals are responsible for their physical (and mental, one should add) well-being (*Recovering* 9). Similarly, one does not just set up appointments at doctors' offices, but visits the "health center," where "health professionals" work. "Health conscious," one works out at the "health club," shops at "health stores," consumes "health products," downloads "health apps" or travels to "health resorts." It thus comes as no surprise that "health craze," too, has recently entered the dictionary.

"Health issues," these examples illustrate, have increasingly begun to dominate public discourse, thereby moving health, disability, and illness from the realm of the extraordinary into the realm of the ordinary and the everyday. Three decades ago, sociologist Sarah Nettleton explains with reference to the seemingly dichotomous word pair health and illness, any mention of these terms would have conjured images of doctors, nurses, hospitals, drugs, or first aid. Nowadays, these images are supplanted by a wide variety of ideas ranging from nutrition and vitamins, exercise equipment, biking, walking, and jogging, to health check-ups, screenings, and alternative medicine (Nettleton 1). 'Fitness,' the buzz word of the 1990s, the popularity of running in U.S. culture, the more recent awareness of depression, as well as the current "farm-to-table" and the steadily growing organic and vegan movements foreground health matters, while simultaneously turning health into a commodity (cf. also ibid. 36). In this vein, Nettleton identifies an "imperative for healthy living" (ibid.).

Yet where does this leave the more than 56 million disabled individuals,[1] who make up 19 percent of the U.S. population? Or the 117 million Americans[2] – 49 percent of the population – who have a chronic condition? While these large numbers of course attest to the great capacities of medical science, they also remind us of its limited power to cure and raise the question of what it means to be ill, disabled, or healthy in today's world, where emphasis lies, Kathlyn Conway argues, on physical strength, beauty, and youth (*Illness* 4). Against this background, it is not astonishing that in recent years, autobiographical[3] writing on illness and disability has increased immensely[4] and has received considerable public and scholarly attention.

No doubt, the proliferation of these stories is also tightly intertwined with the rise, and indeed, to borrow from Leigh Gilmore, the "boom" of the American mem-

---

1   The U.S. Census Bureau released published these estimates on the basis of the most recent Survey of Income and Program Participation conducted in 2010 on the 22nd anniversary of the Americans with Disabilities Act in 2012.

2   No doubt this estimate, gathered in the 2012 National Health Interview Survey (NHIS), overlaps to some extent with the number of disabled Americans. Included in the statistics are twenty chronic conditions, among them cancer, asthma, hypertension, diabetes, coronary heart disease, and stroke (cf. Ward, Schiller, and Goodman n. pag.).

3   My use of the adjective "autobiographical" here and throughout this book does not mean to suggest that autobiographies and memoirs are synonyms or that the terms should be used interchangeably but I use "autobiographical," much like the term "life writing," as an umbrella term.

4   Book-length personal narratives of illness rarely date before 1900 and are still uncommon before 1950 (Hawkins, *Reconstructing* 3). In fact, as Ann Jurecic observes, patients' own accounts were preceded by stories published regularly in professional medical journals, as well as in the popular press during the first half of the twentieth century. They figured most commonly in the personal memoirs of doctors or nurses or as case studies of psychologists and psychiatrists that included brief biographical sketches of their patients' lives (Jurecic 5). Beginning in the 1950s, patients, too, began to publish their own stories that frequently featured the experiences of polio and the patients' isolation in institutions (cf. ibid. 6). It is in this context that Hawkins locates the advent of the first illness narratives which she terms 'testimonial pathographies.' These early narratives tell the stories of patients' experiences with a strong focus on their emotions and thoughts, thus bearing witness to their suffering and at the same time presenting the patient as a model for other fellow patients that the narrative is intended to help (Hawkins, *Reconstructing* 4f.).

oir (2), as the past two and a half decades have seen a tremendous shift in the ways life experiences are recorded: In the 1990s, the memoir began to surge to unparalleled popularity and has now emerged as the dominant cultural mode of telling one's story, presenting arguments and floating ideas, providing justification or (re)constructing reputations, and the sheer number of memoirs has been unprecedented (cf. Yagoda 28f.). Not only does the memoir hence hold paramount cultural currency, but it also "rivals fiction in popularity and critical esteem" and has even supplanted traditional autobiographical writing (Couser, *Memoir* 3, 18). The sharp increase in the production and visibility of illness and disability memoirs is then spurred by the 'memoir boom,' yet at the same time, these stories continue to add to the popularity of the form (cf. ibid. 148).

Moreover, illness and disability memoirs attest to a crucial change in the demographics and body politics of life writing in the United States and generate one of the primary sites through which ill and disabled subjects participate in public discourses (cf. Couser, *Signifying* 3).[5] It is in these texts that writers do not only represent the body with its ailments, anomalies and impairments, but grant a voice to the manifold experiences that discourses of contemporary biomedicine fail to grasp and critically view their experiences, their bodies, and their selves against the backdrop of cultural and social norms. This way, private experiences enter the public arena, a dynamic that in itself subverts the assumption that patients are passive and silent (cf. Frank, "Reclaiming" 3).

Although this is not the first study to include life narratives on both illness *and* disability, this book is the first to elucidate that when these texts are read side by side, structural and aesthetic commonalities become evident that outweigh the factual and sociopolitical differences which separate these conditions and have made a joint discussion of their literary representations a tenuous and fallible matter. Despite the fact that these life narratives are thematically framed by a lack of health, this book departs from previous scholarship to suggest that contemporary illness and disability memoirs abundantly present health and do so beyond its binary relationship to the pathological. The following close readings therefore aim to close a gap in research by bringing into sharp focus the memoirists' representations of cure, recovery, and healing, and, more importantly, their reluctance to bring closure to their narratives and align their stories with traditional notions of health.

---

5   *Signifying Bodies* aptly reflects on the notion of writing in today's life writing, maintaining that writing need not to be taken literally in the digital age if one considers the electronic sites of life writing ranging from online blogs to personal profiles on social networking websites or videos uploaded on Youtube (see Couser's chapter "Introduction: The Some Body Memoir" for a thorough discussion of this issue).

These memoirs challenge health defined merely as "the absence of disease" (cf. e.g. Boorse 63) and therefore treat a pressing and insistent matter in our times – one, however, that has until now unjustifiably been neglected in the study of illness and disability life narratives. This becomes most apparent in the still persistent usage of Anne Hunsaker Hawkins's term '(auto)pathography' (introduced in her 1993 study *Reconstructing Illness: Studies in Pathography*)[6] to refer to the vividly flourishing genre. Sidonie Smith and Julia Watson point out that illness and disability memoirs work to "contest cultural discourses stigmatizing the writer as abnormal, aberrant, or in some sense pathological" (261). Couser, too, despite his frequent usage of the term, criticizes it now for its emphasis on the pathological, arguing that personal narratives of illness and disability need to be seen as "antipathological" because "the impulse to write a first-person illness narrative is often the impulse to depathologize one's condition" (quoted ibid.; cf. also "Genre" 127).

Additionally, previous monograph studies on narrating personal illness and disability have hardly broached the issue of health and have by and large presented it only in contrast to the pathological conditions the memoirists portray and hope to be cured from. Arthur Kleinman's early *The Illness Narratives: Suffering, Healing, and the Human Condition* (1988), for instance, is an ethnographic approach to storytelling in times of illness. *The Wounded Storyteller: Body, Illness, and Ethics*, published in 1995 by sociologist Arthur Frank, delineates several plot structures to frame the analysis of illness narratives and Thomas Couser's *Recovering Bodies: Illness, Disability, and Life Writing* (1997) focuses on bodily dysfunction and narrative authority.

Undoubtedly, this book greatly benefits from the contextual and theoretical frameworks, as well as the models for interpretation developed in the research of these scholars. It is informed by the theories of scholars working in the bourgeoning interdisciplinary field of (Cultural) Disability Studies, such as Rosemarie Garland-Thomson, Lennard Davis, David Mitchell and Sharon Snyder, as well as by Arthur Frank's concept of the 'remission society,' a theoretical framework originating in an autobiographical impulse and affording a fresh perspective on the meaning of 'health.' The remission society, as I will expound in more detail in Chapter 3.2, opens up a discursive space for the plethora of memoirists who may not fully recover from their ailments, but whose stories nevertheless limn healing and a sense of reconciliation and therefore constitute a significant breach of the tradition of storying illness. Building on the existing research, the following chapters then aim to shed light on a subgenre of the illness and disability memoir that has until now been undetected, the 'memoir of well-being.'

---

6 In several of his publications, e.g. in the essay "Genre Matters," Couser claims to have coined the term (126).

This term takes inspiration from the definition of health the World Health Organization has famously devised in 1946 and that is still in use today. The WHO maintains that health is "a state of complete physical, mental and social well-being and not merely the absence of disease or infirmity" (n. pag.), thereby foregrounding the individual's subjective perspective rather than the objective stance of medical professionals. Particularly due to its introduction of "well-being," this definition has since spurred heated debates, for it reduces the power of clinicians to distinguish a healthy from an unhealthy state (Franke 40f.). It is precisely on these grounds that I call the subgenre outlined in this study 'memoirs of well-being.' For memoirists writing in this subgenre, established medical definitions of health no longer hold because they either face chronic conditions, live with acquired or congenital disabilities, or have acute conditions clinicians fail to address adequately. Their stories rewrite the need for a cure and the ways in which well-being may be attained. In doing so, they naturally find themselves at odds with established frameworks, such as medical explanatory schemes, scientific theories, and cultural conceptions of the ill/disabled body.

Classification and categorization, however, only constitute a starting point for my analysis. I strongly agree with Couser who in *Memoir: An Introduction* repeatedly calls attention to the fact that categorization is not an end in itself, but merely a means to understand the conventions under which narratives operate. In line with his argument, I do not merely seek to classify the narratives under analysis here – "find the 'right' or even 'best' pigeonhole" – but I wish to clarify them (cf. 9; 52). Establishing a subgenre as framework is the first step in this clarification, since with respect to life writing in particular, genre does not only circumscribe adherence to a certain literary form. In her classic essay "Genre as Social Action," Carolyn Miller defines genre as "a complex of formal and substantive features that create a particular effect in a given situation. Genre in this way becomes more than a formal entity; it becomes pragmatic, fully rhetorical, a point of connection between intention and effect, an aspect of social action" (153). The rise of a new genre is actuated by social needs. In the past, changing concepts of gender and sexuality, for instance, or re-examined ideas of class or race have turned genres into discursive practices that may rework ideology (Buss 6f.). In using the term 'memoir of well-being,' I attempt to glean what these texts *do* (cf. also Couser, "Genre" 136): They all deliberately seize the power to define well-being from the hands of medical professionals and partake in the construction of alternative narratives of illness and disability.

In many ways, these 'robust texts' may be seen as therapeutic, but, as I aim to show, writing does not only help writers to remediate their individual health problems. In recording their experiences and reflecting on their healing and well-being, memoirists also reconsider and disable the biomedical cure. I argue that by means of recurring motifs, themes, and plot structures, memoirs of well-being challenge the traditional notion of health, as well as the authority of cultural and scientific discourses to account for their writers' experiences. The narratives under analysis thus blur the boundaries between health and illness/disability as their writers may heal, even in the face of a persisting affliction.

The texts analyzed below, representative for a plethora of other life narratives, first of all shed light on the processes of reappropriation at work in these memoirs. These are not limited to the resignification of derogatory terms, such as 'gimp,' 'cripple,' or 'crip' that are now widely used within the disability community as "a testament to the struggle for rights and equity and a reminder of the damaging beliefs and attitudes still held by many" (Baglieri and Shapiro 49).[7] In a number of the texts at hand, metaphors, images, and ideas that have previously been made to work against ill and disabled individuals are reappropriated, thus first of all empowering the memoirists. Indeed, oftentimes the key to attaining a sense of well-being can be discerned in these processes of reappropriation. Secondly, reappropriation in these narratives also has an empowering effect for the entire group of ill and disabled individuals, for it proposes conceptual transformations of illnesses, disabilities, and the (social) status of the people living with them.

Moreover, the texts in this subgenre employ temporality and contingency as recurring motifs and structural tropes to draw attention to the cultural construction of disease, impairment, and health, as well to the plot structures that have traditionally dominated the discourse on illness and disability. In *The Wounded Storyteller*, Frank delineates three plot structures that traditionally serve as a frame for storying illness: the chaos narrative,[8] the restitution narrative, and the quest narrative. The restitution narrative is in fact a story about health, as it begins with the author's memory of good health, recounts the experience of illness and anticipates restored health in the future (77ff.). As a consequence, the dichotomy between health and

---

7   In their chapter "Language, Labels, and Identity" Susan Baglieri and Arthur Shapiro discuss so-called "people first language" and re-claimed labels.

8   The chaos narrative leaves its readers with the conclusion that no improvement can be achieved and illustrates vulnerability in the face of disease and impairment, as well as the futility of efforts to surpass the narrated condition. Chaos in these narratives is frequently underlined by a lack of causality and coherence (Frank, *Wounded* 97ff.). Since it rarely occurs in published life narratives, particularly not in more recent works, it lies beyond the scope of this study. In the context of health, it should, however, be noted that the chaos narrative, too, contributes to the rigid demarcation between illness/disability and health by instilling the fear of disease and impairment in its readers, often perpetuating the stigma associated with certain physical incapacities and the patient's powerlessness, and hence implicitly reinforces the power of 'health.' Moreover, its incoherence distances readers and does not allow for the fashioning of a community amongst other fellow wounded individuals.

illness/disability is reinscribed in the restitution narrative because it explicitly widens the divide between the healthy and the incapacitated, especially due to the fact that most restitution narratives are written once their authors have recovered and find themselves amongst the ranks of the healthy again, looking back on illness and providing a sense of closure.

Yet the restitution narrative is not limited to the storying of acute illness, but may well be detected in memoirs about chronic illness and in disability memoirs. Narrated as triumphant stories of overcoming one's condition, these memoirs aim to leave illness and disability behind and produce disembodied narratives in which the memoirists' bodily realities are silenced and rendered invisible. In such triumph and restitution narratives, medical science is celebrated (ibid. 115), often at the expense of corporeality when the body endures invasive treatment in pursuit of cure or is dismissed altogether as merely a faulty part aloof from the self that needs to be mended. As this study will show, memoirs of well-being write back at and deconstruct triumphant and progressive restitution narratives. Moreover, they supplant the conventional happy ending and disable a diagnostic and medical narrative with concluding passages that defy a sense of closure, pointing at once to the ongoing nature of their writers' conditions and to the instability and inadequacy of traditional notions of health.

Additionally, many of the memoirs analyzed in this study offer valuable clues to an under-studied variant of the so-called quest narrative, the third plot structure Frank identifies and the one he regards as the category encompassing most texts (ibid. 115). This is of course in parts owing to the broad definition of the quest narrative, for Frank notes that in these life stories, narrators hope to gain something from their experience when they confront suffering, accept it, and aim to use it (ibid. 115ff.). Illness and disability therefore incite the memoirists' spiritual journeys, in which the quest to discover one's "true" self and rethink the priorities of one's life looms large. In *A Whole New Life: An Illness and a Healing*, a quest narrative *par excellence*, Reynold Price, for instance, discovers the tremendous benefits of biofeedback and hypnosis for his pain treatment, as well as contemplates the gratitude he feels towards family members, friends and the assistants he needs to hire, but also the creative power that emerges from his illness and that has reinvigorated his life as a writer even as it leaves him disabled. In a similar vein, a host of traditional quest narratives depict illness or disability in its deeply personal dimensions and the insight and solace their narrators hope to gain are conceptualized on an individual scale.

Little attention has thus far been devoted to life narratives that do not only figure as the stories of individuals, but in which the memoirists, either explicitly or implicitly, speak for others or in a chorus of voices and therefore counter both the isolation routinely associated with states of un-wellness and the solitary nature of a (triumphant) quest. As the memoirists take their illnesses and disabilities as trajectories for exploring well-being, their stories constitute a quest for knowledge and agency and – an aspect that has as of yet received far too little attention[9] – powerfully intertwine the autobiographical and the theoretical through a creative and critical engagement with the subjective and the objective perspective. Their memoirs hence become, Carmen Birkle argues, "a new space of communication," one through which doctors and patients (and, along similar lines, clients and service providers), writers and readers may connect (xxvii).

Numerous authors have already attempted to resolve the modalities of the communication processes between writers and readers, and life writers, too, grapple with the nature and the implications of their narratives. In "The Literature of Personal Disaster," for example, disabled essayist Nancy Mairs asks

"what do bookmongers believe will draw readers to [life narratives about illness and disability]? Sorrow? Curiosity? What are they supposed to find there? Solace? Reassurance? Sheer relief that, however wretched their own lives may seem, others are worse? In short: Why do I, and others like me, write this stuff? Why does anybody read it? (Or to put matters more cynically but no doubt more accurately, why does anybody think anybody else is going to pay good money to read it?) And what, if anything, happens when they do?" (125)

According to Anne Hunsaker Hawkins, that which draws readers to memoirs of illness and disability depends on their own state of health. Ill and disabled readers, she claims, will indeed find solace and reassurance because the stories of others likewise affected give voice to their own fears, anxieties, and hopes, and as coherent accounts of these sentiments they offer exemplary ways of coping with illness and disability (*Reconstructing* 11). Many writers make this explicit by dwelling on the epiphany – "in a tone of unmistakable relief, 'Oh, me too! Me too!'" – that the experience that was previously deemed a solitary endeavor is in fact one in which solidarity is possible once the isolated voices become heard (Mairs, "Carnal Acts" 92). Life writing may then indeed foster a sense of community and turn writers and readers into allies.

The feeling Mairs describes is reminiscent of the "nod of recognition" Stanley Fish credits the fellow members of so-called 'interpretive communities' with (485).

---

9 An exception constitutes Franziska Gygax's research in the field of illness narratives. Focusing on the memoirists' conceptions of their self, she explores how the writers' and academics' sense of self changes in the course of their illness experiences. Their texts' theoretical engagements with notions of the self form the center of her work in the project "Life (Beyond) Writing: Illness Narratives." See e.g. her essay "Theoretically Ill: Autobiographer, Patient, Theorist" (in *The Writing Cure: Literature and Medicine in Context*. Eds. Alexandra Lembert-Heidenreich and Jarmila Mildorf. Münster: LIT, 2013. 173-90).

Introduced in his 1976 essay "Interpreting the *Variorum*" focusing on readers' responses, Fish attributes great significance to their processes of decoding texts and, in contrast to "the assumption that there *is* a sense, that it is embedded or encoded in the text, and that it can be taken in at a single glance" (473; italics in original) purports that meaning is created during the reading process (468). Consequently, readers who share knowledge and experiences will share strategies for the interpretation of a text (483) and decode similar meaning.

This is why, according to Hawkins, healthy readers, on the other hand, will find these life narratives invaluable preparatory books, stories that help them brace themselves for the circumstances they might one day find themselves in (*Reconstructing* 11). "I am also trying to draw you into it, to carry you along with it, so that whatever extraordinary circumstances you one day meet – and you will, because all creatures do – you will have, in some way, 'been there' before," writes Mairs in her introduction to the autobiographical essay collection *Carnal Acts*, assuming the existence of other interpretive communities and assigning to her writing a function beyond the cathartic attempt of making her experience with multiple sclerosis "bearable for [her]self" ("But First" 5f.).

One may safely assume that the first interpretive community, though, is larger in size and more attuned to the personal stories of fellow ill or disabled individuals. Like any other genre, illness and disability memoirs are written and published by and for a particular interpretive community, which may in part explain the perceived absence of "classics" in the genre.[10] This, however, Couser concedes, is not a problem inherent in the texts themselves, but a systemic problem, for narratives about illness and disability have long only existed on the margins of the literary market, much like their authors have been socially deprecated ("Embodied" 1). Yet both interpretive communities may detect a strong and powerful message in the texts in the subgenre studied here: "it is possible to be *both* sick *and* happy" (Mairs, "Literature" 127). "This good news, once discovered," Mairs proclaims, "demands to be shared" (ibid.).

Why memoir, one may be tempted to ask in the light of the abundance of fictional works of art that "treat" ill and disabled characters. Yet especially with regard to disability, fictional portrayals have thus far been problematic, since disabled characters have by and large only figured as minor, one-dimensional characters modeled on stereotypes.[11] The memoir form is significant because it enables ill and disabled individuals to speak for themselves and, as Couser argues, to counter pa-

---

10 A number of scholars take this to be a serious shortcoming of these texts, as Couser notes ("Embodied" 1; *Recovering* 7).

11 See Rosemarie Garland-Thomson's groundbreaking study *Extraordinary Bodies: Figuring Physical Disability in American Culture and Literature* on this issue.

tronizing or stigmatizing representations (*Signifying* 31). Furthermore, memoirs are characteristically rooted in the 'real world' and Couser maintains that this is their distinctive source of power, for it allows them to take effect on culture and society more directly (*Memoir* 176). Unlike fictional texts, memoirs rest on different agendas and strive to achieve different aims. In short: they may "*do* things fiction cannot" (ibid.; italics in original).

In contrast to the broad definition of the memoir as a narrative of events in the memoirist's own life, as well as a narrative of the life of "someone known to, and remembered by, the author" (ibid. 19), my choice of texts limits the understanding of the memoir to an account of the writer's own life. Thus consciously excluding the so-called 'relational narratives' currently glutting the literary market in which either children write about their parents or parents pick up the pen to chronicle their children's ordeals[12] (cf. ibid. 21), this study is concerned with the subjective and qualitative experience of illness and disability that a second-hand account is not capable of expressing.

For pragmatic reasons of scope and methodological coherence, this study is selective rather than exhaustive. It is limited to literary memoirs of well-being, although many of the structural and aesthetic elements can also be discerned in the growing body of graphic memoirs. Moreover, I am of course aware of the large – indeed unmanageable – body of self-published work on the experience of illness and disability, photographic and filmic projects, performance art, and the many and popular forms of online life writing that exist both alongside and at the margins of the text corpus I have chosen to include. In restricting the texts analyzed here to professionally published written memoirs, I am conscious of the fact that I have selected the most privileged of life writers, memoirists who have overcome all three difficulties Couser identifies in *Signifying Bodies*, namely "having a life" deemed worthy of an autobiographical account, "writing a life," i.e. having the skills necessary to produce a manuscript, and "publishing a life" and carving out one's place on the literary market where hegemonic scripts may run counter to their self-representations (31ff.).

These memoirists then are professional and established writers and intellectuals. The choice to limit this study to them, rather than to the writers of what reviewer Lorraine Adams has termed 'nobody memoirs,' does not mean to devalue the life

---

12 With respect to writing about disability, particularly memoirs written by parents about their children with autism or Down syndrome, in which the parent-writer aims at humanizing their children and reframing disability, have proliferated, as Alison Piepmeier outlines in her critical survey "Saints, Sages, and Victims: Endorsement of and Resistance to Cultural Stereotypes in Memoirs by Parents of Children with Disabilities" (*Disability Studies Quarterly* 32.1 (2012)).

narratives of first-time writers or presuppose a lack of aesthetic quality, but to show the relevance of the subgenre that comprises well-known and acclaimed texts. Not only does this book aim to complement the body of criticism on these writers and their life narratives, but the choice of texts also connects this study to ongoing research and offers points of connectivity to current discourses in the disciplines of American Studies, memoir studies, and Disability Studies.

In addition, this study is limited to memoirs dealing with physical conditions, such as cancer, injuries and neurological disorders, congenital and acquired disabilities, and therefore excludes mental illnesses and cognitive disabilities, since the latter conditions raise questions pertaining to representation – the ways in which conditions are presented and the ways in which individuals which cognitive impairments or severe and deteriorating mental conditions may present themselves – which simply lie beyond the scope of this book.

Finally, the works discussed here are narrowed down to life narratives published in the 1980s and the first decade of the twenty-first century. Although the following analyses are grouped in temporal order, the structure of this study does not aim to sketch a continuous progress over the past three and a half decades. Rather, the structure aids in the exploration of the political nature of patienthood and disability, as well as the writers' subsequent engagement with questions of health and well-being. I purposefully begin my analyses with Audre Lorde's *The Cancer Journals*, a text published in 1980 because this year marks, as Lisa Diedrich argues, the beginning of a new era, namely that of the 'politicized patient' (*Treatments* 26). The notion of 'politicized patienthood' was originally coined by Linda Singer in the manuscript for her feminist critique *Erotic Welfare: Sexual Theory and Politics in the Age of Epidemic*, a book she was unable to complete before her death from cancer in 1990 and that was edited and published later by Judith Butler and Maureen MacGrogan. For Singer, the politicization of patienthood is characteristic of the AIDS epidemic, when a large number of patients, their friends and families were mobilized in political and organizational networks (106). When activist groups, such as ACT UP, called for patients' participation in decisions on research and treatment of AIDS/HIV in the 1980s, the status of people with AIDS (PWAs) significantly changed, turning passive victims into activists whose interests and expertise constituted "invaluable resources" (ibid. 105). As a consequence, their first-person perspective and subjective knowledge was honored, recognized, and effected change.

The politicization of patienthood is then to be seen as a watershed moment for several reasons. It aided the circulation of knowledge outside the medical establishment, acknowledged individuals other than medical practitioners as significant sources and multipliers of knowledge about diseases, and attributed authority to the qualitative experience of illness, lending a strong voice to personal stories. Secondly, Singer maintains, the patients' activist endeavor also created a new way of speaking about the illness experience (106). She emphasizes the change in language and the coinage of the term "PWAs" – "people with AIDS," but her argument may well be understood as a general shift in the discourse because she also notes how religious logic and imagery, such as the contraction of the disease as a divine punishment for sins is decidedly rejected, as is the attitude of what she refers to as the "good patient" who follows the physician's advice without any questions (ibid.).

Against this background, Audre Lorde's much-lauded *The Cancer Journals* (1980) is not merely an early example of the politicization of the experience of illness, as I will discuss in Chapter 4. A precursor to women's contemporary writing on breast cancer – Diedrich speaks of the prophetic quality of her writing (*Treatments* 38) – Lorde's memoir has already been subject to extensive scholarly critique. In this chapter, though, I aim to shift the perspective. Employing Disability Studies scholars David Mitchell's and Sharon Snyder's concept of the 'narrative prosthesis' as an interpretative lens, this chapter revisits key scenes of the memoir to study how the text, through its subversion of the triumph narrative and its refusal to hide the post-mastectomy body behind a prosthesis deconstructs traditional notions of health and healing, as well as challenges a so-called 'prosthetic' narration. In what I instead call an 'ampu-narrative,' Lorde critically engages with the practice of reconstructing the surgically altered body and her memoir proposes the resignification of the reconstructive process traditionally associated with recovering from breast cancer: In both content and form, the life narrative encourages an alternative reading of reconstruction, and thus of healing and well-being in the midst of the writer's ongoing experience of breast cancer.

Consequently, in the 1980s, activism around health issues proliferates, culminating in the breast cancer movement of the 1990s (cf. ibid. 26). Directly related to this, the politicization of patienthood also spurs new forms of life writing which Diedrich considers counter-narratives to medical discourses and doctors' case histories (ibid.). The patients' growing distrust of the medical establishment incites an increasing number of memoirs that differ considerably in tone from earlier personal narratives about illness (cf. ibid.) and their testimonials begin to give way to what Hawkins terms 'angry pathographies' and pathographies that call for alternative treatment options.[13] Frequently recounting instances of malpractice, these texts evi-

---

13 The publication of Norman Cousin's *Anatomy of an Illness as Perceived by the Patient* in 1979 is commonly seen as the initiation of illness memoirs which function as calls for alternative treatment options (cf. Hawkins, *Reconstructing* 4) and anticipate patients' increasing agency. Cousins, who worked as journalist and author and was later also a professor of Medical Humanities, uses the first chapter of his *Anatomy of an Illness* to intertwine his own experiences of an extremely rare collagen disorder with a critique of institutional medicine, e.g. when he states that he "had a fast-growing conviction that a hospi-

dence their writers' lack of confidence in medicine and their discontentment with treatment protocols and doctor-patient relationships (*Reconstructing* 8). Although Hawkins stresses that these texts are not representative of the genre she outlines, their themes have a lasting influence on many of the works published subsequently. They do not only serve as critical commentaries on medical treatment and patient care (Jurecic 7), but also pinpoint a critical question that has been largely overlooked: the question of knowledge.

Chapter 5 will therefore offer a close reading of the 1984 memoir *A Leg to Stand On* by the renowned physician-writer Oliver Sacks and explore how embodiment and subjective knowledge of the body unhinge the clinicians' authority to account for the patient's recovery process. Beginning to practice medicine in the U.S. in the 1960s, Sacks early on strove to counter what he perceived as the reductionism of biomedicine (Hull 105). In his writing, the relationship between doctor and patient is hence a recurring theme and Sacks's popular scientific prose attempts to merge the doctor's with the patient's perspective, thereby consolidating the biomedical and the humanistic in a new form of clinical narrative (ibid.). Of equal significance is in this context the question of how to reformulate the notions of well-being and healing. While on first reading, Sacks's memoir may resemble the traditional restitution narrative beginning with the celebration of his strong and robust body

---

tal is no place for a person who is seriously ill. The surprising lack of respect for basic sanitation; the rapidity with which staphylococci and other pathogenic organisms can run through an entire hospital; the extensive and sometimes promiscuous use of X-ray equipment; the seemingly indiscriminate administration of tranquilizers and powerful painkillers, sometimes more for the convenience of hospital staff in managing patients than for therapeutic needs; and the regularity with which hospital routines take precedence over the rest requirements of the patient [...] – all these and other practices seemed to me to be critical shortcomings for the modern hospital" (29). His account stresses the significance he attributes to the patient's agency and attitude in the course of the healing process. Being told that his chances for recovery are 1:500, he feels "a compulsion to get into the act. It seemed clear to me that if I was to be that one in five hundred I had better be something more than a passive observer" (31). His narrative, too, critiques traditional notions of cure because Cousins's underlying argument is that the connection between body and mind and the mind's capacity to effect positive biochemical responses needs to be acknowledged in the healing process, something that he puts very simplistically when he states that he "'laughed' [his] way out of a serious illness" (27) but that he explores more thoroughly in subsequent, more theoretical chapters on the placebo effect, pain, and holistic health and healing. At the same time, his narrative reveals the utterly problematic connection between the patients' attitude and their cure (cf. also Hawkins, *Reconstructing* 9), which implicitly puts blame on patients if they cannot attain a cure.

before the accident, recounting the dark abyss of illness, and ending in a spontaneous recovery, it does in fact disrupt the conventional plot through the experiencing I's deep distrust of the medical cure that is accentuated all the more by the fact that Sacks is a medical professional himself. *A Leg to Stand On*, this chapter will demonstrate, writes back at the narrative of biomedical triumph by devoting a significant amount of discourse time to the apparent failure of the surgical cure and revolving around the embodied and qualitative experience of illness. The book eventually displaces cure with healing, for well-being only becomes possible when music unites the mental and the corporeal aspects previously separated in the biomedical realm.

The first two "case studies" therefore exemplarily discuss issues at stake in the early 1980s. The politicization of patienthood, both chapters show, "brings into being various techniques for doing illness in new ways," as well as "new forms of writing illness" (Diedrich, *Treatments* 26). On top of that, these two chapters elucidate the emergence of the memoir of well-being alongside the subgenres Hawkins has identified. The texts discussed here evince a strong consciousness of issues of healing and the inadequacy of traditionally conceived notions of health and cure – remarkably in cases of both chronic and acute conditions. The structural and aesthetic hallmarks I identify continue to shape later texts and become especially prominent in post-millennial texts. Aided by progressive legislation, most importantly the American with Disabilities Act signed into law in 1990 and gradually implemented since then, the conversation on disability has shifted from a focus on participation to a concept of disabled identity and bodily difference in which pride and well-being powerfully resonate.

The 1990s have seen the publication of important memoirs by academics and activists, such as Robert Murphy's *The Body Silent* (1990), subtitled as "An Anthropologist Embarks on the Most Challenging Journey of His Life: Into the World of the Disabled." As the title suggests, his narrative conceptualizes the cancer that damages his spinal cords and makes walking harder and finally impossible as an intellectual quest into "a social world no less strange to me at first than those of the Amazon forests" where he and his wife have conducted participant observation studies (xi). Though also devoting significant time and space to Murphy's qualitative experience of using a cane and later a wheelchair, the memoir explores disability not only as physical condition, but as social identity and "a process set in motion by somatic causes but given definition and meaning by society" (195) and entangles scholarship with personal story. If not overtly politically conscious, this text highlights the social dimension of disability and its understanding as an identity category and may thus well be seen as another precursor to the more explicitly political texts that follow and that I discuss here. *Past Due: A Story of Disability, Pregnancy, and Birth* by writer and Disability Rights activist Anne Finger (1991), for instance, like Michael Bérubé's *Life as We Know It: A Father, A Family, and an Exceptional*

Child (1998), is highly politically charged. Crucial moments in Finger's memoir are her debates on amniocentesis, abortion, and disability with nondisabled women activists, who neither share her experience growing up as a disabled child and living with post-polio syndrome, nor her appreciation of disabled life, as well as Finger's coming to terms with the birth of her potentially disabled son Max. "[W]ell-being does matter," she concludes at the end of her book, yet this recognition is rooted in the fact that "being nondisabled is easier than being disabled" (201) and later texts make clear that once the most pervasive social obstacles that have barred disabled individuals from a social, cultural, and political life are removed, well-being is removed from the binary context of dis/ability.

In a similar vein, a great variety of disability memoirs elucidate the newly emerging consciousness Couser delineates toward the end of his study *Signifying Bodies* and that I discuss in greater depth in Chapter 6. They do so by explicitly referencing disabled embodiment, such as Nancy Mairs in her memoir *Waist-High in the World: A Life among the Nondisabled* (1996) and numerous personal essays that resignify the term 'crip,' and by critically engaging with disability rights or stereotypes. Journalist John Hockenberry's memoir *Moving Violations: War Zones, Wheelchairs, and Declarations of Independence* (1995), for instance, is invested in deconstructing the stereotype of the "man-in-the-wheelchair" (160) which causes him great pain and hatred. The book echoes Audre Lorde's rejection of prostheses for cosmetic reasons (though only in the second-hand account of his grandfather's amputated arm), it stresses, like Kenny Fries's *The History of My Shoes* (Chapter 7), the different perceptions of disability in other cultures when recalling his stays abroad reporting for instance on Israel and Palestine, and shares Simi Linton's preoccupation with disabled sexuality, especially in connection to healing and adjusting to disability. Furthermore, *Moving Violations* bears structural and stylistic commonalities with *My Body Politic*, as it employs temporal references to the Disability Rights Movement and the Americans with Disabilities Act (cf. Chapter 6). It is in his memoir that Hockenberry coins the term 'roll model' to denote other disabled individuals who offer practical advice and hence proclaims a sense of community amongst disabled individuals, as I expound in more detail in the reading of Linton's book. Stephen Kuusisto's *Planet of the Blind* (1998) exhibits a similar argument, since the advocate and scholar sketches his initially reluctant identification with other disabled individuals and illustrates the ways in which he thrives in the community of the 'roll models' Hockenberry describes who offer practical training and guidance. Kuusisto, too, dwells on the image of disability, and, when read side by side with *Moving Violations*, complements Hockenberry's preoccupation with stereotypes by meditating on "the discrepancy between [his] blindness as a symbol for others and the reality that [he is] not all blind people" (180). These books politicize disabled selfhood and exceed mere individual experiences and concerns to address broader social matters and in each of them it becomes clear how tightly well-being, social justice, and identity construction are intertwined. If not explicitly, well-being is broached implicitly in all of these books as the writers mediate their relationship to health, ability or the "normal."

Moreover, many illness memoirs critically comment on progress and the medical cure and counter the (triumphant) quest narrative. Among the most prominent examples is psychologist and literary studies scholar Kathlyn Conway's *Ordinary Life: An Illness and a Healing* (1997) which illustrates that breast cancer is "without redeeming value," and "beyond all else, a misery to be endured" (1) by centering on Conway's fears and anger more than on the friends and family that sustain her in the course of the experience. Additionally, her narrative focuses on uncertainty, as the closure she offers her readers towards the end of the memoir is in the epilogue revoked as a mere practicality that enables her to "get on" with her life, while "the knowledge of illness and death" linger "as ever present possibilities" (260f.).

Such a preoccupation with certainty, contingency and the impossibility of closure is heightened in narratives like *Mapping Fate: A Memoir of Family, Risk, and Genetic Research*, the 1997 memoir of the scholar Alice Wexler. In her story, she contemplates "what it means to occupy a 'third space' outside the categories of either-or that we conventionally use to organize experience" (xv). From its initial pages, her story blurs the boundaries between illness and health, as she does not know – and later, when genetic tests become available, chooses not to know – whether she has inherited her mother's Huntington's Disease. Moreover, uncertainty also applies to the medical research on Huntington's that her father and sister are deeply committed to and that the narrative does not portray as "a straight line from failure to success" (125) but as one with many digressions, dead ends, and open questions, thus highlighting the contingency of advances in medical knowledge. The book harnesses various forms of knowledge, such as "interviews with many scientists, archival materials, and reports in the scientific, medical, and popular press, as well as personal observations at meetings and [academic] workshops […], family papers, scrapbooks, transcripts, conversations over many years, even dreams and memories, diaries and journals," effectively intertwines the subjective and the objective, and lends her a "doubled perspective as insider and outsider, […] participant and observer" (xxi).

These cursory remarks, but more importantly my reading of three exemplary texts from the early years of the new millennium shows that, quite contrary to Diedrich's argument, the politicized patient does not disappear in "a neoliberal mode of being ill and doing illness" in the wake of the emphasis on personal responsibility in the 1990s (*Treatments* 27). While Diedrich holds that discourses of responsibility cover up and displace politicized modes of speaking and writing about illness, that, in other words, the personal ceases to be political and becomes once again merely the personal, a plethora of texts suggest otherwise.[14] The political engagement with illness and disability, Chapters 6 to 8 illustrate, is not only surviving but, to borrow from the words of model, artist, and breast cancer activist Matuschka, is "thriving."[15] This is to be understood in both senses of the word, for the books discussed here, representative of many other memoirs of well-being in the early twenty-first century, have been published with renowned publishing houses, enjoyed economic success, and/or were featured on bestseller lists.

Nevertheless, it is no longer appropriate to speak of politicized *patienthood* here. Neither individuals with chronic conditions nor members of the disability community readily and automatically perceive themselves as patients, and their memoirs strongly attest to this, most of all because they keep aloof from the medical establishment. Franziska Gygax observes that although some memoirs continue to critically comment on doctor-patient relationships, new modes of representing the memoirists' conditions against the backdrop of their academic, intellectual, or activist work are emerging ("Theoretically" 179). However, the formal and stylistic features these texts employ, my book shows, are to be seen in continuity with previous publications. A paramount aspect that Lorde's memoir already illustrates is the turn from politicized patienthood to *politicized selfhood*, an idea strongly pronounced in more recent texts.

Chapter 6 is devoted to the close reading of Simi Linton's *My Body Politic* (2006). In Linton's disability life narrative, well-being assumes personal as much as political significance when the narrating I looks back on three decades of Disability Rights activism and jurisdiction. As a result, her memoir rewrites the conventional progress narrative in which a cure for the flawed body is sought to foreground a narrative of judiciary progress. Similarly, instead of overcoming her condition, the

---

14 I do not mean to say that Diedrich's thesis is entirely unjustified. Within the context of her argumentation that establishes a genealogy of personal writing on breast cancer from Susan Sontag's *Illness as Metaphor* (1978) to Barbara Ehrenreich's "Welcome to Cancerland" (2001), her observation that the emergence of a mainstream and industrial breast cancer culture counters the conception of the disease as a political issue, is quite appropriate, as Ehrenreich's revealing essay demonstrates. Yet Diedrich does not sufficiently honor the fact that the very existence of texts – and popular and widely-circulated texts – such as Ehrenreich's powerfully counters the depoliticization of patienthood. Although she does later concede that "the politicized patient survives in the work of Ehrenreich and others," she immediately objects by questioning whether it is not Ehrenreich's feminist stance but rather her writing style that brought the essay popularity and appraisal (cf. 52; en 36, 183).

15 MatuschkaArt. "Beauty Out of Damage." 23 Feb. 2009. Web. 00:02:28.

writer gradually embraces disability in the community of other disabled individuals, recovers her sexualized body, and celebrates her embodied disabled identity.

While Linton's book is mainly devoted to questions of access – with regard to education, public transportation or the arts – Kenny Fries's 2007 disability memoir *The History of My Shoes and the Evolution of Darwin's Theory* addresses matters pertaining to the quality of disabled life. Consequently, the story that reappropriates Darwin's evolutionary theory revolves around the impaired body and demands that it is accounted for in the critical conversation on disability, but also in society at large. In Chapter 7 I will illustrate how impairment, reconceptualized in the memoir as 'variation,' is celebrated as a variety – part of an ongoing evolutionary process oblivious of the binary dis/ability. To this effect, the narrative undermines the medical model of disability (Chapter 3.1) and throughout the book, ability and disability are portrayed as dependent on place, time, and context, rather than being permanently inscribed onto individual bodies. 'Adaptation,' another term borrowed from evolutionary theory, but substantially resignified in *The History*, is at once personal and political. On the personal level, the memoirist's means of adapting, his orthopedic shoes, foster a sense of well-being and lift the stigma from his impaired body. On a broader, more political level, though, the narrative also makes clear that adaptations are universal, an argument which develops the view of a society in which the binaries of health and impairment are disbanded.

With the analysis of Siri Hustvedt's memoir of an unresolved illness, *The Shaking Woman or a History of My Nerves* (2010), Chapter 8 closes the "case studies." The decidedly intellectual memoir returns to questions of knowledge by revisiting and reworking the traditional case history and intertwining objective and subjective knowledge, as well as science and art. Hustvedt's book silences medical practitioners to a large extent and dissociates her story from the biomedical realm when the narrating I challenges neuro-scientific, psychological, and philosophical discourses about disease, the self, the mind, and the body. The rhetoric of contingency operates here to destabilize established notions of disease and health and the diagnostic medical narrative readers expect eventually doubles back to reveal a therapeutic narrative – however one without a cure – in which well-being is situated outside the realm of professional medicine.

Taken together, the chapters will supplement the analyses of works published mainly in the 1970s and 1980s conducted by Hawkins in *Reconstructing Illness* and Couser's explorations of the 'new disability memoir' in *Signifying Bodies*. They seek to elucidate the experiences of ill and disabled memoirists, members of Frank's remission society. Yet while members of the remission society are often known to pass as healthy when their illnesses are rendered invisible, their life narratives do not permit such passing. Instead, their memoirs of well-being leave a distinctive mark, albeit one which may work to effectively destigmatize disease and impairment and encourage alternative and embodied visions of well-being.

Contextual and Theoretical Framework

2. Illness and Disability in Contemporary Memoirs

2.1 Illness and Disability on the Literary Market: The Age of the Memoir

"No one writes autobiography anymore. At least, no one reads it," Couser pointedly remarks to illustrate the fundamental change life writing has undergone in recent years, both with regard to production and reception (*Memoir* 18). While several words in his quotation may be read with emphasis, I share Couser's argument that traditional autobiographical writing has been supplanted by the memoir.[1] Thomas Larson, too, proclaims that "[i]ndeed, we may be living in the age of the memoir" and points to the "sheer numbers" (21). According to Leigh Gilmore, the number of publications labeled and marketed as 'memoirs' have tripled from the first half of the twentieth century to the 1990s (1) and best-seller lists well into the twenty-first

---

1 Considering that the two terms, 'autobiography' and 'memoir' are frequently used synonymously in varying contexts (cf. also Cheu 104), this distinction appears on first reading not only pedantic, but also difficult, for scholars such as James Olney have noted that the definition of the autobiographical in general has long been complicated, as it has been treated as a subject with fuzzy boundaries to the historical, philosophical, psychological, metaphysical, or sociological (cf. 7, 5). Many of the commonly cited definitions, for instance the entry of the *Oxford English Dictionary* that defines autobiography as the "account of a person's life given by himself or herself," do not strictly distinguish between the two genres and the most frequently cited definition that divides "autobiography" into the morphemes "auto/bio/graphy" derived from Greek does not account for distinct qualities of the genre in contrast to the memoir, either. Julie Rak's "Are Memoirs Autobiography? A Consideration of Genre and Public Identity" (*Genre* 37.3-4 (2004): 305-26) provides a thorough account of the differences and the relationship between 'autobiography' and 'memoir.'

century continue to swarm with memoirs.[2] 'Memoir' has replaced 'autobiography' on the literary market to the extent that it is not only a "term of choice," as Couser purports, but a marker inevitably linked to the production, successful distribution, consumption, and reception of these texts (*Memoir* 3). Ultimately, conventional assignments of literary value no longer hold sway and the memoir has ceased to be regarded as autobiography's "minor," "subliterary," "shallow" or "marginal" cousin. Quite to the contrary, 'memoir' has arguably developed into a prestige term, denoting art (cf. ibid. 18), and nowadays often serves as shorthand for "stylistic innovation" (Larson 17).

Although Gilmore remains undecided in *The Limits of Autobiography*, as to whether this veritable boom in memoirs is being consciously produced by the marketing and publishing sector instead of by the writers themselves, she emphasizes the significance of the civil rights movements in the United States that have given a voice to a wide array of people and their life stories: "Women, people of color, gay men and lesbians, the disabled, and survivors of violence," she notes, "have contributed to the expansion of self-representation by illuminating suppressed histories and creating new emphases" (16). Gilmore's argument elucidates that the memoir decidedly departs from what Julie Rak calls the "'traditional' discourse of the public sphere" (*Boom* 12), as autobiography is commonly understood. Instead, the genre brings forth life stories and lived histories previously marginalized and relegated to the edges of the literary canon and therefore does not only refuse to adhere to the established conventions but, more than that, creates new and alternative stories of self-hood and self-inspection.[3]

---

2   It is only in December 2014 that the Nielsen BookScan report, which tracks books sales on a global scale, shows that sales numbers for memoirs have dropped by 4 % in comparison to previous years (Johnston n. pag.).

3   Further, and no doubt related reasons for the memoir boom include the practices of confession that permeate and shape mass culture in the United States (cf. Gilmore 17, Rak, *Boom* 15). With particular attention to illness and disability memoirs, whose rising numbers, as I have already argued in the introduction, have been made possible by the memoir boom, but at the same time equally contribute to it, the paperback revolution also played a significant role: In the 1980s, the publishing industry underwent dramatic changes as several big trade and paperback companies merged and the differences between cheap paperback generic fiction and literary fiction, as well as between "serious" non-fiction published in hardcover and popular non-fiction published as paperbacks began to fade. Rak explores this development thoroughly in her book and also studies how non-fiction titles are made visible in retail stores and on bestseller lists (69ff.). The paperback revolution allowed mass audiences to purchase publications at a more afforda-

In order to better understand these dynamics, I will briefly define and contrast both forms of self-referential writing. As genre, autobiography has its roots in antiquity and the classical philosophical tradition of self-examination, but the term itself only gained currency during the revolutionary period in the eighteenth century when notions of individualism became of increasing political and cultural significance (Goodwin 3). Sidonie Smith and Julia Watson therefore define autobiography as a work that "privileges the autonomous individual and the universalizing life story" (3). Their literary self-fashionings hence turn the autobiographers into models for the ideal American life. However, not just anyone may pick up a pen, write, and publish their life-story because, as Georges Gusdorf holds in his seminal essay "The Conditions and Limits of Autobiography," the autobiographical tradition is "limited almost entirely to the public sector of existence" (36). For him, the idea of the public is twofold, since public refers both to the content of the autobiography – the linear account of events in one's life that historians, too, may trace – and the status of the writers themselves whom Gusdorf invariably characterizes as public personas:

"As soon as they have the leisure of retirement or exile, the minister of state, the politician, the military leader write in order to celebrate their deeds [...], providing a sort of posthumous propaganda for posterity that otherwise is in danger of forgetting them or of failing to esteem them properly. [Autobiographies] admirably celebrate the penetrating insight and skill of famous men [...]." (ibid.)

The autobiography is hence a narrative written at old age, when one looks back at a life of accomplishments. The writers' "precious capital," as Gusdorf calls it (29), their deeds, insights, and skills are at the heart of their accounts and need to be preserved for the following generations of readers. In a similar vein, Gilmore refers to autobiography as "a monument to the idea of personhood" that constitutes a memorial to the writer "just in case no one else ever gets around to it" (12f.) and in turn, the authors' lives are allocated great social significance (cf. Larson 11). As a result, such public life accounts have helped to establish the master narrative of the so-called 'sovereign self' (Smith and Watson 3), a notion that is quite apt since it carries connotations of the public and political sector and characterizes the authors as independent, exceptional, and surpassing.

Such representations, however, do not do justice to the life experiences of a large number of Americans and the autobiographic endeavor is far from democratic, which is the reason why Gusdorf's essay has prompted a number of critical responses that challenge first and foremost his focus on the Western man (cf. 29ff.)

---

ble price and helped to form and promote various genres, such as therapeutic self-help narratives that recount stories of the patient's triumph over an illness (Jurecic 6).

and argue for the inclusion of marginalized groups.[4] In fact, to return to Gilmore's argument quoted above, the surging number of new publications illustrates a decisive shift in the writership, as well as in content and form that cannot be comprised by the traditional discourse on 'autobiography.' Since the writers of these life narratives are writing from the margins of society, the subject at the center of their stories is not the ideal, autonomous, and celebrated individual, but may well be a struggling individual, or, to borrow Hawkins's term, a self-in-crisis (*Reconstructing* 17). So to refer to "stories about unacknowledged aspects of people's lives, sometimes considered scandalous or titillating, and often written by the socially marginalized" (Smith and Watson 4),[5] critics have recovered the term 'memoir,' a term that in fact predates the use of 'autobiography.'

---

[4] Indeed, many of the early discussions lament the exclusion of female autobiographers: cf. among other studies, Sidonie Smith's *A Poetics of Women's Autobiography: Marginality and the Fictions of Self-Representation* (Bloomington: Indiana UP, 1987), Shari Benstock's volume *The Private Self: Theory and Practice of Women's Autobiographical Writings* (Chapel Hill: U of North Carolina P, 1988), particularly Susan Friedman's essay "Women's Autobiographical Selves: Theory and Practice" therein (72-82), and also Paul J. Eakin's more recent discussion in *How Our Lives Become Stories*. Further points of criticism address Gusdorf's notion of autobiography as the reconstruction of "the unity of a life across time" (37). Constituting more than just "convenient containers for our life stories," to use Paul Eakin's words, life narratives present a crucial part of one's sense of self and identity (*Living* ix). Eakin in fact goes so far as to say that life narratives "are not merely about us but in an inescapable and profound way are *us*" (ibid. x; italics in original). According to him, selfhood and the act of expressing it are inextricably tied to one another (cf. ibid. 2), so that these narratives are not merely descriptions of the unified self, but in fact, as Frank terms it, "the self's medium of being" (*Wounded* 53).

[5] The memoir boom and the so-called 'no-body memoir,' i.e. a story by a first-time writer who needs to create their audience, but may enter the market through the genre of life writing (cf. Couser, *Signifying* 1), are often mentioned in the same breath because for the first time, readers may encounter not only a flood of self-referential writing, but an ever increasing number of these texts are written from beyond the limelight of politics, athletics, and entertainment. For a critical consideration of the genre, see e.g. Lorraine Adams's article "Almost Famous: The Rise of the Nobody Memoir." Barron Lerner sees a direct relationship between the rise in nobody memoirs and illness memoirs and asserts that the publication of one's illness experience attracts attention and helps unknown people to "achieve [...] fifteen minutes of fame" (*When* 14). Even though such parallels have often been drawn (e.g. in Couser's *Signifying Bodies* 2f., 31f.; cf. also his coinage of the 'some body memoir' denoting a memoir portraying "odd bodies" in *Memoir* 148), it should be noted – and my selection of texts clearly underlines this – that illness and disa-

As early as in the 16th century, 'memoir' was used to refer to a "record of events, not purporting to be a complete history, but treating such matters as come within the personal knowledge of the writer" (quoted in Buss 1). This early definition points to significant aspects that still characterize the contemporary form. Most importantly, a memoir does not attempt to offer a "complete history" of the writer's life. In contrast to traditional autobiography, which seeks to record the author's entire life from birth to the time of writing, the memoir focuses on a more limited period of time, a significant event in the writer's life, or a small span of time marked by problems, burdens, challenges, or incitement (cf. Buss 23; Larson 33).

Such periods or decisive events certainly include bouts of illnesses or coming to terms with a disability, so that these topics lend themselves particularly well to a "treatment" in the memoir. While traditional autobiographers have depicted illness as the mere interruption of the life originally intended to be the "proper concern" of the life narrative (cf. Couser, *Recovering* 4f.), the writers of illness and disability memoirs take their ailments and bodily differences as their trajectories and focal points. Particularly in Buss's and Larson's definition of the memoir, negative sentiments, trouble, and suffering resonate and in *The Wounded Storyteller*, Frank, too, imagines the "loss of 'destination and map'" due to illness as the occasion that prompts memoirists to tell their stories (1).[6] Sharing their experiences, these definitions suggest, enables the writers to cope with their conditions and weave them into narratives that give meaning to them.[7] A plethora of early stories about illness, texts

---

bility memoirs must not uniformly be categorized as nobody memoirs. Lerner's argument neglects the growing numbers of illness and disability memoirs written by academics and intellectuals.

6   In *The Memoir and the Memoirist: Reading and Writing Personal Narrative*, Larson uses the term 'sudden memoir' to refer to a work that "examines a most recent life phase" and thereby enables the writers to live through and cope with an immediate experience (79).

7   Particularly the role of coherence in illness and disability (life) narratives has already been widely discussed, for example in Marilyn Chandler's essay "A Healing Art" on coherence as an aspect of therapeutic writing (6) or Catherine Belling's "The Death of the Narrator" (in *Narrative Research in Health and Illness*. Eds. Bruce A. Hurwitz, Trisha Greenhalgh, and Vieda Skultans. Malden, Mass: Blackwell, 2004. 146-55) which studies the need for a coherent account of the narrator's impending death. Other insightful publications include Laurence Kirmayer's "Broken Narratives: Clinical Encounters and the Poetics of Illness Experience" (in *Narrative and the Cultural Construction of Illness and Healing*. Eds. Cheryl Mattingly and Linda C. Garro. Berkeley: U of California P, 2000. 153–80), Maria Medved's and Jens Brockmeier's "Talking about the Unthinkable: Neurotrauma and the 'Catastrophic Reaction'" (in *Health, Illness and Culture: Broken Narratives*. Eds. Lars-Christer Hyden and Jens Brockmeier. New York: Routledge, 2008. 54-

Hawkins coins 'testimonial pathographies,' indeed attest this. These early life narratives, published before the 1970s, tell the stories of patients' experiences with a strong focus on their emotions and thoughts, thus bearing witness to their suffering (*Reconstructing* 4f.). On a personal level, illness and disability memoirs may therefore be cathartic and therapeutic, for the basic patterns and structures that narratives necessitate help writers to reconstruct the fragments of their experiences and weave the multiple stories surrounding their conditions – clinicians' and their own – into a coherent whole (Chandler 6).

Furthermore, like other texts in the memoir genre, contemporary illness and disability memoirs also take their readers beyond the immediate personal dimensions of their experiences. Helen Buss, whose study *Repossessing the World: Reading Memoirs by Contemporary Women* has greatly advanced scholarship on the memoir genre, argues that the events and burdens the writers render are personal, but at the same time pertain to their status in the culture and society of their time because she holds that in the memoir, the subject is never "free from dependence and community" (11). According to Rak, memoirs therefore allow their writers to examine their own life in relation to the lives of others' or to current events and thus aid in the construction of a public identity (*Boom* 12). Similarly, Kathleen Waites sees the memoir as an "insider's subjective view of a historical moment or moments" (379). Her definition should, however, not be read as outlining a testimony of significant historical events, but rather refers to the depiction of the immediate scene that includes individual, local, and communal history (cf. Buss 11) and lends a voice to a particular *cultural* moment. That is, memoirs do not treat their writers' lives in isolation, but conceive them intertwined with time, place, culture, and society.

Accordingly, in contemporary illness and disability memoirs, a wealth of aspects are entangled, ranging from the cultural construction of the writers' conditions and bodily difference more generally, social stigma, activism and advocacy, accommodations and legal repercussions, medical power and the patient's perspective, and, crucial for this study, the significance and definition of health. Unlike Rita Charon, I do not begin from the assumption that stories about illness and disability merely help to bridge the divide between the ones who are ill or disabled and the ones who are well (xi),[8] but maintain that the illness and disability memoirs dis-

---

72), as well as their essay "Weird Stories: Brain, Mind, and Self" (*Beyond Narrative Coherence*. Eds. Matti Hyvärinen et al. Amsterdam: Benjamins, 2010. 17-32), and Cheryl Mattingly's monograph *Healing Dramas and Clinical Plots: The Narrative Structure of Experience* (Cambridge: Cambridge UP, 1998).

8   For Charon's project of Narrative Medicine, this is of course a productive starting point. As a doctor of internal medicine with a Ph.D. in English, it is her aim to develop a form of "medicine practiced with the narrative competence that will more ably recognize pa-

cussed here help to blur this dichotomy. They enable their writers to generate a positive identity and body politics and put forward a sense of well-being that transcends the narrow lines of 'health.'

In the course of the memoir boom and the emergence of contemporary illness and disability memoirs by academics, intellectuals, and renowned writers, we are witnessing "a historic breakthrough in life writing" as these individuals with a reputation actively claim their conditions, thus destigmatizing and depathologizing bodily difference (Couser, *Memoir* 153). While Couser suggests that this is the most important development in contemporary life writing in the Anglophone world (ibid.), I hold that the texts' significance is not just rooted in their writers' claims of their difference, but, beyond that, also in their claims of knowledge and their participation in the discourses that frame their conditions. It is out of these discourses that memoirists are capable of developing the positive identity and body politics their stories showcase, and reform the traditional understanding of the dichotomy of health and illness/disability. These complex workings then do indeed warrant Couser's celebratory outlook because these memoirs of well-being have implications reaching first of all beyond the boundaries of the homogenous groups of people living with the same respective conditions. In the analyses below, the texts evince that the traditional binaries no longer hold across a broad range of symptoms and conditions and therefore are of relevance to the heterogeneous remission society (cf. Chapter 3.2) that marks our historical and cultural moment.

Secondly, memoirs of well-being take readers beyond the boundary of the immediate text by initiating a fruitful dialogue because the reality of their bodies may join imaginative possibility and the factual may meet the theoretical (cf. Buss 2). The texts make full use of the potential of the memoir form to weave together strands of various discourses, to merge the literary and the historical, as well as the factual and the imaginary, and to embed concepts from other disciplines (ibid. 23). The resulting commentaries may then take critics beyond the realm of literature and art and bridge the divide to other disciplines exploring health, such as sociology and the philosophy of medicine. In order to shed light on these complex processes, it is necessary to conceive memoirs of well-being as discursive practices in which the personal and the theoretical or scientific meet, as well as clarify the ways in which conventional plotlines and aesthetics operate in these stories.

---

tients and diseases, convey knowledge and regard, join humbly with colleagues, and accompany patients and their families through the ordeals of illness" (vii). Aware of the lack of humility and empathy and today's clinical protocols, she purports that narrative medicine "will lead to more humane, more ethical, and perhaps more effective care" (ibid.).

2.2 THE PERSONAL AND THE THEORETICAL: MEMOIRS OF WELL-BEING AS ACADEMIC MEMOIRS

The memoirs of well-being studied here are written by individuals who explicitly identify as academics, scholars, and/or activists or writers who have acquired theoretical or scientific knowledge either through earlier academic training or in preparation of their writing. I thus propose to read memoirs of well-being as intellectual or academic memoirs in the widest sense because with Jeremy Popkin I contend that academic training and work significantly shape one's identity and existence ("Academic" 202). The genre of the academic memoir has been bourgeoning since the 1990s (notice the coincidence with the 'memoir boom') when tenured humanities professors in their late or mid-career, began writing and publishing their memoirs in great numbers (Franklin 1; Popkin, "Academic" 198). Popkin maintains that it is one of the fastest-growing life writing genres (ibid. 195). While this is a development that has been celebrated by some critics for its appeal to a broader readership beyond the boundaries of the memoirists' respective disciplines and the realization of the feminist dictum that the personal is political, it has also been harshly criticized by others who see the emergence of such texts as middle-aged academics' self-indulgence and "unfortunate byproducts" of the tenure system (ibid. 195f.).

Thus far, academic memoirs have generally only received little scholarly attention and with the exception of Cynthia Franklin's book-length study *Academic Lives: Memoir, Cultural Theory and the University Today* only a scant number of essays and book chapters attempt to take inventory of the genre.[9] In these critical

---

9   Franklin's book closely examines which insights into the U.S. academy may be gained from reading academic memoirs. She argues that these personal narratives may help to "unmask the workings of the academy" by bringing to the foreground contradictions between one's personal and theoretical writings, commenting on the state of the humanities and the crises in the academy, such as job insecurity and the professionalization of graduate studies (2). Chapter 5, "Disability Studies and Institutional Interventions," examines how Disability Studies as a discipline inspires writers to revise the notions on which, according to Franklin, the memoir genre rests, namely individualism and humanism as defined by ability and extraordinary intelligence (ibid. 23). The chapter studies, among other texts, Lennard Davis's memoir *My Sense of Silence: Memoirs of a Childhood with Deafness*. In "Disrupting the Academic Self: Living with Lupus," Janet MacArthur explores what she terms an "academic body politics," more specifically the ways in which academia denies access to chronically ill and disabled persons (179). In the chapter titled "Joining Heart and Head" in *Repossessing the World*, Buss analyzes contemporary academic memoirs by women writers and in their overview of life writing genres in *Reading Autobiography* Smith and Watson also briefly consider the academic memoir (253f.).

studies, the understanding of the 'academic' is limited to the identity of the memoirist as a person working at a university or holding other teaching positions, so that the analyses have by and large focused on the development of the memoirists' intellectual (and sometimes administrative) skills in connection to larger communal developments in education, such as new directions in the respective field, a new theoretical impetus, or student activism (Buss 170). However, as Rocíco Davis notes, academic memoirs also articulate larger historiographical and intellectual tendencies ("Academic" 441) and therefore enable readers to trace the changes in concepts and ideas, as well as the advent of narratives, both master narratives and counter-narratives.

Academic memoirs, Davis continues, become sites where personal histories and academic – and activist, I would add – commitments intersect (ibid. 442). The analyses in the following chapters will show that these strands do indeed come into a creative and productive interplay, so that not only personal experiences serve as a framework for theoretical understanding, as Davis purports (ibid. 448), but that theoretical and scientific knowledge also inform personal experiences and the ways in which they are recorded. Training in the discipline may influence how narratives are structured (Popkin, "Academic" 197), which symbols and motifs are employed, and how memoirists construct their selves and experiences vis-à-vis dominant discourses. It is because of this interplay that academic memoirs are at once anecdotal and supportive of a certain argument or position (cf. Buss 175) and therefore have the potential to contribute to the memoirists' respective disciplines, as they are capable of shaping disciplinary knowledge (Popkin, "Academic" 197, 195). The memoirs may hence initiate a dialogue between a knowledgeable, outspoken, and involved critic and the reader, who is invited "to participate in the interweaving and construction of the ongoing conversation this criticism may be, even as it remains a text" (Caws quoted in Miller 300).

The personal dimension of these stories, however, does more than merely provide critical arguments with compelling backgrounds: "There is no theory that is not a fragment, carefully preserved, of some autobiography," famously writes phi-

---

Other studies include Gillian Whitlock's essay "Disciplining the Child: Recent British Academic Memoir" (*a/b: Auto/Biography Studies* 19.1 (2004): 46-58), Shirley G.-l. Lim's "Academic and Other Memoirs: Memory, Poetry, and the Body," and the early French monograph study *Essais d'ego-histoire* (1987) by Pierre Nora on the memoirs of French historians (Paris: Gallimard), whose work was followed by historian Jeremy Popkin in *History, Historians, and Autobiography* (Chicago: U of Chicago P, 2005) and other shorter publications. Cf. also the special issue on "Academic autobiography and/in the Discourses of History" of *Rethinking History: The Journal of Theory and Practice* (13.1 (2009)).

losopher and essayist Paul Valéry (quoted in Miller 282), thus invoking a relationship between the objective and the subjective, the theoretical and the personal. Similarly, Gilmore invites her readers to consider the implications of reversing Valéry's quote to read "[e]very autobiography is the fragment of a theory" (11f.). In doing so, Gilmore implies that life writing, too, creates theories of self and identity and helps to determine how one's personal story needs to be seen within the larger contexts of these theories (12). Accordingly, questions of a narrowly defined objectivity are no longer of central concern, since in writing a memoir, memoirists authorize themselves as "the source of valid information" (Davis, "Academic" 442). A significant amount of theoretical pieces of writing by ill and disabled scholars, such as Diane Price Herndl, Jackie Stacey, or Sarah Lochlann Jain, but also an increasing number of illness and disability memoirs intertwine the autobiographical and the critical, bringing forth what Nancy Miller calls "personal criticism," i.e. the "explicitly autobiographical performance within the act of criticism" (282). According to her, this is achieved when critical argumentation is interlaced with or articulated through an autobiographical narrative (ibid. 283).[10]

I definitely agree with Miller when she asserts that personal criticism has its roots in the postmodern crisis regarding representativity, the anxiety over speaking *for* someone or speaking *as* a particular subject (297). Especially in the case of writing about illness and disability, such concerns are indeed central issues: Historically, patients and disabled individuals have been denied a voice and authority in the production of knowledge about their bodies, conditions, and experiences. Speaking from a postcolonial perspective, Medical Humanities scholars Felice Aull and Bradley Lewis maintain that ill and disabled bodies have been medicalized and colonized by institutions, practitioners, and the procedures of professional medicine (92) or the rehabilitative sciences; equally important, the practices and conventions of representation have aided in their construction as 'the other' (ibid. 96), which in turn excluded them from dominant discourses.

At the heart of these exclusionary practices is a vertical power structure (cf. also ibid.) and the conception that "medical discourse is largely a monologue and a mono-logic; clinicians and biomedical scientists create medical discourse, 'patients' do not. In medical libraries or medical records offices one finds almost nothing written by the 'subjects' of medical discourse; the writing is by experts: medical clinicians, researchers, marketers, and administrators" (ibid. 91). Consequently, the status of the patient's voice in the medical discourse is troublesome, since the patient is frequently presented as "saying," or "claiming" something, whereas the

---

10 In her essay "Getting Personal: Autobiography as Cultural Criticism" she lists numerous examples, among them Audre Lorde's *Sister Outsider* and Alice Kaplan's intellectual memoir *French Lessons*.

medical professional may "observe" and "find." However, the latter's actions are not recorded in the active voice of the first-person, but rather in what Aull and Lewis term the "agentless passive," an omniscient stance glossing over the uncertainty of the clinical encounter, to the extent that the text produced in the institutional setting takes on greater authority than the reality it aims to represent (92).

In their project, Aull and Lewis envision a physician-intellectual whose writing will ensure alternative representations of "the weak and oppressed," counter exclusion and stereotypes, and, in a Saidian fashion, "speak truth to power" (98). The personal criticism inherent in memoirs of well-being, though, evinces that powerful counter-narratives are by no means limited to representations by empathetic medical professionals. To a much greater extent, the first-hand accounts conveyed in autobiographical writing work to unhinge hierarchical power structures by not only privileging the account of the illness or disability experience from the inside, but by challenging the foundations on which power in the medical system rests. Memoirs may indeed function, as Mita Banerjee observes, as correctives to the alleged objectivity of science ("Panel" 539).

On the basic level, they refute a belief that is particularly common in the biomedical setting, namely that knowledge can be divided neatly into two categories, i.e. subjective – the patient's subjective perceptions – and objective – data that may be verified. This is highly significant and David Morris stresses that this distinction also entails a value system that devalues the patient's qualitative experiences and places great emphasis on ostensibly more trustworthy sources of knowledge (*Krankheit* 39). Ultimately, such a view grants medical professionals great authority over their patients' experiences of illness and disability (cf. also ibid.). Of course, as Gygax reminds readers, in memoirs, the patient as both the narrator and autobiographical subject assumes particular authority to begin with ("Life" 291). The notion of authority is then reconsidered in memoirs of well-being, when third-person knowledge is claimed by the ill and disabled memoirists themselves and in their stories doctors are, if not portrayed as utterly misunderstanding, to a large extent silent, or even entirely absent. Instead, the memoirists themselves employ objective and theoretical perspectives from their own and other disciplines to explore the cultural and social construction of their conditions (cf. ibid. 292) and to probe and challenge the power of medical, scientific, as well as cultural discourses to account for their experiences.

What is more, these narratives reconceptualize the status of objective knowledge and Banerjee claims that memoirs may reveal or share the uncertainties of knowledge ("Panel" 539). Knowledge, even in the form of data, lab work, and brain scans, ceases to be treated as fixed and stable and is instead historized and depicted as contingent. As a result, the writers' theoretical inquiries into the subject become "exercises in searching [...], charged with uncertainty rather than mastery" and hence breach the conventional idea of theory, as well as established notions of illness and disability (Gygax, "Life" 298). Frequently, such memoirs shy away from definitive answers and rather leave their readers with an open ending, forcing them to accept the instability of health and the contingency of theoretical and professional discourses.

As a narrative strategy, bringing the somatic and the theoretical into dialogue is more than the writers' attempt to "find agency in accidents" (Tougaw, "Autobiography" 15). Their probing transcends individual concerns and instead, as Gygax stresses in her essay, calls attention to the more general issues and questions that their personal stories bring forth ("Life" 298). These personal narratives ultimately not only give shape to the experience of illness, but are capable of shaping medical knowledge and the sociocultural understanding of illness, disability, and health, and therefore constitute empowering resources for ill and disabled individuals (cf. Clarke 3).

In my close readings in the following chapters, I aim to scrutinize the effects of the memoirists' self-representation on the discursive frameworks in which such self-portrayals are located. Questions about how this influences their selves are inescapable, since Nancy Miller notes that personal criticism is voiced by a body conspicuously marked by race, nationality, gender – and disability (284), yet by turning to the personal criticism performed in these texts I seek to explore the ways in which knowledge is (re)claimed or rejected, acts that invariably also involve the memoirists' engagement with and revision of traditional scripts for writing about illness and disability.

2.3 NARRATING ILLNESS AND DISABILITY: CONVENTIONAL SCRIPTS AND THEIR REVISIONS

> Triumph over adversity, redemption, courage in the face of the unknown, recovery, optimism, hope: these sell. Fear, uncertainty, anger, and chaos do not.
> (GARRISON)

When examining illness and disability memoirs and their relationship to health, one will find, as I have already hinted at in the introduction, that they share a number of conventional scripts and plotlines which reinforce the power of health. This innovative perspective brings together life narratives of illness and disability without diminishing the sociopolitical charge of 'disability' and enables readers to gain insights into the ways in which memoirists claim knowledge and agency. In the following, I want to sketch the narrative features and aesthetics common to their stories and, in pointing to alternative narratives, lay the groundwork for the analyses below.

First and foremost, conventional scripts are restricted by the "dominance of the recovery narrative" (Garden, "Telling" 131) or what Couser calls "the tyranny of the comic plot": Since both illness and disability are so negatively connoted, culturally preferred representations follow a progressive narrative of triumph and eventually end happily with the memoirists "overcoming" their ailments ("Empire" 308). They either return to health or transcend their conditions, passing as healthy or 'normal' – either way, "the protagonist is clearly better off at the end than at the beginning" (Couser, "(Un)Common" n. pag.).[11] Inherent in Couser's imagery of the tyranny is the force of this master narrative and, by extension, the potency of health as a concept.[12] These triumphant narratives silence, flout, and suppress the manifold voices who may (need to) tell a different story and instead force them to align the portrayals of their experiences with dominant scripts. Peter Brooks holds that narrative "demarcates, encloses, establishes limits, orders" (quoted in Garden, "Telling" 123). Drawing on his work, Rebecca Garden claims that constraints and order effectively influence the ways in which stories about illness and disability, particularly their endings, are composed: even though a large number of narratives deal with conditions for which there is no cure, happy endings dominate these accounts (ibid.). Conway traces a very similar argument when she holds that the triumph narrative frequently betrays the writer's experience by postulating successful treatment as medical triumph when indeed individuals need to face continued treatment or monitoring, remain susceptible to disease, have been made aware of the contingency of their health (*Illness* 13), and, in short, cannot fulfill the script of the triumph narrative (cf. Garden, "Telling" 127). As a result, the memoir, a form that allows ill and disabled individuals to represent themselves, rather than be subjected to the marginalizing and patronizing misconceptions of third-person narrators, and offers the possibility of challenging stereotypes oftentimes perpetuate the misrepresenta-

---

11 In her essay "Hope in Hard Times: Moments of Epiphany in Illness Narratives" Marilyn Chandler McEntyre's explores how the narration of hope in illness narratives is related to medicine and the cultural construction of illness (in: *The Gift of Story: Narrating Hope in a Postmodern World*. Eds. Emily Griesinger and Mark Eaton. Waco: Baylor UP, 2006. 229-45).

12 This may even be discerned to a heightened degree in therapeutic self-help narratives, books that Jurecic conceives as "cousins of today's narratives of medical triumphs" (6). In these narratives, health is associated with freedom and the realization of the self (Illouz 298f.). See Eva Illouz's monograph on self-help culture for a detailed discussion of this issue.

tion of illness and disability (cf. also Newman, *Writing* 8f.; Couser, "Empire" 305; Couser, "Conflicting" 78).[13]

This, of course, has far-reaching consequences for the status of illness and disability in the public discourse, where the idea that these conditions are tragedies or abnormalities to be corrected and normalized is reinforced (Garden, "Disability" 73). On the one hand, triumph narratives, by climaxing in the writers' cure or a significant improvement of their conditions brought about by medicine, celebrate medical power. On the other hand, in recording the memoirists' successful attempts at transcending the limitations of their conditions, triumph narratives support the – decidedly American – myth that one may pull oneself out by the bootstraps. Such stories frequently employ the archetype of the so-called 'super crip,' a disabled person who, according to feminist Disability Studies scholar Susan Wendell, heroically conforms to able-bodiedness and even exceeds the endurance or physical strength of able bodies in the performance of unusual activities. The super crip exemplifies the possibility of overcoming one's physical limitations, which in reality is a false ideal most disabled people cannot meet (Wendell, "Toward" 271). Super crips are, as Couser reminds readers, by their very definition atypical, but through such narratives nevertheless become representatives of disability to the public ("Empire" 308). Ultimately, super crip narratives increase rather than reduce the otherness of the majority of people with disabilities (Wendell, "Toward" 271).

Both narratives, the medical restitution narrative and the super crip narrative, however, have remarkably similar implications and lead to the individualization of illness and disability because these narratives suggest that an individual medical cure or an individual's right frame of mind may remediate or defy any health problem. Consequently, such memoirs are deprived of political force and impact, since they render accommodations and alternative ways of thinking about their writers' conditions unnecessary. More than that, they stigmatize, or rather perpetuate the stigma of the respective condition for those who cannot tell a triumphant narrative. In her study *Illness and the Limits of Expression*, Conway therefore expresses utter dissatisfaction with the triumph story. Having experienced breast cancer herself, she recalls the desire to read about others' experiences and her subsequent discontentment:

"The writers of triumph narratives tend to reflect on their experience relatively little as they go along, reserving reflection for the end. From a position of authority outside the actual experience, they look back and offer this conclusion: if one battles hard and maintains a positive attitude, everything will work out." (1)

---

13 Susannah Mintz critically discusses this in "Dear (Embodied) Reader: Life Writing and Disability" (133).

Conway laments several issues I will return to in the following close readings. First of all, she expresses her outright disagreement with the optimism that the discourse on illness and disability is steeped in and the myth of a battle and positive attitude that pervades many personal accounts. Triumphant storytelling then, she further criticizes, does not take place within the immediate experience, but only from a considerable distance on the safe side of health, when the memoirists have recovered and prepare to leave their experiences behind, ultimately betraying the life-realities of members of the remission society (cf. Chapter 3.2) and widening the gap between health and illness/disability. Rather than bridging divides, these stories add to the isolation of those who find themselves in the midst of an acute experience or need to adjust to living in remission. As a consequence, these individuals are excluded from the community of those similarly affected, as well as from the community of the "healthy" because returning to health becomes a matter of individual responsibility.

While triumphant and restitution narratives quite explicitly celebrate health as the absence of the pathological or deviant, there are also other narrative aesthetics which carry strong undercurrents of health. Particularly memoirs storying acquired disabilities or illnesses beginning late in the memoirists' lives may feature what Couser fittingly terms the "rhetoric of nostalgia." Removed from the prospects the future may hold, narrators look back on their lives as able-bodied persons and yearn for a return to these "normal" lives (*Signifying* 40). Other rhetorical aspects may be discerned in stories of both congenital and acquired conditions: Disability life narratives, for instance, may employ a gothic rhetoric of horror that turns disability into a dreaded and dreadful condition to be avoided at all costs (Couser, "Conflicting" 80). Consequently, readers are repulsed or feel pity, a reaction that seems at odds with the subjective stance of the memoir, yet engages a similar narrative of progress as restitution and triumph narratives and moves ideas of cure or rehabilitation into the foreground. Memoirists whose impairments are "corrected or transcended" use such rhetoric to look back on their afflictions and celebrate their escape from marginalization (Couser, *Signifying* 34). Similarly, chaos narratives, as also briefly alluded to in the introduction, depict illness as horrific suffering, impotence, and a situation that cannot be imagined as ever improving again (Frank, *Wounded* 97). Much like gothic disability life narratives, chaotic illness memoirs clearly assign positive and utterly negative values to the states of health and illness, respectively. By underscoring the pathological of the memoirists' conditions as well as their suffering, these memoirs implicitly celebrate health and their aesthetic choices at the least work to maintain, but sometimes even widen the gap between health and illness/disability.

Additionally, readers will encounter stories abandoning the realm of the medical and secular in favor of religious and spiritual explorations. In many disability memoirs Couser identifies a "rhetoric of spiritual compensation" which does not only open a discursive realm for the symbolic construction of disability as a marker of sin or God's displeasure, but initially also contributes to the narrators' sense of inferiority (*Signifying* 36). Nevertheless, these narratives feature a consoling comic plot because spiritual compensation is attained when the memoirists recognize that their disabilities have an implicit purpose, e.g. teaching them to be better persons (ibid. 38).

This plot, too, bears great similarities to the quest narrative, a wide-spread mode of narrating illness (cf. also Chapter 1). According to Frank, who has coined the term, writers of the quest narrative commonly take arising symptoms as the beginning of a journey. On "the road of trials," they will encounter suffering, e.g. through medical procedures or stigma, but in their life narratives, this suffering is "progressively understood as teaching something and thus [...] gain[s] meaning" ("Reclaiming" 7f.). Although the focal and climactic points of quest narratives and narratives of spiritual compensation depart from recovery scripts (cf. also ibid.), these plotlines are not without their own sets of problems. Both narratives traditionally neglect the materiality of the writers' conditions in favor of spiritual explorations in which living with the ill or disabled body is the means to a metaphysical end, rather than an end itself. Consequently, quest narratives and narratives of spiritual compensation postulate disembodiment – they render the body silent or assume a dualist stance in which the mind is removed from the afflicted or impaired body.[14]

---

14 Another prominent example is Peter Graham's notion of the 'metapathography,' an extremely problematic classificatory scheme. Graham introduces this term in his analysis of illness and disability memoirs by acclaimed writers (Reynold Price, Norman Cousins and Raymond Carver), arguing that these do not only constitute personal accounts of the writers' illness experiences, but manage to take the reader beyond the frame of the pathography, since the writers "write themselves out of illness and suffering" (73). While he aptly recognizes the potential of these narratives to withstand the silence and passivity that illness may hold for the writers and to endow them with agency and authority (cf. 84), thus stressing the healing dimension inherent in the process of writing, his concept is too idealistic, especially for narratives emerging from the remission society. Graham asserts that in metapathographies, subjects can "[write themselves] beyond illness," in the sense of allowing for their careers to continue despite their diseases (cf. 78; 85). Graham's idea of transcending illness is thus a personal intellectual endeavor, but neglects the corporeal: Although Price, for instance, is able to complete several novels and plays, as well as write poetry in spite of his decreasing health, his illness does eventually leave him disabled and in a wheelchair. The metapathography then reinforces normalcy by depicting the writers' transcendence of their conditions as the desirable theme. The emphasis in recent memoirs on the instability of health, the lack of closure, and the chronicity of illness betrays any notion of truly moving "beyond illness." Furthermore, Graham claims that "in the hands

Conventional narratives fail to destigmatize illness and disability and instead continue to carry medical undercurrents as they revolve around notions of restoration, rehabilitation, cure, or transcending illness or disability. These narratives thus reflect the images that have dominated the representation of disabled persons for much of the twentieth century since the rise of the medical model of disability (cf. Chapter 3.1) and the increasing institutionalization of 'pathological' or 'deviant' individuals. A close inspection of these plot lines and narrative aesthetics elucidates that the audience's fear, revulsion, and pity are driving forces in the construction of these stories. Their rhetoric therefore bears striking similarities to the narratives of progress brought forth by the charity organizations that have controlled and in some instances continue to control the public representation of individuals otherwise entirely removed from the public eye.[15] Though written from a first-person perspective, these life narratives render illness and disability through an objective outside perspective because their subjective stance is permeated by an internalized perspective of marginalization.

Yet although much of the previously published criticism centers on narratives portraying their writers as struggling and coping with or overcoming their constitutions, I absolutely agree with Rebecca Garden who holds that for many disabled individuals (and persons with long-term and chronic conditions I would add more generally), their conditions form a vital aspect of their lives and have quintessential-

---

of the metapathographer, illness itself is diminished [...]. The metapathographer understands illness not merely by taking its measure but by using its dimensions to achieve greater interpretive height above the world of the living" (84f.). Illness is romanticized here and, in line with the traditional quest narrative, depicted as a condition that may provoke deep insight. Leaving pathography behind to "reach for literary life. And immortality" (ibid. 86), may be unruly in the face of the writers' bodily conditions, but Graham's notion of the metapathography rather undermines than exhausts the subversive potential of such narratives.

15 Cf., for instance, the depiction of 'poster children' in charity adds during the Depression era and beyond (esp. for the FDR March of Dimes) or on telethons, particularly the Labor Day telethon of the Muscular Dystrophy Association hosted by Jerry Lewis from the 1960s to 2011 that has prompted wide protests from within the disability community. Invaluable insights are offered in Doris Fleischer's and Frieda Zames's monograph *The Disability Rights Movement: From Charity to Confrontation* (2nd ed. Philadelphia: Temple UP, 2011), Paul Longmore's essay "'Heaven's Special Child': The Making of Poster Children" (in: *The Disability Studies Reader*. 4th ed. Ed. Lennard Davis. New York: Routledge: 2013. 34-41), and the chapter "Pity as oppression in the Jerry Lewis Telethon" in Beth Haller's *Representing Disability in an Ableist World: Essays on Mass Media* (Louisville: Advocado Press, 2010. 137-52).

ly shaped their identities ("Disability" 73). Their narratives reflect this by first of all narrating illness and bodily difference "as embedded within webs of family, community, and culture," and elucidating its sociocultural context (Garden, "Telling" 122), as well as through endings that, in contrast to the comic ending of triumph and restitution narratives, may not be "particularly happy," but "speak of resolution and self-acceptance" (ibid. 124). For Conway, this entails that writers "embrace all aspects of the experience and [...] remain true to themselves throughout" (*Illness* 3).[16] Because comic plots are still so pervasive in the rendition of illness and disability, Couser is absolutely right in remarking that stories which do not feature or even openly refuse a conventional happy ending, carry great weight ("[Un]Common" n. pag.) and this book not only seeks to acknowledge such narratives, but explore the consequences of their writers' unruliness.

To some extent, these memoirs overlap with a category of narratives that Couser, in classifying disability narratives, identifies as stories of "physical and psychological emancipation" (*Signifying* 44). It is in these texts, he argues, that narrators begin to disassociate their experiences from the medical framework and explore the possibilities of accommodation into mainstream society. Despite the fact that a comic plot is not absent in these stories, either, notions of overcoming rather focus on the ways in which societal and cultural obstacles can be grappled with (ibid.). To this effect, disability is not portrayed as a flaw but as a construct rooted in prejudices and normativity, which is a fundamental shift in the representation of disability that Couser does not fully acknowledge here, since he at once asserts that the political critique in these texts is "muted" (ibid. 47). The shift in the perception of deficits and defects from one's own body to society is, as I will illustrate in Chapter 3.1, a powerful and politically charged move and what he alludes to here is in fact the very basis of the social model of disability and the Disability Rights Movement. Hence these texts are capable of resymbolizing disability (cf. Torrell 324).

---

16 In her own memoir of breast cancer, a book she describes as surprisingly "raw," "unrelenting" and "angry" in the afterword (254ff.), Conway closes the final chapter with the direct representation of a conversation between her and her daughter Molly who asks her: "'Is it over. Mom.?' I ask, 'Is what over, honey.?' 'Breast cancer,' she replies. 'Yes, Molly,' I answer, 'breast cancer is over'" (251). The closure and triumph offered in her narrative are, however, revoked in the afterword in which Conway stresses the "knowledge of illness and death as ever present possibilities" (261) and ends with a contemplation of death (264). Her afterword therefore revises the ending of the memoir and exposes, as Garden outlines, the narrative conventions at work in the storying of chronic conditions ("Telling" 122). Cf. also Garden's essay "Telling" (133) and Conway's study *Illness* (120ff.), where she discusses so-called "renegotiated endings."

Notwithstanding the fact that Couser's taxonomy is highly valuable (it is not only the first but probably also to the most extensive to date), it is limited because it first of all overlooks the potential of life narratives to redefine notions of disability and impairment. Secondly, despite the fact that he focuses on contemporary texts, Couser neglects to include many texts that exhibit an alternative conception of disability, one that is not only removed from the medical context, but that works to destigmatize disability by deconstructing the line between ability and disability, emphasizing contingency, and reworking the "normal." The sheer number of recent texts that broach the cultural construction of disability, societal constraints, disability activism, the "taboo" of sexuality, as well as disability and family life turns these texts into more than noteworthy exceptions in a systematic approach to the disability memoir. These texts challenge their readers, particularly their nondisabled readers, because they continue to point to the lack of accommodation that still persists, engage in the discussion of topics deemed absent from disabled persons' lives, such as sexuality and relationships or a life past middle age, and write back at their readers' pity, revulsion, or fear.

Moreover, these narratives frame disability in the context of community (cf. also Torrell 324). Although the narrators do address alienation and – in cases of acquired disabilities – fading bonds with nondisabled people, their immersion into new communities and especially into the community of other disabled people are significant moments in these stories. These narratives stand in stark contrast to David Mitchell's criticism in "The Body Solitaire," where he purports that

"disability life writing tends toward the gratification of a personal story bereft of community with other disabled people. Even the most renowned disability autobiographers often fall prey to an ethos of rugged individualism that can further reify the longstanding association of disability with social isolation." (312)

The problem in Mitchell's argumentation is rooted in the understanding of autobiography, or rather memoir, as a singular story. When an individual is placed at its center, the memoir may, Couser purports in a very similar manner, rather be aligned with the medical and individualizing approach to disability than with a social and political perspective ("Empire" 308, cf. also Cheu 106). A further problem rests in the fact that both Mitchell and Couser see disability memoirs against the backdrop of traditional Western autobiographies (cf. Chapter 2.1), whose values – "rugged individualism" and success – cannot be met by disabled writers and whose focus on the individual's outstanding difference is actually an aspect that both medicine and society tend to devalue as pathology and abnormality (cf. "Empire" 309). While their precautions must not be neglected, they may be refuted when disability and illness memoirs are aligned with the widely-studied tradition of women's autobiography and when they are indeed conceptualized as memoirs, rather than autobiographies.

In their life narratives, women writers have for a long time destabilized the "I" at the center of the traditional autobiography and instead composed stories grounded in a sense of community in which they depict themselves tied to others in multiple ways (Mintz, "Dear" 133; cf. also Torrell 324). The same holds true for disability memoirs, yet I propose not only for the disabled women writers who Susannah Mintz studies (cf. "Dear" 134),[17] but to a large extent also for male writers as well. This may be illustrated by taking Mintz's elaboration into account, for she holds that dominant narratives of a unified and stable selfhood are unhinged when disease or physical impairment are understood as intersecting with other signposts of identity that make allegiance with only one group impossible and therefore rather highlight than resolve ruptures in selfhood and create "disorderly 'I's […] incompatible with unidimensional or essentialized myths of identity" (134f.).

On the other hand, the presentation of community is not limited to frictions and ruptures, but, like in the memoirs of well-being at hand, community may also personally and politically empower the writers, since the groups with which the memoirists associate themselves amplify and authorize their individual voices (Torrell 325). Margaret Torrell maintains that through such references to community, the texts depart from a "purely personal expression" and do indeed help to counter mainstream representations of illness and disability, as well as foster and give voice to a positive identity conception (326). When the subject at the center of the text is therefore seen as the member of a community, memoirs may forcefully highlight the social and political nature of illness and disability (Cheu 107), i.e. politicize bodily difference.

---

17 For a thorough discussion of women and disability, cf., for instance Mary Jo Deegan's and Nancy Brooks's volume *Women and Disability: The Double Handicap* (New Brunswick: Transaction Books, 1985), Michelle Fine's and Adrienne Asch's *Women with Disabilities: Essays in Psychology, Culture, and Politics* (Philadelphia, PA: Temple UP, 1988) or Susan Wendell's *The Rejected Body: Feminist Philosophical Reflections on Disability* (New York: Routledge, 1996).

3. Approaching 'Well-Being'

3.1 Health Problems and the Problem with 'Health'

In recent years, sociologists and philosophers of medicine have struggled to conceptualize 'health,' as it is unclear how exactly the term is to be defined, which nuances are to be accounted for, and which other notions overlap (Engelhardt 42). This is due to the fact that scholarship in these disciplines has previously rather focused on bodily malfunctioning,[1] thus tacitly accepting health as the "absence of illness" or, to borrow from surgeon René Leriche, the "silence of the organs" (quoted in Sontag 44). This understanding of health, commonly referred to as the negative definition, is not only, as Alexa Franke outlines, one of the oldest attempts at defining health, but is also the assumption underlying Western medicine, its taxonomies and practices (39). The debate over the meaning and implications of health, but also of its supposed complements illness and disability therefore has far-reaching consequences for the critical engagement with these terms, as well as for practical medicine and the health care system (cf. Schramme 9). When philosopher Thomas Schramme therefore introduces the debate over an adequate definition in his introduction to the volume on theories of illness, he is certainly right in stressing the significance of these definitions for the practice of medicine and society on the whole: In the practice of medical care, 'disease,' 'impairment,' and 'health' denominate the reasons for clinical intervention, as well as its desired outcomes, while in society, they carry

---

1 Alexa Franke, too, notes that even though particularly philosophers have long been exploring matters of health, a unified theory of health does not exist. Only since the 1970s researchers have begun to develop so-called 'salutogenetic' models of health (Franke 169). Introduced by sociologist of medicine Aaron Antonovsky, 'salutogenesis' rests on two basic propositions, namely (1) that diseases do not constitute abnormalities, but are essentially part and parcel of human life and (2) that health and illness are not polarized ends on a scale (Franke 170).

immense weight, because they are not only descriptive, but also normative notions (cf. ibid.; Engelhardt 41).

In this subchapter, I will clarify 'disease' and 'illness,' as well as the corresponding set of terms 'impairment' and 'disability' and probe their relation to what is traditionally regarded as 'health.' I will introduce what philosophers of medicine commonly refer to as the 'naturalistic' and the 'phenomenological approach,' two avenues of research also widely acknowledged in other disciplines. Although I fully agree with philosopher Havi Carel, who notes that these two approaches should not be conceived as irreconcilable oppositions but should rather be seen as complementing each other (8f.), the texts that I read closely in the subsequent chapters of course privilege a phenomenological position and grant readers insights into the memoirists' lived experience, as well as the perspectives and knowledge emerging from the particularities of these experiences, rather than relying on naturalistic and medical explanatory schemes.

The term 'disease' describes the pathological characteristics of the biological organism that may be explained with references to entities and concepts of the natural world (cf. Schramme 14, 24; Carel 11). Perceived as localized in cells, tissues, or organs,[2] 'disease' is according to Kleinman defined as that which the medical professional "creates" using "theories of disorder" (5). Despite the fact that disease is grasped in the neutral and objective terms of the third-person perspective (cf. also Carel 8), Kleinman's use of the verb "create" is emblematic for the understanding of disease as a constructed entity, a mode of thought shared by a host of other scholars from a variety of disciplines when they refer to the "interaction between social factors – such as attitudes, beliefs, social relations, and ideas – and biological insights that result in the appearance, definition, and/or change in meaning of disease" (Aronowitz 10). This is not to say that scientifically identified causes for diseases, such as viruses or bacteria, do not exist or that diseases do not cause bodily changes, as Rose Weitz is careful to stress in *The Sociology of Health, Illness, and Health Care*. For her, the understanding of disease as a constructed entity rather focuses on the ways members of a community organize their ideas about such viruses, bacteria, and bodily changes (123). As a result, disease is regarded differently in respective cultures, places, and points in time (ibid.).

Weitz's explanation manifests first of all that definitions of diseases are not stable, which becomes evident for instance in the profound changes the entries of the *Diagnostic Statistical Manual* undergo from edition to edition and the medicalization of processes previously not conceived of as pathological. Despite the fact that

---

2   In his essay, Schramme sketches the history of the notion of disease from antiquity, when the entire person was seen as the "location" of disease to the present and the idea that disease may be rooted in our DNA (17ff.).

the classification of symptoms is hardly regarded as problematic, particularly in standard procedures, medical historian Robert Aronowitz emphasizes that the medical knowledge at work is contingent, not only in cases where speculative etiologic ideas are applied, but equally in standard medical classifications (10f.).[3] The underlying assumption of social construction is that the shape disease takes, first of all in medical practice when it is diagnosed, treated and when prognoses are announced, and secondly in a more general sociocultural context when physicians, researchers, and patients give meaning to it, is "neither a necessary nor an inevitable consequence of biological processes, but rather is contingent on social factors" (ibid.).

Statistical considerations in particular, alongside with findings about the physiological functions of an organism therefore account for the categorization of a person as either healthy or un-healthy (Schramme 31). Accordingly, this categorization rests with clinicians and other medical experts (Franke 29) and is thus based on the objective stance. Consequently, patients are excluded from the processes of gaining and interpreting knowledge about their bodies and their subjective perspective is elided, so that this traditional definition implicitly works to maintain the rigid power hierarchies in institutional medicine and restricts patients' participation in the clinical discourse, as well as their authority to evaluate their own condition or state of health (Davis, "Rule" 43).

The second problem is inherent in the fact that statistical data are traditionally applied when checking for disease or its absence and determining whether a person is healthy. A number of scholars, most recently Disability Studies scholar Lennard Davis, have convincingly argued that statistical data are highly problematic when applied to bodies to measure their respective deviance or health, i.e. normalcy. In fact, as Davis's exploration of the history of these ideas reveals, the utterance of the word "normal" in connection to corporeality originated in the advent of statistics approximately 170 years ago ("Crips" 504). In contrast, until the nineteenth century, bodies in Western culture were conceptualized in relation to what was seen as "ideal," an idea dating back to the seventeenth century. Measured against the ideal, all bodies were necessarily found lacking (cf. ibid.; Davis, "Constructing" 10). Hence he finds that the human body was not required to meet the ideal (cf. ibid.)

---

3 In parts, Aronowitz shares historian Charles Rosenberg's critical stance on the notion of 'social construction' in the context of medicine. Rosenberg instead suggests to speak of 'framing' a disease, yet more for the purpose of ridding the discourse of what he sees as a "programmatically charged metaphor" than to develop an entirely new perspective on the ways in which diseases are typically classified and explained (xv). In his introduction to the volume *Framing Disease: Studies in Cultural History* (Eds. Charles Rosenberg and Janet Golden. New Brunswick: Rutgers UP: 1992. xiii-xxvi), Rosenberg elaborates his criticism and outlines his approach.

and a community was united by the fact that none of its members conformed to the ideal. So the form of community Davis sketches here is one in which impaired bodies encounter acceptance and, while they may stand out, are not relegated to the margins on grounds of their bodily difference.

Community, however, was radically altered when statistics became a widely accepted mode of first of all measuring populations and later assessing public health and the distribution of health and disease, culminating in the fiction of "the average man" (cf. ibid. 11; cf. also Davis, "Rule" 39). The average man and with him the majority of the community are contained in the center under the high arch of a Gaussian bell curve. Yet the bell curve, Davis maintains, does not merely establish the exclusive concept of normalcy. Due to the fact that any bell curve shows extreme cases – deviant characteristics – on both sides, it simultaneously introduces the notion of deviance and constructs the ill or impaired body (Davis, "Constructing" 13f.), thereby dividing the community into a large group of "normal," "average," and healthy individuals, and small groups of individuals who lack a certain quality or exhibit too much of it.[4] Models of health and illness, for instance philosopher of medicine Georges Canguilhem's well-established approach to the pathological, often take the same line by conceptualizing disease as a quantitative aberrance (21) and successful medical therapy as either returning something that the patient has been lacking or ridding the patient of what is excessive (19).

Moreover, Davis holds that the concepts of normality and deviance have also established the "imperative to be normal" ("Crips" 504), i.e. to be identified as "constituting, conforming to, not deviating or different from, the common type or standard, regular, usual" so that the average becomes – paradoxically, Davis notes – a new kind of ideal of what the body should be like ("Constructing" 10, 12, 17).[5]

---

4   Davis elaborates that the bell curve was later revised by natural scientist Francis Galton to locate the "normal" not with the average majority and instead introduce a rating of desirable traits and characteristics, so that features falling on the extreme right of the curve, such as e.g. high intelligence, would no longer be considered deviant, but rank highest (cf. "Constructing" 16f.), which ultimately imposes a new ideal on the community.

5   In his essay "The Rule of Normalcy," Davis elaborates these points by sketching the entity of what he terms the 'patient/citizen' and linking the rhetoric surrounding the body to the body politic, more precisely to democracy and capitalism. "[T]he normal tranquil body is silent, operating with its moderate methods. Disease involves excessiveness, excitability, noise, attention, irritation, stimulation," he writes (42) and reasons that much like the "excess" of revolution which needs to be toned down to "moderation, silence, and invisibility," disease must be regulated and "returned to the silent norm" (43). As a consequence, the rule of normalcy creates bodies compliant with both the medical and the political system (44).

On these grounds, any form of variation ceases to be viewed in neutral terms and is constructed as negative and undesirable, which significantly goes beyond the understanding of disease or impairment as biological processes only (cf. also Carel 12). It is therefore this historical development that prompts the association of illness and disability with (individual) problems (cf. also Davis, "Constructing" 9), entailing the processes of exclusion still at work today.

On the theoretical plane, bodies thus constructed as deviant, abnormal, and unhealthy have informed the so-called 'medical model' of disability, the principal paradigm for much of the twentieth century which frames disability as an individual defect or deficit that needs to be cured so that the person suffering from it may achieve the full status of a human being (Siebers 3f.). Disability Studies scholars like Linton remind the community that the medical perspective has substantially contributed to the quality of the lives of many disabled persons, since medical treatment options have improved and frequently saved their lives. On the other hand, Linton emphasizes that the continuing medical attention and the focus on health and the prevention of diseases or impairments are highly problematic (*Claiming* 11). In the context of the medical establishment, as Theri Pickens claims, this perspective has made painful treatments acceptable at the expense of the patients and the quality of their lives (170f.). Pickens's statement reveals a troublesome quandary in the medical model that Linton, too, alludes to, namely that disabled persons continue to be referred to as 'patients' caught in the hierarchical structures of medical institutions aimed at correcting deviance and pathology.

But not only in the context of disability has this rigid and constructed view on health left pathological bodies stigmatized. With regard to illness, too, the statistical underpinnings perpetuate the power of 'health' as both concept and desired corporeal state[6] and thereby foreground the medical cure as the means by which the body may again conform to the standard. Additionally, like in the medical model of disability, disease is framed in terms of the individual. According to Schramme, disease is something an individual "has," thereby implying that the condition may be abstracted from the person afflicted with it (cf. 24). In a similar vein, Kleinman sketches disease as a "diagnostic entity, an 'it'" (5). Through the access to and the application of objective medical knowledge, disease is conveyed as separate from the patient.

However, I do not agree with Michael Bury who purports that this separation frees patients from "the burden of responsibility," enabling them to perceive themselves as "victim[s] of external forces" (173). The association of disease with an in-

---

6   In this context, also see Disability Studies scholar Robert McRuer's insightful critique of 'compulsory able-bodiedness,' the need to conform to "'soundness of bodily health; ability to work; robustness'" (quoted in "Compulsory" 91).

dividual's "problem" is – in our age more than ever before – automatically linked to responsibility. Natural philosopher Klaus Michael Meyer-Abich, for instance points to the veritable cult of physical health that propels the fitness and wellness industries which enable individuals to maintain their bodies' functionality and, as he puts it, "the conveniences" which come with fully functional, i.e. healthy, bodies (22). Wellness and fitness have emerged as pervasive forces and conspicuous reminders of our responsibility to take care of ourselves: "There was a time when the only nod to health awareness in public places was the ubiquitous scale that for a nickel would give you your weight *and* your fortune – an indication of how seriously we took the whole thing," Kay Cook observes tongue-in-cheek before pointing to the ubiquity of "cholesterol screening in shopping centers, blood pressure machines in supermarkets, and 'healthmark' signs on certain food products" ("Medical" 81; italics in original). Similarly, Davis takes note of "the social pressures forcing one to 'have' a doctor; to 'have' regular checkups; to find the hidden diseases that may be incipiently growing without your knowledge" (Davis, "Rule" 47 en 8). These statements pinpoint the social expectation that individuals manage their bodies, assume responsibility for their health, and ward off disease as best as they can. Ultimately, this heavy emphasis on individuality and responsibility depoliticizes disease, turning disease and health into medical and personal matters (Weitz 143), and, as Davis illustrates, prescribes "[d]iet rather than control of pesticides, regular checkups rather than the reduction of pollution, sunscreen rather than ozone-saving measures" ("Rule" 47 en 8).

In contrast to 'disease,' 'illness' is generally understood as the unique phenomenological and existential experience of a condition, of symptoms, and of suffering (cf. Schramme 14, 24; Kleinman 3). In this context, Kleinman focuses on what he refers to as the "lived experience of monitoring bodily processes," i.e. perceiving and judging symptoms, acting on them, categorizing experiences in lay terms, responding to them, and living with them (3f.). While Kleinman's definition certainly addresses key ideas pertaining to the lived experience of the body's materiality, it is very much geared to an understanding of illness in medical terms and may thus only delineate one dimension of a complex experience.

A turn to the lived experience of illness challenges the objective – and, Carel recognizes, objectifying – third-person perspective of the medical professional and privileges the subjective view of the first-person (8). Yet 'illness' is not merely the subjective complement of the objective condition that medical practitioners describe based on their scientific observations and classificatory schemes, as philosopher Evandro Agazzi points out when he offers a comprehensive definition of illness as "reality":

"In the case of illness, [...] even not a particularly serious one, we clearly perceive a global change in our way of being and living: We become unable to perform quite a lot of actions and functions that are absolutely trivial and elementary. We suddenly become dependent on other persons; our spatial and temporal borders are drastically reduced; we live in a palpable way a situation of impotence, limitation, and fragility; our capability of carrying out projects is greatly reduced; our body, that until this moment was one and the same thing with our self and remained "unperceived" and "silent," becomes something that stands in front of us as an external obstacle. In short, we feel that we are no longer ourselves. These general features are greatly magnified when illness increases persistence and seriousness, when it entails important and durable handicaps, and when the prospects for its duration, possibilities of healing, degree of a possible recovery are uncertain. Our experience of illness becomes even more tragic when intense physical pain and the perspective of a fatal end accompany all of the above features." (3f.; italics in original)

In Agazzi's definition it becomes clear that the qualitative experience of illness is one of great complexity. As his quotation elucidates, the experience of illness is indeed a *lived* experience, one that fundamentally alters the ways in which individuals may lead their lives and one that bears influence on all aspects of life. First of all, Agazzi characterizes illness as a form of inability or dis-ability.[7] This may include the mastery of ordinary tasks in everyday life, but also refers to one's professional life, where illness may demand an interruption in the work schedule or may even require individuals to resign from their jobs or discontinue their education.

For him, this entails dependency on others, family members and friends, as well as on medical practitioners or strangers. With regard to the first group of people, Bury holds that the "rules of reciprocity and mutual support" are suspended during the experience of illness (169), thus implying that the structures of reciprocal relationships are unhinged and the ill individual can no longer contribute to the relationship. Therefore, the experience of illness has far-reaching consequences for the patient's social status and a person's sense of self is significantly influenced by the cultural and social connotations which give shape to his/her image of him/herself, as well as determine how the patient is seen by others.

Connected to the patient's need of coming to terms with the corporeality of the body and the materiality of the disease and its symptoms is, as Medical Humanities scholar Howard Brody argues, the urgent necessity of confronting one's vulnerability and mortality (99). Pain and suffering, before seen as either the plight of other people or remote possibilities at the most, become acute forces. As a consequence, illness transforms the awareness of the structures of everyday life, as well as the course of life itself (Bury 169). Established routines and beliefs are re-evaluated and patients are often forced to accommodate new routines, such as doctor's visits, regular examinations, hospital stays, and sick leaves.

---

7 For a reading of illness as dis-ability, also cf. Chapter 3 in Carel's *Illness*.

Illness hence becomes a powerful force in the scope of the patient's life: It may disrupt the presumed or desired plot of a person's life (Couser, *Recovering* 5), or forever alter it. Accordingly, the past needs to be revised and accounted for, and, equally important, a possible future must be envisioned (cf. Garro and Mattingly 2). Especially the latter aspect is difficult due to the uncertainty and unpredictability of the experience. Cultural Studies scholar Jackie Stacey deftly characterizes her own story as one of utter uncertainty where it was "impossible to predict the future, because the present situation might change at any moment" (4). As a result, patient-writers may feel disempowered by the unpredictability of the experience (cf. also Rimmon-Kenan 10) but at the same time, embracing the open-endedness of their story and deliberately foregoing narrative closure may bestow writers with a sense of agency.

While 'illness' serves as the phenomenological counterpart of 'disease,' 'disability' supplements 'impairment' as a term that draws attention to the qualitative and lived experience and has substantially contributed to a change in the perception of impairment. Striving to foster a better understanding of and to improve disabled persons' lives, activists and intellectuals have called for a shift "from the individual to society and from normalization to rehabilitation" (Newman, *Writing* 7), a move that has been coined the 'social model' of disability. In his *Disability Theory*, Tobin Siebers outlines the social model of disability as a perspective that dissociates disability from the medical context and instead considers it a product of political injustice and social oppression, one not in need of medical attention, but one that demands changes in the social perception of disabled persons and the built environment (3f.). In contrast to the medical model, the social model does not assert that impairment constitutes disability. Disability rather arises, as Carol Thomas notes, from the physical and attitudinal barriers that the nondisabled majority has erected in society and that place constraints on the lives of people with impairments or exclude them altogether ("Theorien" 38). Consequently, disability ceases to be a personal matter and the problem of an individual because responsibility is shifted to society (cf. Linton, *Claiming* 11). Furthermore, the social model allows for a distinction between the categories 'impairment' and 'disability': 'Impairment' is seen as a physical fact, while 'disability' is conceived as socially constructed (cf. also Newman 7).

In *Disability Studies: An Interdisciplinary Introduction*, Dan Goodley defines impairment as "a defective limb organism or mechanism of the body," while referring to disability as "the disadvantage or restriction of activity caused by a contemporary social organization which takes no account of people who have physical impairments and thus excludes them from mainstream social activities" (8). Correspondingly, impairment may result in disability (ibid. 5): Deafness, for instance, is an impairment, but ultimately constitutes a disability in a society in which sign language is not a wide-spread means of communication. Similarly, paraplegia is understood as an impairment, yet wheelchair users are disabled by the prevalence of stairs denying them entry to buildings. Although, much like 'disease' and 'illness,' both terms are frequently used interchangeably, their distinction is of immense importance to the project of Disability Studies and the discipline's aim to challenge the essentialism inherent in "the idea that the social and economic status and assigned roles of people with disabilities are inevitable outcomes of their condition" (Linton quoted in Longmore, *Why* 4).

As important as these observations are, the social model does have its drawbacks. Its first stumbling block is the idea of rehabilitation that dominates much of the scholarship on the social model and that the *OED* defines as the "[r]estoration of a person to health or normal activity after injury, illness, disablement, or addiction by means of medical or surgical treatment, physical and occupational therapy, psychological counselling, etc." (n. pag.). While undoubtedly of immense social and personal value, the focus on rehabilitation as pronounced by Sara Newman and other critics is useful for the field of social sciences, yet in context of the cultural perception of disability, it still implies that impairment/disability is a state in need of control and a condition in which individuals lack the skills necessary to function as full members of society. Davis is equally critical of the social model that he aptly refers to as "rehabilitation model" and laments its focus on "repair, concealment, remediation, and supervision" ("Crips" 506). Furthermore, Michael Bérubé stresses that the discussion of disability in the exclusive context of rehabilitation and other "applied fields" of social science fails to grasp the complex and at times intractable link between disability and identity ("Foreword" viii).

Newman is also aware of a second problem with respect to the social model, precisely its strict distinction between impairment and disability, physical reality and social construct. Like all dichotomies, she argues, the binary at the heart of the social model "reifies the very categories it seeks to destabilize" (7). A host of other scholars[8] have begun to criticize and call into question the social model, arguing that it "overlook[s] the material conditions of the body, and the body as a material

---

8   Carol Thomas's essay "How is Disability Understood? An Examination of Sociological Approaches" (*Disability & Society* 19.6 (2004): 569-83) surveys a number of approaches to impairment and disability and provides a concise overview of relevant critical perspectives and their commonalities. Readers might also consult Thomas Shakespeare's and Nicholas Watson's "The Social Model of Disability: An Outdated Ideology?" (*Research in Social Science and Disability* 2 (2001): 9-28) and "The Social Model of Disability and the Disappearing Body: Towards a Sociology of Impairment" by Bill Hughes and Kevin Paterson (*Disability and Society* 12.3 (1997): 325-40), to name just two prominent examples.

condition" (Donaldson 102).[9] The neglect of corporeality and impairment has of course served a strategic purpose in the early stages of the Disability Rights Movement, where showcasing disability and its social implications has effectively helped to pinpoint discrimination (ibid. 111). For many years, scholars have therefore been reluctant to abandon or alter the principles of the social model, foreseeing

> "tremendous difficulty in articulating impairment in ways that do not essentialize disability or reduce it to an individual problem. I think we recognize that outside critics would be willing to latch onto ideas about impairment, and that would deflect attention from the more socially demanding issues such as civil rights or oppression." (Linton, *Claiming* 138)

Linton's concerns here are surely justified yet should not prevent critics from devising ways of thinking more critically about corporeality in the context of disability and fleshing out the disembodied subject at the center of the social model.

What is needed, in consequence, is a phenomenological approach to impairment that does not "treat" the body in medial terms, but opens up a discursive framework for the qualitative experience of the body "over time and in variable circumstances," as Wendell demands, "and any concerns about them that impaired individuals might have" ("Unhealthy" 23). It is important that scholars reckon with the pain and suffering that social justice cannot remediate, but equally important is Wendell's reminder that impairment "is not *only* suffering" (ibid. 31). This means that the physical reality of immobility or bodily deformities, their pain, discomfort, and limitations need to be voiced, but do by no means form the exclusive narrative of disability. When sociologist Irving Kenneth Zola in his seminal essay "Bringing Our Bodies and Ourselves Back In" prompts his readers to reclaim corporeality and urges them to anchor narratives of disability in the gendered, sexual, and impaired body (2f.), he implicates that stories about disability may also reflect acceptance and pride.

Acceptance and pride, of course, are in conflict with cure and the traditional notion of health (cf. also Wendell, "Unhealthy" 31). In accordance with Disability Studies scholarship, such narratives encourage readers to envision a body that does not only permit variation and change, but that may also be imperfect and unruly (Davis, "Crips" 504f.) and hence challenge the "normal."[10] In a similar vein, more

---

9 In "Unhealthy Disabled," Wendell argues that the corporeal body and its impairment have been neglected because they automatically link disability to the medical model and the need for cure (22f.).

10 In *Extraordinary Bodies*, Rosemarie Garland-Thomson probes the politicization of bodily differences, i.e. the means by which "those bodies deemed inferior become spectacles of otherness while the unmarked are sheltered in the neutral space of normalcy" and coins

recent models of illness, disability, and health challenge the firm divide between the former two concepts and the latter and, instead of treating them as dichotomous word pairs, view them as points on a continuum (Franke 33; Schramme 31). These models, prominent among them the remission society discussed in Chapter 3.2, certainly help to accommodate and account for the contingent nature of our bodies – our 'temporary able-bodiedness' – and blur the strict boundaries between health and physical incapacity to substitute sharp contrasts with grey areas. However, they do not help to resolve, and in fact fail to address the dilemma that despite the fact that health and illness/disability may shade into each other in varying degrees, the values attached to each of these conditions remain absolute and hardly permit alternative interpretations.

Most people, Franke contends, would not define health simply as the "absence of disease" but attribute it with a wide range of positive values and images (243). Health is regarded as shorthand for strength (Nettleton 42), beauty (Gilman 51), "a full and satisfactory human lived experience" (Agazzi 5) and, as Howard Spiro summarizes more dramatically, but no doubt accurately, "close relationships with our family and friends, time for contemplation, many of the joys of the living" (Spiro 154). Nowadays inextricably linked to diet, exercise, and general lifestyle (cf. also Weitz 127), health attests to responsibility, will-power, self-discipline, and self-control and is by the same attributes tightly wound up with individualism and capitalism, where it is also a commodity (Nettleton 46). In more spiritual terms, it is seen as a gift (Franke 55). Despite the fact that other scholars define health as a "sociocultural product," dependent on perspective and transformed with the individual's increasing age, as well as by social and cultural changes (Schiffer 36; Loustaunau and Sobo 17), all of these interpretations suggest that health is strongly desired and indeed imperative, so that Nettleton is surely right in claiming that in a culture like the American, where independence and self-reliance are so ingrained, the lack of health is an utterly threatening and undesirable experience (69).

Stories told by members of the so-called 'remission society,' where health is neither the norm, nor the ideal to which patients and disabled individuals strive to return have great potential to change this. On the one hand, this is because in these narratives, as I will elucidate in more detail below, the firm divide between health and illness/disability is refuted when the writers present readers with experiencing Is that are both ill/disabled and well. On the other hand, these narratives provide readers and scholars with what sociological and philosophical scholarship on health has been lacking, namely the phenomenological perspective on well-being. They

---

the term 'normate' to alert readers to "the constructed identity of those who, by way of the bodily configurations and cultural capital they assume, can step into a position of authority and wield the power it grants them" (8ff.).

tell us what it is like to be, in Wendell's words, "healthy disabled" ("Unhealthy" 31), to be chronically ill or have the course of one's life radically altered by grave illness and yet lead a full life.

3.2 REWRITING CURE: THE REMISSION SOCIETY

"You are never cured of cancer; you can only live in remission," maintains sociologist Arthur Frank toward the end of his 1991 memoir *At the Will of the Body: Reflections on Illness* (130). The book relates his recovery from an entirely unanticipated heart attack that is, however, quickly superseded by the diagnosis of cancer and the subsequent treatment. As Frank reflects on his experience of illness in conjunction with his contacts to medical professionals and society,[11] he acknowledges that both diseases leave his body and self forever marked. Yet for Frank – certainly owing to his academic training as a sociologist – such markings take on an entirely different dimension, as becomes evident in the chapter "Ceremonies of Recovery." Rather than constituting stigmata, markings through medical procedures and treatment courses are in his narrative reconceptualized as rituals[12] performed to mark an individual's experience (ibid. 131). Thus, they are material, as well as symbolic: Marking attests to the corporeality of the body, signified by the hair lost during chemotherapy, the line that is now removed from his vein or the incision that is

---

11 Frank's life narrative is significantly influenced by his research as a sociologist and his preceding work with members of the medical profession. Throughout the book, he uses personal events, encounters with his doctors, friends, and strangers as trajectories for mediating larger questions on the perception of illness (particularly the metaphors of war in the discourse on cancer), the nature of the body, as well as stigmatization. I have not included a close and thorough reading of Frank's memoir in this project, for his story is not set in the U.S. but in Canada, a significant difference in location concerning e.g. the experience of the health care system (cf. 116f.).

12 Frank's use of the ritual as a motif in *At the Will of the Body* reflects anthropological thought and cultural studies scholarship. Religious studies scholar Catherine Bell later identifies stages (separation, transition, and incorporation) in the performance of rituals (cf. 94) that reverberate in his narrative, while anthropologist Victor Turner earlier comments on the disorientation and liminality of individuals in the transitory phase of rituals (cf. 95), which manifest themselves in Frank's feelings of being "suspended between the insulated world of illness and the 'healthy' mainstream" (132). A thorough reading of his memoir might therefore focus on the symbolic qualities of medical marking and illness as a rite of passage.

closed with stitches (cf. ibid.), as much as it speaks to the experience and identity of the ill individual, for marking permanently alters one's identity. Through marking, Frank is initiated into what he calls the 'remission society,' a concept he introduces in his memoir and elaborates in his theoretical study on illness, suffering, and narrative, *The Wounded Storyteller*.

In the following, I want to sketch what Frank understands as the fundamental aspects of the remission society by returning to key passages from the end of his life narrative, as well as discussing his theoretical work. Although the concept is now frequently cited by sociologists and medical anthropologists, it has thus far received only little attention in the analysis of creative literary responses to maladies and bodily difference. It is, however, of immense value for a thorough reading of the representations of experiences of illness and disability in the late twentieth and early twenty-first centuries, as it accounts for the changes in the experience of medical care that are taking place due to technological progress and scientific discoveries. More than that, it provides an adequate framework for the critical discussions the primary texts initiate, affording a fresh perspective on 'health' and the specters of disease and impairment by deconstructing the ideal of cure and drafting an in-between state in which well-being may take center stage.

According to Frank, the remission society comprises all who "are effectively well but could never be considered cured" (*Wounded* 8). By describing them as "effectively well," Frank stresses the (former) patients' well-being, implying that they *actually* feel "well" in spite of the fact that their conditions are beyond cure. Although his definition places heavy emphasis on the members' lack of cure and thus attests to the power of the medical institution to name and define states of un-wellness, it simultaneously removes lives in remission from the medical realm, since medical protocols can neither grasp their qualitative experience nor their identity. How exactly well-being is to be understood in relation to medicine's incapacity to cure is, however, left open in Frank's definition and the close readings below serve to shed more light on this issue.

These ambiguities notwithstanding, the remission society signals a momentous turn in the ways in which we read health, illness, disability, and well-being. This is first of all due to the fact that Frank's concept brings together a diverse group of people including

"those who have had almost any cancer, those living in cardiac recovery programs, diabetics, those whose allergies and environmental sensitivities require dietary and other self-monitoring, those with prostheses and mechanical body regulators, the chronically ill, the disabled, those 'recovering' from abuses and addictions, and for all these people, the families that share the worries and daily triumph of staying well." (*Wounded* 8)

The remission society thus provides – at least on first reading[13] – a comprehensive framework for the joint analysis of illness and disability, an endeavor that both Medical Humanities scholars and academics in the field of Disability Studies have so far viewed rather critically. In "Disease versus Disability," Diane Price Herndl even writes about a "disciplinary divide between the medical humanities and disability studies" that makes it impossible to discuss illness and disability within the same context and presents a challenge for "political and intellectual cohesion" (593).[14] Her essay iterates the concerns shared by numerous scholars of the respective fields who maintain that although many individuals are disabled in the course of a life-threatening or chronic disease and many people with disability also face chronic health problems (Wendell, "Unhealthy" 17), "most people in the disability community do not want to be considered ill, and most people who are ill don't want to be considered disabled" (Herndl, "Disease" 593). Both Wendell and Herndl[15] call

---

13 A critical issue is the fact that Frank's framework is limited to somatic conditions and excludes mental illnesses, as Medical Humanities scholar Angela Woods criticizes in "Beyond the Wounded Storyteller: Rethinking Illness, Narrative, and Embodied Self-Experience" (120).

14 In addition to their conceptual problems she criticizes the Medical Humanities for their lack of interest in disability issues and also maintains that Disability Studies scholars are "not overly physician friendly" (596). Her criticism is not shared by Wendell, though, who observes that "many people who are disabled by chronic illnesses are involved in disability politics and contribute to social constructionist analyses, and disability groups have increasingly welcomed into their activities people with HIV/AIDS, fibromyalgia, myalgic encephalomyelitis/chronic fatigue immune dysfunction syndrome (ME/CFIDS), and other chronic illnesses" ("Unhealthy" 19).

15 Herndl's approach to the distinction is of enormous significance for both academic and activist engagements with disability, yet at times remains too simplistic, which is first and foremost a problem of terminology. When she warns that 'disease,' the term denoting a biological condition located in the body, and 'disability,' the social reality of people, may not be conflated, one cannot but agree, but the analogy drawn between the terms here is inherently flawed for it lacks the critical mention of 'impairment' as biological and material and 'illness' as existential and ontological counterparts, as introduced above. As I have shown, 'illness' does in fact realize Herndl's call that conditions be examined with respect to their context and the individuals' experiences, instead of just being located in their physical bodies (cf. ibid. 597). Hence the parameters Herndl devises for an informed distinction between disease and disability prove to be quite problematic on closer examination and frequently rather contrast precarious and ideal situations applicable to both illness and disability. Additionally, the binaries she employs do not take chronic or long-term diseases into account that do not require constant medical attention when patients

for a distinction between 'illness' and 'disability,' most of all because – distinctly speaking from a disability rights perspective and hence in parts neglecting the political nature of illness experiences – they seek to prevent the continuing medicalization of disability and instead foreground its political charge (ibid. 594; Wendell, "Unhealthy" 17). Furthermore, Wendell explains that disability needs to be dissociated from the biomedical discourse, where it is framed in the context of treatment, cure, or prevention, a misconception that has led to the forced institutionalization of "healthy people with disabilities" (ibid.).

Patients with acute and short-term diseases are excluded from the remission society, so that Frank's approach centers on conditions that have a lasting effect on individuals and entail dramatic changes in their life situations. In turn, it also distances the experience of disability from a strictly medical context and therefore resists placing a value judgment on disability and "spoiling," as Cheu writes, disabled individuals' identity (7). More importantly, though, Frank's concept does not rely on or reinforce the differences between the categories of illness and disability, respectively disease and impairment. Rather, it is a common denominator for both groups, resting not on their relation to a medicalized un-wellness and the need for medical care, but on their relation to health. Both illness and disability are uncoupled from cure. For Frank, this is because the members' conditions have taken medical treatments to their limits, rather than the members' active refusal of curative treatments. Without doubt, in this respect the remission society fails to truly acknowledge the experiences of disabled individuals, which clearly need to be more pronounced in the approach, since most of his elaborations are – certainly due to the autobiographical founding of his framework – characteristic of illness but cannot encompass the experience of disability. A shift in perspective, though, which also takes into account the political dimension of disability and conceptualizes the remission status as embodied reveals the full productive potential of the remission society as a framework for analysis.

While Frank's approach has originated in the context of his personal experience of somatic illness and the clinical encounter, scholars must not forget that a similar

---

are in a state of remission and I argue that many of these binaries are effectively resolved when disabled and chronically ill individuals are seen as members of the remission society and do not see their conditions in need of cure. Frank's remission society definitely reflects her call for the subjective perspective (ibid.) and in fact, Frank even goes so far as ridding his project of the medical category "patient" to allow for an identity conception outside the biomedical framework and lays important groundwork for the representation of illness and disability in ways other than "tragedy, end-of-life-as-we-know-it, difficulty" (ibid. 594).

argumentative strand is woven into the critical analysis of disability, too. In *The Rejected Body*, Wendell, for instance, reminds her readers that

> "[u]nless we die suddenly, we are all disabled eventually. Most of us will live part of our lives with bodies that hurt, that move with difficulty or not at all, that deprive us of activities we once took for granted, or that others take for granted – bodies that make daily life a physical struggle. We need understandings of disability and handicap that do not support a paradigm of humanity as young and healthy. Encouraging everyone to acknowledge, accommodate, and identify with a wide range of physical conditions is ultimately the road of self-acceptance as well as the road to increasing the opportunities of those who are disabled now." (18)

Her statement fleshes out one of the fundamental claims of the discipline of Disability Studies that is time and again reiterated by scholars and critics to underline the relevance of a critical discussion on disability matters as issues not merely pertaining to a small minority but as questions which affect a large part of the general population. Especially the term 'temporarily able-bodied' that has gained currency in Disability Studies scholarship pinpoints, sociologist Monika Windisch argues, the contingency and transience of health, understood here as the body's capacity and efficiency. Consequently, the strict dichotomy between "disabled and non-disabled, passive and active, dependent and independent" individuals no longer abides (Windisch 16f.; my translation).

When Wendell's and Frank's quotations are read side by side, it becomes clear that the commonalities between illness and disability his framework suggests are not grounded in the artificial effort to conflate disparate groups, but emerge from shared experiences and lived realities. Like Wendell, who urges readers to disband the idea that we are generally healthy, Frank, too, does not employ the adjective "healthy" in his definition, but rather describes the members of the remission society as striving to "stay well," thereby stressing that traditional notions of 'health' are no longer adequate, just like the idea of 'cure' does not apply. It is precisely this relation that makes his concept so valuable for the study of illness and disability life narratives. Previous analyses have focused on the writers' illnesses and their abnormalities, which is manifested most obviously in the term '(auto-)pathography' initially used to refer to such stories (cf. Chapter 1). Linked to the traditional sense of health, defined above as the absence of disease, the writers were found – and found themselves – lacking, an issue that has greatly impacted many of the common motifs and tropes in their narratives as well as our responses to their stories. After all, the stigmatization of illness and disability and their association with misery, disgust or fear bear on the understanding of the conditions as pathological and abnormal, i.e. undesirable and in need of improvement.

In stark contrast, for individuals in the remission society, health no longer presents a normal or average state, but is exposed as an ideal that many will not attain or return to. Consequently, Frank directly responds to the "postmodern condition of illness" (*Wounded* 4ff.). In his research, "postmodern" is not a label of strict periodization, but serves to pinpoint that "over a period of time, perhaps the last twenty years, how people think about themselves and their world has changed" (ibid.). Two significant consequences of this shift are reflected in the remission society, namely the claiming of voice and the capacity for storytelling and, secondly, the problematization of the notion of the 'health.'

In the modern conceptualization of illness, technical expertise and the complex organization of health care and treatment have shaped personal narratives. Professionalized medicine took control over the definition and interpretation of disease and overstrained patients with specialized language and discourses that excluded them as lay persons (ibid. 5). Moreover, storytelling about illness was limited to the medical chart, the official story of illness, and despite the fact that patients circulated their own stories when they discussed their illnesses with others, "[t]he story told by the physician [became] the one against which others are ultimately judged true or false, useful or not" (ibid.). In this context, Frank coins the term "narrative surrender" to describe not only patients' conforming to the sick role and their compliance in treatment regimens, but more than that, their agreement to adopt the clinician's story as their own (cf. ibid. 6). While I agree with his elaboration, I am skeptical of the term "surrender," since it implies that patients were previously able to share their own stories before they were revised and framed by modern medicine. If one is to understand disease as socially constructed, however, as outlined Chapter 3.1, cultural connotations and systems of belief have always already impacted the ways in which patients made and make sense of their conditions, resulting in culturally and socially conditioned plot lines and narratives, but also in silence. So the individuals' adoption of the medical narrative elucidates a shift in narrative power from the sociocultural to the medical. Such a genealogy clearly shows that until postmodern times, patients' stories have been in accordance with the dominant explanatory schemes that accounted for disease and impairment. This suggests that it is only in postmodernity – aided by the understanding of social construction and the dissatisfaction with the scope of common discursive frameworks – that 'illness' and 'disability' as lived experiences publicly surface, are more fully acknowledged, and produce a plethora of alternative stories which powerfully defy the so-called 'sick role.'

The sick role has been drafted by sociologist Talcott Parsons in his widely-read study *The Social System* in which he acts on the assumption that illness has profound influences on the stability of the social system (cf. also Weitz 147). To retain social stability even if members of the group are afflicted with deviant conditions, the sick role ascribes to them a number of institutionalized expectations. While these individuals may be exempted "from normal social role responsibilities," such as going to work, Parsons does not only consider this to be their right, but also their duty, for he argues that ill people *"ought* to stay in bed" (436; italics in original). Since he acknowledges that patients cannot be expected to "get well by an act of decision or will," thus relieving them of any personal responsibility, he holds that they need to "'be taken care of'" (ibid.). Consequently, people afflicted with a disease are obliged to seek help, and hence cooperate with their doctors, whom Parsons characterizes as *"technically competent"* (436f.; italics in original). Weitz stresses the datedness of the sick role's demand that ill people seek treatment because it neglects the fact that many Americans do not have access to health care since they still lack insurance and because it does not account for the host of patients who find mainstream medicine of little use for their maladies, either (149).

Furthermore, as Weitz points out, it presents doctors as agents of social control (148), while not granting patients authority and agency. Neglecting the individuals' perspective, the sick role, Weitz contends, "confuses the experience of being a *patient* with the experience of *illness*" (149; italics in original), or rather vice versa. In other words, the sick role and the modern understanding of disease emanate from the thought that illness cannot be experienced in any other way than as a patient. The remission society, in stark contrast, challenges this assumption and problematizes another crucial shortcoming of the sick role Weitz mentions in passing: most conspicuously, the sick role does not account for chronic illness (cf. ibid.), a phenomenon that in Frank's taxonomy is decidedly postmodern. In many cases, he argues, disease is no longer an acute crisis which leads either to recovery or to a fatal outcome. Advances in medical practice and care have resulted in an ever-increasing number of patients living with "chronically critical" conditions which occasionally require treatment (*Will* 139).

In contrast to modernity, where people were thought to be either "well *or* sick" Frank sketches the postmodern condition as a state in which "sickness and health constantly shade into each other. Instead of a static picture on the page where light is separated from dark, the image is like a computer graphic where one shape is constantly in process of becoming the other" (*Wounded* 9; italics in original). Hence Frank establishes a striking contrast here: The "static picture" signifies a stable and charged dichotomy between health and illness reminiscent of Susan Sontag's characterization of illness as "the night-side of life" (3). In *Illness as Metaphor*, Sontag has famously conceded a "dual citizenship" to everyone that is recognized both "in the kingdom of the well and in the kingdom of the sick." Although she maintains that eventually, everyone will be forced to report at least briefly to "that other place," thus acknowledging the instability of health, she does envision a separation between the two "kingdoms" (ibid.).[16]

---

16 Cf. Diedrich's monograph study for a critical analysis of Sontag's writing on cancer. Diedrich finds fault with Sontag's "depersonalized way of dealing with and writing about

This clear-cut separation is renounced in the second half of Frank's quotation when he reconceptualizes the relationship between health and illness in a malleable state of flux, shifting its shape to the extent that it is impossible to tell one from the other. Accordingly, the firm borders between Sontag's kingdoms no longer hold sway and Frank imagines either a "demilitarized zone in between them, or […] a secret society within the realm of the healthy" (*Wounded* 9). While the first metaphor suggests that members of the remission society inhabit a neutral, peaceful territory where neither side controls them, the second metaphor implies that members of the remission society live amongst the "healthy" and the 'normates,' yet are most of the time concealed from them and share their own rituals and knowledge.

Although this is an idea that more adequately responds to the members' at times uneasy existence and the tensions between inclusion and exclusion,[17] I have misgivings about both metaphors. After all, Frank initially sketches a fully inclusive framework comprising not only ill and disabled individuals themselves, but also their friends and families (*Wounded* 8). In other parts of his work, though, readers continuously encounter a rift between the remission society and the realm of the healthy, which is a problem also repeated in the works of critics engaged in the reception of his framework, for instance in Paul Stoller's "Cancer Rites in the Remission Society" in which he purports that once treatment courses end, patients "are not reintegrated into a normal social routine" and forever cast out from "'the village of the healthy,' in which health is taken for granted" (n. pag.). These statements reify the dichotomy between health and illness and ultimately present a missed opportunity at rethinking illness, disability, and health in society.

No doubt, reading the remission society as a fully inclusive unity is a radical project that will take further years of social reform and education, as well as more points of contact to be realized. To those residing in Stoller's "village of the healthy," it is also a scary project, since vulnerability and mortality cloud its skies. Nevertheless, with its connotations of community, solidarity, and participation, the remission society is geared toward inclusion and should be read as an attempt to tear down the barrier between "us" and "them" that much research in the Medical Humanities is no doubt built on, helping to design the setting in which, in Herndl's words, "their context is, or at least should be also ours" ("Disease" 596). The voices

---

her illness" and asserts that in her text, the binary between health and illness is maintained (*Treatments* 29f.).

17 Interestingly, both Sontag and Frank use ideas linked to one of the primary categories of identity, namely nationality – Sontag raises the problem of a passport (3), Frank speaks of visa status (*Wounded* 9). Their comparison indicates that a person's status as a member of the remission society, too, comprises a fundamental and, as Frank himself notes, "irrevocable" aspect for their identity (cf. ibid.).

of disabled activists and memoirists are very much needed in this project. As some of the texts analyzed below show, they point to serious social barriers which still need to be overcome but at the same time also lay the groundwork for a more inclusive society that acknowledges, respects, and honors difference.

3.3 RECOVERING THE BODY: EMBODIMENT AND THE REMISSION SOCIETY

The final chapters of Frank's memoir illustrate that for him, remission is essentially an in-between state that blurs the boundaries between health and illness, between a life situated within the realm of biomedicine and an existence removed from the biomedical hold on the body:

"I become less and less a person with cancer, but the continuing schedule of examinations, X-rays, and blood tests reminds me that I remain at greater risk than others. This risk diminishes over time but never disappears. Life remains a remission. But my sense of being a person with cancer is on the level of experience, not of medicine." (*Will* 132)

Frank's paradoxical claim – asserting on the one hand that he gradually ceases to be "a person with cancer" as the acute disease moves into the background, while on the other hand noting that there is a striking "sense of being a person with cancer" as the experience continues to linger and the use of the present tense suggests immediacy – is characteristic of identity in the remission society. While his first statement elucidates that tests and examinations continue to structure his everyday life, entangling the ordinary and the extraordinary and serving as pointed reminders of the ongoing nature of his illness experience, the subsequent sentences make clear that he no longer grasps his identity in biomedical terms.

Moreover, when Frank speaks of himself as "a person with cancer," he points to a significant turn that is emblematic for life in the remission society: By dissociating his life from the biomedical setting and locating his illness instead "on the level of experience" he effectively transcends the Cartesian stance of biomedicine, in which patients may conceive of themselves as "having" an illness, yet do not see their selves essentially connected to their sick bodies (cf. also Meyer-Abich 39). Frank never entertains the idea of embodied experience, but embodiment is crucial to the remission society and in the following I will briefly sketch the fundamental aspects of the concept to illustrate its immense benefit for the theoretical framework. The turn to embodiment, I will show, empowers the members of the remission society and lends a greater argumentative potential to the framework, since it will help to account more fully for the experiences of disabled individuals.

Long a central subject in European phenomenology, embodiment has been extensively discussed by philosophers such as Maurice Merleau-Ponty. Influenced by a broad range of philosophers, among them Edmund Husserl, the founder of phenomenology, Merleau-Ponty's work engages with a vast range of issues but is unified by the questions of how we might conceptualize the relationship between consciousness and the world (Romdenh-Romluc 103f.). In his seminal study *Phenomenology of Perception*, he expounds his notion of embodied subjectivity, writing "[i]n so far as, when I reflect on the essence of subjectivity, I find it bound up what that of the body and that of the world [...] because my existence as subjectivity is merely one with my existence as a body and with the existence of the world" and that that the subject "when taken correctly, is inseparable from his body and his world" (475). This postulation refutes the dualist notion that body and mind are separate and self-contained entities. Generally speaking, phenomenological accounts of the body rest on the basic assumption that "not only does everybody *have* a body, everybody *is* a body" (Svenaeus 100; italics in original) and accordingly distinguish between the objective body, i.e. the physiological entity with nerves, muscles, and bones, and the phenomenal body (Audi 258; Vignemont n. pag.). The phenomenal body, often also referred to as lived body, is the entity through which we experience and understand the world (Svenaeus 100). Kinesthetics and proprioception (cf. Chapter 5) allow for our subjective perceptions and experiences and turn the body into, to borrow from philosopher of medicine Fredrik Svenaeus's words, "the zero-point that makes space and the place of things that I encounter possible at all" (100). The phenomenal body thus determines how we experience the world around us, but at the same time, Robert Audi stresses, also influences the ways in which we experience our bodies (258). Referencing Merleau-Ponty, philosopher Frédérique de Vignemont therefore understands the lived body as our "practical engagement with the world" (Merleau-Ponty quoted in Vignemont n. pag.).[18]

---

18 This is of course an utterly brief sketch of phenomenology as a field of philosophical inquiry and Merleau-Ponty's work with its far reaching consequences for the analysis of perception and intuition or the objectivism of the empirical sciences. For a concise introduction, see *The Phenomenology Reader*, edited by Dermot Moran and Timothy Mooney (London/New York: Routledge, 2002),*The Routledge Companion to Phenomenology* edited by Sebastian Luft and Soren Overgaard (London/New York: Routledge, 2012) and Michael Hammond's, Jane Howarth's and Russell Keat's *Understanding Phenomenology* (Oxford: Blackwell, 1991). Phenomenology is currently experiencing a renaissance (cf. Zahavi 8) and numerous scholars, among them feminist theorists and philosophers of health and illness have significantly expanded and transformed Merleau-Ponty's groundwork. Non-normative forms of embodiment, such as the female and the ill/disabled body, have not figured in Merleau-Ponty's work which has centered on the "standard male em-

When people face illness or disability, these constitute crucial issues that have far too long been neglected in favor of dualist (mis)conceptions of the ill or impaired self in which the mind is split from the sick body. This may be easily explained by returning to established definitions of health, such as the one by Leriche quoted above (Chapter 3.1) that health is "the silence of the organs." Without symptoms the body is rarely consciously felt. Pain and discomfort, when they arise, often prompt us to feel, sociologist Deborah Lupton explains, as though the body is "taking over," so that rather than perceiving illness as essentially connected to the self, patients may conceive of their condition as something entirely separate (20). Diedrich is therefore definitely right in calling illness "a crisis of embodiment" and her study deftly illustrates how this crisis is experienced on the personal level as patient-writers attempt to negotiate their ill bodies and their positions in the world ("Negotiating" 7).

However, such a "crisis of embodiment," a separation between the ill body and the self, is not limited to patients' understanding of themselves, but also one that arises within the context of biomedicine. There, disembodiment has led to a problematic understanding of pathology and its treatment when the body is conceptualized as split from the mind or self and as an isolated entity that can be fixed. Moreover, it has excluded patients from the processes of gaining knowledge from and about their bodies. Since the 1970s and the advent of bioethics, biomedicine has come under heavy criticism (cf. Nettleton 5).[19] Sociologists have pointed to a number of problems, the most severe being what Nettleton refers to as "medicine's *mind-body dualism*" (3; italics in original). This dualism rests in the proposition that

---

bodied experience" (Scully 65). Illness or disability, if broached at all, constituted a disruption of the unified body and "normal embodied" (ibid.) – much like it does in Sacks's memoir (cf. Chapter 5.), yet scholars have more recently made the point that e.g. disabled individuals do "experience their bodies as complete and normal" (Becker 131). In turn, different embodiments may challenge hegemonic ideals and "what being 'normal' means" (ibid.). Especially in the fields of Medical Humanities and feminist Disability Studies, scholars have recognized the potential benefits of re-thinking illness, disability, and health through the lens of embodiment (cf. e.g. Silvers, Havi Carel's *Illness*, Craig Murray's and B. Harrison's work on stroke patients, or Kay Inckle's approach to gender politics and 'disabled embodiment').

19 Cf. the volume *Biomedicine Examined* (edited by Lock, Margaret M., and Deborah Gordon. Dordrecht: Kluwer Academic Publishers, 1988), Elliot G. Mishler's essay "Viewpoint: Critical Perspectives on the Biomedical Model" (in *Social Contexts of Health, Illness, and Patient Care*. Eds. Elliot G. Mishler et al. Cambridge: Cambridge UP, 1981. 1-23), and David Morris's *Krankheit und Kultur: Plädoyer für ein neues Körperverständnis* (München: Kunstmann, 2000).

the body and its parts may be repaired like a machine (ibid.), a comparison that, according to Lupton, permeates both professional and lay accounts (59). Based on this mechanistic understanding of the body and the remediation of its symptoms, biomedicine is inevitably focused on cure (cf. also Morris, "How" 12), which entails severe problems for both ill and disabled individuals: If the body is conceived of in mechanistic terms, there is no other way to account for health and well-being than cure. Consequently, the biomedical framework disregards the experiences of chronically ill and disabled individuals, rendering them disempowered, since "cure" alone presents neither a viable nor comprehensive option. The concept of well-being, in contrast, helps to overcome these deficiencies.

Secondly, the mind-body dualism that disembodiment entails is repeated in the split between subjective concerns about illness experiences, which are devalued in biomedicine, and technical concerns with the categorization and control of symptoms which, in contrast, receive major relevance. Above I have explained in more detail how both patients and disabled individuals have been excluded from the discourses about their bodies (Chapter 2.2). Referring specifically to the biomedical setting, James Wilson and Cynthia Lewiecki-Wilson note in their introduction to the volume *Embodied Rhetorics: Disability in Language and Culture* how the embodied stance is excluded from "scientific objectivity" and "truth" (6)[20] and with Kleinman I lament the disempowerment of patients and disabled subjects in this context (9).

The turn to embodiment and the qualitative experience of illness and disability will thus recognize ill and disabled individuals as experts on their bodies, hence lending them authority and agency. This shift does of course not aim to contest third-person knowledge on the object body – in other words, it will not challenge the knowledge collected in clinical examinations – but it does challenge the assumption that these objective findings may "compensate for, or replace, first-person-perspective explorations of the experiences" (Svenaeus 101). Svenaeus is careful to make explicit that a phenomenological approach to health and illness/disability neither can nor aims to replace research in biomedicine. Instead, taking the lived body into account, he holds, will "enrich our understanding" of illness, disability, and health and help us to explore how ill and disabled individuals lead meaningful lives (ibid. 106). Recent work on disability mainstreaming, such as

---

20 In her stimulating autobiographical critique "Medical Identity: My DNA/Myself," Kay Cook records what she calls her "physiological, organic, hemoglobular, cellular, molecular autobiography" (67). Conscious of the pitfalls of disembodiment, she reclaims her embodied experience from medical discourse and diagnostic tools, but also meditates on what is means to know oneself "in the physical sense": "as my medical tests become more invasive, I am confronted with a material selfhood heretofore invisible to me" (65).

Windisch's study, evinces that this is indeed a path-breaking direction in research. Once society recognizes disabled men and women as knowledgeable authorities on their bodies, she maintains, a dialogue may be initiated that closely examines social environs, realities, and political issues, and joint measures may be taken to effect lasting change in society (106).

As a textual strategy, the storying of qualitative and lived experiences of illness and disability will aid members of the remission society in gaining "narrative control" (Frank, "Reclaiming" 4). From a disability rights perspective, however, the idea of narrative control must be extended to not only refer to patients who, as Frank argues, claim the narratives of their conditions in order to share their experiences not merely in terms of medical language (*Wounded* 6f.), but also to disabled subjects who counter the essentialist view that corporeal differences entirely destine their life chances (Windisch 30). From the narrative control exercised in these texts, alternative identity conceptions[21] emerge which profoundly impact how we read illness/disability and health. Like Frank's body described at the beginning of this subchapter, the memoirist's bodies are marked and, similar to other material features of the body, such as the markers of race and gender Linda Alcoff studies in *Visible Identities*, illness and disability bestow social identities on individuals and profoundly impact the ways in which they experience their "being-in-the-world" (cf. also Lennon n. pag.; Lupton 20). Frank, for instance, becomes aware of his "dual presence," as the embodiment of both risk and survival (*Will* 133), hope and prospect for health and normalcy coincide with the painful reminder of mortality and vulnerability. Yet it is particularly noteworthy that the identity as a member of the remission society is not merely assigned by others, but is inherent in the subjective perspective and rooted in the consciousness of the individual as well. When Frank notes that "[o]n different days I myself emphasize different halves" (ibid.), he asserts agency and power in his own representation.

The following chapters will show that the narratives produced and circulated in the remission society are, as Mintz so eloquently phrases it, "not just manifestos for resisting oppression, detailed accounts of medical conditions, or sociological case histories [...]. They are also open-ended histories of embodiment, tales about anomalous embodiment" which elucidate both the poetic and political dimension of bodies in remission (*Unruly* 4). A perspective developed from the subjective stance, it continuously accentuates the first-person and the political undercurrents in the texts at hand. In drawing attention to the material realities of the memoirists' bodies, the texts bear witness to corporeal difference and unsettle the ideological force of the traditional notion of health.

---

21 Mike Bury and Lee Monaghan term these "biographical reinventions" (75).

The 'Case Studies'

4. Healing Beyond Reconstruction:
Ampu-Narration in Audre Lorde's *The Cancer Journals*

In 2013, the American Cancer Society celebrated their hundredth anniversary, and it is safe to say that the conversation about breast cancer has changed. "Cancer... Dreaded, dreadful word, spoken in whispers when you were growing up, and seldom even whispered," writes Terese Lasser in her 1972 memoir *Reach to Recovery* and describes breast cancer as a subject that "always brought a sad shaking of heads and a pity-filled pause in conversation" (18). Long a taboo subject due to its tight connection to questions of sexuality, breast cancer has now entered public discourses in a way that, as historian Kirsten Gardner outlines, "nothing seems off limits": from the ubiquitous pink ribbons that promote awareness and corporate funding campaigns that benefit research to entire book store sections devoted to the experience of treatment and recovery, the current awareness of the disease seems to suggest that the ways in which breast cancer is conceptualized in contemporary culture have dramatically changed (n. pag.).

However, neither the striking visibility of pink ribbons, the surge of witty campaigns urging women to perform self-examinations, nor the proliferation of writing on the breast cancer experience in print as well as online can conceal the fact that "there is nothing very feminist" about the pink ribbon movement and the understanding of breast cancer in American culture today, Barbara Ehrenreich pointedly argues in her award-winning essay "Welcome to Cancerland" (47).[1] Instead, the

---

1   Cf. the chapter "Ribbon Wars" in Karen Kedrowski's and Marilyn S. Sarow's *Cancer Activism: Gender, Media, and Public Policy* (Chicago: U of Illinois P, 2007) that examines the ways in which corporate America is involved in the fight against breast cancer. Since the 1980s, 'cause-related' marketing campaigns have become an integral part of corporate social responsibility. The essay studies individual campaigns and compares cause-related marketing for breast and prostate cancer awareness. Samantha King's *Pink Ribbons, Inc.: Breast Cancer and the Politics of Philanthropy* (Minneapolis: U of

message spread by institutionalized support groups, Ehrenreich learns when she is diagnosed with breast cancer herself, is one of cheerfulness, infantilization, and obedience (cf. ibid. 52). Moreover, the current focus on early detection, rather than prevention, puts responsibility – and blame – on women and, Stella Bolaki concludes, ultimately turns breast cancer into a private issue ("Re-Covering" 10).

These problems notwithstanding, the 'epidemic' of breast cancer, currently "bigger than AIDS, cystic fibrosis or spinal injury, bigger even than those more prolific killers of women – heart disease, lung cancer and stroke" (Ehrenreich, "Welcome" 45) has also brought to the fore a new wave of activism aimed at unveiling the politics at work in institutional medicine and science (O'Brien, "Theorizing" 149). Such activism finds its roots in Audre Lorde's memoir *The Cancer Journals* (1980) which takes breast cancer not only as an occasion for storytelling but uses her experience to challenge traditional narratives about the disease and establish an alternative discourse.[2]

Minnesota P, 2006) provides a more critical perspective. Quoting Lorde's call for an "army of one-breasted women" to press for political change, King argues that today, this army turns up at health walks and races, yet the institutional structure of such events leaves "little room for politically targeted anger" (36) and "provides no place for those women who cannot or do not wish to view their condition as a lucky gift" (122). For historical perspectives, see Maureen Casamayou's *The Politics of Breast Cancer* (Washington: Georgetown UP, 2001), a book which provides a comprehensive overview of cancer as both a medical problem and a social issue by tracing the development of policies and the history of patient advocacy, and *Bathsheba's Breast: Women, Cancer and History* by James Olson (Baltimore: Johns Hopkins UP, 2002), which outlines the development of treatment in the United States and the changing public discourse on breast cancer.

2 Rose Kushner's *Why Me?* (originally published as *Breast Cancer: A Personal History and Investigative Report*. New York: Harcourt Brace Janovich, 1975) is another early example. It tells the story of her own experience of breast cancer, interlaced with medical research Kushner has conducted into what she calls "the literature," in contrast to simplified reports published in the popular press (255). With the help of her lawyer, Kushner designs a legal document prohibiting the surgeon to perform a radical mastectomy which was the common protocol at the time, i.e. do biopsy and mastectomy in one operation if the lump is cancerous, and instead allowing her to decide on the mastectomy (24). Lorde's book, as Tina Richardson's "Changing Landscapes: Mapping Breast Cancer as an Environmental Justice Issue in Audre Lorde's The Cancer Journals" demonstrates, is also one of the earliest texts to frame breast cancer as an issue of environmental justice (in: *Restoring the Connection to the Natural World Essays on the African American Environmental Imagination*. Ed. Sylvia Mayer. Münster: Lit, 2003. 129-147).

In spite of its title, the memoir does not consist of journal entries alone, but is divided into an introduction and three essays: "The Transformation of Silence into Language and Action," "Breast Cancer: A Black Lesbian Feminist Experience," and "Breast Cancer: Power vs. Prosthesis." Interspersed with selected journal entries, the essays chronicle Lorde experiences, thoughts, and feelings from an initial biopsy of her left breast which proved to be benign, the detection of a cancerous lump in her right breast in 1978 and the ensuing mastectomy, and finally her coming to terms with her altered body. By merging essayistic and personal forms of writing, "combining the strengths of her imagination and intellect," and blending art with feminist theory and sophisticated and subversive arguments about culture and society (Diekmann 157), Lorde meets the silence surrounding women's experience of breast cancer at the time she was writing.

Her decidedly activist stance has been significantly influenced by her work in the academic setting as a poet-in-residence at Tougaloo College in Jackson, Mississippi at the height of racial conflict in 1968, as well as by her later position as lecturer at Hunter College in New York City. "I realized I could take my art in the realest [sic] way and make it do what I wanted. I began bringing together my poetry and my deepest-held convictions," Lorde explains in the documentary *A Litany for Survival* to illustrate how her work has changed throughout the years and began to address political and social concerns.[3] Furthermore, Lorde purports in the documentary that "all poets must teach what they know, in order to continue being," a project she pursues with great urgency in *The Cancer Journals*, where she maintains that "survival is only part of the task. The other is teaching" (40). From the beginning of the memoir, she makes clear that the lessons she has learned throughout her ordeal have been utterly painful. In spite, or rather because of that, it is her primary concern that "the pain not be wasted" but instead voiced and shared so that it may prove of use to others (*Cancer* 14).[4] Accordingly, both her work as a writer and as

---

3   These thoughts are more fully explored in an interview with the poet and feminist Adrienne Rich (Audre Lorde and Adrienne Rich. "An Interview with Audre Lorde." in: *Revising the Word and the World: Essays in Feminist Literary Criticism*. Eds. VeVe A. Clark, Ruth-Ellen B. Joeres and Madelon Sprengnether. Chicago: U of Chicago P, 1993. 13-36). In the interview, the two women discuss Lorde's writing and speak at length about the influence of her stay in Tougaloo. "I know teaching is a survival technique," Lorde states. "It is for me, and I think it is in general; and [writing is] the only way real teaching, real learning, happens" (19). Teaching writing in Tougaloo, Lorde asserts, made her realize, "not only, yes, I am a poet, but also, this is the kind of work I'm going to do" (ibid. 23).

4   This idea, the mantra of *The Cancer Journals*, is introduced in Lorde's biomythography *Zami: A New Spelling of my Name*, where she quotes her older lover Eudora, telling her

an activist figure as important tools in her struggle for a more humane world (cf. Weber 241).

For this reason, the life narrative does not merely voice and show breast cancer, as Bolaki suggests ("Re-Covering" 10). In this chapter, I argue that Lorde's memoir deconstructs the notions of health and healing traditionally put forward in breast cancer memoirs by subverting the 'triumph narrative' and dismantling the prosthetic reconstruction of the post-mastectomy body. In this vein, *The Cancer Journals* reveals the resignification of the reconstructive process that is typically associated with recovery and healing: Both structure and content work to propose an alternative reading of reconstruction, and hence of healing and well-being in the face of cancer. Nevertheless, the altered landscape of Lorde's body, and with it, the "radical absence" that the amputated breast signifies (DeShazer, *Fractured* 13) are at the core of her story and turn the book into an example of what I term 'ampu-narration': a text in stark contrast to the 'narrative prostheses' identified by Disability Studies scholars David Mitchell and Sharon Snyder in their eponymous study.

While Mitchell and Snyder emphasize the capacity of disability to disrupt cultural scripts (*Narrative* 49) and attribute great discursive power to disability used either figuratively or literally in these stories as "a metaphor and fleshy example of the body's unruly resistance to the cultural desire to 'enforce normalcy'" (ibid. 48), their readings of canonized and contemporary texts convincingly demonstrate that these narratives ultimately work to "prostheticize," i.e. correct or resolve, a character's deviance (ibid. 53). One of the prominent examples Mitchell and Snyder use to illustrate their theory includes the children's narrative *The Steadfast Tin Soldier* which opens with the narrator's discovery that in a box of tin soldiers, all figures look alike except for one soldier who has only one leg and becomes the focal point of the story. In this story, as in many others, Mitchell and Snyder identify narrative as a mode of compensation for "a deviance marked as improper in a social context" (ibid.). To be more precise, they find that such prosthetic narratives follow a set of conventions: After initially exposing difference, these stories call for an explanation and proceed to bring difference to the center of attention, before finally "fixing" it (ibid.).

In this vein, the stories may end in a "cure" that repairs and obliterates difference (ibid. 54). Mitchell and Snyder employ the idea of cure in inverted comas, since it does not only encompass 'cure' in the most obvious sense, as medical correction and rescue, but rather because it may refer to any aesthetic or narrative choice that, like a prosthesis, "remove[s] the unsightly from view" and thus eases readers' discomfort (ibid. 8). Other critics, among them David Wood, have referred

---

to "waste nothing [...] not even pain. Particularly not pain" (236; italics in original). See also Weber on this issue.

to this strategy as the "'cure or kill' phenomenon of difference" (n. pag.), which vividly illustrates Mitchell's and Snyder's theory, since for them, prosthetic narration may also exterminate a deviance or efface a deviant character in order to rehabilitate the social body (*Narrative* 54). So instead of accommodating difference, prosthetic narratives either leave disability behind or punish it (ibid. 56) and eventually underscore the significance of health and normalcy, as well as their normativity.

Lorde's writing, on the other hand, posits an elaborate and powerful critique of the prosthetic quick fix that I will explore in detail in this chapter. First of all, on the plane of form, her story subverts the 'triumph narrative,' the prosthetic narrative of cancer that traditionally depicts the experience of the disease as a story about individual triumph and the return to normalcy and health. Instead, Lorde constructs her story as a call for a collective struggle and is sternly aware of the new sense of temporality and contingency that her life has gained through the disease, two issues that I will discuss in the course of this chapter. Although the overall plot of Lorde's narrative is roughly chronological and bespeaks a gradual sense of improvement and returning courage, *The Cancer Journals* departs from the neat linear and progressive plotline of recovery. The selected diary entries interspersed throughout her book create an image which counters the "tyranny of cheerfulness" King identifies in conventional breast cancer narratives (122) and the text is marked by a powerfully articulated anger.

In this respect, Lorde's work does of course overlap with Hawkins's category of 'angry pathographies' (cf. Chapter 1). However, with its sole focus on the patient's lack of trust and confidence in the medical system, Hawkins's definition cannot wholly account for this narrative (cf. *Reconstructing* 5). Despite the fact that Lorde occasionally voices her outrage about nurses and the medical establishment and researches alternative therapy options, her anger is directed at the larger framework that is "american"[5] culture in which these medical institutions operate. Her memoir therefore also writes back at the prosthetic narration on the discursive level: with its intertwining of journal entries and polemical essays, the book challenges the traditional narrative of breast cancer in women by contesting not only the paternalistic perspective of institutionalized medicine, but also the discursive frameworks that regulate cultural views of female, Black, queer and ill/disabled body. Confronting American society and cultural discourses, the text is able to, as Suzette Henke so

---

5   Not only in *The Cancer Journals*, but throughout her work, she spells America in the lower-case, while other locations, e.g. Harlem, are capitalized. Elizabeth Alexander remarks that in her authority of capitalization, Lorde assigns caste or class to locations (704). Like the "Amerika" of the counterculture, her refusal to capitalize America is without doubt to be understood as a derogative marker.

fittingly writes, "dismantle the master's house with none but the poet's tools – honesty, compassion, and clarity of vision" (113).

At the time Lorde was writing, cancer was intricately linked to negative personality traits (cf. Herndl, "Reconstructing" 478), an issue that Susan Sontag illuminates thoroughly in her *Illness as Metaphor* where she discusses the "forlorn, self-hating, emotionally inert creature, the contemporary cancer personality" (53). While discussions about such responsibilities frequently loom large in stories about cancer (and are not entirely absent in Lorde's book, either), placing more or less implicit blame on patients, Lorde strives to make herself 'response-able.'[6] Her attempt to appropriate conventional discourses is tightly related to patients' postcolonial efforts that Frank outlines in *The Wounded Storyteller* to claim a voice in order rescue their stories from medical discourses (11f.; cf. also chapter 3.2), yet significantly goes beyond his notion as it is not limited to the medical discourse, but extended to culture and society. Being response-able entails being capable of responding not only to her condition, but, beyond that, to the objectification of her body, and generating actions from independent and informed choices, thereby deriving authority from the self.

Lorde's way of responding and thus making the personal political, as I will show in the second part of this chapter, occurs on two levels. On the level of language, she breaks with the silence and reworks the metaphoric dimension of struggling with breast cancer. Her book is the memoir of a battle, albeit one in which the common metaphors of the war on cancer are carefully reworked within the framework of the West-African Dahomeyan Amazon myth, a form of resignification introduced by Lorde herself. Not only does this allow for a general reconceptualization of authority in which the doctor is excluded and the patient gains a strong sense of agency. More than that, as I will illustrate, devising new signifieds for the old signifiers of wars and soldiers makes a more adequate representation of Lorde's experience possible and, secondly, enables her to develop a view of her disease that empowers her and makes it possible for her to formulate a raging and rallying statement urging other women to overcome the silence surrounding the discourse on breast cancer.

Third, *The Cancer Journals* also attacks prosthesis as a compulsory quick fix to normalize the post-surgical body when she narrates the exposure of the "unsightly" body marked by cancer and unmasks difference, hence deliberately causing discomfort, particularly in the medical setting. Of course Frank is right in deducing that her amputated body serves as a reminder of the limited power of medical practitioners ("Tricksters" n. pag.), yet a close reading of selected scenes will show that Lorde's

---

6 Herndl also uses this term in her essay "Our Breasts, Our Selves" to describe a "'sense of living out loud'" (225).

refusal to wear a prosthesis is closely intertwined with an alternative notion of healing and well-being. It does therefore not do justice to the complexity of the narrative to state that Lorde eventually chooses to live "outside the Law of the Healthy" (cf. Frank ibid.), for throughout the memoir, she exposes the "unhealthiness" of such normative forces and depicts prosthesis as a hindrance to well-being. Since amputation may only present a therapeutic interference with disease, an attempt to control it, but does not provide a definite cure, the ampu-narration in *The Cancer Journals* is therapeutic, too, and trenchantly reminds readers of the possibility of well-being despite the looming threat of a recurrence. The sense of well-being Lorde sketches ultimately also confronts the biomedical system and its separation of mind from body in the healing process (Knopf-Newman 121). Due to the scope of this chapter, I will limit my analyses to *The Cancer Journals*, but it should be noted that her later collection of journal entries published as "Burst of Light" in a volume of the same name resumes her engagement with social justice issues, as well as continues probing the interconnection of her recurring cancer and her "battle for self-determination and survival" as a Black woman ("Burst" 49).[7]

---

7   "A Burst of Light" begins six years after the mastectomy narrated in *The Cancer Journals* and takes Lorde's fiftieth birthday and her diagnosis of liver cancer just two weeks before as a trajectory, thereby alluding to the significance of temporality – of survival and the contingency of a recurrence – along similar lines as Lorde's first illness memoir. In contrast to *The Cancer Journals*, "A Burst of Light" is a collection of diary entries framed only by a brief introduction and an epilogue; Interestingly, though, her entries do not only list the dates, but also the places in which they were composed, ranging from New York to Berlin, from Arlesheim in Switzerland to St. Croix in the Caribbean. The metastasizing cancer sends Lorde on a journey as she looks for alternative treatment options in Europe, yet more importantly, her travels continue to send her around the globe as a spokesperson for African-American womanhood and social justice and thus undermine the passivity and stillness of the traditional patient role. "A Burst of Light" is hence also powerfully engaged with Lorde's project of turning silence into language and action (Cancer 11ff.). In this vein, her second illness narrative shares significant features with her writing on her experience with breast cancer that I will explore in this chapter, such as the deep sense of struggle that is not merely personal, against her disease, but political and oftentimes transnational ("Burst" 52ff., 59ff., 75, 98f., 107, 110f., 116f., 120f., 126), her eloquent explorations of denial and healing (ibid. 55, 75, 89, 131), her allegiance with other women (cf. e.g. ibid. 101, 109, 130), and experiences of infantilization within the medical establishment (ibid. 112f.). The environmental critique alluded to in *The Cancer Journals*, also through phrases, such as "malignant society," or "environmental madness" is elaborated in "Burst of Light" (also see Mary DeShazer's *Mammographies*, pp. 45ff. on this issue).

When Lorde died in November 1992 of the cancer that had metastasized in her body, women's groups and activists around the world collectively mourned her passing (cf. Diekmann 156) and the immense impact of her work on the feminist community as well as on the cancer 'subculture' is still unabated almost 35 years after its publication. Indeed, many women writing about their experiences with breast cancer reference Lorde as a spokesperson of their feelings. Lesbian playwright Tania Katan, for instance, recounts reading the book while writing a play about her mastectomy at the age of twenty-one and summarizes her initial reaction: "I remember feeling like I had found my pissed-off cancer sister and together we would throw our silly prostheses into the wind, wearing nothing but our collective scars and huge smiles; changing the face of breast cancer forever" ("Lorde" 267).[8] Even feminist critics who have opted for prostheses and reconstructive surgeries feel compelled to reason with Lorde: Diane Price Herndl, for example, begins her theoretical essay on "Reconstructing the Posthuman Feminist Body" by warning her readers that she has not lived up to Lorde (477).

In her essay "Our Breasts, Our Selves" – the title of which echoes the groundbreaking publication *Our Bodies, Ourselves* by the Boston Women's Health Collective in 1973 – Herndl explores the ethical issues inherent in telling and publishing a breast cancer narrative: "to whom, or maybe more to the point, for whom are you telling it," she asks fathoming the ways in which communities emerge (221). Yet Lorde's memoir makes clear that community in the late 1970s was by no means readily available, and much less so to a Black Lesbian Feminist Warrior Poet. *The Cancer Journals*, Herndl claims, has not only helped to make breast cancer more visible, but has also established an ethical imperative: "not only should one write about one's experience of cancer, but doing so is a political act" (ibid.).

Once such a story is told, Frank maintains, it may be turned into a resource for others who wish, but may have difficulties in voicing their experiences ("Tricksters" n. pag.). By posing the question of what it means to say that an individual is empowered by a story of illness, Frank raises a crucial issue, precisely because the

---

8   Katan has published her own memoir *My One-Night Stand with Cancer* in 2005. Notwithstanding her humorist take on the illness, Katan's work certainly shares Lorde's rage. Since the publication of Lorde's narrative, a plethora of first-person accounts have been published that contest social discourses and institutional practices; cf. for example Judith Hooper's "Beauty Tips for the Dead," a sarcastic response to Reach to Recovery's cosmetic advice and the "Look Good, Feel Better" programs (in: *Minding the Body: Women Writers on Body and Soul*. Ed. Patricia Foster. New York: Anchor Books, 1994. 107–37), Susan Love's seminal *Dr. Susan Love's Breast Book* (Reading: Addison-Wesley, 1991), and *Coming Out of Cancer: Writings from the Lesbian Cancer Epidemic*, a volume edited by Victoria A. Brownworth (Seattle: Seal Press, 2000).

answer may appear obvious. "The power of statement – of saying it – should never be underestimated," he holds. According to him, *The Cancer Journals* is an empowering narrative, since even though many of the events and emotions Lorde relates are immediately recognizable to many cancer patients, Lorde puts into words what even today few can and dare say (ibid.).

4.1 AGAINST LINEARITY, CERTAINTY, AND CLOSURE: DECONSTRUCTING THE TRIUMPH NARRATIVE IN *THE CANCER JOURNALS*

Frequently recounting experiences from (early) diagnosis to cure, breast cancer narratives figure as the epitome of the triumph narrative and the traditional representation of the disease bears a set of problems that *The Cancer Journals* powerfully attacks. In her essay on autobiographical representations of breast cancer, Laura Potts observes that women's stories are shaped by key moments: discovering the symptoms, receiving the diagnosis, making decisions concerning treatment courses, confronting death, and continuing life after treatment. These provide the text with a linear and progressive structure and "a sense of being driven through the events – [...] a relentless progression, a story unfolding" (114). What Potts hints at here is the notion that writers are rather passively forced through the narration of these events, without a sense of control. This is underlined by the fact that such a structure corresponds to the medical protocol, i.e. the ways in which breast cancer is detected, diagnosed, and treated (cf. Couser, *Recovering* 42), thereby implicitly locating authority over the storytelling process in the realm of the medical establishment, granting patients little agency and power over the representation of their disease. The story then appears to structure itself, since it is hinged on these decisive moments and a prosthetic ending that leaves breast cancer behind is undoubtedly the culturally preferred narrative.

Lorde's book does of course make reference to all the moments Potts has pointed out in her essay. She recounts how she has discovered the lump in her breast "on Labor Day, 1978, during [her] regular monthly self-examination" (*Cancer* 56) and how she awakes after the second biopsy feeling and instantly knowing that the lump is malignant (ibid. 26). She also explains that she has looked for alternative treatment options, but cannot find any she believes will help her (ibid. 28) and stresses that nevertheless, "[t]he decision whether or not to have a mastectomy ultimately was going to have to be [her] own" (ibid. 29), hence emphasizing her independence from medical professionals and as well as her informed position and agency.

Agency is moreover reflected in the structure of the narrative. *The Cancer Journals* does not chronicle a progressive "drag" from one moment to the next, but may rather be grasped as a conscious pausing. On the one hand this is to be understood literally: imagine one taking the time to write the day's events or one's feelings into a journal. Even in her essay "Breast Cancer: A Black Lesbian Feminist Experience," Lorde remarks: "[f]or months I have been wanting to write a piece of meaning words on cancer as it affects my life and my consciousness as a woman, a black lesbian feminist mother lover poet" (ibid. 24) and the very lines that she offers her readers are evidence that she has finally written it. On the other hand, it is also striking that the events Potts theorizes only figure as brief episodes and, with the exception of Lorde's intuitive knowledge of the diagnosis, are only mentioned in passing. Therefore, instead of providing narrative arcs for her story, detection, diagnosis, and surgery serve as signposts in a plotline that is repetitive at times and revisits crucial moments, such as the incident at the surgeon's office I will discuss in more detail below, where Lorde is berated for not wearing prosthesis. While Theresa Brown reads the memoir as an incomplete book and suggests that its structure implies that one's cancer story can never be "completely told" and may at best be conveyed in a continual narration (90), the fact that Lorde's narrative not only revisits, but also occasionally rewrites repetitive moments evinces her agency and at the same time the significance of tentativeness and temporality in her account.

What is more, the structure of Lorde's text deprives the story of the preconfigured ending – the life after cancer. In contrast to many narratives published around the "five-year mark," the time-span typically associated with survival (cf. Couser, *Recovering* 40), *The Cancer Journals* is far from celebrating recovery in the traditional sense. While stories told in such a manner hold the prospect and ready-made structure for an imagined future (Stacey 10), they promote the idea that cancer can be entirely cured and controlled, through the will and resilience of the mind or by leading a more responsible life, waving aside the uncertainty associated with the experience of cancer. "Whatever I did," Lorde concludes her decision to undergo mastectomy, "might or might not reverse that process, and I would not know with any certainty for a very long time" (*Cancer* 32). In her statement, ambivalence, unpredictability, and tentativeness reverberate and are underlined by the use of the conditional, particularly in the shaky verb phrase introduced by "might or might not" and the subsequent negation of knowledge. Furthermore, the adverbial phrase "for a very long time," moved to the end of the clause for emphasis, resonates and precludes closure.

On numerous occasions, the uncertainty with which she will now continue to live her life is stressed in similar ways. Moreover, by describing cancer as "a chronic and systemic disease" (ibid. 75), Lorde calls attention to the fact that it is impossible to bring her story to a final, definitive conclusion: The adjective "chronic" clearly identifies her as a member of the remission society and reveals the ongoing nature of the disease. This is also reflected in the second descriptive adjective, "systemic," indicating that while the disease may shade into the background as therapeutic measures appear successful, it is by no means a local ailment, but affects the entire body and can therefore not be fully eradicated, which is why Lorde urges herself and other women to be "vigilantly aware" of the contingency of the disease, since "[c]ontrary to the 'lighting strikes' theory, we are the most likely of all women to develop cancer somewhere else in the body" (ibid.). The famous saying that "lightening never strikes twice in the same place," an idiom that suggests the unlikelihood of a bad thing happening repeatedly to the same person and provides solace in the face of misfortune, is refuted here and its false sense of safety overwritten by the contrastive phrase that breast cancer patients in fact "most likely" experience another onset of the disease.

These thoughts are underlined by the great number of journal entries that Lorde includes in her introduction and in the essays. Cynthia Wu asserts that the journal or diary form indicates the sense of temporality, or, to be more precise, the sense of the present that is so significant in this context, both "for those who have cancer as well as for those who are presently healthy" (246). For the latter group in particular, the individuals Wu calls "healthy," temporality adds to the lasting sense of contingency and uncertainty because their status is provisional only. However, the formulation of Wu's statement is too dichotomous, since it allows the firm distinction between the "ill" and the "healthy" to persist and does not acknowledge that these states may well shade into one another, as is characteristic in the remission society, where clear-cut boundaries between health and illness have disintegrated. So in the same journal entry in which Lorde describes the visualization and relaxation techniques she has learned from a book titled *Getting Well Again* and that do indeed appear to help her attain well-being, she points to the looming threat of another malignancy by stating: "*I live with the constant fear of recurrence of another cancer*" (*Cancer* 12; italics in original). The entry situates her in an in-between space where the dichotomy of health and illness may no longer hold and, more than that, it makes utterly clear that her well-being and gradual healing are also portrayed as unstable and temporary, which is reflected first and foremost in the use of the present tense in this entry, in contrast to the majority of journal excerpts that are formulated in the past tense.

In her essay "Filling the Dark Spaces," Cook, too, reminds readers that "one's cancer story is not easily written from a retrospective position, because one isn't sure when the 'retrospect' begins or if one will be around long enough to have the 'distant' take" (92). This is furthermore highlighted by the pervasiveness of dates in Lorde's narrative which stress the present dimension and the fleeting sense of time that inform her writing: not only is each journal entry dated, but aside from that, dates are also given at the end of the introduction, as well as at the end of each essay. Particularly at the end of the essays, the dates imply a sense of accomplishment and attest Lorde's survival, yet also convey the preliminary. In her introduction, she avers that her "work is part of a continuum of women's work, of reclaiming this earth and our power, and know[s] that this work will not begin with [her] birth nor will it end with [her] death" (*Cancer* 15). First of all, she hopes that her experience will help other women in their struggle (Keating, *Women* 47) and secondly, she is confident that it will enable others to continue and expand her project.

Accordingly, the memoir is in line with the feminist dictum that "the personal is political" for the quotes illustrate that, despite the fact that the book serves to chronicle intense and painful personal experiences, it needs to be seen as part of a larger, on-going social and political struggle. In this context, the journal entries also constitute fascinating formal elements with regard to notions of subjectivity and the private vs. the public. First of all, Potts holds, the immediacy and implied authenticity of the journal pose an authority that makes it difficult to question the text (99), hence disrupting hierarchies in the medical institution and the status of knowledge. In a similar vein, Joanne Cooper draws on the long tradition of the journal as a predominantly female genre to argue that the journal exposes a kind of immediacy is that is commonly not part of a memoir. Written daily or in the spur of the moment, journals entries are on that account seen as a more direct reflection of the writer's views and feelings than the renderings of events remembered and rearranged in the memoir (cf. 95). She proposes to conceive journals entries as "raw data" and memoirs as "synthesized memory" (ibid.), an observation that certainly needs further consideration with regard to Lorde's narrative. After all, Lorde states that her book comprises "*selected* journal entries" (*Cancer* 8; my italics). Her statement illustrates that she has decided which entries to reveal and which to keep private and points to the fact that these spontaneous entries are as much involved in the conscious construction of her story as are the more elaborate essays.

Many entries that she has decided to reveal are short and sometimes enigmatic, since allusions to social and cultural events remain without explanations. So at the same time that they assert the privacy of the journal, they also situate Lorde in the public discourse. Not only does *The Cancer Journals* therefore undermine the very idea of a private subjectivity, as William Major argues (n. pag.), but the act of making the private public fully corresponds to Lorde's endeavor of making breast cancer visible. Of course Wu is right in maintaining that the representation of the events in a journal points to the presumed secrecy and silence surrounding the diagnosis of breast cancer (246), yet by including parts of her journal in the published book, Lorde breaks this secrecy and exposes her private, suffering, and defiant self.

The self she constructs in her memoir is therefore also at odds with the triumphant breast cancer survivor, the persona at the heart of the conventional prosthetic cancer narrative which Stacey characterizes as the "heroic struggle against adversity" in which writers draw on all imaginable resources in order to fight the "tragedy" that threatens their lives (1). Betty Rollin's classic 1976 memoir *First, You Cry* is representative with the blurb depicting Rollin, then a correspondent at *NBC News*, as "glamorous, successful, and happily married, ha[ving] it all – and then she learned that she had a malignant tumor in her breast." While the cover of the first edition features *Vogue*'s appraisal and subtitles the life narrative as the "courageous story of her personal triumph over devastating tragedy," the anniversary edition, too, advertises the book as the "inspiring story of one woman's triumph over breast cancer." Lorde alludes to *First, You Cry* when stating that "[b]ut in my experience, it's not true that first you cry" (*Cancer* 40). More than a note on the initial emotional numbness she recounts immediately after her mastectomy, her statement may be read as a comment on Rollin's memoir and its quintessential focus on the triumphant struggle against cancer and the maintenance of her outward appearance at any rate.[9]

Consequently, in her book, Lorde writes back at the triumph narrative, most effectively by documenting – particularly in the immediacy of the journal entries – the despair and loss she feels. Her narrative is a "kaleidoscope of emotions" that demonstrates defiance, fury, and strength as much as fear, sorrow, and resignation (cf. Wear and Nixon 80). Cancer has "knocked [her] for a hell of a loop, having to deal with the pain and the fear and the death" (*Cancer* 25). Her enumeration demonstrates that the consequences of her diagnosis and the ensuing surgical intervention are overwhelming and her narrative revolves around these sentiments. In this vein, her language seamlessly moves between a raw and a sophisticated tone and the first-person and third-person stance, hence tying the respective genres in her work – journal entries and polemical essays – together. Their arrangement is strategic, Wu purports when she observes that topically significant journal entries are placed immediately before or after relevant strands of argumentation in the essays, thus fashioning an argument in which the public and the private spheres merge (246). The merging of both genres therefore underlines Lorde's project of making the private public, the personal political.

In *Recovering Bodies*, Couser has devoted a chapter to the discussion of stories about breast cancer, among them Lorde's account, in which he identifies a dichotomous relationship between "the proximate and the distant, between the emotional and the intellectual." He attributes the emotional qualities of outrage and pain to Lorde's journal entries, while describing the essays as "seasoned, reasoned discourse" (50f.). Although it is true that the journal entries serve a cathartic function, since they help to channel emotions and are in this vein therapeutic, Couser's analysis is highly problematic because it takes a separation of the private and the public

---

9   Though widely praised for her frankness in dealing with issues of sexuality, much of Rollin's concern is limited to appearance and attacks mastectomy on grounds of vanity by exclaiming "I would not like to look hideous if that's possible" (55). In "First, You Cry, 25 Years Later" (*Journal of Clinical Oncology* 19.11 (2001): 2967-69) Lerner also comments on this issue.

for granted and postulates that, when speaking as a "private" individual in her journal entries, Lorde does not comment on political issues, which is clearly not the case. Entries that disprove his argument by taking a straightforward political stand can be found throughout *The Cancer Journals*, such as an entry dated September 1979 in which Lorde refers to Mary Daly's *Gyn/Ecology*, a compendium that does not acknowledge the mythical legacy of women of color, by stating that *"[t]he blood of black women sloshes from coast to coast and Daly says race is of no concern to women"* (*Cancer* 10; italics in original).

For this reason, I agree with Theri Pickens who illustrates that *The Cancer Journals* may not be neatly divided into rational discourse and furious outcries. Pickens emphasizes that Lorde's outcries are very well "reasoned" and that which Couser calls "seasoned discourse" is not only marked, but frequently also brought forth by her outrage. Therefore the journal entries and the essays should not be separated on ground of their emotional distance or proximity, Pickens argues (169). Yet whereas she proposes to see the distance between journal entries and essays rather as a temporal one – an imprecise approach, since both forms of text have been composed in the short time span after Lorde's mastectomy, more or less simultaneously – any notion of distinction needs to be abandoned. Dualistic notions of thinking and feeling, the mind and the body, and the public and the private do not hold in Lorde's narrative (cf. also Wu 246).

Furthermore, the triumph narrative conceives breast cancer as transformative: the disease is gradually understood positively as a source of self-knowledge, wisdom and bravery: "Accepting the fragility of life itself, the cancer survivor sees things others are not brave enough to face," Stacey asserts (1). Cynical as it may read in light of Stacey's own experience of cancer her commentary aptly draws attention to the problem of establishing a hierarchy between the post-illness self and others who have not shared their plight and romanticizing the experience of grave illness. As Frank notes, Lorde is far from romanticizing her illness or even stating that she "feels lucky to have had cancer" ("Tricksters" n. pag.). Sure enough, though, she does ascribe a sense of courage and personal growth to living through her breast cancer. She makes a provocative claim in stating "I am who the world and I have never seen before" (*Cancer* 48), pointing out that her post-mastectomy self is a new self, one that was unthinkable before. Without doubt, her statement refers to the physical change the mastectomy has caused, since Jeanne Perreault infers that the altered body also gives rise to a transformed relationship to the self and the world ("Pain" 7f.). At once she joins others in gazing at this new, unfamiliar self from the outside, and is the newly constructed self who meets their gaze (cf. Perreault, *Writing* 19). Yet in equal measure Lorde's recognition goes beyond her external appearance, for the amputated body also becomes, as I will show below, a tool in her political struggle.

Journal entries, like the one dated May 30, 1980, elaborate this claim: *"I feel like another woman, de-chrysalised and become a broader, stretched-out me, strong and excited, a muscle flexed and honed for action"* (*Cancer* 12; italics in original). By describing herself as emerging from a cocoon, Lorde illustrates a fundamental transformation process. However, in contrast to the image of a beautiful yet fragile butterfly leaving its cocoon, she drafts the notion of her changed self in spatial and physical terms. "[B]roader" and "stretched-out," she occupies more space now, is more visible. Readers need to bear in mind that by the time she was diagnosed with breast cancer, Lorde was already a recognized poet and spokesperson on issues of race and sexuality. Giving a voice to her illness experience may hence be seen as a seamless extension of her previous work (cf. Frank, "Tricksters" n. pag.) but the journal entry also highlights that the illness experience and particularly her acceptance of her post-mastectomy body have well altered the focus of her activist endeavor. Comparing herself to a flexed muscle that is "honed for action," she radiates power, readiness, and control and refers to the sense of embodiment that breast cancer has threatened, but that always remains at the core of her argument against prosthesis.

"I would have never chosen this path, but I am very glad to be who I am, here" (*Cancer* 79) is a conclusion that may at first read like the conventional frame for a breast cancer experience. However, seen in the context of the entire book, a more nuanced reading is necessary. Like in the statement quoted above, movement/place and identity are interwoven, elucidating that the journey through breast cancer has ultimately affected Lorde's self and led her to embrace her identity. Furthermore, Lorde expresses her gratitude for still being "here," an idea that I read very literally as still being alive, for much of her considerations about whether or not to have the mastectomy revolve around the conviction that losing or keeping her breast will constitute a choice between life and death (cf. e.g. 32) and thereby simultaneously introduce the full gravity of mortality into the text, voicing the unspeakable.

While other writers construct the experience of illness as a chance to reflect on the meaning of their lives (cf. Chapter 2.3), Lorde directs her focus to death and the ways in which it influences her decisions. Even though her work imagines death as a terrible threat, it is at the same time aligned with the ultimate freedom and it is *because* she is facing death that Lorde develops the strength she so defiantly expounds in the story: *"What is there possibly left for us to be afraid of, after we have dealt face to face with death and not embraced it? Once I accept the existence of dying [...] who can ever have power over me?"* (*Cancer* 24, Dec. 29, 1978; italics in original). Not only do these rhetorical questions illustrate Lorde's attempt to view death and life on a continuum and deriving her meaning from mortality (cf. Waxman 111) but they also make evident that cancer and its pending threat of death become both "weapon and power" (*Cancer* 53), as they endow her with strength and enable her to fight. In "Breast Cancer: A Black Lesbian Feminist Experience," Lorde wonders "'how do I act to announce or preserve my new status as temporary upon this earth?' and then I'd remember that we have always been temporary, and that I had just never really underlined it before, or acted out of it so completely before" (ibid. 52). Illness finally is empowering and insightful, yet only because it uncovers death, which becomes the catalyst for her social and political engagement.

So for her, breast cancer becomes "a gateway, however cruelly won, into the tapping and expansion of [her] own power and knowing" (ibid. 54). Through her experience, she has been made aware of her mortality and has come to acknowledge "death as a fact" (ibid. 25). In this respect, she does attribute positive qualities to her illness and repeatedly depicts it as an event that has shaken her up from denial and has galvanized her into action. It is of particular significance, though, that the change that has affected Lorde is not limited to her conception of herself as an individual because throughout the text she seamlessly moves from the first person singular to the first person plural or the general notion of "women." There is a sense of plurality inherent in her book, one that is well in line with those of other feminists in her generation who give voice to women's issues and to women (cf. Herndl, "Reconstructing" 478). On the fourth day after her mastectomy, September 25, 1978, Lorde thus determines that her journal entries are not supposed to remain "*a record of grieving only*;" instead she hopes they may prove to be of use for her "*later*," when the immediate crisis of illness has passed. She wishes her memories to be something she can share, "*something that [...] came out of the kind of strength I have that nothing nothing else can shake for very long or equal*" (*Cancer* 46; italics in original) and the repetition of "nothing" reflects her determination and a firm belief in her strength.

Moreover, it is not unusual that stories of diagnosis and cure prompt patients to pause and assess their lives, eventually to decide that they need to lead them differently: "The typical story is of the patient who is unexpectedly diagnosed as having cancer, who plummets to the depths of despair, who reassess their values and the meaning of their life and who rises phoenix-like from the experience a new and better person" (Stacey 1, 12). In *The Cancer Journals*, however, Lorde voices her disillusionment about changing her life. On April 16, 1979, she writes "*I can never accept [...] that turning my life around is so hard, eating differently, sleeping differently, moving differently, being differently*" (10; italics in original) and expresses her frustration over the many aspects of her life in need of change. Her enumeration of verbs that connote the everyday, such as "eating" and "sleeping," escalate to the more abstract "moving" and finally climax in "being." Their repetitive parallel construction, listed without conjunctions implies a sense of being rushed through changes which, as "being differently" suggests, become impossible to implement, not least because the adverb "differently" merely indicates that her previous lifestyle was somehow flawed but does not offer a precise and viable alternative.

In part, her journal entry expresses a feeling of nostalgia and longing for the past. While such a nostalgic rhetoric is frequently found in illness life narratives (cf. Chapter 2.3), it must be noted that Lorde's narration significantly departs from a rhetoric that idealizes the "good ol'days," as Garrison phrases it, as a time without the horror of disease and in the comfort of normalcy (n. pag.). In contrast, Lorde's nostalgic allusions do not revolve around the longing for a return to the healthy body, but rather express the belief that her life before cancer was innocent and had not yet experienced the consequences of the carcinogenic materials she had been subjected to.[10] It is therefore not the glorification and idealization of the healthy body her journal entries register (cf. Garrison ibid.), but the recognition that her dietary and life choices are constrained by the fact that society continues to endorse "radiation, animal fat, air pollution, McDonald's hamburgers and Red Dye No. 2" (*Cancer* 62), ultimately relativizing the idea that illness is conceived as an admonition that spurs individuals to make better choices.

In the absence of a comic plot, Lorde's work finally demands that the very notion of triumph be reconsidered: triumph is not framed as recovery and there is no happily ever-after, for now death has become a "fact" (ibid. 25) and may not be negotiated anymore. In lieu of certainty and the individual's accomplishment, triumph becomes collective when it figures as the end of silence, action, and a profound change in the ways in which society constructs disease and femininity and deals with carcinogens. In this vein, Lorde's story is not hers alone; it is a story in which the presence of those women who cannot speak for themselves – poor Black women in particular – is striking, as well as the presence of women who have not survived the disease.

One of them is Eudora Garret, a former older lover who has undergone a mastectomy. The night before her surgery, Lorde dreams about her and later vividly remembers: "I felt the hesitation and tenderness I felt as I touched the deeply scarred hollow under her right shoulder and across her chest, the night she finally shared the last pain of her mastectomy with me in the clear heavy heat of our Mexican spring" (ibid. 35). Her memory of Eudora is first and foremost an act of witnessing, one that, Gretchen Case notes, is utterly physical, for it involves not only seeing but also touching the mastectomy scar (71). This sensuous moment is accentuated by the repetition of the verb phrase "I felt" as both an emotional and a material experience. In a similar vein the "hesitation" and "tenderness" Lorde perceives when she touches her lover's scarred skin blur the boundaries between the two women, as they refer to Lorde's feelings but may also well be read as Eudora's "hesitation" and the "tenderness" of her skin that the touch discloses. Touching the

---

10 In *Zami*, Lorde reflects in more detail on the radiation she was exposed to while working in a factory in Stamford, Connecticut.

scar thus constitutes a powerful moment and it is only then that the full story of the scar is shared (cf. also Case ibid.), foreshadowing Lorde's later refusal to wear prosthesis since then touching, witnessing, is made impossible. More than merely preparing her psychologically for the impending change of her body, as Barbara Waxman claims (115), the remembrance and revival of the strong bond shared by the women bares the foundations of Lorde's political argument against the reconstruction of the post-mastectomy body in an affectionate and erotic encounter.

In addition, her description of Eudora in this brief scene is sympathetic, yet carries none of the appraisal of courage and dignity Stacey attributes to many narratives in which friends, lovers or relatives resume the task of telling the patient's story after he or she has died (2). "I was 19 and she was 47," Lorde writes. "Now I am 44 and she is dead" (*Cancer* 35). The parallel structure of her sentences suggests that she is well aware of her own mortality, which is also illustrated by the fact that she "carr[ies] tattooed upon [her] heart a list of names of women who did not survive and there is always space left for one more, [her] own" (ibid. 40). These two statements serve as another strong reminder of the temporality and contingency of her state and present a clearly non-prosthetic narrative choice by positing death as a possible outcome of the ordeal rather than effacing it.

According to Conway, life narratives that counter the story of triumph are of utmost significance, for they offer a different cultural conception of illness and disability (*Illness* 3). What makes Conway's concept such a valuable contribution to an alternative framework is the fact that she shies ways from absolute conclusions and readily admits that tensions need not be resolved, but may co-exist: "battling and giving up," "finding meaning and not," "denying and acknowledging death" may become equally part of the experience of illness and disability (ibid.). Lorde, for instance, contemplates this already in the introduction of her book when she announces that she "wish[es] to give form with honesty and precision to the pain faith labor and loving" of these eighteen months of her life (*Cancer* 13). "Pain faith labor and loving," all enumerated without comma, are inseparable from one another. As a consequence, the story is not geared toward success and overcoming disease, but addresses despair or anger in equal measure. Besides recognizing the contingent nature of illness, Conway's approach also presupposes that the story is narrated from "inside" the experience, so to speak, as opposed to an account provided from the safe-side of health and hence adequately responds to the nature of cancer that due to its possible recurrences does not allow patients to speak fully removed from the experience of illness (cf. Chapter 2.3). In the following, I will therefore outline the strategy Lorde's text employs to give voice and power to the particularities of her ordeal.

4.2 SUBVERTING THE (SILENT) WAR ON BREAST CANCER: LORDE'S VISION OF THE 'WARRIOR'

Hasan Al-Zubi purports that over the course of *The Cancer Journals* Lorde creates an alternative role that women can "play" while experiencing illness (857). Although he is right in acknowledging Lorde's alternative conception of the patient and her urge to women to assume full responsibility for their lives, his argument neglects one of Lorde's most fundamental concerns, namely that a woman's reaction to illness is not merely a (or any) role to take up, but is always dependent on how she conceives her identity. This is highlighted in the first sentences of her introduction, for Lorde states that "[e]ach woman responds to the crisis that breast cancer brings to her life out of a whole pattern, which is the design of who she is and how her life has been lived. The weave of her everyday existence is the training ground for how she handles crisis" (*Cancer* 7).

Whereas Wear and Nixon assert that this statement reveals a potential predictability in how women experience breast cancer and mastectomy (89) – an assertion that is problematic in itself – I read Lorde's introduction as a statement that reveals the principle of her approach to healing in *The Cancer Journals*. She goes on to explain that some women will "obscure their painful feelings surrounding mastectomy with a blanket of business as usual" (7). Others may, "in a valiant effort not to be seen as merely victims," deny the reality of these painful feelings entirely (ibid.), while yet a third group of women will take their breast cancer as "the warrior's painstaking examination of yet another weapon, unwanted but useful" (ibid.). These sentences make clear that Lorde not only acknowledges different and individual ways of coping with the experience and finding personal avenues to well-being,[11] but she also emphasizes that whichever direction a woman will choose to turn to will be dependent on how she conceptualizes healing.

Throughout her work on autobiographical writing and healing, Chandler stresses that healing is not universally defined, but always delineated in relation to the problem or condition individuals face: "So, for instance, if we describe a problem as atrophy, the healing act will be to reconstitute; if imbalance, it will be to restore balance; if deficiency, it will be to supplement; if fragmentation, it will be to reintegrate" ("Healing" 6). Healing may then be seen as cathartic, integrative, transformative, or reconstructive and is deeply intertwined with the act of recording one's ex-

---

11 In a similar fashion she acknowledges that some women may choose to wear prostheses after having had time to mourn the loss of their breast. As Weber concludes, Lorde is concerned with women's ability to make autonomous choices, instead of being subject to cultural forces (247). This idea is also explored in Marcy Knopf-Newman's *Beyond Slash, Burn, and Poison* (cf. esp. 119).

periences because writing, too, may be cathartic, integrative, transformative or reconstructive (cf. ibid.). For Lorde, compiling *The Cancer Journals* is certainly a purgative exercise, which is particularly evident in the immediacy of the journal entries, but just as well in the discursive power of her narrative essays. Moreover, her memoir serves as a means of reconstruction, especially against the backdrop of her amputated body. On the one hand, the narrative portrays the gradual development of a new body image, an aspect that plays a crucial role in Lorde's healing process. On the other hand, the healing process detailed in the story is more complex, since Lorde needs to reconnect to her activist work and reconstruct her self as a "warrior."

So it is with pride that she claims inclusion in the third group for herself, outlining the signposts of her identity by stating "I am a post-mastectomy woman who believes our feelings need voice in order to be recognized, respected, and of use" (*Cancer* 7). Her introduction is therefore crucial for various reasons. First of all, Lorde uses the very first sentences of her account to establish the image of the warrior woman and to introduce the metaphorical realm of "war" into her story by speaking of her experience of cancer and breast amputation as a "weapon." Secondly, with its repeated use of the adjective "painful," the introductory paragraph makes evident that any such experience is always permeated by pain and that healing also means coming to terms with this pain. It becomes clear here that cancer in her account is never romanticized, a notion that would also endorse the dualist conception of the ill self in which the mind may flourish while the body is left severely affected. Instead, throughout the course of the book, Lorde outlines her deep pain, both physical and emotional. Yet as a warrior, her explanation makes clear, she does not need to hide or deny the presence of this pain but is permitted to experience and express it openly as a necessary and acknowledged part of her struggle. Only then, she holds, the experience of illness may actually be "useful." By turning her experience and her body into a weapon, she endows them with meaning and purpose, not only in a spiritual sense, but with regard to her activist work.

In *Beyond Slash, Burn and Poison*, Marcy Knopf-Newman makes clear that despite the fact that when she politicizes breast cancer, Lorde considers the body and the environment, two inherently political subjects, her discussion of cancer is political due to the silence and secrecy generally associated with the disease (136). The experience of illness prompts Lorde to redirect her use of language and reconfirm the importance of language in her life (Waxman 107). As she outlines in her introduction, she wishes to attack the kind of "imposed silence" that functions as "a tool for separation and powerlessness" (*Cancer* 7). She conceptualizes silences as imposed by culture and society and a means to obstruct individuals' in general and women's empowerment in particular because it does not permit the exchange of experiences and, as a consequence, the building of a community, and therefore keeps women separated from each other. Accordingly, the first step in gaining power and autonomy is to speak over silence.

"Each of us is here now," Lorde thus appeals to the audience at the Lesbian and Literature Panel of the Modern Language Association for whom the text in "The Transformation of Silence into Language and Action" was originally written, "because in one way or another we share a commitment to language and to the power of language, and to the reclaiming of that language which has been made to work against us" (*Cancer* 20f.). Throughout the course of the book, she strives to utter language in a way that will allow her to put its power to use, a project that is twofold. First of all, reclaiming language entails overcoming silence. Secondly, in reclaiming language which has previously worked to marginalize her, Lorde also reappropriates old metaphors.

Lorde's thoughts on turning silence into language, first explored in the speech delivered on December 28, 1977, have since been published in *Sinister Wisdom* (1978), *The Cancer Journals* (1980), as well as in *Sister Outsider* (1984) and Lester Olson, a scholar of rhetoric, maintains that each of these publications have spread Lorde's message to a readership beyond the audience at the MLA conference (51). Furthermore, placing the speech in the context of Lorde's cancer narrative significantly alters its reading, since her original speech only refers to the biopsy that revealed a benign growth (ibid.). Perreault, too, observes that "[t]here is pathos in these words, written in relief and strength, since the introduction has already told us that a year later a malignant tumor was discovered" ("Pain" 10f.). Yet she is right in professing that Lorde's speech has not been included to allude to sentimentalism or even irony. Rather, it reveals directly how the experience has influenced Lorde in ethical and political terms (ibid. 11). In this respect it is crucial to bear in mind the original format of the essay. As a speech, Lorde has given a voice to these concerns, countering silence with language and realizing the project she outlines in political terms here and whose strength and urgency is drawn from the experience of cancer.

"[W]ithin those three weeks," Lorde speaks about the time between the discovery of the lump and the biopsy, "I was forced to look upon myself and my living with a harsh and urgent clarity that has left me still shaken, but much stronger" (*Cancer* 18). Her experience has made her aware of her mortality and what she has come to regret the most "were [her] silences" (ibid.). "I was going to die, if not sooner, then later, whether or not I had ever spoken myself. My silences had not protected me. Your silence will not protect you" (ibid.). Moving from the personal to the communal, Lorde demonstrates that silence over injustices or internalized shame is not only hurtful but also to no purpose. At the beginning of her speech, it is silence that unites the community of women and she tentatively drafts silence as gendered in so far as it is the result of both socialization and experiences of poverty, violence or verbal abuse (Olson, "Margins" 52).[12] Silence ultimately becomes a political issue rooted in race, gender, sexuality, dis/ability, and class and is thus tightly connected to identity. According to Olson, language is essential to the self, for it is through language that the self is defined. Silence, in contrast, betrays the self and may even have destructive consequences, he asserts (ibid. 58), which becomes evident in Lorde's statement that "[d]eath [...] is the final silence" (*Cancer* 18).[13]

"Of what had I *ever* been afraid?" (*Cancer* 18; italics in original), Lorde asks rhetorically, acknowledging the fear underlying silence, a fear that is used to perpetuate silence, and, to that effect, the status quo (cf. Thatcher 654). As a result, silence is conceived as political, much in the same sense as speech becomes political, yet only speech will generate social change. Olson asserts that even though silence may suggest the illusion of being protected, such an illusion is "endangering the self as undetected cancer endangers the body" ("Margins" 58). This comparison, however, is flawed because it juxtaposes the self and the body as two discrete entities. Lorde herself, though, speaks of her fear of having her ideas "bruised and misunderstood" (*Cancer* 17), thus integrating the corporeal and the verbal.

The physical and the intellectual, as well as the past and the present merge in the memoir and national borders are transcended. Knopf-Newman raises a fascinating thought when she proposes to read Lorde's narrative as an echo of stories written by female slaves that attested to the lack of control these Black women had over their own bodies. According to her, Lorde actively establishes a connection to their situation by means of the autobiographical and through the fact that she links breast

---

12 In view of this argument, the scene in which silence gives way to community when Lorde is introduced to Lil' Sister, the youngest sister of her brother-in-law who visits her after she has returned from the hospital frames a powerful encounter. It is striking that no one in their family has known about Lil' Sister's mastectomy until she announces her visit and Lorde, too, notes that not only has she never met Lil' Sister before, but she also believes that their conversation was the first time Lil' Sister shared her story (*Cancer* 50ff.). In each other's company, the women are able to shatter the silence that surrounds the Black post-mastectomy body (cf. Knopf-Newman 121). Exchanging information about exercise routines, they quickly move into a discussion on "whether or not cocoa-butter retarded black women's tendencies to keloid, the process by which excess scar tissue is formed to ward off infection" and continue their conversation even when Lorde's brother-in-law asks them to change the topic (*Cancer* 51).

13 Olson maintains that today, after the AIDS pandemic and the urge of the AIDS movement to break the silence that surrounds sexuality and AIDS/HIV, readers will not comprehend Lorde's speech the same way as she devised it in 1977. Yet although Lorde's language and action have been appropriated, they remain consistent with her efforts ("Margins" 64).

cancer to a modern form of colonialism, the apartheid in South Africa (112). Lorde begins her speech with the poem "A Song for Many Movements" dedicated to the South African activist Winni Mandela. Ending her poem with the repetition of the verses "our labor/ has become more important/ than our silence," Lorde entangles the racial conflict in South Africa with the ensuing report on her confrontation with breast cancer that has prompted her to reconsider silence (*Cancer* 17). Knopf-Newman may be right when she holds that the urgency of South African apartheid is reflective of the urgency of cancer and thus exemplifies "the myriad ways that silence equals pain, trauma, and death" (112), yet their relationship is also much more immediate. Intertwining apartheid and breast cancer, Lorde unmasks the idea that there are power hierarchies at work in both cases and throughout *The Cancer Journals*, she makes clear that also in the case of breast cancer one of the factors determining power, health, and recovery is race.[14] Furthermore, both intertwine the efforts of an individual with the collective nature of the struggle, and, most importantly, the connection of these two ideas, like Lorde's fear to have her words "bruised and misunderstood" introduces the violence that goes along with speaking against imposed silences. The discourse in which she introduces the notion of herself as a "warrior" is hence one that is permeated by violence already.

"Where are the models for what I am supposed to be in this situation?" Lorde asks, finding only there that are no role models available to a Black lesbian feminist poet: "This is it, Audre. You're on your own" (*Cancer* 28). While her conclusion does of course bespeak a strong sense of isolation and insurmountable difference, it holds at the same time creative potential. Although she voices her yearning for role models on numerous occasions throughout her story, she takes their absence as a reason to devise her own model of how to make sense of her illness and incorporate the experience of breast cancer into her identity, most notably through the metaphorical discourse on the warrior.

In the public discourse on cancer, the experience is traditionally framed as a battle or war, a metaphor that has become internalized and pervades, as Garrison maintains, the very experience of cancer, as well as the ways in which patients themselves and others around them make sense of the disease (n. pag.). It describes medical personnel as actively and heroically fighting against cancer (cf. Wu 246), urges patients to engage in a battle against their selves and their bodies, which are de-

---

14 Maureen Casamayou reports a similar set of problems when she notes that in contrast to white women, Black women are more than twice as likely to die of breast cancer because they often cannot access preventive care, such as clinical breast examinations or yearly mammograms (16). The overall decline in mortality rates that the U.S. Department of Health and Human Services has been observing, Casamayou maintains, does not apply to Black women (ibid.).

clared war zones, pronounces cancer as the enemy and conceptualizes treatments as search-and-destroy missions (Garrison n. pag.). Garrison's "The Personal is Rhetorical" makes a convincing case for the problematic dimension of the war metaphor in cancer narratives, arguing that once cancer is perceived as the "enemy" that "invades" the body, the body becomes a battleground split from the mind and the patient is urged to become a disembodied "soldier" as he/she is forced to make decisions about aggressive treatment options (n. pag.). As a result, the metaphors of war commonly uttered in the discourse about breast cancer enforce a split self whose power rests – if at all – in the patient's mind. The military metaphor is indeed so pervasive that it seems almost impossible to frame the experience of cancer from another standpoint (ibid.).

Lorde's narrative, however, does very well fashion an alternative standpoint, even though it continues to locate the experience of cancer in the metaphorical realm of war. Yet it is not her fight against the cancer in her body that Lorde describes when she chooses to name herself a 'warrior.' Instead of conceptualizing her treatment course as a war and breast cancer as her enemy, her fight is one aimed against medical institutions and, more importantly, American society at large.

At the same time, Ehrenreich, underlining the pervasive nature of the rhetoric of war, calls attention to the fact that a noun that may be used to describe a woman with breast cancer does not exist:

"Instead, we get verbs: Those who are in the midst of their treatments are described as 'battling' or 'fighting,' sometimes intensified with 'bravely' or 'fiercely'-language suggestive of Katharine Hepburn with her face to the wind. Once the treatments are over, one achieves the status of 'survivor' [...]. For those who cease to be survivors and join the more than 40,000 American women who succumb to breast cancer each year – again, no noun applies. They are said to have 'lost their battle' and may be memorialized by photographs carried at races for the cure – our lost, brave sisters, our fallen soldiers." ("Welcome" 48)

Her examples make clear that identity is only assigned to those who leave the experience of cancer behind, transcend their disease, and return to health.[15] The status of

---

15 In an article on The New York Times's "Well"-blog, Susan Gubar, too, voices her outrage over the language employed in conversations about cancer. Besides the medical terminology calling patients "resistant" or "refractory" to certain drugs which ultimately places responsibility and blame on them, she rejects the term "survivor" "because it erases or demeans patients who do not or suspect they cannot survive the disease" (n. pag.). Instead, she proposes "P.L.C. (Person Living with Cancer), cancer veteran, cancer gambler and, given all the hospital trips, cancer schlepper" and references the acronyms used by Eve Kosofsky Sedgwick: "BBP (Bald Barfing Person) and WAPHMO (Woman About

individuals speaking from the immediacy of the experience appears too contingent and, most of all, too frightful to be named, as is the unspeakable situation of a person who dies of cancer. In naming herself a "warrior," Lorde reacts to the striking lack of identification. She assumes the identity of a person diagnosed with breast cancer and Amy Elliot argues that the potential for speech and action inherent in this role endow her with a sense of agency, in contrast to the commonly uttered notion of the victim (163). Moreover, Lorde reappropriates a noun that can be applied as much to the experience of illness as to her struggle for social justice. The warrior metaphor should thus not be read with reference to cancer only, for when Lorde states that "we were never meant to survive," she makes clear that the struggle as a Black lesbian woman involves social constructions of identity just as well as it concerns her illness (*Cancer* 20).

Scholarship on *The Cancer Journals* is therefore frequently devoted to the analysis of the metaphorical language in Lorde's narrative and many critics note that on first reading, the military utterances in the memoir seem to bear a striking resemblance to the problematic use of language Garrison has pointed out. A number of critics, among them Robina Khalid, voice their concern over the fact that militarized language has "a clear masculinist bent," expressing their doubt whether the metaphor is capable of truly grasping the nature of her experiences (700). Resting on stereotypes, Khalid's perspective suggests that by using different utterances, speakers may disengage themselves from the framework of patriarchy. Lorde's book, however, makes clear that patriarchy is inescapable and saturates the experience of cancer, as well as the construction of the dis/abled body. The transgressive potential of her approach thus lies in her appropriation of the conventional metaphorical realm. Attempts, such as Khalid's, to strip the metaphorical dimension of *The Cancer Journals* of the context of war may appear intriguing, yet neglect the effect that the warrior figure has on Lorde's identity and its significance for the genre of breast cancer narratives. So instead of doing away with the metaphor of war altogether, I seek to provide a more nuanced reading that takes into account the relations of mind and body inherent in Lorde's presentation of her battle and herself as a warrior. After all, the metaphor is pervasive in the book and holds great significance, since it makes her aware of her fight as a collective endeavor, while at the same time opening a discursive space for the mourning and loss ultimately connected to any battle that is fought.

---

to go Postal at H.M.O.). [...] PSHIFTY (Person Still Hanging In Fine Thank You) and QIBIFA (Quite Ill, But Inexplicably Fat Anyway) until she settled on 'undead'" (ibid.). All of these terms effectively shift the discourse from a triumphant battle to a bleaker reality.

Lorde does not use the metaphor in the traditional sense, but carefully revises its signifieds. Her image of the warrior is strongly influenced by both classical Greek mythology and the West-African Amazons of Dahomey, who, as Lorde explains in a footnote, are said to have removed their right breasts in order to become better archers (*Cancer* 34), and develop into a fierce symbol of female strength, ethnic identity and difference, and the unity of mind and body. The Amazon warriors of ancient Greece derived their name from the word "amazos," meaning "without a breast" (Conner n. pag.) and it is from the stories surrounding these effective female soldiers that Lorde fashions the imagery of the one-breasted warrior. Nevertheless, her mythological reappropriation rests in equal measure on white myths and on Black roots, thus blurring distinctions and differences and she also associates it with the West African state of Dahomey, where troops of female soldiers were first recorded in written accounts in 1729 and served in combat during the eighteenth and nineteenth century (cf. Dash n. pag.).[16]

Similar to her biomythography *Zami: A New Spelling of My Name* which culminates in Lorde's brief affair with Afrekete, a Black woman uniting the erotic and the maternal, the familiar and the exotic, as well as the present and past, Lorde uses the image of the Amazon warrior to revise both African and Eurocentric archetypes (cf. Ball n. pag.). Drawing from African and European sources, she is hence able to, as Charlene Ball asserts, establish a corrective framework in which existing myths are challenged and displaced (ibid.). However, not only mythical conceptions are confronted in Lorde's writing. In her study "Myth Smashers, Myth Makers," AnaLouise Keating argues that images modeled on non-Western myths also operate to destabilize existing definitions of white heterosexual female identity because they have the potential to disrupt notions of womanhood and therefore provide effective alternatives to the social status quo (75f.). Writing then becomes, according to Keating, not only a means of self-discovery, but likewise a tool for political resistance and social change (ibid. 76). It is consequently because of the metaphor of the Amazon warrior that *The Cancer Journals* is not only a cathartic and therapeutic text, but also a narrative that powerfully reconnects Lorde to her earlier work as an activist and thus incites an alternative notion of healing.

In this vein, Rudolf Käser stresses the feminist stance in her rhetoric but purports that Lorde perceives herself as an heir to the Amazonian warriors "in the fight against the dominance of men in all areas of life" (338, my translation). The similarities the memoir constructs between Lorde and the Amazonian women, though, are much more finely nuanced. The notion of the warrior, then, is not related to an individual, but to a group and the reference to the Amazon warriors establishes a solidarity that transcends time (cf. ibid. 341). In this vein, Roseanne Quinn, too,

---

16 Frank points out that the metaphor also connotes queerness (*Wounded* 129).

stresses the bond between women when she envisions the tight connection between "the grandmother, mother, daughter, sister, aunt, cousin, friend, lover, wife, girlfriend, warrior, woman, women" (280) that Lorde would term 'sisterhood': something "much more than friends or buddies" (*Zami* 178). Rather than employing the metaphor to increase social difference and distance and participate in exclusionary practices, Lorde turns to the Dahomeyan Amazons to foster a sense of unity, equality, and community amongst women who struggle.

Yet Käser criticizes her for supposedly losing sight of the fact that these women did not lose their breasts because of a cancerous lump. He finds fault with her strategy for pushing aside the medical reasons for her mastectomy and in doing so implicitly reiterating the taboo of cancer (341). His line of argumentation, aimed at undermining the project of the entire book, is problematic, as it neglects both Lorde's strong awareness of her cancer and its pathology that threatens her life, as well as the notion of the body that she puts forth. Although the Amazon warriors do not share her illness, they, like Lorde, have turned their body into a tool for combat, thereby bestowing, Frank recognizes, a retrospective necessity on her mastectomy (*Wounded* 130). On the one hand, becoming more effective archers entails having a better chance at surviving the battle and, along similar lines, Gabriella Ricciardi refers to amputation as a sign commonly associated with survival (76), an idea that certainly resonates with Lorde. Beyond that, however, the image of the warrior as the metaphor for Lorde's identity suggests a profound change in the ways in which she perceives her self, since it implies, as Frank convincingly argues, empowerment in the face of incompleteness (*Wounded* 130).

In this respect, already Lorde's first allusion to the Amazon warriors is striking: On waking up from her biopsy, she relates the terrible cold in the recovery room and her fear that the doctor has discovered a malignancy in her breast and interjects: "The Amazon girls were only 15, I thought, how did they handle it?" (*Cancer* 27). Khalid is correct here in stressing that Lorde does not instinctively conceive herself as a warrior after her surgery (701), too great appears to be the distance between "their" bravery and her suffering self. In this scene, the terrible cold, connected to the piercing pain and Lorde's apprehension create an atmosphere of gloom and despair. It is indeed the "love of women" that returns strength to Lorde here:[17] her

---

17 See Weber (242) and Deshazer (*Mammographies* 58) for an analysis of the power of the erotic in this scene. The erotic surfaces on various occasions in the narrative in connection to the healing process, such as when Lorde returns home after her mastectomy and masturbates – reclaims her body and its altered erotic potential (cf. *Cancer* 24, 40). Pickens, too, studies the erotic in the memoir as "integral to healing": According to her, the erotic does not only give a distinct voice to breast cancer patients' sexual concerns but also responds to the sterility of clinical practice and, most importantly, undermines the

partner Frances enters the hospital room "like a great sunflower" and touches Lorde with her "deliciously warm" hands, reinvigorating her from the cold of anesthesia and other friends, too, come to her bed and, learning that the hospital is out of spare blankets, pile their coats onto her bed and provide Lorde with warmth that is physical as well as emotional (*Cancer* 27). "[I]t made self-healing more possible, knowing that I was not alone," Lorde recounts (ibid. 28f.).

The conviction that she is in fact part of a supportive community is a central realization and in contrast to Khalid, I maintain that Lorde's idea of "woman love" is not fundamentally different from the notion of the Amazon warrior, for the latter likewise becomes a means of bonding and establishing a sense of community (cf. 701). Despite the fact that her question of how these young girls handled their surgeries indicates that Lorde feels terribly overwhelmed, it is also open to a more positive reading. Directing her thoughts from the biopsy and the cold to the Amazonian girls, Lorde looks up to them for strength and perseverance and thereby suggests an implicit comparison between their situations so that her question may also be read as one sparked by curiosity. What is more, her question is directly followed by the illustration of the female support network beginning to organize around her bed, hence intertwining the idea of support and community with the Amazon warriors.

Similarly, Lorde turns to the Amazons in the evening before her mastectomy, when she adds to her entry: "*7.30 pm. And yet if I cried for a hundred years I couldn't possibly express the sorrow I feel right now, the sadness and the loss. How did the Amazons of Dahomey feel? They were only little girls. But they did this willingly, for something they believed in. I suppose I am too but I can't feel that for now*" (*Cancer* 34; italics in original). Here, Lorde draws an explicit parallel between herself and the Amazon warriors, assuming they both allow their bodies to be altered "for something they believe in," since Lorde notes that her decision for the mastectomy is based on her will "to live and to love and to do [her] work" (ibid.

---

medical discourse that conceives the post-mastectomy female body as "desexualized and sterile" (179f.). As a result, her narration departs, most obviously in the title of the essay "Breast Cancer: A Black Lesbian Feminist Experience," from the master narrative of breast cancer that portrays patients as asexual and totalizes their experiences. The notion of the erotic is more fully explored in Lorde's essay "Uses of the Erotic: The Erotic as Power." Here, Lorde describes the erotic as a "resource" and a form of "power which rises from our deepest and nonrational knowledge" (53). She urges women to reclaim that what has been "vilified, abused, and devalued within western society" (ibid.) so that they may begin again to "feel deeply all the aspects of our lives, [...] begin to demand from [them]selves and from [their] life-pursuits that they feel in accordance with that joy" (57). Consequently, the erotic becomes a powerful tool, both for the assessment of the self and for the critical examination of the world (cf. ibid.).

32). Even though she cannot yet fully associate herself with their position because her sense of loss is too great, she draws strength from the myth that eventually does enable her to name herself a warrior (cf. ibid. 34). Finally, Lorde's resignification of the metaphor is also significant for another reason. By attesting strength and survival to their physically altered bodies, Lorde reconceptualizes the idea of bodily disfigurement (cf. also Wu 246), an issue that I will probe in the next section of his chapter.

4.3 EXPOSING THE POST-MASTECTOMY BODY: LORDE'S REJECTION OF (NARRATIVE) PROSTHESIS

"Invisibility is to the eyes what silence is to the ears," Lester Olson notes (61). Lorde's efforts to break with the silence surrounding breast cancer and to rework the frameworks in which the experience of the disease is viewed therefore involve not only the verbal, but also the corporeal. For Lorde, wearing prostheses or undergoing surgical reconstruction of the breast after a mastectomy becomes a political issue that is informed by her own experiences and bespeaks the social construction of breast cancer, normalcy, and the female body in American society. That the personal is indeed political is made utterly clear by Lorde's exploration of her post-surgical experiences in the essays "Breast Cancer: A Black Lesbian Feminist Experience" and "Power vs. Prosthesis," on which I will focus in the following. According to Allison Kimmich, the recurring battles Lorde is compelled to fight over the need to wear a "form" prompt her to view the issue from a political and cultural perspective (228). While scholars so far have particularly concentrated on the latter issue, stressing the feminist argument in Lorde's work, I aim to slightly shift the focus and expand the feminist reading of *The Cancer Journals* by combining it with a theoretical impetus from Disability Studies.

In her rejection of prostheses, Lorde turns the concept of stigmatization inside out and takes – in Herndl's words – to "wear" the cancer on her marked body with pride and, most importantly, as a means of exhortation (cf. "Reconstructing" 479). Rejecting the prosthesis is first of all Lorde's personal strategy of coping with the new asymmetry of her body and, secondly, rooted in her refusal to have her marked body normalized and rendered invisible. Although both perspectives are tightly intertwined, it is especially the first that draws on the materiality of the body. Lorde's text then presents both physical and emotional pain not only as an excruciating experience, but as a reminder of embodiment that eventually allows her to see her wound as an honorable marker of difference.

Similar to other narratives, the experience of illness in *The Cancer Journals* threatens the integrity and unity of the self. "*I'm so tired of all this. I want to be the person I used to be, the real me. I feel sometimes that it's all a dream and surely I'm about to wake up now,*" Lorde writes into her journal in October 1978 (*Cancer* 24; italics in original). Her ill self is so removed from what she considers her "real" self, the pre-cancer and pre-mastectomy self, that it appears impossible to acknowledge her new situation, which she conceives as a nightmare from which she hopes to awake in order to leave it behind. In fact, the references to her situation as a bad dream, as well as to a shrill voice telling her that "none of this [is] true" occur repeatedly in the text, illustrating Lorde's inability to accept the reality of her situation and her altered body yet. Her split self becomes even more evident by the fact that she feels that "[a]nother part" of her, like a bird, looks down from the ceiling at the events below, "providing a running commentary" from the distance on what is happening (ibid. 30).

Furthermore, Lorde's alienation from herself becomes evident when she ponders on the mastectomy. "I would lie if I did not speak of loss," she admits at the end of her introduction (*Cancer* 14) and particularly the ensuing journal entries poignantly illustrate the loss that the mastectomy means for her. On October 10, 1978, she writes:

> "*I want to write about the pain. The pain of waking up in the recovery room which is worsened by that immediate sense of loss.* [...] *I want to write of the pain I am feeling right now, of the lukewarm tears that will not stop coming into my eyes – for what? For my lost breast? For the lost me? For the death I don't know how to postpone? Or how to meet elegantly?*"
> (*Cancer* 23; italics in original)

Although it is a distinct form of pain that Lorde wishes to express, illustrated by her repeated use of the definite article, it is a pain that can neither be grasped nor voiced properly. Twice Lorde expresses her wish to write about how she feels, thereby only indirectly speaking about her experience. Her account does not feature adjectives that would describe her pain, translate qualitative feelings into language, and make her situation comparable, accordingly revealing the sense of isolation that pervades her overall argumentation and is part of any experience of illness but especially of the silence and invisibility surrounding breast cancer. Moreover, this journal entry indicates numbness and distance: The experiencing I writes about the "lukewarm tears" that do not cease to come into her eyes, yet she does not speak of crying, and is thus also incapable of controlling the tears. Moreover, her description of her tears as "lukewarm" is striking, as it creates the impression that she experiences them as removed from her body.

The loss of her breast is undoubtedly also a loss of the self, as the parallel form of her questions suggests, as much as it is entangled with the threat of death. Lorde realizes in the face of serious illness that she cannot protract her death and prolong her life, a feeling of powerlessness that is ultimately reinforced by her last question of how to meet death "elegantly." Despite the impression of helplessness that her diary entry conveys, her final question mediates this to some extent, as it foreshadows the project of *The Cancer Journals* in which she not only comes to terms with the temporality of life, but takes great power and relentlessness from this new urgency. In fact, as Knopf-Newman holds, after her diagnosis, the word "urgent" appears in this book, as well as elsewhere in Lorde's work with great frequency (123).

On the other hand, terror and fear frequently give way to an utterly rational perspective, for instance when Lorde envisions the decision whether to undergo mastectomy or not to be an intellectual endeavor: "What was the wisest approach to take having a diagnosis of breast cancer and a history of cystic mastitis?" she wonders, giving weight to all possible rational factors and digesting the reading "material that concerned women" have brought her (*Cancer* 30f.). A turn away from her embodied reality can also be observed when Lorde recalls her feelings before her first biopsy:

"I had grown angry at my right breast because I felt as if it had in some unexpected way betrayed me, as if it had become already separate from me and had turned against me by creating this tumor which might be malignant. My beloved breast had suddenly departed from the rules we had agreed upon to function by all these years." (*Cancer* 33)

The threat of cancer has dissolved the unity of body and self and Lorde sees her self aligned with her mind, directing her anger at her breast. In this scene, the body is depicted in strikingly negative terms when Lorde accuses her breast as having created a tumor and thus having "turned against" her and violated the rules of their relationship.

Like in Oliver Sacks's and Siri Hustvedt's narratives, the unity of mind and body comes as an epiphany. Yet whereas in *A Leg to Stand On*, music unites mind and body (Chapter 5.3), and automatic writing helps Hustvedt in *The Shaking Woman* to uncover the unconscious past, thereby merging mind and body, present and past (Chapter 8.3), Lorde's narrative does not derive unity from artistic practices. Instead, Lorde reaches a decisive moment when she faces herself in the mirror wearing the temporary prosthesis that does not fit at all and determines: "either I would love my body one-breasted now, or remain forever alien to myself" (*Cancer* 44).

Meeting the altered contours of one's body in the mirror is a key moment in mastectomy narratives. Lorde's acknowledgement of her body, however, does not resemble the sense of alienation, horror, disgust, fear or mutilation that Potts writes about with regard to other breast cancer stories (123). When Lorde faces her amputated body, she takes note of a "strange and uneven and peculiar" sight, but one that she characterizes as "ever so much more myself, and therefore so much more acceptable, than I looked with that thing stuck inside my clothes" (*Cancer* 44).

Alexander deduces that the prosthetic is rendered unnecessary and deforming compared to the new shape of her body that Lorde is beginning to accept, stressing the need for creating one's own sense of body-image rather than conforming to an ideal of symmetry (705).[18] Her decision to embrace her altered body is of course in line with the feminist stance Lorde and her contemporaries have promoted that women love and acknowledge their bodies. On top of that, she also defies the ideology of cure, for Garland-Thomson notes that when aimed at the disabled body, 'cure' concentrates on changing the "abnormal" or "dysfunctional" body so that it will adhere to the norms of beauty and normalcy ("Integrating" 499, 495).

The inadequacy of the prosthetic "cure" is exemplified when Lorde accentuates that "[w]here 'normal' means the 'right' color, shape, size, or number of breasts, a woman's perception of her own body and the strengths that come from that perception are discouraged, trivialized, and ignored" (*Cancer* 66). The normalization of women's bodies, and directly connected to this, the pressure to assimilate to what Bolaki calls a "universal or unmarked body ideal" ("Challenging" 55) have nothing to do with the reality of their lives and deny women agency. As their bodies are objectified and fragmented – for despite the fact that prostheses are intended to repair the body and restore its wholeness, the focus on breasts leaves a breach – post-mastectomy women come to be regarded, in Quinn's words, as "damaged goods" (276). Lorde therefore exposes that the prosthetic "cure" and its deception of wholeness bears no relation to the healing process she hopes to initiate. In contrast, she claims that "in the process of losing a breast, [she] ha[s] become a more whole person" (*Cancer* 56), a paradoxical assumption, as Weber observes, yet one that becomes possible precisely because she faces all her pain and fear with brutal honesty (246).

In this respect, pain becomes a recurring trope in her narrative, particularly during the first months after the surgery. In April 1979, Lorde writes: "*I must let this pain flow through me and pass on. If I resist or try to stop it, it will detonate inside me, shatter me, splatter my pieces against every wall and person I touch*" (*Cancer* 10; italics in original), thus highlighting that she feels the need to give in to the pain. Only when she surrenders herself to it, it will eventually pass. As a result, pain becomes a necessary trouble and a rite of passage. What is remarkable about the diary entry quoted above is certainly the language in which Lorde refers to her pain, more precisely, the violent characteristics she attributes to it if it is interrupted: then the pain will "detonate," "shatter" her, and "splatter [her] pieces," a graphic imagery that calls forth the context of war again. Yet on her 46th birthday, on February

---

18 Alexander compares the rejection of prosthesis to Lorde's decision to omit the "dangling y" in her first name to arrive at a "new and natural shape of the name" that is "indeed wonderfully even AUDRELORDE" (705).

18th, 1980, her journal reads: *"Fear and pain and despair do not disappear. They only become slowly less and less important"* (*Cancer* 11f.; italics in original). Like she has anticipated, her pain begins to fade, but traces of it remain. In contrast to her earlier statement about pain, this journal entry reads reconciliatory and illustrates that healing has begun to take place.

Throughout the book, prostheses are depicted as a hindrance to healing. Although Lorde repeatedly aligns her mastectomy with a deep sense of loss, describing it as a "recurrent sadness," she concludes her introduction by stating that it is "certainly not one that dominates [her] life," demonstrating that she has acknowledged her loss and integrated it into her sense of self as both physical and emotional reality (*Cancer* 14). Directly opposed to this new "reality," Lorde outlines the practice of wearing prostheses as a "mask" and breast reconstruction as a "dangerous fantasy" (ibid.). It is important to understand the prosthesis, as anthropologist Sarah Lochlann Jain reminds readers, as material artifact, as well as discursive framework ("Prosthetic" 32). For Lorde, prostheses constitute a means of deception, not only for anyone allowing the cancer patient to 'pass' as healthy or cured, but most importantly it presents a form of self-deception for any woman trying to heal.

The image of the mask lends itself particularly well to a comparison with the prosthesis: as foreign bodies made of inorganic matter, both are attached to the body to shield it from the gaze. In this context, Lorde speaks of hiding, a verb that can – and should – be interpreted as denoting both seeking protection and yielding to cowardice. Prostheses allow women, as Al-Zubi observes, to "return undetected to the ranks of the healthy" and thus to the status they inhabited before they became ill, which in turn leads to a denial of the disease and allows them to "pretend that their bodies are whole, unflawed" (860). Couser associates a sense of hypocrisy with such attempts in 'passing'[19] and claims that due to her racial and sexual identi-

---

19 Disability memoirs frequently exhibit parallels to ethnic life narratives in which writers recount passing for white. An impairment not instantly visible, for instance, may allow writers to pass as able-bodied, but passing here may also involve downplaying the significance or the implications of an impairment by refusing accommodation. In Chapter 6.3, I analyze passing in Simi Linton's memoir. Kuusisto's *Planet of the Blind*, for instance, depicts the experiencing I as trying to pass by refusing mobility training and accommodations that may help him complete the workload in his literary studies classes, while the narrating I comments on these futile attempts at "masquerading like a seeing man": "In the meantime I'm a tired kid. It's preposterous to live as though you can see. Looking back, I can scarcely imagine the energy it took. […] There are headaches that spread from my skull to my stomach. My entire body is uninhabitable. I have backaches from leaning and straining to see" (103, 43). His embrace of blindness, too, is a gradual and lengthy process aided by mentors and role models when he recognizes that "[s]o thoroughly has

ty, Lorde is utterly aware of the inefficacy of such practices (*Recovering* 51). In a similar vein, Garland-Thomson remarks that while the pursuit of normalcy may give comfort to others, it denies limitations and pain (*Extraordinary* 13).

The prosthesis in Lorde's argumentation is then not enabling, but in fact disabling, as it promotes women's silence and isolation and prohibits the creation of a community and an open conversation about women's health (cf. *Cancer* 14f.). As I have discussed above, silence, much like invisibility, maintains the status quo. The post-mastectomy body Lorde chooses to not only embrace but to expose, however, demands that its story is told and thus figures as a crucial part of her efforts to disrupt the silence and secrecy surrounding breast cancer. Through "wearing" her cancer, Lorde becomes visible to other women, thus encouraging the building of an alternative support system. Furthermore, her marked body also makes Lorde visible to society as a constant reminder of things awry in "america."

In *Narrative Prosthesis*, Mitchell and Snyder likewise conceptualize the prosthesis as an illusion when they assert that a "body deemed lacking, unfunctional, or inappropriately functional needs compensation, and prosthesis helps to effect this end" (6). Despite the fact that prostheses in the general sense may enhance the functionality of the impaired body, allowing for instance for greater physical mobility, Mitchell and Snyder are absolutely right in pointing out the ideological assumptions underlying the use of prostheses, for they presuppose notions of normalcy and pathology/deviance. By producing the "semblance of an originary wholeness," prostheses then help to make deviance tolerable, or visibly disappear (ibid. 6f.). Consequently, prostheses become a "quick fix" to remove impairment from sight, and as critics aptly note, from public vigilance and concern (cf. ibid. 8). Lorde's ampunarration, in contrast, makes her deformed body present and visible, an issue that has a clearly discomforting effect (cf. ibid.), as numerous encounters both within and without the hospital walls show. In the following, I will illustrate how Lorde's mastectomy body bears transgressive potential by inhabiting both a troubled and a troubling space within culture (cf. ibid.), disrupting notions of normalcy.

In "Breast Cancer: A Black Lesbian Feminist Experience," Lorde describes the visit by a woman volunteering for Reach to Recovery[20] shortly after her mastecto-

---

my life been spent in the service of passing, I have almost no blind skills" (131). See also Jeffrey Brune's and Daniel Wilson's volume *Disability and Passing: Blurring the Lines of Identity* (Philadelphia: Temple UP, 2013).

20 Reach to Recovery, the first organized support program for breast cancer survivors, was founded by Terese Lasser in 1952, after she had experienced breast cancer and a radical mastectomy herself. Hoping to give other women in the same situation the support and guidance she had lacked, she began visiting patients while they were still in the hospital. Lasser recounts her own experiences and the objectives of the program in *Reach to Reco-*

my. Never mentioned by name the woman may be seen as the epitome of institutionalized support networks for female breast cancer patients, and, Kimmich argues, of the sexist, racist and heteronormative forces of oppression operating in contemporary American society (126). The exchange presented in this scene exposes the mechanisms at work in constructing the experience of breast cancer as white, homosexual, and compliant, which is countered by the title of Lorde's chapter. Her experience with prosthesis makes it clear that traditional support networks cannot accommodate and indeed do not approve difference, but aim to normalize and regularize the experience of illness. The presentation of her account as a "Black Lesbian Feminist Experience," does invoke difference and singularity; after all, her account is significantly shaped by the composite aspects of her identity and the respective discourses that give rise to them and Lorde's insistence on these differences is a means of affirming them (cf. Perreault, "Pain" 12). In addition, Margaret Morris points out that Lorde's essay is saturated with references to race, skin color, "woman love," and the potential sexual consequences of the mastectomy that are merged to a unified experience (n. pag.). Yet Lorde's account constitutes in equal measure an attempt to fashion an alternative support structure when it crystallizes that in the face of difference, conventional networks fail her.

Although Lorde is intrigued by her visitor, whom she initially describes as a "kindly woman" spreading an "upbeat message" with "admirable energies," already her first description of the volunteer demonstrates aversion, since Lorde sees the woman's "admirable energies" devoted to "uphold[ing] and defend[ing] to death those structures of a society that had allowed her a little niche to shine in" (*Cancer* 41f.), depicting the volunteer as reliant on society to provide her with a "niche" for her existence that mainstream society will no longer accommodate and in turn de-

---

very, a book that blurs memoir and self-help book (with William Kendall Clarke. New York: Simon and Schuster, 1972). The narrative is clearly dated now, yet provides an interesting perspective on key aspects that Lorde criticizes: Lasser establishes a narrative which foregrounds heterosexual marriage with children and a middle-class life. The return to health Lorde considers impossible is of outmost importance to Lasser who provides her readers with "7 signposts to watch for along your personal road back to health" – no. 6 urges women to cooperate with their doctors and warns not to "outguess" them (59). When she speaks of healing, her notion is limited to the physical healing of the surgery wound. Despite the fact that both her story and the support program are initiated by her own devastation, the loss of the breast as an emotional issue is never articulated. In the chapter "You and the Art of Grooming," she highlights that a temporary prosthesis, however "unrealistic" it may look, should encourage women to "make of this an effective camouflage until healing is complete" and a real prosthesis may be fitted that will "achieve a 'natural look'" (89).

mands that she repeat the social dictum she has internalized. In her reading of the scene, Kimmich particularly focuses on the "structures of society" that suggest that the boundaries between the subject and the Other are socially constructed (127). What has begun as an expression of admiration is therefore turned into an uncommonly hostile view and Lorde articulates from the start that bonding between the two cancer patients will not be possible.

Despite the fact that she raises an important issue by drawing attention to the visual differences between the women that highlights especially the racial boundaries separating them, Kimmich certainly overstates the contrast between the two women in the scene by focusing on the volunteer worker's white skin, light hair color and clothing, the idealized image of femininity that sharply clash with Lorde's Black post-mastectomy body "spilling over the white hospital bed" (226f.). Although Lorde comments in passing on the woman's "trim powder blue man-tailored jacket" that reveals a blue pullover and an extortionately big gold embossed locket[21] (*Cancer* 42), she does not dwell further on their differences in appearance. This is a crucial issue, since community is not made impossible by skin color or clothing and neither by age or sexual orientation, for Lorde mentions earlier in the text that during the time between the discovery of the lump and the biopsy that would determine whether it was malignant, a diverse group of women has "sustained" her: "black and white, old and young, lesbian, bisexual and heterosexual" (ibid. 19). Instead, in this scene, the women are separated by a more profound difference, namely their differences in language and the ways in which they choose to frame their experiences of cancer, mastectomy, and healing.

"Her message was," Lorde continues, "you are just as good as you were before because you look exactly the same" (ibid. 42). Interestingly, the first issue the volunteer worker addresses is the question of self-worth, implying that the procedure has inflicted damage on how Lorde sees her value as an individual. Self-worth is hence tied to appearance and reconstructing this appearance as quickly as possible will, in this line of argumentation, return self-worth. The disruptive nature of illness and the surgical invasion is cast aside and silenced to immediately restore an outward form of normalcy and continuity, since the woman suggests that Lorde use the lambswool now and get a "good prosthesis as soon as possible," implying that "nobody'll ever know the difference" (ibid.).

However, Lorde does not seek to hide difference, but in fact wishes to affirm it, and through her difference, make herself visible to other women (cf. Perreault,

---

21 If one wishes to engage in a further discussion on the visual differences between the two women, this may be interpreted as an indicator of class – which is a significant marker because Lorde frequently refers to Black poverty and the consequential disadvantages in cancer treatment and cure.

"Pain" 14). Perreault recognizes that while many other women live in silence, Lorde's body has the potential to voice the difference (ibid.), which is a crucial observation given Lorde's deep immersion in language as a tool for action and social change. Lorde's body is permitted to "speak its own difference" when Lorde vehemently resists the prosthesis (ibid. 13). This resistance is crucially entangled with the idea of difference: it will make difference visible because it sets Lorde apart from other women who have not undergone mastectomy (ibid.), but it will also create a feeling of sameness amongst those women who have suffered from cancer.

On the one hand, Kimmich is right in maintaining that the volunteer worker is apparently oblivious to the difference in their skin colors that does not make the pink lambswool a permissible substitute for a Black woman's breast (227). The scene indicates that the experience of breast cancer is racially preconceived as a white experience and throughout the course of their conversation Lorde is cast as an outsider due to every aspect of her identity – race, sexuality, and political conviction. On the other hand, the suggestion also reveals the struggle about knowledge and the self that is at stake in framing well-being, for Lorde continues: "But what she said was, '*You'll* never know the difference,' and she lost me right there, because I know sure as hell *I'd* know the difference" (*Cancer* 42; italics in original). The volunteer's well-intentioned advice reflects the idea of the mask operating to hide the woman both to the outside and to herself and is entirely unacceptable for Lorde, who is clearly outraged. Proposing that Lorde will not be able to tell the difference between a prosthesis and her real breast, the volunteer promotes a view of the body that is not only entirely removed from the woman's knowledge and feeling, but in addition one that conceptualizes the body as a purely material object, to be decorated, accessorized, and improved.

When the volunteer then turns to Lorde and asks her whether she can tell which of her breasts is a prosthesis, Lorde writes "I admitted that I could not," yet her statement is by no means a compliment. Instead, she finds "[i]n her tight garment and stiff, up-lifting bra, both breasts looked equally unreal" (ibid.), thus exposing the divide between the women's realities and offering a telling characterization that pictures the woman as entirely subject to constraints: restrained by her clothing as well as by the social convictions she embodies.

The divide between their life-worlds is further highlighted by the subsequent conversation about their love lives, when Lorde can only answer that she is divorced but does not "have the moxie or desire or the courage maybe to say, 'I love women'" (ibid.). At other times utterly outspoken about her sexuality, she is exceptionally silent here, both uncomfortable and unwilling to share her identity that will undoubtedly explode the "heterosexist domain" in which, Elliott notes, lesbian identity is overtly oppressed by limiting the conversation to heterosexual partnership constellations and hence also covertly prohibited (181). Lorde's white lie and her decision to conceal her sexual orientation behind the mask of half-truth demonstrate that within the structures of the heteronormative support network that fosters physical recovery, communication is flawed and women are unable to trust each other and share their stories.

On the formal level, too, the scene reflects their different realities. While the volunteer worker continues talking about "forms" and where to purchase the silicone prostheses that she deems best, Lorde's own thoughts blend over the woman's loud posture:

"I was thinking, 'What is it like to be making love to a woman and have only one breast brushing against her?' I thought, 'How will we fit so perfectly together ever again?' I thought, 'I wonder if our love-making had anything to do with it?' I thought, 'What will it be like making love to me? Will she still find my body delicious?'" (*Cancer* 43)

Compared to the woman's preceding impersonal description of her sexual relationship – "There is nothing that I did before that I don't still do now. I just make sure I carry an extra form just in case" (ibid. 42f.) – Lorde's concerns are uttered in a sensual language that highlights the warmth and intimacy between partners as well as acknowledges Lorde's altered body and its possible implications for their love life. Although these words are never uttered aloud, they carry great significance for they signify the refusal to treat sexual relations in silence and they allow Lorde to begin mourning the loss of her breast and come to terms with her new body. Again, it is the erotic that fosters healing. Her thoughts hence challenge the notion that the disabled body must be 'enabled' to pass for a sexualized and normalized one through prosthesis or concealment (cf. Garland-Thomson, "Integrating" 496).

Nevertheless, she does examine the lambswool and even tries it on. That it is indeed "the strangest part" of the package the volunteer leaves her with becomes evident in Lorde's description of it. Nothing like a real breast or anything organic, the lambswool is a "blush-pink nylon envelope with a slighter, darker apex and shaped like a giant slipper shell" (*Cancer* 43). Highlighting its synthetic make-up, Lorde stresses that is does not share any human properties, let alone the erotic qualities of a female breast. Alexander purports that Lorde's rejection of the prosthesis is also rooted in the fact that, unlike a prosthetic arm or leg, the breast prosthesis does not "perform" and is neither "its own erotic world," nor "erotic unto itself" (710).

In a similar vein, her abstract description has a defamiliarizing effect and exemplifies how alien and strange the lambswool appears to her, which is underscored when she actually tries to wear it:

"It perched on my chest askew, awkwardly inert and lifeless, and having nothing to do with any me I could possibly conceive of. Besides, it was the wrong color, and looked grotesquely pale through the cloth of my bra. Somewhere, up to that moment, I had thought, well perhaps they know something that I don't and maybe they're right, if I put it on maybe I'll feel entirely different. I didn't." (*Cancer* 44)

Like the heteronomative ideology inherent in the prosthesis, Wu asserts, the lambswool does not fit (253), and not just because the volunteer worker has given Lorde a prosthesis in the wrong size, thus waving the knowledge of her own body aside and implying that details do not matter, the scar just needs to be covered up quickly. Most importantly, in Lorde's rendering of the incident, not disability and amputation become that which disfigures and brings out the grotesque, but the prosthesis – unfitting, sluggish, without life, and in the wrong color. It does not create normalcy, but rather foregrounds deformity and otherness. In this scene, whiteness and what Elliot terms so fittingly "heterosexual mimicry" intersect to produce a feeling of extreme discomfort and marginalization and remind Lorde of her status as 'Other' (179; Kimmich 227). Along similar lines, William Major suggests that Lorde's body is both incapable of speaking "the social language of health" and conforming to racial norms (n. pag.). Quite literally, the silence engendered by the prosthesis does not fit Lorde, much like it cannot conceal her altered body. Instead, it rather highlights difference and exposes compulsory able-bodiedness and compulsory heterosexuality (Garland-Thomson, "Integrating" 504).

In her manifesto "Power vs. Prosthesis," Lorde elaborates on the political dimension of her rejection of prostheses. Much of her outrage, as Sharon Barnes notes, is directed at the conceptualization of breast cancer as a mere cosmetic issue that may easily be effaced by means of prosthesis (770). In this essay, as the title foreshadows, prosthesis and power are seen in contradistinction to one another. Power in her narration stands for the right to claim and define one's body (cf. Ricciardi 77) and acknowledges that a refusal to conform to the normalizing prosthesis requires great strength and resilience. When she decides not to wear prosthesis, Lorde has to face accusations (cf. also Pickens 186). Additionally, the prosthesis robs one of visibility and the subversive potential that Lorde locates in the marked body. Lorde is one of the women whom Garland-Thomson celebrates as "nonconformity incarnate" (*Extraordinary* 130). Her book *Extraordinary Bodies*, as its title suggests, is an effort to see the disabled body not as abnormal, but rather as extraordinary, thereby stripping it of its modern conception of deviance. While Garland-Thomson focuses on the reading of fictional works and Lorde's autobiomythography *Zami: A New Spelling of My Name*, her approach to these texts is equally well suited for the analysis of *The Cancer Journals*. The marked body, she maintains, is appropriated for cultural work and can thus help the subjects to regain the power that has been suppressed by the sameness of standardization inherent in mainstream culture. Their bodies are no longer colonized, but disclose a positive identity politic (130f.).

At great length, Lorde recounts an incident that takes place when she visits her doctor's office ten days after her mastectomy, having carefully prepared herself: after a friend has washed her hair, it looks "black and shining" (*Cancer* 59) and she decides to wear "the most opalescent" moonstone that she owns, as well as an African kente tunic (ibid. 60). Not only does Lorde carefully tend to her body, but she embraces its brightness and vitality.[22] Particularly striking is the "single floating bird dangling from [her] right ear in the name of grant asymmetry" (ibid.), a beautifully conjured image that portrays Lorde as regal and dignified and celebrates the new shape of her body. While Mitchell and Snyder speak of leaving "the wound of disability undressed" (*Narrative* 8), Lorde goes one step further by enunciating asymmetry through her choice of clothing and jewelry.

In his seminal study, sociologist Erving Goffman defines stigma as the "bodily signs of physical disorder" and a mark that an individual should be avoided, for their presence will cause discomfort (1, 19). Yet this uneasiness, Goffman claims, may be reduced when individuals who bear a mark attempt to either pass or resort to 'covering,' a practice similar to passing in that attention is drawn away from the stigma and the mark is concealed so that individuals may still participate in social interactions (102). For him, covering is an assimilative technique as it does not merely aid in passing but also prevents the stigma from taking up the center of attention (103). Consequently, covering the marked body allows individuals to blend in and for Goffman it is such a significant practice because it makes stigmatized bodies less visible, identifiable, and obtrusive, therefore turning covering into a practice that greatly benefits society at large, as it apparently eases discomfort.[23]

The passage evinces that Lorde consciously chooses not to assimilate and attempt to pass as "healthy," i.e. physically restored. Instead of covering or hiding her amputated body or deflecting attention from it in order to evade the stigma of disability (cf. Weitz 172) and put others and their gazes at ease, she embraces the emp-

---

22 In her comparative reading of Lorde's autobiographical works and texts by the homosexual Italian director, writer, and intellectual Piere Paolo Pasolini, Ricciardi compares this image to the cover photograph of the original edition of *The Cancer Journals* on which Lorde is seen wearing an African turban. The shot takes up the entire space on the cover, placing the smiling Lorde center stage: "The joy is there, the strength and vitality, the bird dangling from one ear and the African Kentecloth tunic" (122).

23 Goffman acknowledges that this sense of comfort is very much one-sided for individuals who attempt to cover their stigma may face severe psychological conflicts (87ff.) yet he does not elaborate on the implications of this. This view is certainly owing to the time Goffman published his book and, accordingly, to his dichotomous perspective: more than once he explicitly aligns himself with the "normal" in stark contrast to the blind, lame, amputated, or plain "ugly."

tiness of the amputation, since any attempts to cover it have caused her discomfort. What is more, her body is marked by Blackness to begin with and therefore cannot fully pass. She then makes clear that covering and passing are not the only options for disabled individuals and inverts the negative notion of stigma Goffman devises by exhibiting an orderly, carefully groomed and attended to, as well as proud post-mastectomy body that demands respect and admiration. Similarly, she attributes a sense of peacefulness to her body when she bears witness to the wound after the surgery and does not encounter a "ravaged and pitted battlefield of some major catastrophic war" but only the "same soft brown skin, […] smooth and tender and untroubled" (*Cancer* 45). Mastectomy, her statement clearly shows, has not disfigured her but left her with a body that is still familiar to a certain extent, and, as the climax elucidates, surprisingly comfortable.

She then stresses her returning well-being, as well as her beauty, when she concludes "I knew I looked fine, with that brave new-born security of a beautiful woman having come through a very hard time and being very glad to be alive" (ibid. 60). This thoroughly positive image of pride, self-confidence and an emerging feeling of recovery and healing, however, is utterly disrupted when Lorde goes on to recount that the nurse at the doctor's office berates her for not wearing a prosthesis:

"the nurse now looked at me urgently and disapprovingly as she told me that even if it didn't look exactly right it was 'better than nothing,' and that as soon as my stitches were out I would be fitted for a 'real form.' 'You will feel so much better with it on,' she said. 'And besides, we really like you to wear something, at least when you come in. Otherwise it's bad for the morale at the office.'" (ibid.)

The nurse's assurance that prosthesis, however makeshift and temporary, will be "better than nothing," exposes a disparaging view of the body Lorde has so carefully tended to and begun to make peace with. Her urge to cover the "nothing" in the right side of her chest suggests that the new body is seen as incomplete and in need to be restored to a "whole." Above all, prosthesis is made compulsory, which Lorde finds entirely illogical, given that she is in a room crowded with women who have shared or may potentially share her plight (cf. ibid.). Prosthetic covering will normalize their bodies, thus making them invisible to one another and silencing any conversation about breast cancer, whereas her argumentation has revealed the need for social discomfort. Ultimately, as Frank observes, the argument in this scene is not limited to the right to claim one's body, but also addresses the right to claim the visual recognition of other women who share her experience. The marked body is thus not to be concealed, but to be affirmed (*Wounded* 121).

However, a paternalistic dichotomy between the first-person and third-person stance is invoked in which Lorde's personal perspective is cast aside when the nurse emphatically speaks for her, telling her that she will feel better with a prosthesis on, despite the fact that Lorde has just established that she feels good and looks "fine." In her account of the incident, she therefore makes clear that women, too, perpetuate the patriarchic structures of institutionalized medicine and hegemonic society that reduce the female body to an object in need of restoration and improvement so that its appearance can be seen in public. Her personal sense of self-esteem and her idea of femininity clash with the conditioned view that the body needs to be seen through the gaze of others rather than in terms of how oneself feels (cf. Elliot 187f.). Lorde is denied the nurse's confirmation that she is fine just as she is, but instead encouraged to masquerade as "recovered" or "feeling better" (cf. ibid.), an issue that underlines the lie that, according to Lorde, is inherent in the prosthesis. *The Cancer Journals* therefore powerfully illustrate the difference between physical reconstruction, but at the same time also point to a further meaning of reconstruction, namely the reconstruction of Lorde's activist self.

In speaking about the "morale" at the office, the nurse has used an ambiguous term that may of course be understood as the psychological and emotional state of the women in the waiting room, yet may also be read in military terms. Lorde then picks up on this military subtext by calling her urge to wear prosthesis an "assault" on her right to her body (*Cancer* 60). This scene, too, makes clear that it is not possible to eliminate the war metaphor from a reading of the book. Lorde's outrage brings forth, as Weber holds, a cleverly chosen political analogy to the former Foreign Minister of Israel, Moishe Dayan, and his trademark eye-patch that he has worn since a war injury caused the loss of his eye (247) and who exhibited his altered body with pride (Katan, "Lorde" 270). "Nobody tells him to get a glass eye, or that he is bad for the moral of the office. The world sees him as a warrior with an honorable wound, and a loss of a piece of himself which he has marked, mourned, and moved beyond" (*Cancer* 61). Of course the idea that a male, white, heterosexual politician is not inclined to see his body as a reason for discussion is, Knopf-Newman claims, a revealing point of comparison (120). Yet what is more striking is the question under which conditions it is acceptable to expose the marked body:

"Well, women with breast cancer are warriors, also. I have been to war, and still am. So has every woman who had had one or both breasts amputated because of the cancer that is becoming the primary scourge of our time. For me, my scars are an honorable reminder that I am a casualty in the cosmic war against radiation, animal fat, air pollution, McDonald's hamburgers and Red Dye No. 2, but the fight is still going on, and I am still part of it. I refuse to have my scars hidden or trivialized behind lambswool or silicone gel. I refuse to be reduced in my own eyes or in the eyes of others from warrior to mere victim, simply because it might render me a fraction more acceptable or less dangerous to the still complacent, those who believe if you cover up a problem it ceases to exist." (*Cancer* 61f.)

Lorde makes clear that she understands herself and her fellow breast cancer patients as warriors who are, not unlike Dayan, engaged in an ongoing fight that concerns the entire country and it is the acknowledgment of this status that she claims for herself and other women. This sense of community is clearly evoked in the comparison that not only she herself "has[s] been to war, and still [is]" but likewise "every woman" who has undergone mastectomy. Again, Lorde plays on the dichotomy between casualty and warrior, illustrating that breast cancer patients have fallen victim to environmental, chemical, and institutional causes, yet continue their fight for visibility. The anaphora "I refuse" powerfully expresses the gist of her manifesto against prosthesis and, along similar lines, against the cultural discourse on the dis/abled female body. When she states that "the fight is still going on, and I am still part of it," Lorde laments the fact that nothing has changed in society as of yet, while the second mention of the adverb "still" underscores her activist endeavor and her active involvement in the social struggle.

The Cancer Journals, as my reading shows, illustrates the opposition between prosthetic reconstruction and the notions of healing and discomforting "reconstruction" Lorde crafts, since the memoir suggests that comfort may only be found when the alleged discomfort is accepted and she may tell her story without the prosthetic reconstruction of the female body that, according to Bolaki, is deemed mandatory ("Re-Covering" 10). Instead, her memoir becomes an ampu-narration not only because it refuses to spare readers the unsightly and unspeakable – death as a possible outcome in contrast to the conventional triumphant illness experience, the contingent nature of her disease, and the struggle that affects hundreds of thousands of women annually – but also because amputation shifts readers' gaze to the body that, although perhaps incomplete, is full of erotic and resistant potential. In this vein, Lorde's book is more than a "narrative of patient resistance" (cf. Frank, "Tricksters" n. pag.), but amputation as the aesthetic and rhetorical choice to unhinge prosthetic narration actively works to depathologize difference.

While Lorde assembles fragments of her breast cancer experience into a coherent political argument, she succeeds in telling her story, which Chandler sees as a fundamental aspect of healing (4). The memoir situates Lorde in a community of women and also turns her into someone who may offer her help to others, as Herndl notes. Beyond that, she also frames recovery as the creation of a sense of self beyond the passivity of patienthood, but this does by no means entail leaving the cancer experience behind (Herndl, "Breasts" 229). In firmly rooting her writing in the painful experience of cancer that she is never removed from, she is indeed able to continue her work as an activist and advocate for social justice. For Lorde, well-being in the face of breast cancer becomes the ability "to live and to love and to do [her] work" (ibid. 32).[24]

As Henke notes, Lorde's "scriptotherapy" has offered a narrative of healing "for those who come after her and for all women engaged in political, economic, psychological, and physiological struggles (118). One among the early autobiographical texts on breast cancer, it remains a pivotal work of art on a disease that has become, as DeShazer notes in the introduction to *Fractured Borders*, "the topic of our times" and the number of both professionally published and self-published testimonies has increased exponentially in the 1990s and the beginning of the twenty-first century (1). Many of these narratives respond to the metaphors which are commonly woven into the discourse on cancer and broach responsibility and terror. *The Cancer Journals*, as my reading has shown, cannot escape the metaphoric dimension of cancer as a war or fight, yet the power of her memoir lies in Lorde's reappropriation of the metaphor by referring to herself as a "warrior." In the ensuing years, many women have followed her, from the feminist poet Deena Metzger who, on the 1980 photograph titled "The Warrior" taken by Hella Hammid, spreads her arms and exposes her mastectomy scars (cf. also DeShazer, *Fractured* 33) to a large number of writers and scholars, some of whom are referenced in this chapter.

Consequently, in the twenty-first century, breast cancer is no longer silenced or rendered invisible but has become "*hyper*visible" (cf. Waples 163; italics in original) through breast cancer awareness months, fund raisers and campaigns. However, responsibility, the detection rather than the prevention of the disease, and an upbeat rhetoric amongst patients continue to loom large in contemporary discourses on breast cancer and survival (DeShazer, *Mammographies* 1). Contemporary verbal and visual texts, such as Sarah Lochlann Jain's personal and scholarly essays "Living in Prognosis" (2007) and "Be Prepared" (2010) or Miriam Engelberg's 2006 graphic memoir *Cancer Made Me a Shallower Person: A Memoir in Comics* follow Lorde and challenge these hegemonic discourses, as well as what DeShazer has so fittingly called a "consumer-oriented breast cancer culture" marked by "'pink kitsch'" (*Mammographies* 9). Today, the question is no longer centered on the issue of prosthesis, as Herndl outlines in her essay on "Reconstructing the Posthuman Feminist Body," yet recent cancer memoirs profess that the significance of Lorde's memoir endures in the face of prosthetic narratives of cancer.

---

24 Incidentally, this reflects the definition of health frequently attributed to Freud, which however, cannot be identified in his works or correspondence.

5. Musical Cu[r]e:
Reconnection in Oliver Sacks's *A Leg to Stand On*

In the second half of the twentieth century, as I have outlined above, the perception of medicine begins to change, both in the public eye, as patients and their caregivers grow skeptical of the capacities of institutional medicine to help them, but also within the profession itself: An increasing number of professionals strive to renew the vision of medicine as a practice of art, rather than merely a form of science and technology (Greaves 14). Their concerns have given shape to the field of Medical Humanities, an interdisciplinary approach to medicine borrowing from the humanities, arts, and social sciences and applying these texts and theories to medical practice and the education and further training of physicians, clinicians, and nurses. On these grounds, the editors of the volume *Medical Humanities* call for "philosophical methods of critical reflection" in the practice of medicine, so as to "refocus on the meaning of 'the human'" (Evans and Finlay 8). This entails a shift in focus from data and lab work to the human condition of illness – the story of the individual patient suffering from the disease.[1] Over the past decades, the medical community has therefore become increasingly drawn to narratives as a means of foregrounding the human "drama" that illness entails (cf. Garro and Mattingly 8f.). Narratives by patients strongly articulate the subjective and qualitative experience of illness (cf. Chapter 2.2) and Medical Humanities scholars have therefore begun to value them as a means to foster empathy in clinicians.

Throughout *Medical Humanities*, several contributors return to the writings of the renowned neurologist Oliver Sacks, who, according to Greaves, applied such a "philosophical" outlook, blurring the boundaries between art and science (17), thus spurring many of the debates surrounding humane medical care and the significance of patients' narratives that are currently taking place in Medical Humanities pro-

---

[1] In his essay, Greaves provides a comprehensive introduction to the goals and nature of the Medical Humanities.

grams in the Anglo-American context. It is not surprising that Sacks's name is associated with patients' stories of disease and impairment, for these narratives – 'clinical tales' as he himself termed them – are indeed at the core of his professional life as both medical practitioner and writer. It is because of his patients and their narratives that he has gained fame and recognition, even though interestingly enough his reputation seems far more established in the art world than in the world of medicine.[2]

Historian of medicine Andrew Hull foregrounds Sacks's turn to patients' narratives and claims that beyond bearing witness to individuals' suffering, they aid in the reconceptualization of 'disease'/'illness' and 'health' because they foreground the fact that the concept of 'disease' as a functional impairment, localized in the body and measured in relation to general norms does not exhaust patients' difficulties in coping with their conditions and their efforts to envisage an alternative way of living in order to mend the disruption caused by disease (105; cf. Chapter 3.1). What Hull describes here is first of all the capacity of narratives to complicate the notion of 'disease' and turn medical professionals' critical attention to their patients' subjective experience of illness. In the past, it was well acknowledged that the symptoms accompanying neurological dysfunctions are unpredictable, individual, and often quite "curious" (Howarth 105) so that diagnosis required careful attention to the patients' symptoms and their stories. William Howarth argues that with the rise of computer-operated CAT-scanners, though, diagnosis has experienced a radical shift toward a statistical and technical study that ultimately turns neurologists away from a holistic view of the patient (ibid.). It is the turn back to his holistic view that Sacks in his oeuvre coins 'neurology of identity.' Not only does it aim to transcend what he refers to as the "mechanical" approach of classical neurology, but also the discrepancy between science with its attempt to be as objective as pos-

---

2 Although the life narrative is also discussed in medical journals (see, for instance, Jon Stone's, Jo Perthen's and Alan Carson's review article "'A Leg to Stand On' by Oliver Sacks: A Unique Autobiographical Account of Functional Paralysis" [*Journal of Neurology, Neurosurgery and Psychiatry* 83 (2012): 864-67]), its author's primary audience was and remains an educated readership. This audience cherishes his popular scientific writing and literary critic Curt Schleier aptly notes that Sacks is better known for these texts than for his medical successes, and the royalties on his books, together with honoraria for lectures, by far outnumber his medical income (n. pag.). Besides, in April 2013 the inaugural festival of "Live Ideas," an interdisciplinary annual festival hosted by New York Live Arts, was devoted to "The Worlds of Oliver Sacks." Theater, dance, and music performances, as well as film screenings on a variety of neurological topics treated in Sacks's books complemented discussion panels on philosophy and writing to celebrate his career.

sible, and the patient, who as "a human being, is first and last *active* – a subject, not an object" (*Leg* 164).³

Beyond that, Sacks's writing is particularly revealing in matters of health. As critic Kevin Shapiro holds, cure is a problematic issue in neurology, since the neurologist's therapeutic capacity is limited and does commonly not permit the cure of diseases or impairments (Shapiro 73; Cassuto, "Uncanny" n. pag.). Many of the patients Sacks encountered in the clinic and subsequently portrayed for his readership are members of the remission society, so 'health' ultimately requires reconceptualization. I certainly agree with William Hunter, who in "Your Friendly Neighborhood Neurologist" observes that for the majority of Sacks's patients, there is no avenue to return to health; instead, the neurologist may help them to come to terms with their conditions and adapt to their new lives (100). Yet I heavily disagree with the conclusions he draws from these observations. Rather than reading "failures in returning his patients to normal" (ibid.) into Sacks's writing, readers will encounter stories that do not enforce normalcy and set out to reframe the understanding of health, thereby substituting "cure" with various forms of healing, compensating, and well-being. Sacks himself called for a redefinition of "the very concepts of 'health' and 'disease,' to see these in terms of the ability of the organism to create a new organization and order, one that fits its special, altered disposition and needs, rather than in the terms of a rigidly defined norm" (*Anthropologist* xviiif.). As a consequence, statistical notions of health are deconstructed in Sacks's writing and supplanted by a highly individualized concept of well-being.

Not least because of this, Sacks is frequently referred to as one of "the most gifted and problematic" of contemporary writers of illness narratives (Howarth 105). On the one hand, critics admire his "characteristic combination of clinical insight, intellectual curiosity, and linguistic dexterity" (Shapiro 75) and hail him as "a one-man bridge" between science and art (Cassuto, "Conversation" n. pag.). In his essay on "Oliver Sacks's Neurology of Identity," Murdo McRae, too, praises his "philosophically sophisticated prose" and points to the numerous allusions to neurologists in Sacks's writing, such as Henry Head, philosophers, like Gottfried Leibniz and René Descartes, and poets, such as W.H. Auden and John Donne (97). While science itself often assumes a prominent role in his texts, Sacks attributes great importance to the question of how individuals understand themselves in relation to science (cf. Pitts 249). Howarth hence introduces him as "a vernacular phi-

---

3 In *Awakenings*, Sacks refers to the neurology of identity by describing "the inseparability of a patient's illness, his self, and his world" (22), thereby resisting a separation of neurology and psychology. Instead, he calls for a more meaningful integration of their interpretational methods (cf. Howarth 105) and presents a strategy that will overcome the divide between doctors and their patients (cf. Tougaw, *Strange* 210f.).

losopher" of medicine, devoted to translating academic abstraction into ethical and spiritual experience (105) and Couser also speaks of him as an "interpreter of neurological disorder" (*Vulnerable* 74). In other words, Sacks's writing makes information accessible to those who do not 'speak the same language.' In this context, he is internationally known for his popular scientific writing that includes the acclaimed titles *Migraine* (1970), *Awakenings* (1973), *The Man Who Mistook His Wife for a Hat* (1985), *Seeing Voices* (1989), *An Anthropologist on Mars* (1995), *The Island of the Colorblind* (1997), *Musicophilia: Tales of Music and the Brain* (2007), *The Mind's Eye* (2010) and his most recent book *Hallucinations* (2012). In these works, Sacks's role as a writer may indeed be understood as that of a translator who renders neurological processes and peculiar symptoms for an educated lay audience, even though these books are less concerned with the workings of the brain than with his patients' qualitative experiences.[4]

This is also precisely why his writing is frequently met by criticism. A number of scholars have noted that in these clinical tales, Sacks participates in the practice of 'othering' neurologically impaired patients (Berger 347), an issue which has prompted particularly harsh criticism from scholars in the field of Disability Studies.[5] Furthermore, William Hunter maintains that the books reveal a vertical power structure, since Sacks, though overtly appearing as a "fatherly, beneficent physi-

---

4   Shapiro, too, develops this argument in his review of *Musicophilia* (75f.), and – perhaps with the exception of his early *Awakenings* in which he assumes a decidedly authorial and professional voice – this holds true for all of his popular scientific writing.

5   See especially Tom Shakespeare's review of *Anthropologist on Mars* in which he famously characterizes Sacks as "the man who mistook his patients for a literary career" and accuses him of "violat[ing] every existing principle of disability equality" (137) and Simi Linton's more moderate criticism in *Claiming Disability*. Although Linton acknowledges Sacks's attempts to "dissociate 'disability' from 'problem,'" she finds fault with the construction of the doctor-patient relationship in his writing and argues that patients are reduced to "objects of aesthetic interest" while "the doctor's competence in diagnosis and interpretation is valorized" (140f.). For a contrasting view, Leonard Cassuto's critical engagement with Sacks's work is also highly interesting because he explicitly addresses the criticism the books have received from the Disability Studies community and argues that despite that fact that Sacks himself has never responded to his critics, an implicit response may be detected in his writing, which over time has not only become increasingly personal, but has also turned to understand and portray neurological difference against a more detailed social backdrop. As a result, the concept of disability inherent in Sacks's writing, Cassuto contends, in fact shades off into established Disability Studies conceptions of 'difference' ("Conversation" n. pag.; cf. also Cassuto's essay "Oliver Sacks and the Medical Case Narrative" in *Disability Studies: Enabling the Humanities*).

cian," covertly constructs his professional role as the more superior one and therefore sustains authority in the discourse about disease and impairment (98, 93).

However, in his 1984 autobiographical narrative *A Leg to Stand On*,[6] the book that recounts Sacks's own injury after a hiking accident in the Norwegian mountains and his eventual recovery, this criticism is difficult to maintain. In this book, Sacks is forced from the bedside into the sickbed and needs to resign himself to the process of "becoming a patient," as well as to a seemingly slow recovery during which he fears he has completely lost all feeling for his injured leg after the surgery and, more than that, has entirely forgotten how to use it. Like other life narratives published at the time, his book strongly focuses on the representation of the qualitative experience of illness and healing Sacks attempts to convey to his doctors – who are unwilling to listen, though – and later discusses with the Russian neuropsychologist A. R. Luria, contemplating them through the lens of neurology. Neurological literature provides him with the objective and abstract notions to explain what has caused his odd sensations, while at the same time exposing a serious shortcoming: the neglect of subjectivity. The retrospect perspective on illness enables the narrating I to not only intertwine these experiences with his knowledge of clinical terminology and comments on the state of neurological research and the clinical encounter, but also allows him to make connections to philosophy and art, thereby constructing his illness as both a subjective and aestheticized experience. His story highlights and stylizes the experience of patienthood, illness, and healing and both the great despair of illness and the epiphany of healing constitute rhetorically fascinating passages that I will explore below. Aesthetics are then finally not an end in itself in Sacks's work, but also a means to remediate health.

This cursory summary already makes evident that Sacks's status as a medical professional who slips into the role of the patient for a brief time complicates the way in which first- and third-person knowledge, subjectivity and objectivity, generally operate in the biomedical setting. In the preface to his book, Sacks describes *A Leg to Stand On* as a "neurological novel or short story [...] rooted in personal experience and neurological fact" (*Leg* viii), a description in which experience is highlighted and reconciled with "neurological fact." As a consequence, both the

---

6 The accident that initiates the story happened in 1974. In "Oliver Sacks: The Ecology of Writing Science," Howarth states that Sacks retained a journal of the events and recorded them in letters before they were later published, first in the article "The Leg," then in *A Leg to Stand On* (110f.). In the course of subsequent publications, Sacks returned to these experiences, most prominently in *Musicophilia* (cf. also Wallace-Wells's article "A Brain with a Heart"). Excerpts from the book have also been anthologized in collections of nonfiction writing, such as a part of the first chapter in *The Norton Book of Personal Essays* under the title "The Bull on the Mountain."

subjective and the objective perspective on illness/disease and restored health will be of significance in the memoir and will thus receive particular attention in this chapter. In the memoir, they need to be studied on two levels: First, Sacks's own account illustrates a split between the two perspectives when he recounts the qualitative experience of his injury while attempting to reason in objective terms. Second, the subjective and objective perspectives also refer to the hierarchy within the hospital walls where Sacks finds himself as a patient forced to assume the 'sick role'[7] when the attending surgeons and doctors dismiss his subjective experiences.

His story may on the one hand be aligned with a tradition of physician-writers[8] publishing the stories of their own illnesses and concluding, as Garro and Mattingly phrase it, with the "hard-won realization that there is more to the story of being a patient that can be captured by a medical synopsis or charted medical history" (9). On the other hand, it also goes considerably beyond the tradition of the physician-writer. Despite the fact that *A Leg to Stand On* stands out due to Sacks's status and reputation, it is nevertheless representative for a plethora of illness life narratives published in the 1980s which share Sacks's criticism of the hierarchical doctor-patient relationship, the traditional biomedical view on the body, as well as the ways in which health is restored (cf. Chapter 1).

Tightly connected to this is a philosophical discussion of the self. Although Sacks encounters a dualist conception of the self in this own thinking as a patient,

---

7   Sacks's concept of his patienthood mirror's Talcott Parson's 'sick role' outlined in *The Social System* and critically discussed also in Chapter 3.2. Life narratives about illness as such generally challenge the passivity Talcott links to the social role. Though at first conforming to the role by following his doctors' advice and accepting medical care thankfully, he does later criticize it, for instance when he recounts the ceremoniousness of Grand Rounds in which he can finally speak with Dr. Swan and concludes: "Both of us were forced to play roles – he the role of the All-knowing Specialist, I the role of the Know-nothing Patient" (Leg 73), hence exposing the construction and artificiality of their roles and the inadequate hierarchy they enforce (cf. also Hunter, "Your" 98; Aull and Lewis 102 on this scene).

8   In his essay "Physician Autobiography. Narrative and the Social History of Medicine," Donald Pollock analyzes a number of twentieth century autobiographies by physicians. His approach, though, follows the classical model of the autobiography which depicts the life of an extraordinary individual, as he cites various cultural stereotypes, such as the doctor as a heroic figure, the drama of the medial encounter, and the intellectual challenges of dealing with diseases and curing them as influential to these autobiographies. He studies the heroic stories of surgeons, women doctors and doctors in training, yet does not mention the stories of doctors as patients that would well fall into the given time period, – an issue that is likely due to his theoretical approach to autobiographical writing.

by probing what it means to have and *be* an ill body, his narrative works toward a subversion of the dichotomy between mind and body. In this chapter, I aim to show how science – the notions of body-image and proprioception – and art, especially music, are employed to transcend the dualist concept of the self that figures so prominently in the context of biomedicine and its conceptualization of 'disease.' As a result, the narrative promotes a holistic notion of identity that foregrounds embodiment. I argue that as a consequence, *A Leg to Stand On* skillfully crafts an alternative notion of healing that significantly goes beyond the biomedical and mechanical conception of curing and repairing the injured body. In this light, the narrative becomes an 'unruly text' as it challenges the simplicity of the biomedical cure by demonstrating that the objectified body essentially involves an individual self, as well as traditional life writing by foregrounding the fact that the individual self is also a body.

5.1 "Bringing the Body Back In": Embodiment in Sacks's Memoir

A fundamental part of these aesthetics is the return to the embodied self. Through its strong focus on the self as the unity of mind and body Sacks's story does not only subvert the conventional mode of writing in the field of classical neurology, but also breaks with the traditional autobiography that has tended to neglect the body in favor of the writer's intellectual or spiritual journey. Indeed, a number of scholars, most prominently Hawkins, have read *A Leg to Stand On* as a quest story, chronicling a journey into a strange world. Sacks himself no doubt invites such a reading by referring to the idea of a journey several times throughout the narrative, for instance by calling his friends his "traveling companions on the journey of life" (*Leg* 34) or when remembering the words of the captain who flew the plane that brought him back to England and reminded him to "'[t]ake it easy! The whole thing, going through it, is really a pilgrimage'" (ibid. 81). Moreover, the state of limbo, too, becomes a journey for Sacks, "a journey of the soul" (ibid.).[9] Although the idea of a

---

9   Hawkins observes that Sacks's journey corresponds to the three realms of Dante's *Divine Comedy* – hell, purgatory, and heaven. The beginning of Sacks's story bears close resemblance to the prologue of the epic poem: Like Dante's speaker, Sacks attempts to climb a mountain and where he encounters the bull, runs from him and falls, while the speaker of the poem is confronted by three beasts that force him to leave the mountain, upon which he falls into despair (cf. "Oliver Sacks's" 233). Unlike Dante's speaker, however, Sacks's journey is a lonesome one, since he lacks a guide or companion, an issue that Hawkins reads as a critical comment on his doctors' behavior who refuse to "enter the patient's

quest or journey permeates the narrative, it is not a purely intellectual endeavor: it is the body that propels the journey, both on a literal and figurative level. The injured body forces Sacks to "travel" into the world of the patient, it confines movement and therefore leads to spiritual crisis, its acknowledgement leads to insight and allows Sacks to leave the patient's world, though, through his vision of the neurology of identity, not leaving it behind entirely.[10]

In the context of life writing, this is extraordinary because, as Roger Porter notes, life writing has traditionally placed a strong focus on the writers' beliefs and thoughts and thus neglected the physical nature of their lives. Porter asserts that even Rousseau's autobiography, a foundational text of the genre, despite undermining "existing standards of autobiographical decorum," rather highlights Rousseau's relation to society than represents his body (122). When the body is in fact foregrounded in the conventional autobiography, Porter continues, it is employed as a metaphor, serves to discuss issues that are concerned with questions of consciousness, or mentioned in passing because it has been temporarily stricken by illness (ibid.). In their investigation of more recent life narratives, both Shirley Neuman and Couser hold that the body is rarely prominent and, if represented at all, is related to the writer's private or professional life (Neuman 1). Couser argues that memoirs which do treat their writers' bodies are mostly written by movie stars or professional athletes, thus pushing to the fore the sensual qualities of the body, ideals of beauty, athletic skills, and fitness (*Signifying* 3). Ultimately, he concludes, these memoirs do not only construct success and celebrity as directly linked to exceptional beauty or fitness, but also imply that iconic status in our culture may be attained by exceeding physical norms (ibid.). What these memoirs suggest, then, is that the body and the writer's physical qualities and capacities are to be perfected

---

world" (ibid.; cf. also *Reconstructing* 83). The parallels to Dante's epic poem contribute to the stylization and anesthetization of Sacks's illness experience. Furthermore, like the Divine Comedy, Sacks's account links art and science (cf. e.g. the volume *Dante: The Critical Heritage*. Ed. Michael Caesar. New York/London: Routledge, 1989). For another close reading of the narrative as a quest story, see Frank (*Wounded* 123f.).

10 Sacks's story may in this vein also well be read as a conversion narrative. Conversion narratives, according to Smith and Watson, revolve around the dramatic transformation and improvement of the self who first experiences downfall and confusion and is then gradually transformed, before eventually journeying to a "place of membership in an enlightened community of like believers" (266). While conversion plot lines have figured prominently in religious storytelling, they are also frequently invoked in stories about illness and disability. The protagonists of conversion narratives, Lisa Kerr holds, are separated from their familiar world but may later return more insightful (97).

and regulated, hence aligning these narratives of able bodies with the tradition of autobiographical writing.

Similarly, Neuman claims that in conceptualizing the self as a coherent individual rather than as a "subject-in-process," conventional life narratives tend to repress the body as a site of cultural construction (1). According to her, the "near-effacement of bodies" in autobiographical texts is rooted in the Platonic tradition that privileges the spiritual over the corporeal by aligning the self with the spiritual, as well as in the Enlightenment tradition with its Cartesian notion of man as the thinking being (ibid.). Although Sacks is drawn to the spiritual over the course of his narrative, the experience of illness constitutes, in his words, "reason's scandal," a crisis of rational thinking and intellectual reasoning, "and the humiliation of mind" (*Leg* 130).

In her essay on "Academic and Other Memoirs," author and critic Shirley Geok-lin Lim decidedly speaks against the traditional notion "that life writing is only or chiefly about writing – or, using related terms, only about discourse and textuality." Instead, she claims that life writing is first of all "about bodies, about memories that are embodied" (30). While Lim is mostly concerned with the nature of memory and its creation through people's bodily interactions, perceptions and actions, thus foregrounding questions of trauma und flashbacks, many of her statements are also valid in a broader context. Attempting to formulate an answer to the question of what it is like to be writing a memoir, she confirms that her memoir is "more than the identity of the text" and also comprises the identity of the body: "I tell the story that my body has lived through," she summarizes (29). In a similar vein, critical approaches to the memoir now attribute importance to the body as both the "textual surface upon which a person's life is inscribed" and as the "site of autobiographical knowledge" (Smith and Watson 49). In this respect, autobiographical knowledge, e.g. memory, needs to be seen as embodied knowledge. Images, sensations, and experiences of the external world are perceived and internalized by the body (cf. ibid. 37) and bodies therefore represent means of acting with the external world.

Despite this fundamental claim, it is not until recently that the body has received prominent status in life writing (cf. Couser, *Recovering* 4f.). Frank adds that although social scientists have been invested in studying the role of the body for years, scholars are still confronted with the problem of how to avoid reducing the body to a "thing that is described" (*Wounded* 27). In the context of illness and disability, the body 'lives through' a crisis that considerably shapes both the context and the form of the story. Although Lim's statement grants the body the status of an agent that has experienced the past, her formulation remains ambiguous with respect to the question of whether she has accepted the body as a part integral of the storyteller or whether she regards it as a separate entity about which she, the self, writes. Frank, in contrast, is very clear about the role of the body, one that foregrounds illness as a distinctive characteristic of the storyteller emerging from the wounded body, rather than just being the topic of the story. He argues that the body thus becomes at once topic, instrument, and cause of storytelling (ibid. 1f.). Storytelling is hence an embodied practice, yet one that extends beyond the obvious sense of the physical nature of writing: the body as the entity which tells the story is also prominent in the language, style, and rhetoric of the narrative. For Frank, this is self-evident as "[o]nly a caricature Cartesian would imagine a head, compartmentalized away from the disease, talking about the sick body beneath it" (ibid. 2). Descartes's dualist stance – "I think, therefore I am" – is what the concept of embodiment transcends (cf. Poirier 524f.). Sacks makes this clear when he states that he "had fallen into an abyss, with the breaking apart of [his] tissues, [his] perceptions, the natural unities of body-soul, body-mind" (*Leg* 131). In this statement, he creates a vivid image of the rupture in the body's texture that opens up a spiritual abyss, thus elucidating that the physical and the mental/spiritual are deeply intertwined.

It is because of this that I aim to read Sacks's narrative as an account that goes beyond the mere representation of the "bodily, somatic dimension of selfhood," as Eakin holds (*Touching* 182). More than constituting a painful reminder of the vulnerability and mortality of the embodied self (cf. Couser, *Recovering* 295), *A Leg to Stand On* highlights the ways in which the subjective body becomes a fundamental source of insight and knowledge. In contrast to the outside perspective of the third-person which objectifies and fragments the body so that it is reduced to the dis- and then reconnected nerves and tissues, the subjective perspective brought forth by embodiment – feminist scholar Elizabeth Grosz speaks here of "the very 'stuff' of subjectivity" (quoted in Avrahami 2) – results in a more holistic view of the self. Consequently, the cultural norms about bodies and embodiment are negotiated, revised, and contested. Additionally, the discourses defining and distinguishing the normal from the pathological body are at times reproduced, yet at other times highly contested (cf. Smith and Watson 41f.).

"Thus many themes are interwoven here," Sacks describes his narrative in the preface,

"the specific neuropsychological and existential phenomena associated with my injury and recovery; the business of being patient and of returning later to the outside world; the complexities of the doctor-patient relationship and the difficulties of dialogue between them [...] – all this leading, finally, to a critique of current neurological medicine, and to a vision of what may be the neurological medicine of the future." (*Leg* viii)

On first sight, Sacks's account of his injury and recovery seems to combine the elements of the categories of 'pathographies' Hawkins defines and that have been introduced above (Chapter 1). His narrative is decidedly a 'testimonial' of what has happened to him after the accident and throughout the process of recovery and features an altered perception of time that is characteristic for stories of illness (cf. also Brody 90), as well as the utterly bleak visions of the present and future that he can only overcome when recovery sets in. *A Leg to Stand On* also shows traces of Hawkins's 'angry pathography,' as Sacks's descriptions of doctors and nurses, as well as the conversations he recalls imply the "difficulties of dialogue" he experiences and the rigid hierarchies he cannot "stand up" to in his attempts at communicating his experiences to his doctors (cf. *Leg* 77). Finally, his story also contains an explicit call for 'alternative treatment options,' as he envisions a "neurological medicine of the future." While his story can be read in terms of either and all of these categories, they, as categories so often, do not fully exhaust the central issues in Sacks's story, because they can neither account for Sacks's particular situation as a both patient and doctor – a trained professional with a long history in clinical practice and research on neurological diseases – nor for the vision of well-being his memoir sketches.

This considerably changes the way in which the hallmarks of Hawkins's categories are reflected in the story. The account of Sacks's illness is not merely a personal and subjective account of a patient, but is saturated with the objective perspective of the doctor. As a consequence, felt experiences are brought into a dialogue with neurological knowledge. Yet at the same time, Sacks's narrative also illustrates that the capacity of clinical knowledge, even though it is knowledge he himself has acquired, to explain his frightening experiences is very limited. Knowledge from "the outside," so to speak, ceases to be absolute. Likewise, the knowledge of other physicians and surgeons loses its validity, as it excludes Sacks's qualitative experiences and only turns to the objective view on his body. Not only does this cause Sacks's alienation from the doctors who treat him, but also from common neurological practice: 'Old' knowledge no longer suffices to grasp his situation, so that eventually 'new' knowledge is needed, a form of knowledge that emerges first and foremost from the body. Commenting on the subject's lived experience of the body, Einat Avrahami argues that it defies discursivity and illustrates that the available means of describing experiences are inadequate to account for qualitative experiences of illness (4), and, one may add, of well-being. In Sacks's case, this holds particularly true for the discourse of medicine, which he explicitly challenges when he begins his answer to the physician's question about his state of health by stating that "surgically speaking" he is well (*Leg* 72). The ways in which he experiences his body thus dispute the clinical vision of medicine. By coining the neologism and concept of the neurology of identity, Sacks then begins an alternative discourse. As I will illustrate in the following, the body becomes an agent in the creation of knowledge (cf. Avrahami 163). It is crucial that the insight of the embodied position is the resource for Sacks's professional authority: it provides him with knowledge and understanding where intellectual capacities, contemporary science, and reason fail, so that the Cartesian hierarchy between mind and body is unhinged and the body – particularly the wounded body – becomes powerful.

5.2 Encountering the Doctor: Sacks, Dr. Swan, and the Disappointment with the Biomedical Cure

Although the narrating I establishes a coherent account of illness and recovery, a close reading of Sacks's story reveals that the experiencing I is not a coherent and unified persona. However, this is not only a problem owing to Sacks's unique position as both doctor and patient, but an issue that highlights the initial problematic understanding of his injured self. The accident, it should be noted, leads to an immediate and utter detachment: "My first thought was this: that there had been an accident, and that *someone I knew* had been seriously injured. Later, it dawned on me that the victim was myself; but with this came the feeling that it was not really serious" (*Leg* 6, italics in original). While his self-perception is of course severely distorted here and his sense of body ownership is lost, this fulfills a crucial strategy, namely to keep the self in safety, unified and untouched by serious illness. This kind of detached attitude does not collapse even when Sacks begins to examine his injured leg in the mountains after the accident: "Very professionally, and impersonally, and not at all tenderly," he treats his leg, looking at it "as if [he] were a surgeon examining 'a case'" (ibid.). Sacks's attitude remains detached, void of any feeling and self-reference when he takes on the professional role of the physician.

In this particular situation, Couser argues, medical jargon may in fact express the experience of illness accurately and subjectively and figure as the way in which bodily experience is normally constructed. It is hence by means of the professional perspective that Sacks moves from the vulnerable patient to the status of the privileged physician (*Recovering* 27). Not only does he pretend to examine his leg, employing the vocabulary from anatomy and neurology and thereby maintaining a connection to his status as a doctor (cf. also Hunter, "Your" 100), but he also imagines himself standing in front of medical students who follow him at rounds and for whom he illustrates and comments every examination move, thus increasing his authority: "No movement at the knee, gentlemen, no movement at the hip … You will observe that the entire quadriceps has been torn from the patella. But though it has torn loose, it has not retracted – it is wholly toneless, which might suggest nerve injury as well […]" (*Leg* 6). William Hunter is certainly right in stressing the significance of Sacks's use of medical vocabulary, which he does not define or explain, neither for his intratextual audience, nor for his lay audience on the extratextual level. Consequently, it creates a divide between writer and reader that ultimately contributes to his authority as a physician (cf. Hunter 100). In this particular scene, however, a similar divide also powerfully influences the relations on the intratextual level and separates professional from injured patient.

In retrospect, the narrating I reflects: "I murmured my findings aloud [...], as if for a class of students" (ibid.). His repeated use of the phrase "as if" in this scene refers in both cases to Sacks's assumed role as an objective doctor. In the immediacy of the events, it helps to downplay the seriousness and the reality of the situation. Uttered it retrospect, it also points out that Sacks is well-aware that his professional role is only a façade. This façade collapses, however, when Sacks realizes that he himself is the "fascinating case" as he finishes his examination and lecture. Early on, the narrative indicates that a division of the self cannot hold. Howarth argues that in Sacks's realization it becomes clear that he is forced to see the parts of his identity as a whole: scared victim and deliberate physician conflate, just as the story later also merges the other dichotomous identity constructions Howarth identifies: child and adult, as well as athlete and intellectual (111). Turning to the side, "awaiting a round of applause," Sacks realizes that he is "entirely alone [...] so alone, so lost, so forlorn, so utterly beyond the pale of help" (*Leg* 7). His dramatic realization is of course owing to the fact that he is still in the mountains and far removed from the village and any chance for help. Beyond that, it also indicates that in his role as a doctor, Sacks has always perceived himself as part of a community. Finding himself now injured and alone foreshadows the isolation he associates and in fact later does experience as a patient until he enters the convalescent home.

In addition, medical terminology, as Frank tellingly illustrates in *At the Will of the Body*, reduces the body to its physiological states and processes that can be observed and measured and hence appear to be objective: "Thus in disease talk *my* body, my ongoing experience of being alive, becomes *the* body, an object to be measured and thus objectified. [...] [B]ut in using medical expressions, ill persons lose themselves: the body I experience cannot be reduced to the body someone else measures" (12; italics in original). Although Sacks's initial reaction is to assume distance from the injured body and objectify it so he can assess the injury, it is evident that the body does not allow this and that subjectivity permeates Sacks's third-person perspective. More specifically, it is by means of proprioception, or in Sacks's words "the eyes of the body, the way the body sees itself" (*The Man* 46), that awareness of the body figures. Proprioception here clearly dominates over visual perception, as even Sacks's professional objective examination of his leg features attributes of proprioception, such as "toneless" and "flimsy" (*Leg* 6). Subjective proprioception hence eventually undermines the professional outside perspective when his examination moves cause the experiencing I to scream in pain (cf. ibid. 7).

Yet the dichotomy between the first- and third-person perspectives does not only emerge in Sacks's own account of his accident. The subsequent chapter titled

"Becoming a Patient" begins with a quotation by John Donne: "I cannot rise out of my bed till the physician enable me, nay I cannot tell that I am able to rise till he tell me so. I do nothing, I know nothing, of myself" (ibid. 21). The patient is conceptualized here as passive and powerless, incapable of moving, acting and knowing, and fully relying on the power and knowledge of the physician. This quote sets the tone for the following accounts, as Sacks is subjected to the control of various nurses and doctors and brought into the London hospital that he bleakly compares to the Tower of London and its "notorious torture chamber" (ibid. 28). Indeed, he compares his new status as a patient to that of a prisoner, observing that he "is no longer a free agent" (ibid.), an observation that is underlined by his now frequent use of the passive voice which portrays him at the mercy of others.

Interestingly, Sacks also compares his hospitalization to the first day of school (ibid.), implying that he is now subject to new rules, does not possess knowledge, and needs to comply to the authority of others. Thus when the surgeon prepares Sacks for the upcoming operation, he does not grant him a spinal anesthesia:

"For then I could *see* what was happening. They said, no, general anesthesia was the rule in such cases, and besides (they smiled) the surgeons wouldn't want me talking or asking questions all through the operation!

I wanted to pursue the point, but there was something in their tone and manner that made me desist. I felt curiously helpless, as with Nurse Solveig in Odda, and I thought: 'Is this what 'being a patient' means? Well, I have been a doctor for fifteen years. Now I will see what it means to be a patient.'" (ibid. 29; italics in original)

The surgeons humorously, yet paternalistically allude to Sacks's own medical professionalism that may interfere with their authority. Here, Sacks experiences what it is like to be a patient, in the sense Donne's quote has foreshadowed. Through the general anesthesia Sacks does indeed "see what it means to be a patient," i.e. he cannot "see" what happens to his leg during the operation. As a result, his perspective shifts in this scene from that of a medical professional who recommends anesthesia options to the patient who wants to object, but feels too helpless and is therefore forced to give up both control and consciousness during the operation.

This scene is crucial for the unfolding events, since it is at this point that a rupture occurs. On waking up from the operation, Sacks is strikingly disoriented: "There was no sense of any 'nextness' or 'in-between'," he states (ibid. 31). Yet not illness is presented here as an interruption, but the attempt to restore health. Anesthesia has brought the temporal sequence of events in disarray, but being unconscious has also broken the continuous story of illness and healing: "I thought of these, for a time, as two separate stories, and it was only gradually that I came to see that they were essentially connected" (ibid. 23). The idea of connection is of utmost significance here, as it is relevant in Sacks's story about his illness, just as well as with regard to the injury itself. As Howarth holds, both surgery and writing depend on anatomy, on the "tension and connection" that establish structure (112). The operation connecting the two stories –although Sacks is only capable of "seeing" this in retrospect – is intended to reconnect the torn tendon in his knee, or as the surgeon reassures him, to "'[r]estore continuity. That's all there is to it ... nothing at all'" (*Leg* 30). *A Leg to Stand On* therefore stresses the role of narration for the process of healing, a process Hull characterizes as both physiological and psychological when patients create a revised story of their bodies and their selves (110). In the biomedical setting, though, Sacks's memoir at this point illustrates, there is no room for a story other than the triumphant narrative of surgical reconnection, which ultimately impedes healing.

Though an uncomplicated procedure, the medical intervention complicates storytelling because after the operation Sacks's subjective and objective perspectives are ruptured despite the fact that the narrating I renders the events from the position of an authoritative subject, whose health has been restored. Asked to explain the "'salient facts'" of his accident and injury, so that his medical history can be recorded properly, Sacks notes that "[he] wanted to tell them everything – the entire story" because he is not sure which information the doctors would consider "salient" (ibid. 29). On the one hand, Sacks is entirely removed from this role as a doctor, incapable of deciding which information will be essential for his physicians. On the other hand, this scene also illustrates that the very process of storytelling is disrupted: While Sacks feels the need to tell the "entire story," the doctors are only interested in fragments of his account, a tension that also implies that traditional medicine is a "bad narration" (cf. Howarth 112f.).

But "there was to be another story," Sacks explains (*Leg* 23). Denied the conscious experience of the operation and the process of reconnecting the tendon, Sacks can no longer draw on his own professional knowledge, but increasingly turns to the first-person perspective. Diedrich highlights that this "other story" that needs to be told is, though neurological, a phenomenological account ("Treatments" 132). The speculations on the nature of his injury from the perspective of a medical professional he continues to entertain often lapse into panic and hypochondria, e.g. when he fears his perception may be altered because he has suffered a stroke or other anesthetic complications. Yet more frequently he begins to turn to comparisons with patients he has encountered before, and, most importantly, to his own view of his injury. The objective view on his illness, in contrast, is now located in the domain and authority of other doctors, who repeatedly tell him that there is nothing wrong with him.

In her article "Tenacious Assumptions in Western Medicine," sociologist Deborah Gordon illustrates that subjectivity is generally considered to exist "in there," while objectivity is "given, out there" and distinct from its observer (25). As a result, the patient's subjective perspective is often seen as unreliable. She argues that this is why health and illness are not defined by the patient's experience, but rather through the objective data that an examination of the body reveals (ibid. 25f.). In *A Leg to Stand On* it becomes clear that Sacks's doctors regard the publicly observable third-person stance as the only way of expressing the nature of his injury and recovery accurately, an issue that becomes the source of strong tension in the narrative, as they neglect his contrasting qualitative experiences.

The development of Sacks's phenomenological impressions first of all points to the fact that qualitative experiences are specific to the person experiencing them. According to philosopher Thomas Nagel, they are "so peculiar that some may be inclined to doubt their reality, or the significance of claims about them" (437). This certainly holds true for Sacks's initial perceptions, for instance when we touches the leg and fails to feel any muscle mass at all, but instead feels as if he is touching "soft inanimate jelly or cheese" (*Leg* 34). His idiosyncratic statement evinces that he is not sure how to frame his perception and looks for similes and points of comparison that may provide a reference to the familiar. Moreover, expressing the opposites of the physical qualities "hard/strong" and "animate" Sacks celebrated before his accident, it highlights the contrast between the injured body and the body he is familiar with. As he ascends on the mountain trail, Sacks constructs his body as vigorous and infallible, for instance when he holds that he "was as strong as a bull, in the prime, the pride, the high noon of life" (ibid. 3). The simile which presents an overt comparison to the bull that stands in for strength, masculinity, and force (ironically of course the very force that leads to his accident) aids in Sacks's celebration of a body unsurpassable in power and health. His celebration of the healthy body culminates in an essentialist statement when Sacks is

"blessing my energy and stamina, and especially my strong legs, trained by years of hard exercise and hard lifting in the gym. Strong quads, strong body, good mind, good stamina – I was grateful to Nature for endowing me well. And if I drove myself to feats-of-strength, and long swims, and long climbs, it was a way of saying 'Thank you' to Nature and using to the full the good body she had given me." (ibid. 4)

Nature, emphasized here not only through capitalization but also by means of a personification, bestowed on Sacks the gift of a good and healthy body which he therefore, so his argument, needs to use to full capacity and exercise rigorously. "Good" is in fact repeated several times in the passage for emphasis, as is the adjective "strong" and in the parallel sentence structure of the enumeration, strength and the functioning body become inextricably linked to that which is "good."

The beginning of the narrative may thus well be criticized as an attempt to construct his body in opposition to a body that is at best below average, at worst pathological, and hence draws a stable line between health/normalcy and a state of illness and deficiency. This serious shortcoming in the narrative notwithstanding, the good and healthy body is in these scenes rather seen from the outside than actually experienced qualitatively. The vocabulary employed in the quotations is strikingly limited, with "good" and "strong" presenting the only variations and describing objective observations. Not only does this illustrate historian Rolf Ahlzén's reiteration of the dictum that "health is seldom experienced before it is threatened and lost" (326), that one is hardly aware of the body in times of health, but the strong contrast between the experiences of the healthy and the injured body simultaneously exposes the significance of the subjective stance in times of illness, the richness of experience that ill health triggers, and that is neither represented nor encouraged in the biomedical context.

In this vein, Sacks's quickly turns to other thoughts, assuring himself that in the morning he will find that he was absurdly mistaken and all is in fact well (*Leg* 34), or trying to calm himself when we cannot flex the muscle and move the leg by blaming the drinks he had with a friend to toast the successful surgery: "'It's the champagne. You're delirious, you're excited. [...] Go back to sleep – deep restful sleep – and you'll find that everything's OK in the morning'" (ibid. 36). In a paternalistic tone he scolds himself, like a doctor his patient, and the split in perspective – Sacks addressing himself in the second person – elucidates that in his attempt to be rational, he continues to fight against his subjective perception.

Similarly, he greatly affirms the authority of the objective stance and the role of the doctor when he initially longs for the "quiet voice of authority" with which the surgeon Dr. Swan will speak and explain the problematic symptoms he experiences, the lasting numbness in his leg after the operation (*Leg* 63). "Authority" in this quotation is used as a metonym for the physician, which underlines that his position as a medical professional is inextricably linked to authority and the power to speak in the medical discourse. Despite the fact that Dr. Swan's authoritative voice is "quiet" it will be heard in the discourse, but Sacks's direct characterization of his ideal surgeon (for until then he has not spoken to Swan yet but only imagines their exchange) also makes clear that for him, authority is equally linked to resolution as it is to calm and respect.

Furthermore, Sacks aligns authority with "simplicity" and "conviction," two nouns that grasp the directness, clarity, and transparency he seeks in the imaginary dialogue with the surgeon whom he expects to reply: "'Yes, I understand. It happens. Don't fret. Do this! Believe me! You will soon be well'" (ibid.). The short sentences indeed reflect the conviction and clarity Sacks hopes for. Moreover, they illustrate that Dr. Swan is expected to provide reassurance and his authority derives from his experience in the profession (Heifferon 47). In the demand "Believe me!" on the other hand, the surgeon is imagined almost like a priest, thus transmuting his voice to "the ultimate authority, an authority that tells us what to do, how to act" (cf. ibid. 48). While there is slight criticism inherent in Barbara Heifferon's reading of the scene, I do not share her reservations, because it is crucial that not Dr. Swan himself is speaking to Sacks but Sacks is imagining an ideal encounter taking place. Associating the surgeon with a priest-like figure then also bespeaks the trust and faith Sacks as a patient wishes to put in his surgeon and in his capacity to cure his body and do away with his fears.

Upon Swan's arrival at his bedside, Sacks hopes to receive the answers to, as he states, "[w]hat I could not do for myself in a hundred years, precisely because I was entangled in my own patienthood and could not stand outside it" (*Leg* 63.). The subjective perspective of patienthood is at first perceived as problematic because it "entangles" Sacks, the professional, in a web of immediate and idiosyncratic experiences in which he is passively caught and lacks the detached and removed perspective that would be necessary to disentangle the situation. Patienthood, Sacks indicates, has rendered him passive, playing here, as well as on several other occasions throughout the story, on the meanings of the verb "stand" because, like his injured leg does not permit him to stand, patienthood does not allow a removed, objective perspective. Heifferon thus observes in her analysis that Sacks is depicted here as both physically and psychologically paralyzed and turns to Dr. Swan as a voice detached from his panic (45).

The surgeon is in fact portrayed as a heroic figure, emphasized and contrasted to Sacks himself through the use of italics, when Sacks envisions that "*he* [Dr. Swan] could cut across at a single stroke, with the scalpel of detachment, insight, and authority" (*Leg* 63; italics in original). Essential for Dr. Swan's capacity to act heroically, he implies, is his role as a surgeon because the scalpel becomes a sword-like weapon with which the physician may forcefully disentangle him from the web of frightening experiences. By foregrounding Swan's occupation as a surgeon, Sacks initially attributes great significance to the surgical cure. Moreover, it is not the scalpel alone that aids in Sacks's rescue, but it is "the scalpel of detachment," a metaphor echoing the ordnance of heroic epics and highlighting that the singular quality distinguishing the hero is in this case his removed perspective and emotional distance. In the climactic sentence structure the surgeon's scalpel and his insight culminate in his authority.

This scene illustrates that the narrative does not criticize the precision, determinacy, and power of conventional institutionalized medicine, but in the beginning rather works to underline it. However, the ensuing scenes show that the actual encounter between Sacks and his surgeon has little in common with the exchange he imagined and drew strength from. On the contrary, the meeting is utterly devastating for Sacks since Dr. Swan refuses to listen – indeed hardly hears his concerns – and refuses to discuss any of the symptoms and fears his patient mentions. Instead, the surgeon focuses solely on the body that, according to him, has been skillfully repaired (cf. ibid. 72f.). In a paternalistic fashion similar to his own reaction, Dr. Swan eventually dismisses Sacks's qualitative experiences by exclaiming: "'Nonsense, Sacks'" (ibid. 73). Dr. Swan shrugs off Sacks's concerns in an utterly direct and impolite way, as both the declaration of "nonsense" and the surgeon's omission of Sacks's title (his refusal to acknowledge their equal status), or in fact any polite form of address indicate. Indeed Dr. Swan replies in the short and decisive sentences that Sacks has envisioned, yet his answer is rather sharp and condescending than reassuring when he iterates that "'[t]here's nothing the matter. Nothing at all. Nothing to be worried about. Nothing at all!'" Through its anaphoric usage, "nothing" receives particular emphasis in the surgeon's statements and the repeated utterance "[n]othing at all" signifies the physician's unwillingness to deal with Sacks's objections.

His reluctance to engage in his patient's worries becomes all the more clear when he interrupts Sacks's attempt to voice disagreement with a revealing gesture, as Sacks recounts: "He held up his hand, like a policeman halting traffic" (ibid.). Dr. Swan's gesture, underlined by the simile, grants him authority in the discourse, thus constituting indeed what Heifferon terms "vertical rhetoric" in the context of institutional medicine (29). Not only does the gesture signal Sacks to stop, but it also erects a barrier between doctor and patient, effectively closing down, Heifferon observes, any exchange of information between them (56). The fact that the surgeon talks down to Sacks is finally underscored by the opposition between "nonsense" and reason he establishes when he appeals to Sacks's rationality and, in an almost threatening manner, enquires "'You *understand* that [there is nothing wrong], don't you?'" (*Leg* 73; my italics). While the subjective perspective is disqualified in such statements, the rationality of the third-person stance is emphasized.

The ensuing conflict between Sacks and his surgeon then reveals the importance of the surgical cure and its medical triumph in traditional biomedicine, since the doctor does not allow the patient to see the operation as unsuccessful (cf. Conway, *Illness* 35). Dr. Swan hence exposes a restricted view on health by postulating that health is restored and the patient is on the road to recovery through the successful clinical intervention that repairs the object body only. Over the course of the story, though, it becomes obvious that the objective explanations given by his doctors and devised by Sacks himself can neither account for his personal illness experience nor can they reassure him that his recovery is proceeding. Consequently, Sacks becomes one of whom Conway identifies as "untriumphant writers," authors who do not downplay the catastrophic dimension of their illness experiences, but instead revisit and mediate their most devastating moments (ibid. 55). In *A Leg to Stand On*, Sacks therefore deconstructs the triumph of the biomedical cure by exploring his catastrophic experiences at great length.

As reason fails, Sacks begins to construct a vivid representation of his distorted body image and lost sense of body ownership. Because the leg does not function properly, it is erased from Sacks's "inner image" of himself (cf. *Leg* 55). On the verbal level, this disconnection is illustrated by an absolute negation of the injured leg as part of his body, when Sacks describes it as the "non-leg" (ibid. 64) or at best a "life-less replica" attached to his body (ibid. 80). His "non-recognition" then leads to the conclusion that the injured leg is "not-me" and impossibly "continuous with [him]" (ibid. 47f.), ultimately leaving him entirely alienated from his leg:

"In particular, it no longer seemed a 'home.' I couldn't conceive it 'housing' anything, let alone part of me. [...] The flesh beneath my fingers no longer seemed like flesh. It no longer seemed like material or matter. It no longer resembled anything. The more I gazed at it, and handled it, the less it was 'there,' the more it became Nothing – and Nowhere. Unalive, unreal, it was no part of my body, or anything else. It didn't 'go' anywhere. It had no place in the world." (ibid. 48f.)

This traumatic scene stresses that the objective third-person view from the outside loses its strength: even though Sacks can look at his leg and touch it and is therefore objectively aware that it is still there, he cannot help but feel deeply alienated from it. In this and subsequent scenes, the first-person perspective is brought to the fore and clearly dominates over an outside view of his body. Additionally, alienation for him entails a sense of disembodiment. While the leg at first appears to be merely lifeless flesh beneath his hands, it soon loses all of its material qualities and becomes "Nothing – and Nowhere," with the capitalization here adding emphasis and dramatic moment to the significance of these two ideas. As Malcolm MacLachlan states, Sacks has lost the feeling of, as well as the feeling for his leg. Any experience of embodiment, he continues, is essentially linked to emotions and actions (40), which are precisely what his disembodied state now lacks.

Bodily movement is of particular importance for Sacks, as a preceding scene demonstrates in which he is able to do chin-ups in his bed and recalls: "Lovely movement, lovely muscles – their action gave me joy" (*Leg* 37). Next to transcending the passive state of lying in bed, movement links his body to health, since it reassures him that he is "still in good shape" and capable of recovering (ibid.). When the body is able to move him and be moved by him, Sacks speaks about it in terms of his "good body," linking it to the strong and well-trained body at the beginning of the story (ibid.); when he fails to move the leg, however, he loses the emotional connection to it and is also unable to assign any emotive qualities to the leg, finding that it looks neither "friendly," "hospitable" or "warm" (like something that may house him), nor "nasty," "unfriendly," or "hostile" (*Leg* 48). Consequently, his sense of body and self is utterly disrupted.

The narrating I renders this disruption in scientific terms, more specifically, in terms of proprioception: "One has oneself, one *is* oneself, because the body knows itself, confirms itself, at all times, by this sixth sense. I wondered how much the absurd dualism of philosophy since Descartes might have been avoided by a proper understanding of 'proprioception'" (ibid. 47; italics in original). Proprioception, in the literal sense the perception of "one's own," refers to the ability to perceive the relative position of, for instance, one's limbs.[11] Sacks's observation elucidates that, when proprioception is functional, one understands oneself as a material, corporeal object, instead of merely an immaterial, thinking being. Although Eakin asserts that Sacks uses the verbs "have" and "be" interchangeably with respect to his body and his self (*How Our Lives* 29), in this statement, the embodied stance of his identity is clearly foregrounded and the verbs are by no means intended to suggest interchangeability. As McEntyre observes, Sacks's writing is marked by a distinct style in which he often uses several adjectives or verbs in one sentence as a means of "probing" for an adequate and appropriate expression (238). Additionally, the italic typeface in particular suggests emphasis and this way supports the idea that Sacks foregrounds the notion that proprioception defines the self, thus intertwining self and body, rather than merely suggesting that one "has" a self, seemingly separate from the body.

Along similar lines, Kleinman deftly defines what he terms the "divided nature of the human condition in the West": persons affected by illness realize that they *have* (i.e. experience), but at the same time also *are* their bodies, with the former meaning that they perceive that they have a sick or injured body that is distinct from their selves and that they may observe objectively, as if they were someone else (26). When a sense of embodiment is missing, the relationship between the patient's mind and body is ruptured and the self is conceptualized as the Cartesian thinking mind that may observe the injured or sick body, to an extent that it may even be completely alienated from it, which is exactly the case during the beginning of Sacks's recovery.

Right after the operation Sacks feels, to his own surprise, reinvigorated and ready for a quick recovery, since he believes in his body, "its strength, its resilience, its will to recovery" (*Leg* 37). Although he does not treat his body with the same lack of self-reference as his injured leg, the qualities he considers necessary for a speedy recovery are solely attributed to his body, despite the fact that they would generally be applied to both, body and mind. This evokes the impression that at this point in the memoir, Sacks views his body as the object that needs to be restored in the process of recovery.

---

11 The way in which the body appears during proprioception is commonly referred to as body image. Body image is crucial when it comes to issues of ownership and agency in movement, i.e. generating a willful action, and therefore plays a significant role in the understanding of embodiment. According to Shaun Gallagher this underlines the assertion that control is an essential part of any sense of selfhood. Another important aspect is the visual perception of the body which validates the fact that one's body is one's own (56).

This impression is underlined by a statement following his expression of confidence. Preparing himself for the first visit of his physiotherapist, Sacks concludes that she will help him get the leg "ship-shape" again, pondering on the implications of this proverbial phrase:

> "I somehow *felt* like a ship when I said 'ship-shape' to myself, a living ship, a ship of life. I felt my body was the ship in which I travelled through life, all parts of it – strong timbers, alert sailors working harmoniously together, under the direction and co-ordination of the captain, myself." (ibid. 38; italics in original)

It is in brief scenes, such as this one that the experiencing I slips into a dualist stance. He distinguishes between his body, the material home of his self, and his mind, to which he attributes the power to direct and co-ordinate the workings of the body. Laurence Kirmayer describes mind and body as two contrasting poles in the human experience, since they symbolize the voluntary and intentional as opposed to the involuntary and accidental. He argues that it is this opposition that assumes a central role in forming both a private sense of self and a public concept of the person and that is thus responsible of the powerful persistence of the mind-body dualism in the Western conceptualization of illness ("Mind" 57).

In his study *Nervous Acts*, George Rousseau points out that especially the alleged separation of body and mind is a crucial issue in the representation of illness, purporting that in everyday conceptualizations of the self, the separation of mind and body facilitates life. This is not only true in times of health, when each part has its functions, but even more so in times of illness: Rousseau asserts that "when things go wrong, you fix the part rather than the whole." According to him, we like to forget that any illness of the body is likewise an illness of mind and hence of the entire self (341). Ultimately, his approach stresses the unity and inseparability of mind and body in the self. However, when Sacks considers himself the "captain," he connects the capacity of think and the ability to control the body to his self and, as a consequence, believes he is capable of assuming control over his body. According to philosopher Daniel Dennett, who uses the same metaphor to refer to the relationship between self, body, and mind, this exposes the persistent dualist view that one is not one's body, but the body's owner (cf. 77).

However, Sacks's optimistic vision of the ship-shape body is repudiated when he is not able to move the leg in physiotherapy:

> "The image of myself as a living ship – the stout timbers, the good sailors, the directing captain, myself – which had come so vividly to my mind in the morning, now re-presented itself in the lineaments of horror. It was not just that some of the stout timbers were rotten and infirm, and that the good sailors were deaf, disobedient or missing, but that I, the captain, was no longer captain. I, the captain, was apparently brain-damaged [...]." (*Leg* 44)

This fearful recognition makes evident that he first of all realizes that he is no longer in control over his body. This powerlessness is highlighted through the repetition "I, the captain," a phrase at once emphasizing his presumed power and the utter incapacity to exert any control that is revealed during the therapy session. A rhetoric of pathology hence pervades this scene, beginning with the ambiguous usage of "infirm" that may refer to the weak rotten timbers, as well as to fragility and invalidism, the accusation of the sailors being "deaf," and the fear that he himself may be "brain-damaged" and hence aligns the loss of control with pathology and abnormality. Yet at precisely this deeply problematic point the dualist notion is transcended, as Sacks realizes that it is not only his body that is affected, but also his mind. Up until then, he has assumed that his injury in no way affected his "essential being" (ibid.), but now he comes to the conclusion that his inability to move the leg is *"not just a lesion in my muscle, but a lesion in me"* (ibid.; italics in original), recognizing his embodied condition.

Since his ability to move the leg does not return, Sacks's emotional situation deteriorates dramatically. For him, the leg has become unreal, so that he is repeatedly haunted by nightmares in which he dreams that the cast protecting the leg is in fact either completely solid or empty. He imagines his leg to be made of "chalk or plaster or marble" or of something entirely inorganic (ibid. 64). Finally, Sacks is even convinced that he has lost his leg and that recovery is inconceivable:

"The leg had vanished, taking its 'past' away with it! I could no longer remember having a leg. I could no longer remember how I had ever walked and climbed. I felt conceivably cut off from the person who had walked and run, and climbed just five days before. There was only a 'formal' continuity between us. There was a gap – an absolute gap – between then and now; and in that gap, into the void, the former 'I' had vanished – the 'I' who could thoughtlessly stand, run and walk, who was totally thoughtlessly sure of his body […]." (ibid. 58)

In these passages, he connects the loss of the feeling for his leg also with a loss affecting his entire self. Enumerating verbs of movement, such as walk, run, and climb, he stresses the self's capacity for movement and action, its embodiedness. All of these verbs illustrate that it is of course also a self that stands in an upright position, not a patient whose "head lies as low as the foot" (Donne quoted in *Leg* 21). However, in his current situation, he can no longer establish a connection to the self capable of performing all these actions, claiming that the continuity between him and this past self is merely "formal," much in the same sense as the nerves and tissues that were surgically reconnected. Furthermore, it becomes obvious here that the embodied practice of memory is of crucial significance in Sacks's conceptualization of his self.[12] His situation thus constitutes the opposite of the phantom limb condition: in the latter, the limb is missing, yet memory persists that the limb is a functioning part of the body, while in Sacks's case, the leg has been erased from memory, although it is still part of this body (cf. also Wallace-Wells n. pag.).

5.3 Recovery in Action: Sacks's "Muscle Music"

His recovery eventually sets in when Sacks experiences the first instances in which his nerves are reinvigorated, moments he describes as an "electrical storm" (*Leg* 86). Though overwhelming and powerful, these "lightning flashes" also set the scene for a Gothic[13] spectacle: "I could not help being reminded of Frankenstein's monster, connected up to a lightning rod, and crackling to life with the flashes" (ibid.). After this first comparison that serves to elucidate the uncanny feeling of the nervous system reverting to motion, Sacks quickly corrects himself, stating it is not him, but his nervous system that is "electrified into life" (ibid.). He, however, "played no part in these local, involuntary flashes and spasms," which he describes as lacking any personal quality, intention, or volition (ibid.). On numerous occasions, Sacks then compares himself to a puppet, illustrating his passivity and inabil-

---

12 Israel Rosenfield's study on consciousness titled *The Strange, Familiar and Forgotten* points to the significant connection between a sense of self and memory. In the chapter on "The Counterfeit Leg and the Bankruptcy of Classical Neurology," Rosenfield cites the famous case of Madame I who continuously needed to touch herself in order to "know that she was herself" and interprets it as the patient trying to create a self and assure herself of her existence. Madame I's case receives particular attention because she is also unable to recollect the memories of her family and her past, leading Rosenfield to the conclusion that memories cannot exist without a sense of self (41).

13 The idea and aesthetic of Gothic is at the core of Couser's criticism of the narrative. In *Vulnerable Subjects*, he notes that both the rhetoric of conversion and the rhetoric of Gothic have "historically operated at the expense of disabled people" (101), bringing forth an argument that is certainly valid for disability narratives in general (cf. Chapter 2.3) but that should not be employed to generalize all accounts that make use of such rhetoric. Significantly, Gothic rhetoric is employed not in "Limbo," the dramatic account of the passivity of patienthood, but first and foremost pervades the initial moment of Sacks's recovery, thereby undermining the association of Gothic, dread, and impairment Couser proposes. Freadman also responds to Couser's criticism, pointing out that it reveals "traces of discourse determinism [...], according to which a discourse's ideological freight will inevitably trump the innovative power of the individual writer who employs the discourse" (396f.).

ity to control his leg that is instead moved by his nerves only. These comparisons, too, point out that he still at times perceives his willing mind to be cut off from his body.

Though often lapsing into such a Cartesian dualist stance, Sacks gradually develops an alternative strategy, for instance when he awakes feeling what he terms "an odd impulse" to flex his left leg and is – immediately and for the first time since his accident – able to do so (cf. ibid. 94). "The idea, the impulse, the action, were all one," the narrating I recounts, attributing his active contraction of the muscle to his ability to remember how to move the leg (ibid.). It should be noted that only at this point Sacks considers his self to be involved in the bodily movements, hence tying the concept of his self tightly to movement. Movement in particular is significant here, as it is concrete and opposed to the abstract idea of muscles tensing and contracting, or, to quote Sacks's physiotherapist during their exercises: "One needs to think of a movement, not a muscle. After all, people move, they *do* things, they don't tense their muscles" (ibid. 39; italics in original). Consequently, movement denotes purpose, action and agency, in contrast to passivity. Moreover, as the quotation highlights, movement involves the entire person, not merely a part of their body. Movement is therefore crucial to Sacks as it finally not only involves his body, but also his mind. He consequently celebrates the muscular sparks as uniting his mind and body, "the unity which had been lost since [his] disconnecting injury" (ibid. 95) and a unity that may be attributed to movement and, as I will illustrate, to music.

When listening to Mendelssohn's lively and lighthearted music, Sacks recounts that he feels more hopeful "that life would return to [his] leg – that *it* would be stirred, and stir, with original movement, and recollect or recreate its forgotten motor melody" (ibid. 87; italics in original). The developments Sacks envisions here correspond to the muscular sparks that first move passive nerves and then finally also involve his own movement, a movement he terms "original" – "natural" and originating from him. This passage therefore allows for direct parallels between his reinvigorated nerves and music. Music is presented as the means by which Sacks is able to not only "recollect" – remember – movement, but also recreate it, and hence constitutes a powerful metaphor for the unity of thought and action, mind and body. In the same passage, Sacks celebrates his immersion in the music as the moment in which "the animating and creative principle of the whole world was revealed, that life itself was music, or consubstantial with music; that our living moving flesh, itself, was 'solid' music – music made fleshy, substantial, corporeal" (ibid.). For Sacks, a unity of mind and body is not only expressed metaphorically through music, but is by analogy also inherent in "life itself;" it is a unity that becomes embodied.

Looking back at his injury, Sacks then explains that not only nerves and muscles were disconnected through his injury, but at the same time also the unity of body and mind: "The 'will' was unstrung, precisely as the nerve-muscle. The spirit was ruptured, precisely as the body" (ibid. 96). In a similar vein, he remembers himself being animated by music earlier, with the exception of his injured leg, "that poor broken instrument which could not join in and lay motionless and mute without tone or tune" (ibid. 14). Here, too, Sacks describes his mind and body borrowing from musical terminology, thus intertwining music, the mental, and the corporeal. Music ultimately allows for a direct connection to the body that language cannot provide (Frank, *Wounded* 107).[14] Vice versa, verbs denoting the corporeal are also employed to describe Sacks's relationship to music, for instance when he feels he had been "panting and thirsting for" a reaction to Mendelsohn's music (*Leg* 87), as well as in the chapter titled "Limbo" that recounts Sacks's dramatically low mood. In this scene, the experiencing I turns to the passages in Goethe's *Dr. Faustus* which meditate on hell and music: "'No man can hear his own tune,' [...] I yearned, hungrily, thirstily, desperately – for music" (ibid. 78).[15] As a result, music is conceived as the force that may rehabilitate the lost sense of embodiment, and, eventually, even well-being.

So Sacks's recovery accelerates when he practices walking with his therapist and suddenly hears what he terms his "own personal melody" (ibid. 109), the music of Mendelssohn:

"I found myself walking, easily, *with* the music. [...] [I]n this self-same moment *the leg came back*. Suddenly, with no warning, no transition whatever, the leg felt alive, and real, and mine, its moment of actualization precisely consonant with the spontaneous quickening, walking and music. [...] I was absolutely certain – I *believed* in my leg, I *knew* how to walk..." (ibid. 108, italics in original)

---

14 Cf. also James Berger's essay "Falling Towers and Postmodern Wild Children: Oliver Sacks, Don DeLillo, and Turns against Language" on the ways in which music brings Sacks into "contact with some part of reality that is deeper than language" (348).

15 "Limbo," rendering a phase that lasted 10 days and therefore almost half of the time it took Sacks to recover, is surprisingly brief, a formal characteristic that alludes to the passivity during the time and Sacks's inability to move/be moved. It is a state in which communication is impossible, because there is "no leg to stand on" (*Leg* 77), and, along these lines, no moral or spiritual support to overcome the deep sense of Nothingness. Most importantly, limbo for Sacks is a state of disembodiment, for, as he recounts "[his] powers and faculties had no locus of action" (ibid. 80).

In her essay "The Soul of Oliver Sacks," Ella Kusnetz harshly criticizes this climactic moment of recovery, imputing inauthenticity to Sacks (193),[16] yet neglecting the function of this scene. As the climactic sentence structure elucidates, music aids in returning the leg to life, "reality," and to Sacks's own image of himself. The passage begins with Sacks's unawareness of what is happening, how he began moving the leg "easily," and what exactly initiated his movement. More than that, the realization that the leg is part of his body again occurs "suddenly, with no warning, no transition," but is entirely "spontaneous." This supports the idea mentioned above that Sacks narrates "two separate stories" bearing no connection (*Leg* 23). Beyond that, it also mocks the idea of surgical reconnection and cure: even though the nerves and tissues had already been reconnected before and their continuity had been re-established, the medical intervention neither improved Sacks's psychological situation nor achieved holistic well-being. As Medical Humanities scholar Martyn Evans therefore notes in "Medicine and Music," the musical epiphany that occurs transcends the mechanistic and posits "both music as healing and healing as music" (140).

Describing the outcome of this scene as the mere restoration of health and well-being, however, would not do justice to the narrative. Berger is right in stating that the condition Sacks has reached through music is not just a recovery of the things lost due to the injury, but an entirely new condition (348). Sacks terms this new condition "Grace" (*Leg* 112f.), a noun that unites the physical and spiritual and enables Sacks to grasp his body in terms other than medical or mechanical (cf. Berger 348). By introducing a new term for his state of well-being and recovery, Sacks's memoir bears striking similarities to the ending of Frank's *At the Will of the Body*, were Frank comes to the conclusion that the word "health" cannot encompass his status after finishes his treatment for cancer and enters the remission society. Instead, "[i]n recovery," Frank holds, "I seek not health, but a word that has no opposite, a word that just is, in itself" (135). For him, this is "gravy," a word he borrows from a poem by Raymond Carver of the same name to illustrate the utterly positive, desirable, and exquisite qualities of having recovered, as well as the materiality,

---

16 Kusnetz accuses *A Leg to Stand On* of being "a false book" (191) and contends that the use of music as a spontaneous principle of organization may possibly not be Sacks's original idea. Pointing out that the 1983 version of *Awakenings*, a book originally published in 1973, features the story of a former musician suffering from Parkinson's disease who states that he is "unmusicked [and] must be remusicked" (294f.), and that *A Leg to Stand On* was not published until 1984, although Sacks claims to have written it in the 1970s, she states that "the complicated process of projection and expropriation in Sacks – as well as the elaborate fictionalizing, fantasizing, and metaphysicalizing – that in all the books it is virtually impossible to discern whose material is whose" (192f.).

corporeality, and warmth of the body. Yet at the same time, the adjective "grave" also resonates and serves as a reminder that his well-being is temporary only (ibid.). Both words, "gravy" and "Grace," effectively locate the newly-found state of well-being outside the binary of health and illness. As a result, music is of immense importance in the memoir because it eventually triggers a paradigm shift in the conception of both the body and well-being.

This moment of revelation can be aligned with Sacks's effort to descent the Scandinavian mountain after his accident with his injured leg, where the experiencing I suddenly hears music and finds himself not being "muscled along" anymore, but rather "musicked along" (*Leg* 13). I do not agree with Diedrich who claims that Sacks's rowing downhill movements compromise his "human-ness" because he is no longer able to stand in an upright position (cf. "Treatments" 135). Although Sacks does complain about the shortcomings of his now "crippled" body that needs infinitely longer to descend the mountain than it took for him to "stride" (*Leg* 16), this scene clearly privileges the account of the body's capacity to move with the help of music, despite the severe injury. On the one hand, music fulfills the purpose of making Sacks's effort to descent the mountain before sundown "less like a grim anxious struggle" (ibid. 13) and is therefore of crucial value for his emotional well-being. In *Musicophilia: Tales of Music and the Brain*, where Sacks revisits his accident and recovery, he adds that while Mendelsohn inspired his rehabilitation, his descent from the mountain was accompanied by "The Volga Boatman's Song" (262). A shanty, this song is sung to accompany labor and bring it into a common rhythm; as such it adequately represents the hard physical labor of "rowing" oneself downhill, and, as Sacks elucidates, articulates a dynamic movement (ibid. 282). At the same time it also imagines a community and may therefore be seen as a way to counter the desolate and forlorn feeling he experiences in the mountains.

Hence music is not only, as illustrated above, throughout the narrative tied to the body, but essentially linked to movement. During his descent from the mountain, for instance, Sacks observes that "the musical beat was generated within [him] and all [his] muscles responded obediently" (*Leg* 13). Music is understood as a force organizing and coordinating bodily movement, an idea also inherent in Sacks's notion of the "muscle-orchestra" (ibid. 14). Moreover, he apprehends his own involvement in the process when he notes that he himself "became the music" (ibid.), explicitly referring – repeatedly – to the verses of T. S. Eliot's "Dry Salvages" that read "You are the music/ While the music lasts." Sacks suggests here that he is entirely saturated by music, in complete unity with it. Yet rather than characterizing himself merely as a passive object through which music passes, he stresses that he is the one capable of coordinating movement. Music finally also powerfully links to agency.[17] It is therefore no coincidence that Sacks perceives music as "quickening" his body and simultaneously his mind – returning moral and spiritual fortitude, and, again, reinforcing the unity of body and mind (cf. ibid. 111).

So not only does his story come full circle at the point of his recovery, but it also stresses the role of music as a spontaneous and transcendental power that brings body and mind in tune by merging the cognitive, the sensual, and the physical. In *Musicophilia*, Sacks invokes a passage from Nietzsche – "We listen to music with our muscles" – to illustrate that music does not only have an auditory and emotional effect on the listener, but a motoric effect as well (xii).[18] In her study *Music in Everyday Life*, cultural sociologist Tia DeNora holds that for this reason, music becomes a "prosthetic technology of the body" (159), enabling Sacks to stand up (both in a literal and figurative sense) and walk again. *A Leg to Stand On* eventually attests to the transcendental and corporeal powers of music that lift Sacks out of the passivity and posture of the patient, unite mind and body, invite movement, and restore agency. When discussing Sacks's encephalitis lethargica patients in *Awakenings*, DeNora reminds readers that the role of music is by no means metaphorical only. On the contrary, she asserts, "music provides a basis of reckoning, an animating force or flow of energy, feeling, desire and aesthetic sensibility that is action's matrix" (151f.). The surgeon's fleeting remark quoted above that nerves and tissues have been reconnected falls far short of the processes at work in Sacks's healing, or, as Wasserstein so aptly concludes, that art succeeds where reason fails (443). In a similar vein, MacLachlan notes that Sacks's work explores music and art as "tools to living and rehabilitation that reach beyond rationality"[19] and thus well mirror the "richness of life" Sacks's writing seeks to capture (41).

Fittingly, the title of this chapter is "Solvitur Ambulando" – "it is solved by walking." When the experiencing I before tried to move his leg that appeared so

---

17 The role of music as an implicit way of creating agency is more fully explored in Tia DeNora's *Music in Everyday Life*.

18 Cf. "Keeping Time: Rhythm and Music," a chapter in *Musicophilia*, where Sacks describes his own experience with motor-music and also refers to several of his patients for whom music served as an "activator" and triggered "quasi-automatic responses" (256).

19 This idea is also expounded in Evans's "Medicine and Music: Three Relations Considered" in which he postulates three possible points of connection between medicine and music: most obviously medicine's work in explaining the physiological basis of music, music as a diagnostic and therapeutic means and, much less obvious, what Evans calls "music's illumination of medicine" (136). He conceives both music and medicine to constitute "practical practice," experienced both by the person performing and the person listening. Furthermore, medicine and music address individual and singular conditions and enable "individual flourishing in creative and restorative ways" (143).

strange, so lost and clumsy, he wondered: "Will I be forced, from now on, to think out each move? Must everything be so complex?" (*Leg* 108). Whereas mental capacity is at first idealized as the controlling force, it now appears as impeding, as it turns the automatic process of walking into an activity in which cognitive processes are foregrounded, thereby complicating it to the extreme and unmanageable. The music which Sacks perceives, however, serves as "'motor' music," a "kinetic melody" simulating the "natural, unconscious rhythm" of walking (ibid. 108f.). Instead of a series of isolated movements, walking regains its fluency, for, as Sacks illustrates in *The Man Who Mistook His Wife for a Hat*, "every moment in music and arts refers to, contains, other moments" (41) and therefore finally becomes a means of establishing a new sense of continuity. Sacks depicts this moment as an "abrupt and absolute leap" (*Leg* 109) and it is then through the power of this inner rhythm that Sacks is able to – quite literally – overstep the gap in his self-conception.

Music as a tool for rehabilitation and well-being, as my reading has shown, enables Sacks to recognize his embodied condition and accounts for his movement. His time in the hospital, in contrast, is to a great extent marked by thinking only because he recounts that he was "motionless, as if paralyzed, for eighteen days in [his] room, eighteen days of intense thought, but without *doing* or *going*" (ibid. 117). The memoir shows that is it impossible "to think the leg back into life and reality" (ibid. 188) but recovery is only made possible through action and movement. Similarly, when his physician criticizes that Sacks still does not move the leg naturally, he sends him to the local pool, instructing a life-guard to race Sacks, who describes himself as "a natural" in swimming and does indeed emerge from the pool being able to move more easily. This scene is surprisingly brief, with the only sentiment Sacks describes being outrage about the life-guard who dares to race an injured man, so that the moment of full recovery is hence depicted as elusive. Most importantly, recovery takes place in social interaction, thereby breaking with the isolation of the hospital. Sacks later explains this in reference to his exchange with Luria, as "[t]he alienated part, so to speak, is deceived into action, by being made a part of, participating in, some complex activity" (ibid. 163).

5.4 MERGING THE OBJECTIVE AND THE SUBJECTIVE: SACKS'S 'NEUROLOGY OF IDENTITY'

It is finally through the distance and Sacks's exchange with A. R. Luria that the overwhelming feeling of his distorted body image is not only transformed into language, but also located in the context of neurological research and medical tradition. Particularly the ending of *A Leg to Stand On* has prompted scholarly criticism. Diedrich asserts that at the end of the book, Sacks, having not only his leg, but also his status restored, returns to what she assumes is "his rightful position [...] in the doctor-patient binary" ("Treatments" 136). Although I agree with her claim that Sacks's ability to tell his story in this manner rests in his privileged position as a doctor (ibid. 136f.; cf. also Frank, *Wounded* 129), the criticism voiced in her work and elsewhere[20] is too drastic. Diedrich purports that Sacks's narrative neither changes the position of the patient within the medical establishment, nor challenges the role of the doctor (ibid.). This, however, is not possible because both doctor and patient are, as Diedrich acknowledges, part of the medical system. For their relationship to change, then, the system needs to be reformed – which is indeed what the narrating I proposes with the introduction of his neurology of identity.

The afterword to *A Leg to Stand On* closes with an annotated bibliography and Sacks's critique of classical neurology. Here, Sacks argues that the existing neurological terminology is inadequate to describe his loss of body image (161). What is needed in neurology, he also notes in *The Man Who*, are notions that transcend static functions and that may encompass the dynamic and kinetic inherent in ideas, such as 'will' and 'impulse' (92). It is important, though, that these concepts are not intended to substitute the terminological inventory of classical neurology, but are supposed to serve as a corrective. This conclusion triggers his effort to establish what he terms a 'neurology of identity,' a new form of medical understanding that will help to "escape from the rigid dualism of body/mind" (*Leg* 178). Generally, Kleinman credits Freud with including the interpretation of the patients' biographies and their personal experiences of illness in medical treatment, maintaining that this practice has influenced a number of medical professionals, amongst them Sacks, and helped to form new ways of speaking about health and disease that incorporate the "deeply private significance of illness" (42f.). Kleinman's notion of the "deeply private" also highlights that the 'neurology of identity' eventually aims at reconciling the dichotomy between objective classical neurology and individual subjective experiences, between the abstract and the concrete.

In his discussion of Sacks's writing, philosopher Colin McGinn, however, voices doubts about the nature and purpose of the neurology of identity, arguing that physical injuries should be treated as physical problems, because "they do not have psychological causes or an intelligible psychological history: they have brute physical causes" (176). He goes on to purport that any psychological problems that may arise in the course of such an illness are "entirely impersonal" (ibid.). His overall argument, namely that neurology should not apply methods of psychoanalysis because the immediate causes for the respective disease differ and need appropriate responses, is a valid concern. Nevertheless, the concept of self that lies at the root of it is dubitable. First of all, Sacks's narrative elucidates that the inner world and sub-

---

20 Cf. especially Couser's *Vulnerable Subjects*, 102f.

jective reality of illness are a vital part of the experience of an injury and the subsequent recovery, thus significantly influencing how diagnosis and treatment are conceived by the patient and how rehabilitation progresses. The experience of illness, Sacks's story has shown, involves both mind and body, as it is not enough for the body to be restored but the patient's spirit needs to be "quickened" as well. Sacks thus emphatically writes back at McGinn's proposition that people "must be treated as machines – for the simple reason that the brain is a machine and hence is prone to the breakdowns that are the lot of all machines" (176).[21] Instead, Sacks holds that "we are in no sense machines or impersonal automata" and in his afterword he illustrates that what "has always been intuitively clear" is now "becoming formally clear" (*Leg* 188), subjective and objective knowledge may merge in the neurology of identity.

While the entire narrative powerfully illustrates this, the afterword to *A Leg to Stand On* is particularly revealing in terms of Sacks's contextualization of the new form of neurology he envisions. Howarth points out that the final chapter discloses the book's "double plot" consisting of the narration of the events and the thoughts that followed. Joint together, they guide Sacks's exploration of the connection between actions and ideas (cf. Howarth 111), an exploration that can encompass both the subjective and the objective perspective. Kusnetz criticizes Sacks's emerging concept of neurology as "mystical" and "overridden by emotions" (178), hence raising a frequently voiced concern Sacks himself addresses in his article when he quotes the philosopher Carol Feldman asking him "'Why do all you neurologists go mystical?'" (quoted in "Neurology" n. pag.). Admittedly, Sacks never clarifies the neurological basis for his recovery through music, but rather presents it, as analyzed above, as a climactic moment of epiphany. The foundations of his neurology of identity, however, are delineated in strongly rational and scientific terms that move his intuition to the realm of neurological science. Here, he briefly turns to the founding figures of classical neurology, such as Jean-Martin Charcot, Silas Weir Mitchel, and Joseph Babinski, outlining how they all employed a dualist standpoint and categorized symptoms of alienation as either 'hysterical', i.e. mental, or as the consequences of brain damage, i.e. physiological. At the same time, he points to the shortcomings of their approaches, elucidating that understanding alienation as 'hys-

---

21 Although Sacks uses the terminology of computer science in a footnote of his afterword when he discusses the story of a colleague who had to "'reprogram' her brain" after losing many movements she considered 'automatic' while recovering from a broken ankle, he argues that these movements are not "'practiced' internally" and cannot be thought through (cf. *Leg* 173 fn*), implying, much in the same sense as in "Solvitur Ambulando" that they need to be carried out. He therefore understands them as tied to the person acting and moving, instead of inherent and fixed in the brain.

terical,' for instance, has initially prevented further investigation on the physiological nature of the condition (cf. *Leg* 176f.). He therefore exposes that the dualist categories inevitably restrict the progress of neurological research. The rhetorical strategy Sacks employs in this chapter deserves attention, as it is by means of renowned studies and the reference to key figures of classical neurology that he places himself at once within and beyond traditional neurological discourse.

Pointing to the emergence of 'body-image' as a scientific category that has reformed the understanding of the workings of the body and the mind, as well as to the technological advances of his field that now allow the recording of neuronal activity and thus prove that parts of the body are in fact represented on the sensory cortex and effectively erased when sensory input stops (cf. ibid. 180), Sacks highlights that there are recent neurological explanations for his own loss of feelings for and memories of the leg. His own story is thus presented as a prime example and simultaneously validated by the neurological explanation now available. Contrary to the belief of his doctors, he demonstrates that his qualitative experience after surgery is by no means singular. However, he notes, these scientific findings fail to explain why he also felt so strangely alienated from his leg (ibid. 181), which is why he introduces the notion of consciousness in the sense of Gerald Edelman's 'primary' and 'secondary consciousness.' While the former encompasses, among other things, perceptual sensations and the distinction between self and non-self, the latter involves language and thought processes, affirming Sacks's notion that consciousness "is essentially personal; it is essentially connected to the living body" (ibid. 185f.). When Sacks's asserts that his narrative "is not just a story of a leg, but an account from inside, of what primary consciousness is like," he suggests that he is also aiding in advancing the study of consciousness, presenting his story as a unique opportunity to gain more insight into the workings of consciousness that "an account such as the experience of alienation, and nothing else, can provide" (ibid. 187). Not only does this strengthen the relevance of *A Leg to Stand On* for scientific discourse, but it simultaneously attributes great authority and scientific value to the first-person perspective.

In this context, he joins the early neurologist Joseph Babinski in arguing for a kind of neurology capable of transcending the dualism of classical neurology that has previously left the study of consciousness to psychiatrists, reiterating the criticism that such a division between the mental and the physical has inhibited scientific progress (ibid. 183). Scientific progress is presented in this chapter as a natural course of events. By emphasizing that Babinski "wrote at a time before" the concept of body-image had been coined or that only generations after Babinski, Head, and Sherrington could in fact "grasp the actual mechanisms whose principles they intuited" (ibid. 177), the narrating I makes clear that scientific discovery is a dynamic and ongoing process that with each step sheds new light on existing problems and questions. In this spirit, his urge for a neurology of identity is conceptualized as a part of this continuous progress.

Earlier case studies, he suggests, do not pay attention to "the full subjectivity" of the patients' accounts of their experiences, although "[the patient] can articulate a state of radical perplexity, a total breakdown in his inner sense of identity, memory, 'space'" (ibid. 185). While *A Leg to Stand On* is a response to this lack of subjectivity, Sacks's neurology of identity may be seen as the attempt to theoretically conceptualize "identity, memory, 'space'" in patients' experiences. The afterword consequently merges the voice of the doctor with the subjectivity and experience of the patient. Finally, Sacks returns the idea of the patient's identity and self, of personhood and subjective experience to the discourse of clinical neurology. His dual perspective as neurologist and patient enables him to reassume authority arguing not only from an ethical perspective that the voice of the patient needs to be heard, but also from the perspective of a scientist.

McRae contends that the strong appeal of the neurology of identity certainly rests in the fact that human identity is marked by individuality and uniqueness, and stresses the irreplicable. Nevertheless, his article voices profound criticism when he reminds readers that "Sacks's repudiation of abstract and impersonal thinking should not blind us to the equally abstract and impersonal character of his own thinking" (97). In this vein, he accuses Sacks of viewing not only his own patients, but also himself when he is a patient in ways that reproduce "the conceptual, even ethical, fault in traditional neurology," namely treating individual patients as replicates of other patients (ibid.). A possible explanation that McRae offers is based on the assumption that Sacks was influenced by thinkers such as Leibniz and Pythagoras who generally favor the abstract over the concrete, turning the individual empirical instance into a synecdoche for other instances and their general form (97f.). These points of criticism are problematic and several of the text passages McRae cites to support his argument are in fact open to a contrasting interpretation, such as the one in which the narrating I is reminded of a childhood experience and recounts: "For it was then, in the summer of 1938, that I discovered that the whorled florets were multiples of prime numbers, and I had such a vision of the order and beauty of the world as was to be a prototype of every scientific wonder and joy I was later to experience" (*Leg* 16). Whereas McRae interprets this passage as an instance in which individual parts disappear into the whole (100), this passage may well read to intertwine the vivid and detailed experience of the flower garden with sober mathematical abstraction. In uncovering the principle of the golden ratio, the key to aesthetics, Sacks merges both formulaic abstraction and the concrete experience of nature.

Furthermore, McRae repeatedly criticizes Sacks for intertwining his own experiences with the case histories of other patients, arguing that "his fellow patients' identities resided not in their uniqueness but in the way each served as a synecdoche for an abstract form: the alienated, the excommunicated, cast-out patient" (107). McRae thus reads Sacks's use of other patients' neurological problems as a means to underline his own alienated status, accounting for the immediate function of these case histories. Since the attending physicians have repeatedly stressed the uniqueness of Sacks's situation, they have ultimately alienated him from the community of patients and knowledgeable doctors and complicated any form of communication between medical professionals and the patient. Through experiences similar to his own, Sacks emerges as a member of their community, a community in which he is capable of sharing and making sense of his experiences, as well as giving voice to his own moral fallacy. He proudly declares: "I was no longer alone, but one of many, a ward, a community, of patients. I was no longer the only one in the world, as perhaps every patient thinks in the ultimate solitude of sickness" (*Leg* 124). In the context of subjective experiences and objective observations, however, Sacks's strategy loses some of its critical connotations. At first sight, the narrating I's representation of other patients does correspond to the classical case history, as the scene describing a young male patient whom Sacks encounters as a medical student on the ward elucidates. Sacks describes his encounter with the patient at length, beginning with a brief report on his admission and a thorough observation of the patient who refuses to go back into his bed, since "someone's leg" is in there (ibid. 50). However, once the patient offers Sacks an explanation for his strange behavior, objective professionalism is intertwined with empathy:

"He [patient] felt the leg gingerly. It seemed perfectly formed, but 'peculiar' and cold. At this point he had a brainwave. He now 'realised' what had happened: *it was all a joke*! [...] but feeling that a joke was a joke, and that this one was a bit much, he threw the damn thing out of the bed. But – and at this point his conversational manner deserted him, and he suddenly trembled and became ashen-pale – *when he threw it* [the strange leg] *out of bed, he somehow came after it – and now it was attached to him.*" (ibid. 51; italics in original)

The mode of representation is certainly noteworthy in this scene. In free indirect discourse, Sacks's narrating voice mixes with the patient's voice and view of the situation, adapting not only his diction when speaking about the "damn thing," but also tracing the patient's train of thoughts when he comes to the crucial realization that the entire situation can only be the result of a cruel joke played on him by the hospital staff.

On the one hand, stories of encounters between him and patients in earlier contexts allow Sacks to maintain his status as expert and medical professional: on the surface, they enable him to assume the voice of medical authority at a time when he is severely injured and not granted an objective voice in front of his attending physicians. On the other hand, the mode of representation in these accounts show that in these case histories, Sacks merges the objective and subjective perspective, for instance by paying close attention to the patient's qualitative experience of his leg. What leads to insight in this situation is not a mere comparison to the patient's diagnosis, but to him as an individual, when Sacks states that "although I called myself a neurologist I had totally forgotten him, thrust him out of my consciousness until – until I found myself, apparently, in his position, experiencing [...] what *he* had experienced, and, like him, scared and confounded to the roots of my being" (ibid. 53; italics in original). It becomes clear here that Sacks finds fault with his practice of neurology for having forgotten this patient's peculiar story and in fact credits his own disturbing experiences as a patient for returning these memories and, most importantly, for great insight and an understanding of his own condition. Stories such as this one hence foreshadow Sacks's call for the neurology of identity.

In "Neurology and the Soul," he recounts that when he first started treating patients, his thinking was "mechanical, physiological" (n. pag.). Yet, he asserts,

"it soon became clear that I needed always to address myself to the individual person and to his needs, and that I could not understand what was going on without this. More and more I started to think of medicine as not just treating the lesion, or the disease. One has to treat the lesion, but one has, equally, to pay attention to the entire individual. This is not only ethically so, but it seems to me to be scientifically so as well." (ibid.)

In a similar vein, Sacks alludes to Luria who frequently quoted Marx by stating that science presented the "ascent to the concrete" and that "an idea of the full richness of life" is a prerequisite to treating patients successfully (ibid.).

Likewise, this scene also shows that the recollected encounter with the patient and the subjective experience of his illness enable Sacks to learn from his patient – not in terms of reaching an apt diagnosis of his own state, but rather in terms of understanding his status as a patient, when he then notes that "then, as on the Mountain, I suddenly realized that this 'fascinating case' *was* myself – not just a 'case' for Dr. Anton-Babinski-Pötzl-Sacks to demonstrate and write up, but a very frightened patient [...]" (*Leg* 55). While Kusnetz interjects that Sacks in fact renames the disease he apparently suffers from after himself (196), Sacks decidedly distances himself from the professorial figure he has invented, and in turn also from his own status as a physician by refusing to be a case study the physician may put in writing and claiming his status as a "frightened patient," an individual affected by illness. Indeed, this recognition does aid Sacks in restructuring the doctor-patient-relationship that his neurology of identity envisions. Viewed through this lens, his concept of medicine implies a "richer, more personal, more intimate vision of the relationship" between the patient and his attending physicians (Kusnetz 176).

Finally, another kind of comparison also adds to the emotional rehabilitation I have alluded to earlier, namely Sacks's comparison to literary characters. When he is utterly frightened by the prospect of not being able to return to the foot of the mountain and find help, he recalls his experience of reading Tolstoy's *Hadji Murad*:

"This strange, profound emotionless clarity, neither cold, nor warm, neither severe nor indulgent, but utterly, beautifully, terribly *truthful*, I had encountered in others, especially in patients, who were facing death and did not conceal the truth from themselves; I had marveled, though in a way uncomprehendingly, at the simply ending of *Hadji Murad* – how, when Murad had been fatally shot, 'images without feelings' stream through his mind; but now, for the first time, I encountered this – in myself." (*Leg* 10; italics in original)

In the past, Sacks has observed the ways in which his patients have come to accept their impending deaths, yet has not been able to entirely comprehend it, as is illustrated by his attempt to find an appropriate description for the experience. His use of contrasting adjectives suggests that he is incapable of pinpointing the quality of this experience. When he finally concludes that it is "truthful," he establishes an incomparable und personal description. It is then through his memory of Tolstoy's novel and the representation of Murad's dying consciousness that Sacks may grasp the qualitative dimension of his own experience, thus gaining new insights. This passage, too, ultimately highlights the importance of the connection of aesthetic representations of qualitative experiences. Budge notes that emotional experiences, both through music and literature, serve as teachers in understanding illness (ibid. 135).

In his influential study *Two Cultures*, Charles P. Snow outlines a cultural schism between science and the humanities that for many years hindered scholarly endeavors in the Medical Humanities (cf. also Hull 105). Science and narrative are here seen as having an "opposite version of history": in working toward prospects, science orders past events into a chain of causes and effects that turn them logical and predictable. Narrative, on the other hand, is retrospective in nature and adheres to the "eccentric pace of memory and understanding" (Howarth 106). Acknowledging patients' stories requires a reconciliation of the two conceptions of history. Equally, Sacks's article on "Neurology and the Soul" addresses what he conceives as the "split between science and life, between the apparent poverty of scientific formulation and the manifest richness of phenomenal experience" (n. pag.). He characterizes this split as a vast discrepancy caused by our "desire to see ourselves as something above nature, above the body," a desire which spurs dualist conceptions of the self (ibid.). So while his recognition of proprioception may be seen as a theoretical, scientific strategy to transcend this dualist notion, music certainly serves as a practical and subjective strategy to reconstruct and feel the unity of his mind and body. Once the Cartesian view of the self is suspended, the scientific study of the body as a mechanical entity loses its legitimacy (cf. Eisenberg 10).

In spite of his illness experience, which has caused deep trouble in Sacks, the closing of the story turns him into the "autonomous individual," whose life is celebrated in the classical autobiography (cf. Smith and Watson 3). This is, most importantly, a self that emerges from the illness experience as a more insightful and knowledgeable physician whose view of illness is arguably altered and who has succeeded in transforming illness into meaning, which is why *A Leg to Stand On* may indeed, as Couser holds, be described as an illness memoir moving to an autobiography (*Vulnerable* 100). In his study, this conclusion has a critical ring to it, reading as though the autobiography would constitute a step back from the potential "progress" that the illness memoir may grasp. In fact, however, Sacks's story has subverted crucial elements of the conventional life narrative, most significantly by constructing the narrative of the embodied self and a body that is not marked by health. The self in the conventional autobiography is a character marked by wholeness and integrity that speaks in a unified tone (cf. Porter "Figuration" 134). When a conversion takes place, the writer's life and story take a new direction: the conversion narrative, Porter holds, "invokes an old life and a new life," and through the turning point in their lives, the writer has gained "epistemological certainty that brings self-knowledge," knowledge that should also inspire others to follow the writer's path (ibid.). The understanding Sacks reaches is in the end not merely personal and subjective, but receives social relevance as it helps to establish a new medical discipline. The ending of the story thus reestablishes Sacks as the professional that his audience is already familiar with and medical authority is eventually re-established, albeit in a different form. Rather than undermining the doctor's position per se, the memoir therefore problematizes the role of the physician by juxtaposing the rich qualitative account of his symptoms with the straightforward and neutral description offered by his surgeon. At the heart of the critique that the life narrative offers, is then the biomedical quick fix of surgery that, though vital for Sacks's recovery, disregards his individual healing process.

In *Vulnerable Subjects*, Couser is particularly critical of Sacks's narrative since he composes it years later, "from the perspective of complete recovery," and therefore "tends to reinscribe, rather than erase, the line between disability and nondisability" (102). His criticism is problematic because it is primarily based on the hard facts of Sacks's accident and his injury, which was "merely" temporal, an injury after which his problems could be remediated, but not a lasting impairment. His story would therefore betray the nature of his condition if recovery did not receive a prominent role, and as Richard Freadman points out, audiences in this case expect a narrative of recovery (396f.). Yet Sacks's memoir also highlights that knowledge is not merely inscribed onto the sick body after the experience has passed, but that the body itself figures as an agent in the perception and understanding of the illness experience, recovery, and well-being and therefore adds substantially to the subgenre outlined here.

6. "She Rides It Like an Untamed Pony":
The Politics of Well-Being in Simi Linton's *My Body Politic*

Simi Linton dancing in her wheelchair in the midst of both disabled and nondisabled scholars and activists at the annual conference of the Society for Disability Studies (SDS) is one of the pivotal moments in her 2006 memoir *My Body Politic*. Over several pages, she creates a collage of moments, when, "after all the papers have been read and all the issues raised and put to bed," the participants gather on the dance floor (*Body* 149ff.). Recalling several conference nights since the 1990s, she takes readers to the locales of their dances, hotel suites where a small crowd, initiated by Linton and her husband David, begins to dance, and later larger dance floors in a meeting room of the convention center, when the more organized dances have become major events in the conference program. In all of these moments, Linton describes the varieties of dance styles her friends and colleagues display: Paraplegic dancers bounce in their wheelchairs, crutches twirl, a scholar's child slides out of her wheelchair to crawl-dance amongst the adults and sheds "big tears" when her parents finally try to convince her that it is already well past her bedtime. A dancer in an electric wheelchair starts a conga line and takes the frolic crowd along the hotel corridors and around waiters still clearing the tables from the conference dinner. A quadriplegic scholar dances with his tongue to the tunes of music turned "way up" so that the deaf and hard-of-hearing dancers can feel the beat (ibid. 151).

Linton's anecdotal rendering of the heterogeneous group's nights on the dance floor is, like many other scenes narrated in the book, humorous and affectionate; like no other scene, though, these pages weave together the overarching themes of Linton's life narrative: community, pleasure and well-being, as well as the reappropriation of the discursive space in which meaning is attributed to disability and the impaired body. It is in this scene that the writer repeatedly uses the first person plural to count herself in the group of disability rights activists and disabled people, a process of identity formation that, as the narrative which spans more than three decades vividly illustrates, has taken many years to unfold.

The memoir begins with the day in 1971 when, on their way hitchhiking from Boston to Washington D.C. to protest the Vietnam War, Linton, her husband John, and her best friend Carol were involved in a car accident that injured both Carol and John fatally. This day marks the day Linton, who survived yet suffered severe trauma to her spine, has become impaired and introduces her life as a disabled woman in what Couser describes as "a kind of disability bildungsroman" (*Signifying* 186). Against this background, the dance at the SDS conference is the climax of a sequence of scenes in which the disabled body yields her pleasure and in which the dichotomy of ability and disability is dissolved as dancing is re-defined, since the dancers do not attempt to imitate standard forms of dance or mask their difference (*Body* 153), but instead create and celebrate alternative forms of movement.

With Torrell, I therefore see the memoir as a powerful – and successful – attempt to resymbolize disability (328), an act visible in the form and content of her book. In the following, I will argue that the memoir politicizes well-being by narrating disability and pleasure not only as deeply personal, but at the same time as social, particularly legal, issues, thereby imagining well-being as an embodied form of disability advocacy. As a political narrative, *My Body Politic* contextualizes many events within the framework of legal issues and disability rights laws to supplant the conventional progress narrative propelled by cure or the correction of the flawed body with a narrative of judiciary progress. As a narrative of embodiment, the memoir similarly resists the triumphant narrative of overcoming disability (cf. Chapter 2.3) and instead turns to recovering and embracing the disabled and sexualized body. I will unite both strands in the third section of this chapter where I will analyze the dance scene introduced above and its (narrative) aesthetics as a way of both celebrating an embodied disabled identity and performing activist work.

Criticism on Linton's book has been surprisingly sparse thus far, given her position as one of the leading activist and scholarly voices in Disability Studies in the United States. Her study *Claiming Disability: Knowledge and Identity* (1998) is highly praised and among the most widely read texts in the discipline, her articles have appeared in numerous scholarly journals, and she continues to hold speaking engagements at universities. After leaving a teaching position in psychology at Hunter College to pursue activist and cultural work on a larger scale she founded the consulting organization Disability/Arts that offers advice to artists, filmmakers, and cultural institutions, among them the Smithsonian, on the representation and depiction of disability in the arts (Nario-Redmond 1). Her most recent work includes the 2014 film project *Invitation to Dance*, a documentary jointly produced with the German-born director Christian von Tippelskirch that is loosely based on

My Body Politic[1] and explores the significance and power of dance for the disability community.

For Rosalía Baena, the memoir is a success story, because it depicts Linton and many other disabled individuals at her side leading "fulfilled and satisfactory lives" (136f.). Although Baena makes explicit that she does not utter the notion of the success story in the traditional sense, where it is connected to cure and the return to a "normal" life, her approach is problematic. After all, the idea of the success story turns the individual way of life into an achievement and her argumentation therefore echoes the ableist subtext of "making it" *despite* one's disability and aids the impression that to live happily and contentedly is exceptional when one is disabled. This, however, is precisely what *My Body Politic* counters by narrating happiness and contentment as commonplace and by positing well-being as an integral part of Linton's disability identity politics. This does by no means entail that feelings of shame, fear or loss are silenced. Quite to the contrary, they are voiced in various contexts for both the narrating I and the reader to bear witness to. Throughout the book it is in the community of others that they are abated and transformed into a positive body politics, which effectively challenges the notion of success as a solitary endeavor because Linton's book comprises the stories, joys, and struggles of other disabled individuals.

As I have shown in Chapter 4, a similar dynamic is at work in Audre Lorde's *Cancer Journals*, where the personal becomes the political as Lorde speaks for a host of other women and for a generation of writers and scholars. Linton's memoir at times inverts this as the narrating I not only speaks on behalf of other members of the disability community, but frequently recounts being spoken to, both directly and indirectly. Friends, acquaintances, and colleagues ultimately assume a fundamental

---

1 Nevertheless, von Tippelskirch emphasizes that the film is "not Simi's story, it's the biography of a very big issue in this country" (quoted in Hill n. pag.). Tracing Linton's process of becoming a disabled woman through video footage from her childhood, youth, and later speaking engagements, archival material of disability rights demonstrations, and the voices of numerous friends as well as fellow activists and scholars, the film reaches out to the disability community, but also well beyond it to tell the story of Americans claiming their disabilities and "their rights to 'equality, justice, and a place on the dance floor!'" (Linton and von Tippelskirch n. pag.). The film has been partially financed through crowd funding and premiered at the ReelAbilities Film Festival in March 2014. See http://www.invitationtodancemovie.com for a trailer. Previously, Linton has produced and toured with a theatrical adaption of her memoir titled *My Body Politic: An Illustrated History*, a play in two acts. In the performance, Linton enters the stage as the narrator of both her own life and the disability culture and politics that have emerged since her accident (Linton, "My Body Politic: An Illustrated History" n. pag.).

role in her narrative as mentors and *roll* models[2] who guide her growing political awareness and her gradual process of "claiming disability." In his foreword to Linton's critical study, Disability Studies scholar Michael Bérubé muses that the act of "claiming disability," undertaken both inside and outside of academic contexts, will become "one of the most politically sensitive endeavors" over the coming years and decades (vii). He elucidates the tight and intricate connection between the personal act of claiming a disabled identity and the political and social implications of doing so, for claiming disability will at once unmask difference and work to erase the stigma of the impaired body, fostering a positive identity conception. Ultimately, this not only amounts to a personal and individual act, but a political one as well, influencing the ways in which disability is conceived and represented in public, and, finally, claiming disability, the act of embracing difference, demands participation and calls for an inclusive society.

This is also reflected in the title of the life narrative, *My Body Politic* which may be read to foreground either the individual body or a community of people. When read as a noun phrase with a postpositive adjective, the title implies that the individual body, Linton's impaired body, is political. Comfortably placing it in the public eye, tending to it and being yielded the pleasures it affords, Linton, as Baena purports, mediates the personal and the political (128) and claims disability with this title. Reminiscent of a Whitmanian "body electric," which in fact resonates in one of the chapter titles of her memoir, *My Body Politic* is simultaneously a celebration of embodiment and the disabled body. In this vein, the cover of her memoir, too, has been read as an act of "claiming disability" in which Linton not only meets the public eye but has successfully negotiated a new body and a new form of visibility (Garland-Thomson, *Staring* 195). One amongst the few memoirists to have a photograph of themselves printed on the cover of their books, Linton smiles at her readers with what Disability Studies scholar Bruce Henderson calls "a smile of triumph" (460). The large scale portrait photographer Ruth Morgan has taken for the book jacket shows her in her electric wheelchair (see figure 1).

The reader's eye meets the writer from a slightly higher angle, the perspective of those of the "walking world" (*Body* 15), as she approaches the camera in her motorized wheelchair, the obvious signifier of her disability, her right hand pulling the

---

[2] 'Roll model,' as I have briefly noted in the introduction, is a term that disabled journalist John Hockenberry uses in his 1995 memoir *Moving Violations: War Zones, Wheelchairs, and Declarations of Independence* to refer to "[c]rips [who] have few pieces of advice for other folks in chairs" (135), "who have hung in there, who have taken the airline flights, gotten a real job, and found the unfindable public bathroom" (137). According to him, they can offer practical advice and thus present an alternative to the popular disabled role models ranging from FDR to Stephen Hawking.

control to come to a stop just inside the frame of the photograph. The setting, an open space outside in the sun, as well as the movement captured in the photo illustrated by her hair streamed out behind her, the blurred ends of her long scarf, and the flaunting rose-colored jacket that falls in drapes over her black shirt and pants counter the most obvious stereotypes of disabled individuals as passive, isolated, and confined. Instead, dressed "for work and play, love and sport," Linton is indeed portrayed here as a representative of what she terms the "new cadre of disabled people" who "wield that white cane or ride that wheelchair or limp that limp" (ibid. 108). Both Linton's portrait and the quotation elucidate what Garland-Thomson has so fittingly described as *"relish*" (*Staring* 196; italics in original), the sense of well-being that the photograph radiates.

Figure 1: Book cover My Body Politic

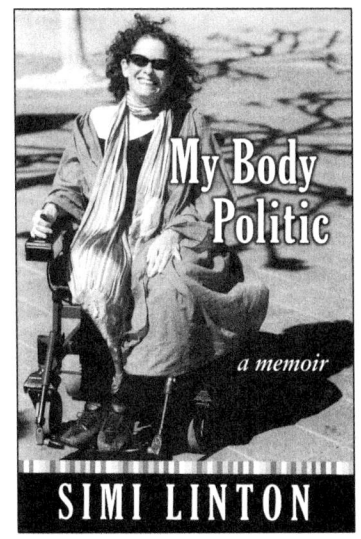

My Body Politic: A Memoir. Ann Arbor: U of Michigan P, 2006.

It is actually with this photo of the writer that Garland-Thomson concludes her study *Staring: How We Look* on a celebratory note, describing it as one in which the sitter meets "the startled eyes of a public made insensate to the spectacular range of human variation by the social pressure toward visual conformity" (ibid.). The body Linton showcases is certainly not as nonconformist as the aesthetics of other bodies Garland-Thomson surveys over the course of her study, but the photograph posits an alternative conception of the disabled body as robust, an adjective Linton herself uses several times, and pleasurable. Furthermore, the scarf and jacket she wears in the photograph blur the boundaries of her body, making it difficult to discern where her body ends and the wheelchair begins and hence makes the two inseparable from one another and suggesting that the wheelchair is a significant aspect of her embodiment. To that effect, the portrait unveils a new understanding of disability and the impaired body and sets the tone for the story. Especially the sunglasses Linton wears in the photograph are significant in this respect, for they allow her to stare[3] back at prospective readers and buyers of the book while at the same time shielding her eyes from their gazes, thereby reversing the power structure traditionally at work in the depiction of disabled individuals.

Secondly, the memoir's title may also be read as a metaphor, since "body politic" is commonly used to describe "a nation regarded as a corporate entity" or, in more general terms, a society of otherwise organized groups of persons ("Body politic" n. pag.). In contrast to Torrell and Couser, who both read the title of the memoir as pertaining exclusively to the disability community, illustrating Linton's position "along with a myriad diverse others, on the margin of what is usually understood as the 'body politic'" (Couser, *Signifying* 188) and hailing a community "bonded together by a common culture" (Torrell 327), the body politic delineated in the memoir is also open to a broader definition. Read along these lines, the title foreshadows Linton's vision of a kind of remission society, a society comprised of disabled and able-bodied people who enjoy equal and full participation that becomes prominent towards the end of the book. At times, her memoir offers a bleak view on the lack of accommodation and the prejudices that have restricted disabled individuals' participation in American society; Much more often, though, the life narrative crafts a powerful perspective on well-being and asserts that contentment, pleasure, and ease are not dependent on the healthy and intact body. Well-being, as I will show in this chapter, is therefore not only conceptualized as personal and individual but exhibits a strong communal and political dimension.

6.1 *My Body Politic* and the 'New Disability Memoir'

Linton's memoir may certainly be grouped, alongside other texts, such as Stephen Kuusisto's *Planet of the Blind*, Anne Finger's *Elegy for a Disease: A Personal and Cultural History of Polio*, Ben Mattlin's *Miracle Boy Grows Up: How the Disability Rights Revolution Saved My Sanity*, and Harriet McBryde Johnson's *Too Late to Die Young: Nearly True Tales from a Life* into the subgenre Couser has recently termed the 'new disability memoir' (*Signifying* 164ff.). Around the turn of the cen-

---

3   In this context, cf. Garland-Thomson's *Staring* for her exceptional theorization of the communicative processes inherent in practices of looking and staring that she supplements with a plethora of compelling analyses, most of them of visual material representing disability.

tury, he notes, numerous life stories have been published which no longer focus on impairment but instead self-consciously revolve around issues of disability and deliberately attempt to depart from "failed or counterproductive formulas" of conventional disability memoirs (ibid. 164f., 172). Gothic rhetoric, pity, the language of inspiration, and the conception of disability as a horrific fate (cf. Chapter 2.3) are absent from these narratives which portray disability, both congenital and acquired, as a significant aspect of the memoirists' identity.

Beyond that, Linton's life narrative serves as a representative example for the subversion of progressive plotlines that have catered to notions of compulsory able-bodiedness and depicted the protagonists' (re)entrance into normalcy, for instance through a cure or an otherwise significant medical improvement of the impaired body. *My Body Politic* defies such a notion of progress that focusses on the affected and oftentimes medicalized body and the normative force of the medical system. In line with Linton's orientation on the social model of disability (cf. Chapter 3.1), her memoir instead reverts both the narrating I's and the reader's gaze to scrutinize the idea of progress in relation to disability, exclusion, and human rights legislation.

"Let the shameful wall of exclusion finally come tumbling down," President George Bush heralded when he signed the landmark Americans with Disabilities Act (ADA) into law in 1990 (quoted in Longmore and Umansky 1). Although historians Paul Longmore and Lauri Umansky call the ADA "hardly a panacea" to discrimination and exclusion, they affirm its significance as a comprehensive law that "promises [disabled individuals] access to the public sites where their fellow citizens conduct their everyday lives: subways and snack bars, offices and auditoriums, jury boxes and gymnasiums" (ibid.). They make clear that the ADA does not call for a "special treatment," but demands basic civil rights and disabled people's access to mainstream society (ibid.; Russell 1). In five titles, the law therefore sketches specific situations and environs, such as employment, public services and transportation, as well as communication technologies, in which "reasonable accommodations" (Sec. 12111) must be made, e.g. by making facilities accessible, modifying equipment, or reorganizing work schedules. – Unless this "would impose an undue hardship" on employers, businesses, or service providers (ibid.), which is the reason why the interpretation of the ADA is still highly contested.

Moreover, Emily Russell points to another significant aspect of the legislation when she turns to the definition of disability the ADA establishes. According to the ADA, disability denotes "A) a physical or mental impairment that substantially limits one or more life activities of such individual; B) a record of such an impairment; or C) being regarded as having such an impairment" (Sec. 12102.). The first part of the definition of course complies with standard medical definitions of disability as a condition that may be diagnosed and treated, yet Russell is quick to stress that in the subsequent parts of the definition, the ADA acknowledges disability as embodiment by extending it to individuals who live with a "record," in other words have a history of a condition, such as cancer, and people whose scars or other bodily markings may reveal them as disabled (2). In a similar vein, she notes that later amendments also recognize the episodic impairment that individuals in remission experience (ibid.).

"So it seems," Longmore and Umansky conclude, "that *disability* is no longer hidden and taboo; that disability issues will get, must get public attention; that people with all sorts of disabilities have presently emerged from the shadows to assert their citizenship" (2). Over the course of Linton's narrative, the implementation of disability laws, most importantly the ADA, is imagined as essential to progress in American social life and therefore powerfully counters the view that disability impedes social progress (cf. also Chapter 7). As a consequence, issues of autonomy, physical appearance, perfection, and health are rethought (cf. Linton, *Claiming* 118).

This crucial shift in perspective, as Couser aptly observes, corresponds to the foundations of Disability Studies as an academic discipline and it is thus no coincidence that all of the memoirs he analyzes in the epilogue to his *Signifying Bodies* have been composed by writers actively involved in the field. Nevertheless, he decidedly turns away from the conception of these texts as academic life narratives, arguing that calling them 'disability studies memoirs' would betray their informal tone and lead readers to expect a theoretical treatise of disability (165). In contrast, he purports, "[t]he memoirs may read at times like advocates' or activists' autobiographies, but rarely like academics'" (ibid.). While this distinction registers the tone of these texts, it betrays their writers' voices, since Couser neglects that a number of Disability Studies scholars are as deeply committed to research and teaching as to doing activist work and that the foundations of the discipline rest on the interconnections between intellectual engagement and advocacy.[4] For instance

---

4   Simi Linton is of course a particular case in point, but numerous critics have remarked that work in Disability Studies "is more than theoretical," most importantly because scholars, many of whom are disabled, have directly linked their theoretical research to political actions (Bickenbach 1174). One might for instance consider the late Paul Longmore, a disabled historian who has greatly advanced research on the history of disability but has also acquired fame for publicly burning his first book in front of the L.A. Federal Building in 1988 to protest the restrictive Social Security policy that threatened to cut his financial aid if he were to receive royalties from the book. He later recounts the incident in *Why I Burned My Book, and Other Essays on Disability* (Philadelphia: Temple UP, 2003), a book that in itself intertwines scholarship and advocacy. Similarly, the esteemed sociologist Tom Shakespeare has not only researched Disability Rights but has long been involved in the Disability Rights Movement in the UK and served on the Arts Council England to promote disability arts, while Christopher Bell, a Black Disabili-

the distinction between 'impairment' and 'disability' and a critical examination of disability and society within the scope of the social model has, as Linton outlines in her essay "Disability Studies/Not Disability Studies," "benefitted the development of scholarship on disability, and has benefitted disabled people" (535) and is consequently as much a scholarly as an activist effort. In turn, many theories spurring current debates in the field are generated by disabled individuals who are active in the struggle for civil rights (Shakespeare 139). Couser's disregard for the academic dimension is ultimately too hastily pronounced and Linton's memoir demonstrates how the personal, the political, and the academic may merge.

In this vein, reviewer Cory Silverberg has praised the life narrative as "an excellent crash course" in matters of disability culture, identity, and politics (188), stressing the strong didactic stance inherent in Linton's writing. According to him, the memoir form invites readers to join the writer in contemplating the concept of disability and the ways in which her experiences and inner conflicts may influence its definition and hence contributes substantially to the project of educating and raising consciousness (189). Clearly, the book is targeted not only at disabled, but even to a greater extent at able-bodied readers, since it features many scenes in which Linton carefully describes how her impairment has affected various bodily functions or how she uses New York public transportation in her wheelchair in order to give readers an idea of the qualitative experience of impairment and disability, thus fashioning a space in which able-bodied readers may encounter disability on her terms. Like all first-person accounts, *My Body Politic* transforms the representation of disability from the subjective perspective to present a newly emerging disability consciousness (*Signifying* 164) and – another novel aspect of the 'new disability memoir' – makes the effort to reach out to others in an attempt to raise their consciousness and reinscribe disability with new values and connotations.

---

ty scholar who contracted HIV/AIDS, was active in HIV/AIDS education and issues of race and disability. One of the leading international journals in the field, *Disability Studies Quarterly* (DSQ) of the Society for Disability Studies, publishes submissions by scholars and activists side by side and it is the Society's declared aim to enhance the critical understanding of disability, foster greater awareness, and advocate for social and political changes "[t]hrough research, artistic production, teaching and activism" (n. pag.). Similarly, Disability Studies scholar Mairian Corker characterizes research in her field as "emancipatory" and cites Collin Barnes who maintains that scholarly work on disability "is about the systemic demystification of the structures and processes which create disability, and the establishment of a workable 'dialogue' between the research community and disabled people in order to facilitate the latter's empowerment" (quoted in Corker 628).

Yet I do not share Couser's overgeneralizing observation that the "work" of these memoirs takes place on the plane of content only, for he dismisses their form as "not innovative, much less experimental," without specifying what innovation and experimentation might mean in the established memoir genre (ibid.).[5] The emerging disability consciousness these 'new' stories typically render, particularly through recurring references to disability legislation (cf. Couser, *Signifying* 182f.) also influences the form of a life narrative like Linton's. In *My Body Politic*, the use of adjectival constructions to indicate temporality is conspicuous. Similar to the other memoirs analyzed here, some of these direct the reader's attention to the future and the prospects and uncertainties it may hold as Linton becomes aware of the contingent nature both of her own and other bodies. Yet these are by far outnumbered by instances in which the narrating I turns back to the past.

The function of temporality in her narrative is therefore twofold: First, it aids in illustrating and frequently also celebrating the changes Linton has witnessed throughout the Disability Rights Movement, and, second, in contrast to traditional progress narratives in which disability is overcome, temporality is employed to make clear that Linton gradually adopts a self-conscious perspective on her disability. The narrative begins with the linear and chronological narration of her initial months and years of living with disability and although the chronology is maintained over the course of the entire book, later chapters chronicle Linton's life in

---

5 My reading of Kenny Fries's *The History of My Shoes* in the subsequent chapter of this book will illustrate that 'new disability memoirs' may just as well feature innovative plot lines and structural choices. Consider also comparative and French literature scholar Evelyne Accad's memoir of breast cancer and amputation, *The Wounded Breast: Intimate Journeys through Cancer* (Melbourne: Spinifex, 2001), in which Accad not only mixes her experiences with scientific research and scholarly quotations, but also incorporates her two editors' comments as direct speech in her text. These are at times in accord with her arguments, reinforcing the significance of her words, while at other times raising further questions or expressing disagreement. On the one hand, her narrative provides a meta-textual commentary on the process of writing and publishing a memoir. Beyond that, the writer's inclusion of and engagement with her editors' interjections encourage readers' dialogue with Accad's experience and the scientific evidence she presents, generating an innovative sense of plurality and community in the reading experience. Another fascinating example is poet Jennifer Bartlett's 2014 *Autobiography/Anti-Autobiography* (Palmyra: Theenk Books), a life narrative comprising sections written in brief lines of free verse and passages of narrative prose. Starting from the assumption that the narrative poem is "a symbol of able-bodiedness," Bartlett's exploration of her identity as a woman with cerebral palsy aims to deconstruct "stereotypes of disability not only through content but through form" ("Interview" n. pag.).

more episodic terms, focusing rather on brief moments in which other disabled individuals are introduced or events that initiate the contemplation of broader questions, such as the shortcomings of the special education system or the representation of disability in the arts. These different focal points notwithstanding, these chapters are held together through the recurring motif of temporality.

6.2 FROM CURE TO ACCOMMODATION: INTRODUCING DISABILITY RIGHTS INTO THE PROGRESS NARRATIVE

The car accident in the early 1970s that leaves Linton disabled serves as the trajectory for the memoir, since it emphasizes the numerous obstacles she faced in its aftermath despite her privileged social position. Statements, such as the following, illustrate that this privileged position is highly contingent and she has,

"by the collision of a tinny Volkswagen bus into a cement embankment on Interstate 95 become a marginal citizen, her rights and liberties compromised, and her economic advantage, white skin, and private school education weakened currency in this new world she inhabited." (*Body* 3)

Factors that have previously denoted a stable life in the upper middle-class, such as "economic advantage," "white skin," and her "private school education" cease to provide stability from the moment of the accident. Instead, they are reduced to "weakened currency" and the capitalist diction illustrates the economic consequences of Linton's disability, since she later notes that "[l]ife was bound to be more expensive now" (ibid. 19) and recounts that her mother paid for her new apartment and sent her housekeeper to live with her during the time she still required help in accomplishing the tasks of everyday life (ibid. 22). Moreover, her choice of words in this phrase evinces that her impairment will now make it harder to participate in capitalist society, where neither her financial and educational background, nor her whiteness may continue to secure easy avenues to success.

The causality expressed in this sentence suggests that it is due to the accident, which is shorthand for her resulting impairment, that all of the actual and potential privileges have been erased. This train of thoughts, certainly rooted in the fact that Linton's disability is not congenital, permeates the initial chapters of the memoir and Linton's early years as a disabled woman during which she repeatedly shies away from complaining about a lack of accommodation and accessibility, thinking of her impairment as her own, personal problem. Another significant aspect that this quotation highlights is the fact that, at the time of Linton's accident, disability legislation is still in its infancy and critics, scholars, and advocates have yet to frame disability in other than medical or rehabilitative terms.

Her story, as Silverberg holds, coincides with key moments in disability activism in the United States and is therefore suggestive of the issues that have changed over time, as well as those that have remained problematic (189). In this vein, the memoir devotes little space to the writer's physical improvement and is quite explicit in stressing early on that she is uninterested in having her impairment corrected, fixed, and cured. When her mother hesitantly tells her about a potential cure for spinal cord injury she has learned about in the media, Linton is quick to decline, later reflecting: "I meant what I said, but the telling of it surprised me. It made me realize that I had made a commitment – to live this life the way it was" (*Body* 68). Living as a disabled woman is hence linked to choice, both by means of the active syntax and the verb phrase that expresses Linton's own commitment to using a wheelchair. Beyond that, the noun "commitment" also implies obligation toward others on her part and hence imagines a community whom she would abandon if she were to look for a cure for her condition. Hence "cure" is posited as a solitary achievement in the narrative, while disability is early on associated with community.

Similarly, the communal is highlighted when she reasons that rather than striving to have her body cured and "get [her] legs moving," she wishes to discover "a way out of the tunnel [she has to use to access certain buildings on campus], doing away with tunnels, building accessible campuses and laws to insure them" (ibid.). In contrast to a medical cure, "doing away with tunnels" and ensuring access for all would improve the situation for many people and effect lasting changes in society. The book therefore centers on redemption, yet not brought about by a cure, but by community (Garland-Thomson, "Shape" 118).

Moreover, this scene also highlights the ineffectiveness of cure when Linton maintains: "there is no cure for this condition I have. [...] Not a get-up-out-of-bed, stand, get-dressed, walk-to-the-supermarket kind of cure. Not a Christopher Reeve kind of cure, which he told the public would be right around the corner if we just donated enough money" (*Body* 69). There is no medical improvement, the activities she enumerates illustrate, that will facilitate her everyday life, ensure she can lead an independent life, and enable her to fully participate in the same routines as able-bodied people. Additionally, the repetition of the noun "cure," or rather a "kind of cure," in the negated statements not only points to the inadequacy of potential medical improvements, but finally also reveals that such forms of corrections are not what Linton strives for. So instead of focusing on the question of overcoming impairment and fixing the paraplegic body, the life narrative revolves around the social aspects of disability to highlight the political and legislative achievements from the 1970s onwards, often referring directly to the enactment of disability laws.

In his essay "Undoing Hardships: Life Writing and Disability Law" Couser analyzes the connection between legislation and the disability memoir, envisioning three possible relationships between first-person narratives about disability and legal repercussions. According to him, the first constitutes an "anticipatory relation" because these narratives serve as testimonies in which narrators complain about the injustices they face on account of their disabilities and hence exemplify the lack of jurisdiction and call for disability laws (73). He describes these stories as having a proleptic relation to legislative acts, prescribing laws that have not gone into effect yet and attempting to advance the conception of disability in society, since discrimination, exclusion or oppression may only be barred when they are recognized (ibid.). Whereas these narratives demand laws, the second set of personal narratives Couser identifies may be read as calling for amendments of the laws that have already come into effect (ibid. 75). These either confirm or disconfirm disability legislation, often denouncing violations of the laws and turning their narrators into legal plaintiffs, often before courts, who carefully craft their narratives in accordance to legal terminology (ibid. 74). In both cases, Couser surveys short and oral accounts, contending that particularly in the second category of life narratives, readers will find the case stories of individuals seeking justice in the courtroom, stories that may become precedents for future legislation (ibid. 75).

With regard to written, book-length memoirs that address disability legislation he argues that they are far and few between and commonly narrate the writers' lives as having been shaped by disability laws (ibid. 79). While Couser is right in maintaining that only a scant number of narratives focus exclusively on their authors' experiences in connection with the legislation that has greatly impacted many areas of their lives and that particularly younger writers tend to take these laws for granted because they have not witnessed the time before the Disability Rights Movement, I do not share his opinion that such narratives often leave it up to their readers to infer a connection between the story and disability legislation (ibid.). Quite to the contrary, the presence of a not so distant past is revealing in many narratives: Even though their stories may appear to be entirely removed from legal contexts, many memoirists explicitly recall growing up and coming-of-age before the Disability Rights Movement and retell their parents' efforts of enrolling them into "regular" or inclusive schools. In addition, a large number of writers problematize the question of quality of life, inevitably shifting the discussion to legislation pertaining to the "right to die," as well as to questions of abortion and the social implications of prenatal diagnosis. Finally, numerous stories broach disability history in the horrific context of eugenic programs. To date, disability laws have had such a crucial and lasting impact on the lives of disabled people, precisely because, as mentioned above, it has considerably contributed to a revision of earlier concepts of disability and exclusion so that it appears impossible to not moot legal issues and repercussions at least marginally in 'new' disability life narratives. The writers' lives have benefitted from disability legislation and in some cases laws have shaped the courses of their lives, which is why Couser classifies these narratives as bearing an "existential relation" to the law (ibid. 79).[6]

Ultimately, these stories take up a retrospective perspective (cf. ibid.) and Linton's narrating I, too, writes looking back on events that have taken place earlier while assessing them from the perspective of the advocate the experiencing I has yet to become. Adverbial phrases, such as "not yet" or "over the coming years" are therefore recurring markers of the temporality in the life narrative that intertwines past, present, and future. On the one hand, this temporality serves foreshadowing from the initial pages of the memoir. When Linton gets into a fight with the staff psychologist at the rehab facility a few months after her accident over an IQ test he administered, she remarks that the outrage she voiced then was similar to "the kind of opinion-rendering [she] would one day get paid for" (*Body* 9), pointing to her future work as an activist. Through explicit links to the future, such as the one quoted here, the narrating I effectively influences the perception of the experiencing I's present time, stressing first of all that there is the prospect of action and a strong voice ahead of her, which powerfully unhinges the narrative of disability as passivity and bleakness. Foreshadowing thus becomes an effective narrative strategy to not only foster a sense of well-being in the experiencing I, but to also affirm its possibility for others and hence significantly influences readers' perception of the expe-

---

[6] In *Miracle Boy Grows Up: How the Disability Rights Revolution Saved My Sanity* (New York: Skyhorse, 2012), former poster child Ben Mattlin makes this existential connection explicit not only through the title of this memoir, but also by introducing his story as one that "tracks a surge of unprecedented advances in medicine, technology, and civil rights that people with disabilities have enjoyed and harnessed. Indeed, the synchronicity between that movement and my own is surely more than coincidental" (xi). In this regard, readers may find it interesting to consult the collection of literary first-person narratives in *Voices from the Edge: Narratives about the Americans with Disabilities Act* edited by political scientist Ruth O'Brien (Oxford: Oxford UP, 2004). Grouped according to the individual sections of the ADA, the autobiographical stories featured in the book demonstrate the significance of disability legislation in the lives of disabled individuals, even though the law is oftentimes only alluded to or referenced implicitly. An explicit contextualization within the framework of the ADA is only provided after each set of stories in an analysis and commentary section (cf. O'Brien 5). Moreover, the 2005 memoir *Too Late to Die Young: Nearly True Tales from a Life* by attorney and Disability Rights activist Harriet McBryde Johnson reflects on the significance of the Americans with Disabilities Act for plaintiffs in the courtroom, as well as other disabled friends and fellow activists and offers a compelling discussion of the right to die legislation and philosopher Peter Singer's call to abort disabled fetuses (New York: Picador).

riencing I. Beyond that, foreshadowing also contributes to continuity in her narrative and Linton's self-portrayal, for it illustrates that while disability does impact her belief system, it does not transform her into a different person.

Similarly, the turn to the past, i.e. the time before her accident as well as its circumstances, works to strengthen the sense of coherence and continuity in both the memoir and Linton's self-presentation as an activist and advocate for social justice, since the narrative repeatedly links Linton's involvement in the Disability Rights Movement to her earlier participation in anti-war demonstrations.[7] Most important with regard to this, the context of war frames the story and the thirty-five years it spans and connects Linton's accident to the anti-war demonstrations in Washington before ending in 2005 with a reflection on the wounded and disabled veterans returning from Iraq. Although the importance of the context of the accident is not lost on critics because none of the reviewers and scholars discussing the memoir fails to include a reference to the event in passing, it has hardly received critical attention so far, despite the fact that it has significant functions for the narrative. The thematic frame of U.S. military operations and soldiers returning from their missions with severe long-term injuries, amputated limbs, and psychological traumas render the discourse on disability an urgent social and political matter. In this vein, disability ceases to be merely an individual's condition and singular life story, but enters the public arena, touching the lives of many Americans, becoming increasingly visible, and insisting on legislation and accommodation.

Secondly, while the accident that leaves her disabled undoubtedly constitutes a harsh and dramatic break in Linton's life and momentarily seems to mark the end of her hippie life-style, the narrating I, now turning to the past with the eyes of a Disability Rights advocate, uses the accident to engender a sense of continuity in the life so radically altered by disability. Indeed, readers are introduced to a self who has always voiced her opinions and spoken on behalf of others and will continue to do so throughout the course of her story and through the publication of her book. This

---

7 In many ways, Linton may be seen as a typical member of the generation of baby boomers, who, being born shortly after WWII, have come of age in the mist of social and political turmoil and have been deeply committed to effecting change during the civil rights movements. A self-proclaimed member of the counterculture, she repeatedly references drug use, pot (*Body* 47, 197), "tripping on LSD" (6), rock-n-roll, Bruce Springsteen, and Jimi Hendrix (in the chapter "I Sing My Body Electric," Linton recalls how she, the "young nondisabled hippie chick," snuck into "Jimi's dressing room" at a concert in 1970 and was awarded a kiss on the right cheek [ibid. 103f.]). Additionally, at the beginning of her memoir, she posits an experiencing I who has dropped out of college to organize against the draft and the Vietnam War.

thematic frame presents Linton as a witness and conscious observer of these historical events and firmly roots her life narrative in American society and politics.

In retrospect, her transition from the anti-war movement to demanding her rights as a disabled woman is seamless, for Linton notes that while she is "on leave" from the demonstrations and has "left the skewering of the big guys at the Pentagon to others," she notices another form of systemic injustice around her when looking at the medical professionals in the rehab facility, "the mischief in their brand of power-wielding and the hierarchies they impose on others" (*Body* 15). Consequently, Linton begins what Roulstone calls a "low key rebellion" (741): "Even in the forest of overseers, where every move I made was scheduled and every quantity of liquid I drank and eliminated was measured, I had opinions. I was cowed by the outside world, the walking world, but here inside I had a role and a point of view" (*Body* 15). The power hierarchy Linton sketches in which she is subjected to the staff's rigid control (she calls them "overseers" which hints at their perceived ruthlessness and their lack of rapport) whose supervision neither allows her agency nor privacy, is broken by the short revelation that she "had opinions," even if they initially only implicated agreeing or disagreeing in basic matters. – It is not yet a form of rebellion that may hold in the "walking world," but within the walls of the rehabilitation center it does, and Linton is able to transform herself into a subject with opinions of significance to others, especially when it comes to her efforts to implement sex education in their rehabilitation courses (cf. ibid. 12ff.). Therefore Roulstone is right when he notes that the time in rehab is the "seedling" for her later active participation in the movement (741).

Initially, she does not see these parallels, distinguishing between the anti-war protests and the call for accommodation on grounds that while former are based on systemic injustices, inequality, and false representations, the latter pertains "just facts of life, random incidents, not governed by any principle" (*Body* 27). Over the course of the narrative, however, Linton's acceptance of the lack of accommodation is rewritten, beginning with her summer in Berkeley in the mid-1970s when she becomes frustrated over the fact that her apartment is "designed for walking people" and anticipates that "in the course of the summer [she] would grow increasingly impatient with the effort it took to squeeze [herself] into their world" (ibid. 41). Her assertion voices a strong sense of discontentment and discomfort illustrated by her growing impatience and the imagery invoked by the verb "squeeze" which evinces that like the narrow doorways, maladjusted counters, and tiny rooms in her rented apartment the world of the able-bodied constrains and confines her and will only house her if she makes the effort to fit in. More than that, for the first time, Linton's memoir separates her from the able-bodied population through the use of the first-person singular in opposition to the third-person plural, indicating that she is no longer willing to mask her difference.

It is also here that a tentative active stance develops when Linton notes that "[a]s time went on, I wondered, might I play a part in reconfiguring the world to let me in?" (ibid.). For the first time, the issue of disability activism is raised, though only tentatively here, because the question she poses is not yet a question of how she might change her environs but the question of whether she "might," and the use of the conjunctive adds to the tentativeness of the quote. Nevertheless, there is momentousness in her question, expressed through the verb phrase "reconfiguring the world" that points to the magnitude of the project ahead of her and is aimed at challenging both visible and invisible forms of discrimination. Although she experiences Berkeley as a place by far more accessible and inclusive than New York City,[8] "over the course of the summer," she learns that public transportation there is by and large inaccessible and that other accommodations, too, are limited and restricted to certain areas of the city, though noting that "it would take [her] a while longer to learn how entrenched the patterns of discrimination are" and realizing, as she "would come to learn more precisely in the coming years, that each of the changes that had been made had taken enormous effort, and involved struggle and demonstrations and time in jail" (ibid. 54). In pointing to the future and the years it will take her to fully understand and act on the discrimination she encounters, Linton stresses the long duration of the struggle for disabled people's rights. The climactic structure of "struggle and demonstrations and time in jail" in which arrests receive particular emphasis highlights the opposition the disability community has faced over the years in their attempts to ensure their civil rights.

Linton's narration, however, does not lapse into moralizing lamentations. Within the story, she does not appear as a plaintiff, but rather as an educator who illustrates what ensuing legislation has made possible and how it has impacted her life and her perception of disability. Due to the scope of this chapter, I will limit my analyses in this subchapter to passages from one chapter of the memoir, the chapter ambiguously titled "A Special Education" which relates Linton's studies at Columbia University, since it is representative for other moments in the life narrative in which disability legislation is explicitly referred to and interlaced with com-

---

8 The contrast between the two cities described in two consecutive chapters highlights, as Torrell claims, the contrast between Linton's gradual alignment with the disability community on the West coast and her isolation in New York City where a disability community has not yet visibly surfaced (328). In turn, the two chapters also emphasize the impact of Disability Rights activism on the perception and definition of disability and Rachel Adams pointedly remarks that "[t]o ask that a class be moved, sidewalks equipped with curb cuts, or bathroom stalls expanded seemed embarrassingly narcissistic" ("All" n. pag.).

ments about both the past and the future.⁹ As she has difficulties navigating between classes in her wheelchair, she begins complaining to her advisors and the Dean, who eventually asks her to join the committee that was then "looking into what he called 'these matters'" (ibid. 50). The Dean's utterance quoted verbatim signifies the school's detachment from questions of access in his inability and unwillingness to name it and accordingly reflects an only half-hearted effort to make the campus more accessible. Looking back, the narrating I underscores the committee's unsuccessful work by contextualizing it as the forced reaction to the introduction to

"the Rehabilitation Act, Section 504, that went into effect in 1973 requiring colleges that receive any kind of federal money to make their programs and facilities accessible to students with disabilities. These laws were largely ignored until the '90s when the more rigorous provisions of the Americans with Disabilities Act (ADA) went into effect, requiring not only access, but reasonable accommodation to students and employers." (ibid. 59f.)

Linton assumes a didactic stance, offering a piece of disability history by outlining the basic statute of Section 504 and explaining the ineffectiveness of the committee by referring to the lax legal hold early jurisdiction provided. Here, too, the long duration of the struggle becomes obvious because Linton notes that from 1973 on, another twenty years would pass until more comprehensive change was effected. Additionally, her choice of words highlights society's reluctance to follow legal provisions, since Section 504 was "largely ignored" and only "the more rigorous" jurisdiction of the ADA eventually proved more successful.

Thus the committee, though understanding of Linton's difficulties, is of little help: The statutes of the Rehabilitation Act are not fully implemented on campus but the committee tells Linton that like "those few disabled people who had over the years 'made' it at Columbia," she "would make it too, because they know [she]

---

9   In a similar vein, the subsequent chapter "Going Away" about Linton's trip to France that appears to be already spoiled at the check-in counter when the ticket agent refuses to address her directly but only talks about her in third person to the friend who accompanied her to the airport to say goodbye comments on the progress made with regard to the attitudes towards disabled people, for Linton notes that "had this trip occurred in 1997 rather than 1977, she would have received the systematic training that most airline employees now receive, teaching them to directly address disabled people if they are the customers" (*Body* 72). In "Pleasures and Freedoms," the narrating I retrospectively links the famous dictum "nothing about us without us" to her and her friend Glenn's efforts to mobilize other disabled people who might help lead their initiative that later developed into the National Coalition on Sexuality and Disability (ibid. 81, 84).

would persevere even in the face of these obstacles" (ibid. 60). The committee thus portrays the inaccessibility of the campus buildings as a rite of passage and "making it" at the school as a disabled student is ironically not based on academic merit but becomes a matter of enduring hardship.

In this chapter, Linton also makes explicit that her relation to disability legislation is indeed "existential," to return to Couser's concept of disability law and life writing ("Undoing" 79). "What I didn't understand at the time was that there was a filtration system that allowed so few of us to breathe in this rarified atmosphere," Linton takes note of her privileged education at Columbia looking back on the mid-1970s (*Body* 61): "I was at Columbia from 1975 to 1977. Public Law 94-142 was passed in 1975, the legislation that mandates free and appropriate education for all children" (ibid.). Her juxtaposition of the two events taking place around the same year is meaningful, since while Linton began her undergraduate studies in 1975, it was only then that disabled children were legally granted access to and inclusion in the general education system.[10] In other words, had her disability been congenital, it is highly unlikely that she would have been able to pursue the same education, and the narrative doubles back on its ambiguous chapter title "A Special Education."[11]

---

10 Similar passages can be found in Mattlin's memoir, whose chapters titles are supplemented with the respective time period. Steven Kuusisto's *Planet of the Blind*, too, uses temporality in similar ways and also refers to mainstreamed education, for instance when the narrating I outlines the problems he and his family face upon returning to the U.S. after his father's sabbatical in Scandinavia: "Back in the States, my mother must fight with the local district to gain my admission into an ordinary first-grade classroom. I am a legally blind child, and it is the era of Kennedy. It will be another thirty years before people with disabilities are guaranteed their civil rights in the United States" (12). Like Linton's memoir, his life narrative intertwines legal progress and especially the improvement of adaptive technology and "becoming" disabled through the extensive use of temporal markers. While he is in college, a blind mentor urges him to stop trying to read the assigned books with his face pressed against the page – attempting to pass as an able-bodied student – and instead use a computer that scans the page and reads it. Marveling at the technology, Kuusisto notes: "It's 1980, and I've never heard of computers being used for anything other than missile tracking at the Pentagon or snooping at the IRS" (ibid. 110). Although "[a]nother decade will pass before this machine can read Eliot, and it will be another decade before [he] unfolds the white cane" (ibid. 113), he begins using the computer regularly.

11 The mainstreamed college education she receives at Columbia, the life narrative demonstrates, has a crucial impact on the course of Linton's life, because it is during a psychology class in the Women's Studies program at Barnard that she begins questioning her "automatic connection of the word 'problem' with women's issues" and in a similar vein

Moreover, the "special education" she receives at Columbia is also significant in a third way, since it is here that she experiences social discrimination to a much greater extent than before and begins to act on it. While her body and story are removed from the medical setting and its individualizing perspective on disability early in the narrative once Linton leaves the rehab facility that has arguably prepared her for an independent life, it is with a growing political awareness that her story ceases to be hers alone.

The memoir hence shares with Audre Lorde's *The Cancer Journals* a strong sense of community that becomes evident in the writer's linguistic move from the first person singular – initially often even uttered in opposition to the othering "they" – to the first person plural, as well as in the decidedly political stance of the narrative and the resulting identity politics, a lengthy process that not only requires time, but also a significant change in perspective, as I will show in the following. In Chapter 4 I have shown that Lorde's strong political consciousness is heavily influenced by her marginalized position as a Black lesbian woman whose body and ordeal do not conform to the markedly white and heterosexual breast cancer experience. Though initially located in the center of society through her white skin color, the stable economic background of her family and the college education she has briefly pursued, Linton finds herself in a marginal position after her accident and is made aware of her status as a member of a minority group whose accommodation is not seldom denied. Despite the fact that she might readily be identified as a member of the remission society, she needs to claim her status as a citizen with equal rights.

It is in this sense that temporality in the narrative also serves a second function, namely to illustrate Linton's gradual identification with other disabled individuals and the formation of her own identity as a disabled person. In contrast to narratives of overcoming disability, the book chronicles her process of *becoming* a disabled woman, for she notes that "the paralysis in my leg was instant. Becoming disabled took much longer" (*Body* 3). The two separate sentences elucidate that the acquisition of impairment and the fashioning of a disability identity do not go hand in hand; adopting the perspective of a disabled woman is a lengthy process, juxtaposed to the instantaneousness of the accident through the parallel syntax and acknowledged repeatedly throughout the memoir:

"For it wasn't some time after I sustained the injury to my spine that immobilized my legs, after I learned to use a wheelchair, and after I had reckoned with myself and the world for a while in this new state – it wasn't until then that I gained the vantage point of the atypical, the out-of-step, the underfooted." (ibid.)

---

realizes that "'disability' might not be a 'problem' in the way that most people view it" (63).

6.3 BECOMING DISABLED: COMMUNITY, SEXUALITY, AND THE "BODY POLITIC"

Since Linton begins her book with the car accident and even in the flashbacks withholds most of her life before the accident, Couser observes that the memoir shies away from expressing nostalgia for her able body (*Signifying* 186). Indeed, several passages in the text support such a reading.[12] However, when reflecting on the further implications of the memoir's beginning, Couser's analysis is troublesome, because he asserts that in contrast to the conventional bildungsroman, this "structure replaces [Linton's] birth and development as a unique *individual* with her birth and development as a *disabled* person" (ibid.; italics in original). While it is absolutely sensible to point to this structural difference as it is certainly in line with the project of Linton's memoir, the phrasing is deeply problematic here because it establishes an opposition between "unique *individual*" and "*disabled* person" that is not only incoherent with the life narrative itself but also reflects the ableist and essentialist assumption that a person is defined by their disability and their other, unique characteristics are consequently overlooked.

Similar to other 'new disability memoirs,' *My Body Politic* tells the story of her disability on Linton's own terms (*Signifying* 178). Although the accident commences the narration, the book does not obey the script of the conventional disability memoir that narrativizes impairment and thus anticipates readers' questions of "what happened to you?" Instead, the beginning of the narrative offers merely the bare facts of the car crash and her friend's and husband's deaths. The temporal distance of more than thirty years, as well as Linton's own critical condition and, in

---

12 It is the loss of John and Carol that dominates the first few pages of the book and the word "lost" is repeated numerous times as Linton attempts to see their deaths from different angles. From her own perspective, she writes: "I lost my husband [...]. And I lost Carol [...]," mourning their deaths (*Body* 2). The parallel structure of the sentences introducing them and the fact that she devotes about the same amount of space on the page to stress the extraordinary personalities of both her husband and her friend illustrate that she holds them equally dear. Subsequently, she expands the view to think about Rick, Carol's partner, and, moving from the first person singular into the plural, holds: "Carol and John were lost to us," thereby creating a bond between her and Rick. Rick and Linton are indeed for a period of time united in their mourning and loss as they enter a relationship once Linton leaves the rehab facility and moves to New York City. Their romantic involvement which may be, in Katherine Wallis's words, seen as "oddly incestuous" (42) is of utter significance for Linton because it is with Rick that she begins to feel more at ease with her altered body and has sexual intercourse for the first time. Rick therefore assumes a significance role in her healing process.

consequence, the impossibility of memories, is implicated in the narrating I's account and in her conclusion when she states "I never saw him. Or, if I did, I don't remember. I've blotted it all out" (*Body* 2). Through short, isolated sentences she makes clear that composing a coherent narrative from the fragments of the day is not possible, but more than that, it is also not what Linton wishes to do for her readers, which becomes evident when she lists "[t]he crash, the ambulance, the airlift in the helicopter, and the emergency room" as possible sites from which to recall memories, but determines that they "are locked up somewhere, I hope never to be found" (ibid.). Her hope to never be able to recall all the particulars of the accident is at once also a determinate statement to the reader to seek no more details and in this respect the brevity and absoluteness of the utterances about Carol's and John's death also have a clearly alienating effect and permit no further questioning.

Beyond that, Linton does not resort to medical terminology to refer to any aspects of her condition, neither in her account of the accident nor in the narration of her ensuing hospitalization and the months spent in rehabilitation. She withholds any detailed medical information and instead merely characterizes the injury she sustained as one "that immobilized [her] legs" (ibid. 3). In doing so, she remains in control over the discourse on her body, in contrast to surrendering herself to the objectifying language of medicine (cf. Chapter 3.2). Early on in the narrative it is hence manifested that Linton strives to distance her body and herself from the binary thought inherent in the medical establishment and does not view her impaired body as a lasting pathology. The core of her narrative is accordingly not constituted by her individual, medical problem, but at its center are "the life [she] grew into," her body's "new shape and formation," and the meanings this body would take on over the years following the accident until the time of writing (ibid.).

To this effect, *My Body Politic* exhibits two narrative strands that, according to Garland-Thomson, are commonly rendered silent and invisible in stories about disability, namely sexuality and community ("Shape" 114). This is due to the fact that in our culture, disabled people are rarely perceived as sexual subjects, as I will explore in more detail below, and disability is generally regarded as an individual experience that isolates people from one another (ibid. 115). However, precisely these two aspects, the erotic and the bonds created within a sustaining community, are what she refers to as "principal fonts of exuberant human flourishing" (ibid.), and are central elements to an individual's sense of well-being. Consequently, Garland-Thomson argues, if these are introduced into the plot of a disability narrative, a new story is created (ibid.). Such a new story challenges stereotypes and preconceptions about disability and the disabled body on part of the reader and, with respect to Linton's memoir, also on part of the writer herself. On the most fundamental level, a life narrative like Linton's may thus be read as a response to the ways in which disabled individuals have traditionally been misrepresented (Couser, "Disability, Life Narrative" 604).[13]

Yet grasping disability life writing in terms of deconstruction cannot exhaust the full potential of Linton's text because her memoir is invested in more than responding to or writing back at dominant discourses on disability, in part because her book assumes such a decidedly didactic stance, as illustrated above. Assigning significance to issues of sexuality and community is therefore also a constructive endeavor, serving to create – and this is implicated in Garland-Thomson's idea of a "new story" – a definition of disability in which well-being is not counterintuitive. The community with other disabled individuals and the power of the erotic are ultimately not presented as mere antidotes to individualizing and objectifying conditions, but it is precisely through community and sexuality that a new definition of disability may emerge in which well-being is self-evident.

Especially the issue of community has thus far been neglected in autobiographical narratives. Torrell problematizes the memoirist's singular voice in the context of disability life narratives, an issue Mitchell also discusses at length in his essay "Body Solitaire: The Singular Subject of Disability Autobiography" in which he laments the fact that many writers comply with autobiography's call for "rugged individualism" narrating rather a personal story than their community with others and ultimately consolidating the link between disability and isolation and inadvertently reinforcing the notions of the medical model that disability issues are personal but do not relate to society at large (Mitchell 312; Torrell 321; cf. Chapter 2.3). Nevertheless, Torrell argues that the singular voice of the memoirist may fashion a community by telling her story alongside the stories of other disabled individuals. Their stories, however, have long been only incompletely acknowledged because they have been treated as aides to the memoirist's identity construction and their reading has therefore been limited to what they add to the narrator's sense of self, which is why Torrell urges scholars to shift the focus to the stories included in the life narrative in order to more fully recognize the sense of community very well inherent in these texts (321f.). This in turn, she argues, revises the notion of disability as an isolating experience because the stories of other disabled people produce an image of disability as comprised of manifold experiences by a heterogeneous group comprised of people of different ethnic backgrounds and genders, with a range of disabilities and different sexual orientations. Consequently, disability narrated in such a way becomes a political and social issue when the singular voice of the memoirist is aligned with that of a host of other people who substantiate or elaborate her experiences (ibid. 322). The story told in the memoir is then not the story of a single life,

---

13 In his essay "Disability, Life Narrative, and Representation" Couser offers a cursory outline of these issues.

a "body solitaire," but "the story of disabled lives" which pictures the disability community as an empowered group (ibid., ibid. 327).[14]

It is in New York City in the rehabilitation institution that Linton first engages with other disabled people and the six months she spends there are portrayed as the first instance in which she and other disabled individuals forge a sense community, even though it is a community born out of necessity rather than choice and conviction. On her first day she is greeted by a group of young men and women in wheelchairs who enter her room joking and laughing in order to welcome her. For Torrell, the group radiates happiness (329) and even though Linton is conscious that some of the group's exuberance may only be a show for her benefit, it is already then that she voices the wish "to be like them" (*Body* 5). The group embodies what has thus far been unimaginable for Linton, namely movement, rapport and, at least on first sight, also the ease with which the young adults move in their bodies.

Nevertheless, she cannot yet fully identify with them, too great is both her helplessness in the new situation and her memory of her identity before the accident, as a flashback cutting into the first encounter with the group shows:

"Had it been just weeks before that I had been splayed out on my living room floor in Cambridge, tripping on LSD, entranced by the oily purple globules rising and falling in my lava lamp?

And had it been just a couple of years before that when I stood tall on the roof of my apartment building in the East Village, with the New York City skyline rising up behind me? Dressed in John's black V-neck sweater and a pair of tattered jeans, I was having my picture taken for an underground newspaper, the *East Village Other*. I would be the centerfold for the

---

14 Similarly, Nancy Mairs' memoir of multiple sclerosis, *Waist-High in the World: A Life among the Nondisabled* (1996), contrary to its title, constructs a vivid disability community. The book is divided into two sections – "Home Truths" and "The Wider World" – which feature short chapters on private issues in Mair's life and on larger social issues respectively. The sense of community, however, permeates both sections: Mairs begins her memoir by recalling the phone call from a young woman suspecting she may have MS and an early chapter in the first section ("Plunging In") is devoted to participants of the water-exercise class of the Multiple Sclerosis Society Mairs describes as "one of the high points of [her] week" since she "no longer avoid[s] others with disabilities" (15). The later chapter "Young and Disabled" recounts her work for *Glamour* magazine when she is asked to compile the voices of hundreds of young women who responded to the magazine's prompt to write about their disabilities, friendships, and love lives. Reproducing some of their letters, Mairs not only expresses deep admiration, but also creates a diverse community of disabled women (127ff.).

next issue, with a bold caption over my head: SLUM GODDESS." (*Body* 6; capitalization in original)

These two memories, while each confirming Linton as a self-styled outsider to society and conformist ways of life, also focus on her able body as the epitome of her hippie identity. In the first episode, a scene is sketched in which Linton lies "splayed out" on the floor to produce a stereotypical image of psychedelic drug use in the early 1970s, while the second episode likewise characterizes her as deeply immersed in the counterculture, even serving as its icon when her photograph is taken for the newspaper that entitles her the "SLUM GODDESS." The caption merges the horrific and other with strength and beauty to fashion an alternative notion of what Linton terms the "ethereal" (ibid.) and connects her outsider position to her body.

"[S]tanding tall" on the New York City rooftop against the backdrop of the city's skyline, this body signifies ability, freedom, and defiance and literally stands in harsh contrast to the body Linton finds herself inhabiting now, the "slight, horizontal body draped in a loose white hospital gown" (ibid.). Several opposites are at work in this passage to elucidate that Linton's body and identity before and after the accident are entirely incompatible: her pre-accident body is rendered as "standing," while her new body is "horizontal," and in a similar vein, it is no longer the "tall" and forceful body of a goddess, but the "slight" shape of a patient. Likewise, her black clothes have been substituted by the white institutional garb that "opened in the back so if a doctor or nurse approached my bed, I would be available for their examinations and ministrations" (ibid.). Particularly the patient gown relinquishes Linton's freedom and defiance, subjecting her to the constraints of the medical institution and indubitably replacing her self-fashioned identity with that of the patient.

Tellingly, the rooftop again becomes a place of relative freedom from the institutional constraints as the group begins to regularly gather there to drink, smoke, and exchange thoughts and ideas. The rooftop becomes a crucial setting in the first chapter of the memoir because it is here, aloof from the "antiseptic" halls of the rehab facility (ibid. 6), that the group discusses their bodies and sexualities and where "furtive fondling with girlfriends and boyfriends" takes place (ibid. 11f.). This passage is significant for two reasons, first of all because it outlines sexuality as the single one issue that ties the otherwise diverse group of young women and men together. The group Linton portrays on the rooftop transcends the lines of gender, family background, political convictions, and class consisting of

"a college student who smacked up his sports car on spring break, a country boy thrown from his horse, a construction worker who toppled off a high rigging, a young woman who fell off the back of a motorcycle, and me, a college dropout, a young widow, kind of drifting, kind of working, kind of OK, sideswiped on her way to an anti-war demonstration." (ibid. 11)

Moreover, she notes that on the rooftop of the facility, "scotch drinkers" and "pot smokers," previously "divided along party lines," are united, tolerant of each other since "there was only one party" (ibid.). Playing on the homonymous political "party" and their nightly gatherings, she establishes that the group members' previous lives and convictions have become unhinged as their impaired bodies and their consequences now form their common ground.

Secondly, the passage demonstrates the contested nature of disabled sexuality that may only be addressed, and in fact, as Katherine Wallis argues, reclaimed (41), outside the halls of the facility and the group's open discussion of disability and sexuality and their exchange of information and knowledge challenges the power of the medical, respectively rehabilitation system. The rooftop becomes the site of intimate relations as the virtual strangers share their experiences with masturbation and their bodies' responses to sexual stimulation. The group serves as an interpersonal space in which the lived experience of sexuality is validated and from which Linton derives her authority to voice her own sexuality, since Torrell argues that if Linton were to speak from her own subject position only, she might not have been able to link disability and sexuality in such a positive and liberating manner in her memoir (330). The chorus of the voices of other disabled individuals is therefore necessary to facilitate abled-bodied readers' understanding of the writer's yearning for pleasure. Yet the fact that the group's discussions may only take place outside the rehab institution bespeaks a much greater problem, namely that sexuality is silenced in the medical and rehabilitational setting.

That sexuality is indeed not only in harsh opposition to established discourses on disability but at the same time also utterly powerful is demonstrated when Linton recalls finding great strength in the moment her brother candidly asks her whether she "'[b]een doin' them horizontal exercises'" at the rehab center (*Body* 14). His outspokenness and humorous approach to her body and sexuality is what she remembers as "the sweetest memory" of her time in the rehabilitation program (ibid.) because it reverberates the message to "[g]o ahead, enjoy your life" (ibid.). Ultimately, her brother's question is an invitation to well-being, more precisely a form of well-being to which sexuality is integral. Time and again, Linton therefore returns to sexuality, because it helps to rewrite the dichotomous dis/ability by "challeng[ing] accepted ideals of sexual prowess" (ibid. 82) and to simultaneously shift the focus to embodiment: "What was clear and uniform across the group was that we had strong desire. We felt lust in our hearts, and our bodies tingled and stretched out toward sex, toward pleasure" (ibid. 11f.). In her assertion, Linton foregrounds the sensations felt in and through the body, such as tingling, and, more than that, attributes attention to the movement the body can perform. Not only does the "stretched out" body occupy more space, but it is also an active body reaching for the pleasure she desires and the posture as such of course attributes sensual and erotic qualities to the disabled body. For Linton and the entire group, sexuality therefore becomes an affirmative notion.

The third chapter of the memoir recounts Linton's experience in Berkeley, California in the summer of 1975. Berkeley, both the campus and the city, have played a highly significant and pioneering role in the Disability Rights Movement, oral historian Susan O'Hara reports. In the 1960s, a number of disabled students, all of whom were wheelchair users, began to live independently on the UC Berkeley campus, therefore "profoundly chang[ing] the rules of living with a disability" and defying the institutionalization of disabled people (n. pag.). Their struggle for an independent life rested on the premise that "people with even the most severe disabilities should have the choice of living in the community" ("Disability Rights" n. pag.). First of all, this could be achieved through the creation of personal assistance services which enabled people with disabilities to manage their own care at home, work or attend school, and participate in community life. Secondly, architectural barriers needed to be removed to grant disabled people full access to all aspects of communal life (ibid.). In fact, as early as 1958, the first architectural changes, such as ramps and curbs cuts were made to improve the accessibility of the Berkeley campus ("History" n. pag.). In the early 1970s, the disabled students then also moved out from campus into the Berkeley community and founded several organizations and institutions run by and for people with disabilities, among them most notably the Center for Independent Living (O'Hara n. pag.).

A number of disabled memoirists mention Berkeley's involvement in the Disability Rights Movement in their books and many of them recall moving or spending time there and coming into contact with the disability community. Linton is no exception and this chapter in her book is revealingly titled "Coming Out in the West" to signify how profoundly her identity and self-conception change during the summer in Berkeley. On these grounds, *My Body Politic*, along with numerous other 'new' disability memoirs, has been read as a coming-out-narrative in which writers chronologically trace their process of openly claiming their disability. In her comparative reading of Linton's memoir and Mary Felstiner's life narrative *Out of Joint* in "Disability Memoirs in the Academic World" Baena, for instance, reads these texts as coming-out-narratives in which the subjects reassemble fragments of their story in a continuous narrative after a turning point has given new meaning to their lives (134f.). However, it is necessary to demarcate several key moments that gradually influence Linton's identity, such as her time in Berkeley and the yoghurt "affair" analyzed in detail below or her introduction to wheelchair dancing, the topic of the final section in the chapter. The narrative does not suggest that there is a single radical turning point and, in sharp contrast, the temporality employed throughout the book underlines the slow gradual process of becoming disabled.

Nevertheless, there are certain parallels between 'new' disability life narratives and the coming-out-memoirs that have their origins in the 1960s, when early texts aimed at making formerly invisible queer subjects visible (Smith and Watson 152). Often, Smith and Watson expound, these stories relate the narrators' solitary attempts to pass in a heteronormative society, a sexual awakening and transformation of the self, and eventually the liberation of disclosing and finding validation in their sexual identities. Contemporary coming-out-narratives, on the other hand, go beyond these issues to depict aspects of community, committed relationships or family lives to protest marginalizing and stigmatizing perspectives and to challenge the discourse on queerness (ibid. 152f.). This is a parallel that the two subgenres, disability and queer memoirs, share in their development, one that is inarguably due to their subjects' initially marginalized position and the stigma and sense of pathology that has previously been attached to their identities and that is now being overwritten with stories of a positive identity construction and narratives that position both groups as full-fledged members of society.

In the following, I will therefore turn to the issue of passing, or more precisely, Linton's decision to no longer attempt to pass in the able-bodied world. Her "coming-out" is then marked by her decision to choose to refer to herself as a "disabled woman," become active in the struggle for disability rights, and use her disability in the classroom (cf. e.g. *Body* 118). In becoming visible and demanding inclusion, she seeks to reform the understanding of disability, so that when reading the memoir as a coming-out-narrative, it is crucial to look beyond the most obvious characteristics of the subgenre and pay particular attention to the last aspect Smith and Watson outline, namely the destigmatization of the disabled body. As the remainder of this chapter will show, this is achieved through a narrative that is not only didactic and strongly political, but that also highlights embodiment.

Originally planning on moving to the West coast to study and, most of all, finally immerse herself in the community of hippies again, "'recapturing the '60s'" and hoping to be welcomed into their circle and recognized as one of them despite her wheelchair (ibid. 38), Linton soon learns that the university town is a veritable hotbed of disability rights activism, where disability is much more visible and the term 'crip' is gaining currency. Her "coming out" then denotes her first hesitant attempts at embracing her disability and identity as a disabled woman in contrast to her earlier eagerness to 'pass' and thus signals the emergence of her political consciousness as she gradually understands how her disability may be read in other ways than merely individual. Relating several key moments, the chapter thus decidedly turns away from the medical model of disability and exemplifies the social model by situating Linton not yet quite in but close to the disability community.

My reading of the initial chapters of the memoir departs from Couser's, who asserts that since her wheelchair makes the paralysis instantly visible and exposes her disability to others, passing is not an option for Linton (*Signifying* 188). However,

Linton does attempt to pass by limiting accommodations to an absolute minimum and by explicitly distancing herself from other disabled individuals. Although she does contact the Disabled Students' Office to find a wheelchair accessible apartment in Berkeley, she is unwilling to ask for further accommodations, firmly stating: "Each thing I could do without accommodation [...] indicated how unfettered and normal my life would be" (*Body* 39). The conceptual world Linton inhabits before coming to California is, as her statement indicates, a nondisabled world in which normalcy reigns and she takes the constant pressure to prove her abilities for granted. It is particularly striking that she views her disability as a potential restriction and hindrance in her life that needs to be overcome by adhering as closely to the standards of nondisabled living as possible.

Likewise, she dismisses her friend's hint that she will "'really like'" Berkeley, because she will be able to get in touch with "'a lot more handicapped people'" thinking that this "was not what [she] was looking for" and stressing that when talking to her friends about spending the summer there, she is careful not to tell them about the disability community in Berkeley: "People might think I did everything because of disability, that it ruled my life" (ibid.). To the experiencing I, disability is a specter that she feels threatens to take over her life, forcing her to surrender and give up activities she may have participated in as an able-bodied woman. When she fears that her life may be conceived as "ruled" by disability, the tension that pervades the first three chapters of the book is disclosed. Already in rehab and to a greater extent in the second chapter "Brave New World" which begins with her release from the rehab facility and the beginning of her life and studies in New York City, Linton recalls the many instances in which her everyday life is heavily influenced by her impairment and she designs new routines, so that in this sense, many aspects of her life are certainly "ruled" by disability. It is already then that Linton carefully avoids letting others in on the troubles she goes through to find accessible routes to class or to the only bathroom that can accommodate her and her wheelchair to avoid "call[ing] attention to how hard things were" (ibid. 27).

In her early years, this scene and many similar passages from the beginning of the memoir demonstrate, disability causes a fissure in her sense of self, for the experiencing I well accepts her dramatically altered and impaired body but refuses to see herself as a disabled woman. Instead she assumes that incorporating disability into her identity will drain her strength and expose her weakness, a fear that is rooted, as the narrating I notes in retrospect, in her understanding of the category 'disability.' "I thought them to be flat, reluctant people," she describes the ways in which she has formerly interpreted disability, "not the sort to stir up the pot, to be juicy and interesting" (*Body* 47). The identity category 'disabled' is grasped in negative terms and comprised of "flat" people who lack personality and edge. Again, binary opposites are used to distinguish between disabled and able-bodied people, with the latter being "interesting," in contrast to "flat," and able to "stir up the pot" as opposed to the reluctance disabled individuals supposedly exhibit. However, the binary opposition does not merely operate on the lexical level, but also on the semantic, because the Linton utters by far less expressive words to refer to disabled identity to denote uniformity and monotony, than to illustrate the features she ascribes to non-disabled individuals, whose characteristics are more diverse, not just described in more words, but also using adjectives which may be read in many different ways. This is especially true for the adjective "juicy," the only word in the list of traits which does not have a clear opposite and therefore stands out, even more so due to its sexual connotations and the material dimension of its meaning.

In line with the dichotomous character traits, Linton expresses the irreconcilability of disability and "all those things" she hopes distinguish her "daring and crazy" personality through the use of the pronoun "them" which distances herself from the group and turns disabled individuals into a uniform group of 'others.' Furthermore, her detachment is also underlined when she confirms that she will stay true to her old self in spite of "this disability thing" (ibid.). Used repeatedly in the first three chapters, the phrase elucidates that the experiencing I cannot yet put disability into words and certainly not into any words that would relate to herself, instead seeing it as "this thing" separated from herself and her concerns, since disability is ultimately tied to "the unfortunates of the world" who "were suffering" and whose "lives had fixed boundaries and held few pleasures" (ibid. 48).

However, upon meeting other disabled individuals, Linton learns that her negative definition of 'disability' may no longer hold. As she leaves the grocery store early into her stay in California, she witnesses a strange but ultimately genuinely pleasurable event:

"There on the corner, facing me, was a man sitting tall in a sporty black wheelchair. Wavy blond hair fell down his bare back. He wore only tattered jeans and leather sandals. He was not alone. Three women swirled around him, dancing and skipping. Each woman held a container of yoghurt, and each, with gusto, was throwing handfuls of stuff at him. He answered them. He scooped up the cream from his naked chest and off his sun-burnished shoulders, and lobbed it back. There was yoghurt in their hair, running down each and every chest, dribbling down one woman's thigh, another's forearm. It lingered in bellybuttons, between toes, and in the spokes of his wheels." (ibid. 42)

Short main clauses epitomize Linton's staring while she notices more details about the disabled man and the encounter taking place in the street. She places emphasis on the constellation of the group that is turned to her, symbolically inviting her in, first noticing the man's upright posture and "sporty black wheelchair," which suggest a new way of showcasing disability, then the rest of his body, his long hair and naked upper body that characterize him as attractive, and finally highlighting that he is in the midst of a circle of women, which underlines his apparent attractiveness. When she later recalls the event a second time, this aspect clearly dominates, for Linton there refers to the women as "frolicking nymphs" and to their yoghurt fight as an "affair" (ibid. 43), and therefore attaches explicit sexual connotations to the group, their bodies, and their movements.

Likewise, in her first rendering of the incident, the entire narration of the scene revolves around the pleasures of corporeality, not only indicated through the yoghurt thrown "with gusto" and bare hands at the man's and women's bodies but particularly accentuated through detailed descriptions of these bodies and their actions. Using a variety of verbs, the experiencing I creates a vivid image in which bodily movement is finely nuanced: The women "swirled," "danc[ed]," and "skipp[ed]," and the man "scooped up" and "lobbed" the yoghurt to respond to their throws. For the first time, the disabled body and its pleasure – pleasure that directly pertains to the body – is flaunted in public and the lavish food fight that holds Linton's attention for a considerable amount of time, since the discourse time in this passage is longer than the story time, serves to pin point the audacity and boldness the event has in her eyes.

Beyond that, Linton renders the incident as one in which all the participants are equal: "each and every chest" is smeared with yoghurt and in the final sentence she notes how its remnants stick "in bellybuttons, between toes, and in the spokes of his wheels." The enumeration seamlessly connects able and disabled bodies, first of all by not distinguishing between their "bellybuttons" and "toes" and, secondly, by linking the bodies and the man's wheelchair. The "wheels," a synecdoche for his wheelchair, are not presented as alien in this enumeration but seen as a part of his body, from which, like from all other body parts, yoghurt drips.

Tellingly, the first time pleasure is publicly connected to the disabled body is also the first time Linton slips into the first person plural, wondering whether "people like us" may "survive" (ibid. 43). Of course her question is still hesitant and her identification with the disability community rather tentative, which is also due to the fact that she has only been a bystander watching the event from the sidelines, alone both in Berkeley and with her role as a disabled woman. The latter in particular concerns her, for her observation of the yoghurt fight makes it utterly clear that she lacks "guideposts for this life" (ibid. 44), other disabled people who might serve as role models.

In lieu of such friends, Linton decides that the man is to become her "first mascot" (ibid.), which is an interesting choice of words because mascots are carried along for good luck and in order to represent a group of people. Choosing an attractive young man who publicly displays bodily pleasure to represent her and her life, Linton does not model her identity on the stereotypical view of other disabled individuals she has detailed before but maintains her sense of self, rather adjusting the definition of disabled life so that it may be brought in line with the identity she has fashioned for herself. "If that's disability," she proclaims, "I can do that. He made it look fun and sexy. Not woeful and sick-like" (ibid. 43) and although binary thinking – the contrast between "fun and sexy" and "woeful and sick-like" – still shapes her statement, the quotation discloses the recognition that disability cannot be grasped in negative terms only.

Likewise, not only the new friend she makes on campus needs to be exempted from the group of the "unfortunates" on account of him being "too much like" her but similarly also Linton's "neighbor, the blind woman with the cleavage, and the smiley guy in the health food store, the gorgeous blond yoghurt tosser, and [her] friends from the roof at rehab" (ibid. 48f.). All of the people she enumerates in this list exhibit at least one feature that disrupts her earlier definition of disability, be it sex appeal, happiness, or a beautiful outward appearance and the freedom from constraints. Yet whereas most of these people are strangers she has only admired from the distance, her list culminates with the mention of her "friends" from the rehab facility and thus ends with a sense of close connection and community. This growing awareness of herself as part of a community is then made explicit when she muses "[m]aybe I was like them, and they were like me, but we are not like we were supposed to be" (ibid. 49) and the dichotomy between "I" and "them" is dissolved as they merge into "we" to showcase their commonalities and their collective difference to common belief. On the other hand, there is also challenge and provocation inherent in the final clause, even though the end rhyme renders them playfully[15] because the meter does not match and therefore disrupts the flow of the sentences, inevitably highlighting their falling out of the "norm" for disabled people.

Over time and as the story proceeds, the ways in which Linton introduces herself to others – opposed to the previous scenes in which her musings on disability have been largely silent – change. Instead of responding to people's inquiries about her body by explaining: "'I was in an accident,'" thereby not only limiting her condition to "an event that occurred in one moment in time" (ibid. 110), but inevitably also responding to dominant scripts, her initiation into the discipline of Disability Studies and her self-conscious identity conception profoundly change the ways she mediates her body and self in public. She even goes so far as abandoning the 'people-first' term "woman with a disability" and begins her class by introducing herself as a "disabled woman," telling her students that she "identif[ies] as a member of the

---

15 In California, she adopts a more playful approach to her disability and "show[s] off" her impaired body for the first time when she befriends a traveling group of pantomime actors who decide to incorporate her into their performance and have her "create a spectacle using [her] chair," the adaptive device she previously attempted to "minimize" and purposefully left undecorated (*Body* 46, 28).

minority group [...] and that is a strong influence on my cultural make-up, who I am, and the way I think" (ibid. 118).

Finally, becoming a disabled woman also essentially entails transcending the hierarchy and dichotomy between ability and disability. This is foreshadowed quite explicitly when Linton first enters an independent living center in California, noticing to her great surprise that "[t]his wasn't like the rehab center. That had a clear line of demarcation – the disabled people were the patients, pretty much everybody on the staff was nondisabled" (ibid. 50). In the independent living center, the category of patient does not exist and the lines between disability and ability blur as disabled employees take charge and provide services to fellow disabled individuals. Eventually, Linton therefore decides to not pursue a career in the rehabilitation sciences (ibid. 80), but to transcend the dichotomy inherent in the medical and rehabilitation system altogether, engaging in activist work amongst the disability community.

6.4 BEHOLDING (THE PLEASURES OF) DISABLED BODIES

The chapter "Citizens in Good Standing" focuses on Linton's involvement in the Society for Disability Studies which also situates her in the community of distinguished Disability Studies scholars such as Rosemarie Garland-Thomson[16] or the late Paul Longmore (cf. also Roulstone 742) and, most importantly, posits dancing as a cultural practice capable of destigmatizing the disabled body. In this chapter, Linton introduces a host of friends and scholars on the dance floor to illustrate a positive, jolly, and frolicsome view of disability, in which her friend Devva, who has a neurological impairment not further explained in medical terms, may be read as a synecdoche for the other dancers – although each of them are later imagined in vivid and loving detail – since "Devva hasn't 'overcome' this condition, she rides it like an untamed pony" (*Body* 147). As this statement foreshadows, the chapter

---

16 Garland-Thomson, too, emphasizes the significance of dancing at these conferences, closing her essay "Shape Structures Story" with a section that constitutes a hybrid form of personal narrative and academic essay about the time when the conference speakers covered the dance floor in bubble wrap to send of loud noises with each of their moves. She posits these dances, particularly "tongue dancing," as the community's "very own ethnic folk dance" with arises from a shared experience, history, and sense of identity: "So we all dance the night away in our peculiar ways. It's our culture, our ethnic distinctiveness. Tongue dancing is our jig, our tango, our hora, our Virginia reel. And like the macherena, it's our contribution to mainstream culture" ("Shape" 120ff.).

awaits readers with a wild and fun crowd at ease with their bodies, bodies which continuously afford them pleasures.

Torrell understands dancing as a form of bonding and a means of fashioning a community and reads the dance scenes in the book – Linton as a "novice dancer" dancing for the first time at her friend Glenn's party and later as a coordinator of dances at the conference – as a metatext that parallels Linton's gradual empowerment and her growing identification with disability culture (333). Yet the dance scenes also serve a further, crucial function. In *My Body Politic*, dancing articulately signals embodiment and, secondly, the depiction of the disabled dancers in the book invites readers to behold the disabled body and its pleasures, ultimately urging them to redefine both disability and standard forms of movement.

The first time Linton introduces her readers to the subject of dancing is in the chapter fittingly titled "Pleasures and Freedoms," about half-way through the narrative. The chapter begins with her assertion: "Everything I know about dancing I learned from a quadriplegic" (77), which sounds paradoxical at first, but captures the spirit of her project in which standards are re-defined. Dance moves are reappropriated because Glenn shows her that dancing is not a right and pleasure reserved for able-bodied people (cf. also Mihirad 130). The discursive power of dancing is reinforced when Linton draws parallels between dancing and both their activist work and disabled sexuality:

"This dancing was the public equivalent of what Glenn and I had been saying at the desk that afternoon. If sexuality is the individual expression of any person's desires and needs, not bound to a particular set of people who possess physical and psychological traits deemed worthy, and if sexual activity needn't follow a measured recipe of arousal, intercourse, orgasm, in more or less that order, engaged in only between two people of the opposite sex, then dancing shouldn't be restricted to people on feet, people who can see, people who are young, and thin, and popular, or people who can perform all the moves." (*Body* 86f.)

Like their activist work, dancing becomes a "public" act expressing "desires and needs." In their efforts to reform views on disabled sexuality, Linton and her friend strive to redefine sexuality so that it is no longer limited to "normal" bodies or restricted to a sequence that fulfill (hetero)normative desire alone. In a similar vein, the parallel indicates, dancing is not restricted to "all the moves" – standard forms of movement dancers need to be capable of performing – and is a practice open to anybody and any body.

The bodily pleasure Linton herself experiences as she is drawn to the group of dancers at Glenn's party after years of merely watching others dance becomes evident when she recalls opening her mouth to a joyful scream "as if I had been holding my breath for a very long time" (*Body* 86). Portrayed as breaking a long period of silence and holding her breath, the recovery of a loud voice comes as a great relief, and so does dancing. The power of dancing in this chapter is made all the more obvious through the fact that it is aligned with voice and thus receives connotations of agency. In the context of the memoir, this is a momentous connection, since bodily realities have generally been avoided in the discussion of disability as a social issue (cf. Chapter 3.1), which has led to a form of disabled identity that is disembodied (cf. also Torrell 335). This may be countered, Torrell expounds, by narrating identity as "at once personal, corporeal, and sociopolitical" (ibid.).

However, several critics have read the chapter as exposing a rupture between the educational voice in which Linton recounts listening to a paper by Garland-Thomson on the representation of disability in literature, art, and the academic curriculum (*Body* 137) and the intimacy with which she narrates the scholars' nightly gatherings on the dance floor. Disability law scholar Elizabeth Emens, who briefly discusses the life narrative in her response to Garland-Thomson's narratological inquiry in "Shape Structures Story" notes that the scenes depicting the SDS dances frame a "world unto itself, not created to communicate to the outside" (129). For Roulstone, too, these pages put readers into a "slightly voyeuristic" position, making them feel "as though intruding on a private reflection" (742). Such criticism may surely be grounded in Linton's thorough description of her friends' and colleagues' bodies and movements, a narrative choice that is strategic. On first reading, readers may well gain the impression that the narrative that has until then spanned many years comes to a halt, pausing in a series of affectionate moments in which other bodies are closely eyed and put on display.

Yet I do not share the concerns expressed by both critics that readers are intruding into a private gathering unrightfully staring at the writer's friends from the outside. Regarding the conference and the dance, which is, after all, printed in the program to draw in participants (*Body* 152), as exclusive gatherings removed from the public is to first of all misinterpret the overtly political and activist work conducted at the SDS meetings. "SDS isn't just some safe haven – a refuge from the prejudice and stares of the nondisabled world," Linton rectifies attempts to downplay the importance of the organization and their gatherings for the community, stating that instead of representing "a place to lick our wounds, it is a place of action. Our objective isn't to hide ourselves or mask disability," she firmly clarifies (ibid. 150) and moves from signifiers of withdrawal and passivity to action and agency. Moreover, the inclusion of these meetings in the memoir is politically significant in its own right, for Linton could have chosen to render the dance scenes in less detail or omit them entirely had she apprehended them as the private moments inside an inner circle. Rather, readers are invited into the scene, for it is in this chapter that she repeatedly uses the second-person pronoun "you" to address readers directly and include them (cf. e.g. *Body* 141f.).

Similarly, the detailed description of the dancers' bodies and movements in this chapter may well be read as an invitation to behold the disabled body, giving readers all the more to "see." Garland-Thomson defines staring as an either intentional or involuntary response to a startling, unknown sight that attempts to "make the unknown known" (*Staring* 3f., 15). Such stares and gawps may of course be disrespectful, voyeuristic, and inappropriate, yet her study also convincingly demonstrates that they are not always tantamount with the starer's "surrender to sensationalism" (ibid. 186). In the following, I therefore aim to apply her theoretical approach to the ethics of staring to passages of Linton's life narrative to illustrate that these, much like the portrait on the book cover, defy a sense of visual and textual intrusion and instead serve to project an alternative vision of disability.

When we stare at others, our intense gazing may, according to Garland-Thomson, mark a "productive aspect of our interpersonal, even our political, lives" (ibid. 185), which leads her to the conclusion that the key question in the discourse on staring is not whether one should or should not stare, but rather how we gaze at the extraordinary body (ibid.). "Good staring," as she calls ethical practices of looking, may in fact be transformative and ask for political engagement (ibid. 187). In this context, she writes extensively about starees in portraits who enter the communication process initiated by others' stares by meeting their gazes in demand of "extending equity to fellow humans" (ibid.).[17] Although readers do not encounter the disabled dancers in a strictly analogous fashion in the life narrative, since they are not portrayed visually and do not stare back in a literal sense, their bodies and dance moves in these scenes well account for a form of staring back: In the widest sense, staring back implies that starees take charge of the encounter (cf. ibid. 189), assume agency in the communication process, and retell dominant narratives of "unbearable pain, insurmountable adversity, a diminished life, and a fervent desire for a cured body," thus implicating that starees channel or control the effects of others' stares (ibid. 191). In the memoir this is achieved by several textual strategies, namely through (1) mocking the medical gaze on the defective body and its language, (2) allowing, but at once disabling the voyeuristic gawk, (3) presenting the disabled body as overtly sexual, and (4) framing the disabled scholars' dance as an activity with political, social, and cultural momentum.

The first strategy Linton employs to take control of the reader's curious "stares" as she introduces the members of the SDS community is the eloquent mockery of

---

17 Among the contemporary images she discusses are the photograph of model Matuschka and her mastectomy scar on the cover of *Time Magazine* in 1993, Chris Rush's life-size crayon portrait of disabled men and women, and painter Doug Auld's oil portraits of burn survivors from the series "State of Grace" (especially "Shayla," the painting shown in the Smithsonian National Portrait Gallery) which invite viewers to "[g]o ahead and stare" "without voyeuristic guilt" so that they may see beyond the grotesque (Newman, "Facing" n. pag.).

the medical gaze and the language commonly used to refer to disabled individuals' bodies and their striking characteristics or physical features. When introducing her friend Harilyn, for example, who "has a touch of cerebral palsy" (*Body* 147) she observes:

"Some of the most pronounced symptoms of her impairment are incisive political acumen and expressions of unbounded joy in the presence of paintings by Matisse. [...] Due, in part, to difficulty in fully controlling her musculature and because she finds herself helpless in the presence of my wry wit, she cannot keep a straight face around me. My clinical training and long standing interest in such cases prompt me to evoke such responses when we meet. I have observed a strong correlation between Chardonnay and eruptions of uncontrolled facial movements, and the symptom seems particularly acute when our mutual friend and playmate, Rosemarie, is present." (ibid. 147f.)

In this affectionate description, Linton avails herself of phrases, such as "some of the most pronounced symptoms," typically used to enumerate the corporeal deficits caused by an impairment, to point to Harilyn's sharp understanding of political matters and her love for modern art, shifting attention from the isolated and in its pathology fragmented body to the unique woman Harilyn is. As a consequence, her introduction does not satisfy readers' potential curiosity about what may actually be "wrong" with her friend, focusing instead on the characteristics she cherishes and turning the expectation of deficiency into a pronouncement of ability and pleasure. Likewise, she mocks the scientific and neurological explanation of Harilyn's symptoms by emphasizing her own professional training, evoking authority, and explaining "a strong correlation" between her taste for wine and "eruptions of uncontrolled facial movements," because the seemingly neutral and professional third-person description is ridiculed, not only due to the mention of alcohol, but also because of the ambiguity of Harilyn's "eruptions of uncontrolled facial movements" which may point to her tics but in this context far more likely denominate fits of laughter. Again, the pathological and extraordinary is turned 'normal' and ordinary.

Next, Linton challenges not only the language of science but also that of voyeurism when she moves on to introduce her fellow scholar Rosemarie Garland-Thomson as "a very unusual subject of study": "She possesses six or seven fingers, distributed between her two arms; [...] Her left arm is half as long as the right, and her hugs therefore form a complete circle, without the usual crossover pattern seen in the 'normal' hug" (ibid. 148). In her observation, Rosemarie is not reduced to an "object of study," but remains a subject, a noteworthy phrasing that allows her to maintain agency. In contrast to Harilyn's description, Rosemarie's does account for the extraordinary body in very explicit terms, has readers imagine it, and allows them to "stare" at it, i.e. linger in her close description of her hands for a moment. Readers' stares, however, are not the distant "peeping" of strangers, but reconceptualized, because they are connected to the scholar giving a hug, a context that reframes the encounter and stages a fond and affectionate situation in which one may imagine coming close to her body in an intimate gesture.

The third strategy repeatedly employed in the close depiction of other disabled men and women is depicting their bodies and movements in an overtly sexual tone. On the most basic level, this portrayal counters the stereotype of disabled individuals as asexual beings that may perhaps make it such a strange sight to behold for able-bodied readers subscribing to this prejudice. A number of scenes, though, work to not only establish sexuality as an integral aspect of the disabled body, but also utilize sexual connotations and explicit links in order to associate the disabled body with pleasure and a positive body politics.

There is Corbett, for instance, who, though claiming to be "100 percent queer" makes Linton "feel a twinge of jealousy" every time she dances with her husband David (ibid. 150). Prefacing her friend's depiction with these words, Linton makes clear that her movements and her body are to be read in strongly sexual tones. The lesbian Corbett is described as embodying heterosexual desire, passion, and lust when dancing with David, instead of merely pretending, thus mocking, the physical closeness of potential lovers. Desire, lust, and passion are intensified when Linton portrays their dance: "I see Corbett shimmy up to him and watch David straddle her Big Mama thighs and slide onto her lap. He wraps his legs around the back of her wheelchair and she takes him for a spin around the dance floor" (ibid.). Shimming up to David, shaking her shoulders and setting her upper body in motion, Corbett and her dance moves are detailed as openly sexual movements and her "Big Mama thighs" bespeak a voluptuous body. In addition, it is Corbett who leads their dance as David, in an interesting role reversal, sits on her lap with his legs wrapped around her and her wheelchair and she wheels them across the dance floor. Since the information that Corbett uses a wheelchair is momentarily withheld, her lead on the dance floor is highlighted. While they dance, the experiencing I gazes at Corbett's body and the dancers' movements from the side of the dance floor and twice explicitly refers to her role as an onlooker using the verbs "see" and "watch." Her description thus invites readers to join her gaze and look at the disabled dancer through her eyes and Linton accordingly determines the way in which readers will perceive Corbett.

Along similar lines, the experiencing I calls the poet, actor, and dancer Neil Marcus "a sight to behold" (ibid. 152), hence again encouraging readers to "stare" and imagine his dance style as he "rise[s] up from his wheelchair, in a spurt of excitation, and achieve[s] a full-body erection" (ibid.). Neil's upright posture, too, receives sexual connotations through the use of nouns such as "excitation" and "erection." Disability, Linton's description of his body makes clear, has not compromised his masculinity; far from that, her choice of words foregrounds and heightens it. Like the account of Corbett's dance, that of Neil's movements writes back at the commonly articulated fear of the sexual disabled body (cf. Wilkerson 193) by allowing readers to imagine and engage with it. Social scientist Abby Wilkerson rightly observes that the sexualities of disabled individuals have frequently been denied (ibid.) and they have been portrayed as people without sexual desire and as those who are not sexually desired. Yet sexuality, she argues, is of immense significance, because it provides "pleasure, interpersonal connection, personal efficacy, and acceptance of one's body and of self more generally" (194). Consequently, sexuality needs to be seen as an integral part of a positive body and identity politics and, as she maintains, has a liberating function for disenfranchised groups (197). By moving sexuality into the foreground when looking at disabled bodies, Linton therefore not only regulates readers' "stares," but also re-inscribes such bodies with a sense of pleasure.

The most overtly sexual representation of disabled bodies dancing, however, is that of the quadriplegic John Kelly. Readers learn that John "is a brilliant theorist by day [...], but at night when the lights are low, he is a dancer" (*Body* 154) and his introduction invokes a superhero-like figure who goes about doing ordinary work during the day, but becomes an extraordinary person at night. Admittedly, readers will find, though, that John's work during the day – devising "brilliant" sociological approaches to disability – is already far from ordinary, which inevitably accentuates his role as a dancer even more. Since his tongue is the part of the body that "has great control and strength," his dance style is the "tongue dance" and to this already markedly sexual style Linton adds further sexual connotations when she holds that "this thrusts and wiggles are nuanced and expressive" (ibid.).

In the dance scenes analyzed here so far, the multiplicity of the disabled dancers' bodies and movements has already become evident. An array of further glimpses onto other dancers underlines this: Emma, David Mitchell's daughter, is observed sliding out of her wheelchair, "crawl[ing] around" and, "perched up on her knees, rocking back and forth and clapping to the beat" (ibid. 151f.). Educator Joy Weeber, who uses a motorized scooter, initiates a conga line "with the whole crew snacking down the corridor" (ibid. 155), and political advisor Jonathan Young is portrayed "bouncing side to side in his wheelchair, each wheel coming up off the floor and each rock leaving him balanced at about a forty-five-degree angle from the floor" (ibid. 151). A plethora of verbs of movements of all forms is used synecdochally in these passages for the heterogeneity within the group, which has lead Torrell to appropriately call the dance floor "a microcosm of the larger disability community" sketched in the memoir (336). Torrell also points out that there is cohesion in the group's dancing (334), which Linton elucidates through her frequent use of the first-person plural, for instance when she notes: "our wheelchairs bounded across the floor, our crutches twirled in space" (*Body* 151). This sense of cohesion is crucial, for in spite of the variety of dance styles the dancers showcase, great importance is attributed to their collective dancing which for the memoirist epitomizes much-needed social, political, and cultural work.

In a like manner, the narrative's rendition of the dancers' bodies has performed such social, political, and cultural work by acting as the telephoto lens that bridges the distance between (able-bodied) readers and the SDS community and close captioning disabled bodies on Linton's own terms. The scenes abandon the boundaries between the private and the public, powerfully making the personal political. Moreover, in these scenes, readers are confronted with what may on first sight appear odd because it does not comply with standard forms of dancing[18], yet Linton invites readers to cast a second look and linger in moments where standards cease to hold sway. On reading, readers may become "ethical starers" who not only register the presence of the odd, the repulsive or beautiful, but who sympathetically "bea[r] visual witness" and, as a result, come to recognize new sights as something transformative (Garland-Thomson, *Staring* 188). Ultimately, like the dancing itself, these pages of the memoir "challenge every assumption about the shame and displeasure that supposedly shadow disabled people's lives" and "exploit and expand on the quirkiness of our form" (*Body* 153f.). The individuals Linton so vividly describes in the chapter metaphorically return the gaze and make staring back a politically and socially productive act of communication that, as Linton's quotes show, is capable of rewriting the dominant narrative of disabled bodies.

On the whole, *My Body Politic* presents a vivid and powerful counter-narrative to the dominant biomedical, political, and cultural discourses on disability and difference. In the final chapter, these issues move again into sharp focus when Linton points to the shortcomings in the current legislation and the prejudices disabled individuals are frequently exposed to and deny the memoir full closure. The book seemingly comes full circle at the end when Linton protests the war on Iraq and reflects on the soldiers returning to the U.S. with injuries and impairments. Reminiscent of the beginning, the final pages of the narrative sketch disability as a pressing issue: As medicine and technology ensure that more soldiers survive their war wounds, "we have a growing veteran population with significant impairments" (*Body* 242). While the beginning has conceived the disabled body as a symbol of the failure of the Vietnam War, thus availing itself of one of the commonly employed symbolic readings of impairment in the charged context of war and antiwar protest, the ending re-appropriates another, namely the impaired body as a symbol

---

18 In this context, also see the chapter "The Cripple Girl and the Blind Boy Go to the Museum," in which Linton urges readers to rethink how art is presented as her blind friend is allowed to transgress the rules and conventions at the museum and touch the bronze sculptures and humorously reappropriates the word "blind" as it is explained in the dictionary.

inspiring continued fighting (cf. Russell 100). At the end, the bodies of returning veterans become a symbol for the continuous fight for disabled citizenship:

"For disabled veterans and other disabled women and men, it takes legal measures to guarantee the right to get on a bus, go to college, get a job, and live on one's own. While the transformations over the last thirty-some years have afforded many disabled Americans opportunities and pleasures that would astound earlier generations, there are persistent obstacles – systemic and pervasive – that structure inequality. These veterans will, I hope, benefit from the advances, but will not be exempt from the ongoing discrimination." (*Body* 243)

Undoubtedly, Linton maintains, veterans of the war on Iraq will benefit from the "opportunities and pleasures" legislation has made possible, yet her statement is far from celebratory here. When she reminds readers that "it takes legal measures" to ensure disabled people's access to education and public transportation, a career and independence, the pervasiveness and persistence of obstacles to equality does indeed become evident.

Moreover, Linton appropriates the language of war, hoping that disabled veterans will meet a "battalion of workers and friends" who, if in any way similar to the group of individuals she "was conscripted into," will invite them to dance – and as my reading of the chapter "Citizens in Good Standing" has demonstrated, dancing is at once connected to well-being and to the performance of cultural and political work. As such, dancing becomes the epitome of the disability identity Linton has fashioned. Additionally, the significance of the disability community is stressed, in the scenes rendering the scholars' dance as much as in these sentences, since a major political task is still ahead: "to convince the public that the burden of proof can no longer rest on our shoulders. It is not our job alone to point out inequities, frame legislation, and defend our rights. It is the responsibility of the nation" (ibid. 244). In pinpointing the "responsibility of the nation," Linton calls out to disabled and able-bodied people alike, erasing the boundaries of dis/ability in the "body politic" that needs to ensure equality and inclusion.

My Body Politic does therefore not offer closure but explicitly highlights the issues that still need to be tackled, ranging from low employment rates amongst the disabled to the large number of households who live below the poverty line to draw the conclusion that "this remains, largely, an intolerant society with respect to disability" (ibid.). Turning to the future and the need for "affirmative actions of a new and as yet unwritten form" (ibid. 245), the memoir denies readers the comfortable stasis of a progress narrative arrived at its end-point but instead opens up a vast legislative, social, and cultural space readers are invited to fill. Although the epilogue – a few paragraphs from scenes at an amusement park – in parts glosses over the seriousness of the previous pages, their message is not suspended. "Are you a ride?" a child turns to Linton in her motorized wheelchair (ibid. 246) and her question concludes the book and hence remains unanswered. Perhaps it is another teachable moment that presents itself here, signaling Linton's continuous work; but maybe it is also the light-hearted invitation to join her ride.

7. Variation and Well-Being:
Rethinking The Impaired Body in Kenny Fries's
The History of My Shoes and the Evolution of Darwin's Theory

In 1997, Kenny Fries published his first memoir *Body, Remember*, a narrative about the intricate connection of memory and the body that chronicles his coming-of-age as a young gay Jewish and disabled man and his quest to fashion an identity in which homosexuality, Jewishness, and disability may merge. *Body, Remember* also insinuates a shift in Fries's perception of his disability from living as a "disabled person who internalized the misinformation and stereotypes of disability, to being in community with others, disabled and nondisabled, who have a more accurate understanding of disability, and to a growing understanding of disability as a social construct" (*Body* xii). This perspective is then further explored in Fries's second life narrative, *The History of My Shoes and the Evolution of Darwin's Theory* (2007).

Although Fries is primarily known for his work as a playwright and poet,[1] particularly the publication of his life narratives has turned him into a noted spokesperson for Disability Rights within the disability community (cf. Beam 172). He has written numerous editorials and is the editor of the prominent anthology of writing on disability, *Staring Back: The Disability Experience from the Inside Out*. Howev-

---

1 In "Exposing the Scars," Fries describes his poetry as "first-person narrative" (quoted in Troxell 6). From the publication of his second collection of poetry, *The Healing Notebooks*, which broach his lover's infection with AIDS/HIV, his writings also begin to assume a social and political perspective. *Anesthesia* renders bodily disfigurement and surgery, sexual abuse, as well as love and beauty, thereby confronting, often in an autobiographical mode, queerness and the disabled body, as Mintz convincingly outlines in her essay "Lyric Bodies: Poets on Disability and Masculinity." Fries's fourth volume of poetry, *Desert Walking*, links the natural to the spiritual to explore mortality and the body's frailty (*The Healing Notebooks*. Berkeley: Open Books, 1990; *Anesthesia*. Louisville: The Avocado Press, 1996; *Desert Walking*. Louisville: The Avocado Press, 2000.).

er, Fries's literary work, especially *The History*, has so far been largely overlooked by both literary and Disability Studies scholarship despite the fact that his writing bears great potential to transform the aesthetics and politics of the representation of disabled identity. In this vein, critic Jeffery Beam celebrates Fries for transforming disability into a means for personal growth while at the same time developing a critical stance against stereotypes and prejudices against disabled individuals, thus intertwining the perspectives of the poet and the social critic (174). This chapter offers the first in-depth close reading of the memoir from a literary and Disability Studies perspective and thus seeks to begin filling the gap in the critical apprehension of his memoir and contribute to current scholarship on the conceptualization and representation of the impaired body in life writing.

The perception and portrayal of the impaired body is a recurring theme in Fries's oeuvre. Close to the end of *Body, Remember*, he recounts how his lover Kevin asks him to model for a picture about "*[d]emythologizing difference*" and "*[t]he perception of beauty*" in which Fries will be wearing his orthopedic shoes (*Body* 207; italics in original). Despite Kevin's best intentions, the experience is utterly humiliating for Fries, echoing the questions of "Why are your shoes so big? Why do you walk that way?" posed at random by strangers' children in the street. These demands to narrativize corporeal difference linger and *Body, Remember* closes with the question "How do I tell them that some questions have no answer?" (222). The issue of how to explain the extraordinary body then hovers over the ending of the memoir and seamlessly links it to the theme of *The History* in which the impaired body and its adaptations take center stage.

As the title of the memoir announces, Fries's orthopedic shoes are recontextualized within the framework of Darwin's theory of evolution. On the one hand, the shoes are of course significant on the personal level, increasing Fries's mobility, ensuring his access to social life, and allowing him to travel. Yet as they "conjure unseen worlds" (*History* xvii) in Indonesia, Thailand, on the Galápagos Islands or on the Colorado River, they also fulfill an additional function as they produce links between chapters and ideas. Connecting past, present, and future, culture and biology, the shoes become a synecdoche for notions about the body and physical difference.

Linking Fries's experiences to episodes of Charles Darwin's biography and his theory of evolution, as well as to the findings of the lesser known naturalist Alfred Russel Wallace in this way, the story probes, Disability Studies scholar and poet Laurie Clements Lambeth purports, the definition of the 'fittest' (n. pag.) and provides a corrective reading. What emerges from the story is hence not only the history of an idea, but also, as literary critic Yasmin Nair holds, the history of a body (n. pag.). The life narrative shows, though, that neither can exist independent of context. Darwin's theory is portrayed as the result of meticulous work and the consideration of its moral implications, as well as strategic publication and the engagement with other scientists. Similarly, Fries considers his impairment in the context of living in the United States in the twentieth, respectively twenty-first centuries. As a consequence, "what constitutes impairment" or "who determines disability" are questions that permeate the narrative as it builds on the motifs of difference and sameness, dependence and interdependence, stigma, and adaptation.

In this chapter, I therefore aim to show how *The History of My Shoes* reframes the understanding of impairment and creates a narrative in which physical difference is not the story of an individual pathology, but is envisioned as a necessary and integral part of all human development. To this end, this chapter will read Fries's second memoir as a creative reappropriation of Charles Darwin's theory of evolution expounded in his 1859 *On the Origin of Species by Means of Natural Selection, or the Preservation of Favoured Races in the Struggle for Life*. Since its publication, Darwin's theory has been received beyond the boundaries of the natural sciences. Both his contemporaries and ensuing scholars have deemed his work revolutionary: In the decade after its publication, *The Origin* dramatically changed the ways in which the educated public fathomed evolution (cf. Carroll, *Literary* viii) and a number of scholars have highlighted its profound and lasting influence on our understanding of life (cf. Engels, "Person" 9). In his *Reading Human Nature*, Joseph Carroll even presents the *Origin* as "one of the two or three most significant scientific works of all time" and praises both its scientific vision and its "eloquent," "evocative," and "compelling" rhetoric, as well as the rigorous consistency of its argumentative structure (197). Interest in Darwin's writing is therefore unabated and particularly the bicentennial of his birth and the 150th anniversary of the publication of his *Origin* in 2009 have spurred a veritable Darwin hype amongst scholars of disciplines as diverse as philosophy, political science, psychology, linguistics, and literary studies (cf. Carroll, *Literary* ix).[2]

Gillian Beer characterizes our culture as "dominated by evolutionary ideas" and attests to the profound imaginative power of these ideas on our understanding of the

---

2 In *Literary Darwinism: Evolution, Human Nature, and Literature*, Joseph Carroll explores the intersections of evolutionary theory and literary studies in a vast array of close readings. He asserts that Darwin has not only had a lasting effect on Victorian writers, such as Thomas Hardy and George Eliot and naturalists like Émile Zola and Jack London, but traces Darwinian thought and motifs in the writings of Aldous Huxley, William Golding, Kurt Vonnegut, and Ian McEwan (ix). Other studies proclaiming a paradigm-shift in narratology and literary theory include Jonathan Gottschall's and David S. Wilson's *The Literary Animal: Evolution and the Nature of Narrative* (Evaston: Northwestern UP, 2005), *On the Origin of Stories: Evolution, Cognition, and Fiction* by Brian Boyd (Cambridge: Bellknap, 2010), Robert Storey's *Mimesis and the Human Animal: On the Biogenetic Foundations of Literary Representations* (Evaston: Northwestern UP, 1996) and the journal *Evolutionary Review: Art, Science, Culture*.

world (2). Fries's narrative is a particular case in point for it not only painfully exposes a significant aspect of Darwin's legacy, but also *reworks* its imaginative power. Living with congenital deformities in both his legs that necessitate custom-made orthopedic shoes, Fries is haunted by the notion of the "survival of the fittest." The phrase famously misattributed to Darwin[3] reverberates throughout the memoir as Fries strives to make sense of and come to terms with his impairment, and carve out his identity in a society that at times proves to be a rather hostile living environment. As a consequence, his memoir provides a rather narrow and, to a certain extent, biased reading of Darwin's evolutionary theory, particularly of the processes of natural selection and the 'survival of the fittest,' which foregrounds what he initially perceives to be the precarious and uneasy place of disability in society. Though aware of the positive ideas of for instance interdependence and morality inherent in Darwin's work, Fries rather glosses over them and his memoir therefore strongly engages with the misattribution of eugenic thought, as well as with the sense of perfection and progress so pervasive in contemporary society.

The life narrative hence significantly expands the discussion on well-being, as it narrates well-being both in the context of a condition that cannot be cured – multiple surgeries in childhood have left Fries physically and emotionally scarred so that when he is later offered a surgical procedure to increase the length of his right leg, he declines – and in the face of the memoirist's gradually deteriorating health and ability. In this vein, the life narrative takes up ongoing discussions on disability by broaching the issue of quality of life and the question of whose life is worth living. It thereby moves the impaired body into the foreground and demands that it is accounted for and integrated into the critical conversation on disability. Consequently, well-being in *The History* is linked to the body and its changing capacities, and rests, as I will illustrate, on the revision of the impaired body's place

---

3   The notion "survival of the fittest" has been coined by the British philosopher Herbert Spencer a decade before the first edition of *The Origin* was published to "describe the mechanism employed by nature to assure the survival of the only part of the population able to adapt to the conditions of existence" (Beck 196). It should be noted that Darwin never intended his Origin to elucidate human evolution and was therefore reluctant to adopt the term as a means to clarify his metaphor of 'natural selection.' Also see George L. Levine's *Darwin, the Writer* for a discussion of the early critical responses to the metaphor that led Alfred Russel Wallace to urge Darwin to substitute his term with Spencer's less metaphorical expression for the sake of scientific authority (8f.). Darwin hesitated, yet in the fifth edition, he did finally introduce Spencer's phrase (cf. Hoquet 159) and used it alongside 'natural selection': "But the expression often used by Mr. Herbert Spencer, of the Survival of the Fittest, is more accurate, and is sometimes equally convenient" (Darwin 63).

and status in society. I will argue that by reconceptualizing impairment as 'variation,' the narrating I is enabled to craft a sense of well-being not in contrast to his impaired body and dissolve the dichotomy between ability and disability. 'Variation' is employed to disclose the contingency of both the body and its development in the light of an ongoing evolutionary process. To this effect, Fries's life narrative responds to the call reverberating throughout Linton's *Claiming Disability* that 'disability' should be dissociated from 'problem' (141).

At the beginning of the memoir, the introduction of the notion of 'variation,' undermines the medical model of disability and its conception of the impaired body as an individual's tragic and pathological flaw and posits impairment as a variety worthy of celebration and one in which the binaries of ability and disability disband. This also becomes evident in the structure of the book that first of all defies the super crip narrative which traditionally reinforces normalcy, and secondly, reworks the story of the impaired body defying linearity and making alternative cause-and-effect relationships possible. Here, Fries's encounter with the blue-footed booby is constructed as a powerful turning point when the recognition that their curious feet need not be narrativized fosters a sense of well-being and relief. Third, the idea of variation is also used to point to the contingency of the impaired body by stressing that ability and disability are strongly dependent on place, time, and context, and that impairment is at times utterly beneficial and indeed necessary. Finally, the orthopedic shoes – provided they fit – help to advance a notion of adaptation beyond the scope of Darwin's theory and thus help to lift the stigma from the impaired body. The recognition that adaptations are virtually universal, then, further spurs the view of a remission society in which impairment is not a flaw, but merely another variation.

At the same time, though, the book also complicates the social model that has come to be widely accepted in Disability Studies (cf. Chapter 3.1). Like Linton's *My Body Politic* Fries's book may well be read as another recent example of what Couser terms the 'new disability memoir' (cf. Chapter 6.1) and shares with her text a deep commitment to disability consciousness. My analysis has shown that for Linton, well-being is inherently connected to questions of equity and access and her memoir is strongly oriented on social, political, and cultural activism as the groundwork for a more inclusive society. Although Fries, too, repeatedly references the Disability Rights Movement in his memoir, particularly the shift from the medical to the social model of disability spurred by activist and scholarly work,[4] *The*

---

4   Growing up in the 1960s and 1970s, he witnesses exactly this shift in perspective: "In 1960, years before the disability rights movement, disability was seen solely as a medical issue. It was over a decade before disability, spurred on by the growing disability rights movements, as well as the field of disability studies, would be viewed from a civil rights

History does not depict the movement as equally influential to his well-being and positive identity construction, due to the fact that the narrating I shares his story against the background of his gradually decreasing mobility and increasing back pain, hence moving the physical reality of impairment into the foreground and demanding that the body's corporeality is accounted for. Well-being becomes at once an urgent political, theoretical, and deeply personal matter and his experience recounted in the memoir thus demands that disability is not only read in terms of structural barriers, but that pain, exhaustion, and emotional distress are equally taken into account (cf. Malhotra and Rowe 199).

The History therefore points to a fundamental problem in the social model of disability, namely its neglect of the corporeality of impairment. The social model, as I have outlined above (Chapter 3.1), has, legal scholars Ravi Malhotra and Morgan Rowe summarize, fostered the understanding of disabled identity as the membership in a minority group and social movement, similar to the identity constructions of people of color or the LGBT community (4). Current academic discourse in the discipline, however, has met criticism on grounds of "failing to deal with impairment" (Shakespeare, "Disability" 144).[5] In his essay on "Disability Studies Today and Tomorrow," Tom Shakespeare asks how scholars may find more adequate ways of theorizing disability, maintaining that disability can neither be defined in medical terms only, nor may fully be explained by social exclusion and oppression (ibid. 147). Similarly, Malhotra and Rowe, in a growing chorus of other Disability Studies scholars, lament the absence of the body from the social model,

---

or cultural perspective" (*History* 92f.). This particular comment is interwoven with a childhood experience in the vignette "Something about You Kids" where Fries remembers a fight between his mother and a neighbor at the community pool. Although the reason for the fight is never revealed, neither to Fries nor to the reader, the subtext hints at the idea that the neighbor has complained about young Fries exposing his deformed legs and surgery scars at the pool. Shame and fear echo in the passage as Fries ponders the reasons for the fight and considers his mother's unpreparedness "to raise a child with a disability" (ibid. 92), yet he also highlights the sense of pride on his mother's part that he now understands to be "a missed opportunity […] to untangle the feelings surrounding the situation we found ourselves in as I grew up" (ibid. 93).

5   Shakespeare's critique of the social model also urges scholars to re-think the role of biomedicine and the technological advances in medicine and rehabilitation, since he argues that "Disability studies has valuable work to do: distinguishing between appropriate and normalizing medical therapies; challenging doctors' tendency to define a disabled person's health and status totally with reference to their impairment; analyzing the potential, and dangers, of new treatments, such as stem cell research, gene therapy, pharmacogenetics" (ibid. 145f.).

strongly recommend the theorization of impairment and the impaired body, and stress the importance of "acknowledge[ing] that physical impairments have very real and occasionally subtle implications on the quality of life of disabled people and need to be fully analyzed" (4). Only then, they argue, can the Cartesian split between mind and body be transcended (ibid.) and the experience of disability be conceptualized in its entirety.

Yet so far, as I have illustrated in greater detail above, the impaired body has largely remained unarticulated in theories about disability to either avoid sidestepping civil rights issues or succumbing to an essentialist view, reducing impairment to an individual problem (Linton, *Claiming* 138), and hence replicating the shortcomings of the medical model. In devising his own – personal and political – theory of impairment, Fries successfully straddles this divide, and his memoir does, like Malhotra and Rowe demand, "bring the body back in" (4) by intrinsically tying well-being to the body and the reconceptualization of impairment.

7.1 Rethinking Impairment beyond the Medical and Social Model

"Still Disabled" is the first vignette of *The History* and recounts Fries's visit to Dr. Mendotti, who, on behalf of Social Security, is supposed to examine his feet in order to determine whether he is "still disabled." "*Still disabled?*" Fries reiterates their concern ridiculing the idea that his condition which doctors – short of a medical term – have defined as "congenital deformities of the lower extremities" may have changed (*History* 1; italics in original). It is therefore a telling illustration of the fact that the term 'disability' is socially constructed, as Linton outlines, to "arrange people in ways that are socially and economically convenient to society" (*Claiming* 9f.). Not only accidents or degenerative diseases may change an individual's status, but also precedent-setting legal rulings (cf. Bérubé, "Foreword" viii). Yet more than merely pointing to the social construction of the disabled body, the initial chapter of the narrative also raises material concerns because Fries depends on the physician's assessment to confirm his status as legally disabled so that he may continue to receive health care and benefits. "Still Disabled" therefore reveals the push and pull between the corporeal reality of disability and its social construction, and by the same token the clash of first- and third-person perspective when the authority for definition rests with persons other than Fries himself.

I consciously avoid the term 'doctor-patient relationship' in the close reading of this passage, because it is significant to note that Fries has not come to Dr. Mendotti for treatment, care, or even cure. Garden appropriately characterizes the physician here as a "gatekeeper" to social services ("Disability" 70), a notion that spells out the administrative dimension of their meeting, as well as the asymmetrical power relationship. Although this is not the only scene in which Fries discusses his body with a doctor[6] it is the only passage that is narrated with such immediacy and that paints such an unsympathetic picture of the physician. A prime example of the clashing perspectives on disability in the context of institutional medicine, this scene first of all illustrates, as Garden maintains, the bias and mistaken assumptions that frequently shape encounters between the disabled and nondisabled (ibid.). Dr. Mendotti, here the epitome of the medical model, perceives disability as a flaw in the individual and, later in the chapter, allows the extremely biased subtext to emerge that the disabled life is not worth living. The first chapter of the book then aims to deconstruct the medical model of disability, which proves to constitute a framework too limited to grasp Fries's situation and too normative to allow for a neutral perception, let alone foster the acceptance of impairment.

Inside the examination room, Fries becomes an object to the medical gaze of Dr. Mendotti who, though apparently "a specialist in the field," is so surprised to see his legs and feet that he looks at him twice upon entering the room (cf. *History* 2). As he examines Fries's body, his statements – "Wow" and "You can walk on those?" – express surprise at "those" deformed feet, place Fries's bodily difference outside of language, and reverberate astonishment, pity, and revulsion. "'How can I describe this to [Social Security]? They won't believe me,'" Dr. Mendotti ponders, resolving that his secretary should "come in and see this" and bring an old Polaroid camera so that he can take a photo (ibid. 4). On grounds of the syntactic ambiguity of the isolated remark yelled through the hallway, it does not become clear whether the demonstrative "this" points to Fries's legs or to Fries himself, hence intensifying the already dehumanizing encounter. Under the gaze of the physician, Fries is turned into a wondrous specimen that may be described neither in ordinary language nor in the register of medical terminology so that only a photo can serve as evidence of his existence.

The encounter in the clinical context thus frames impairment in utterly negative terms. Exposed to the stares of the doctor, the deformed body becomes a source of shame: "I wish I could recoil my legs, like the legs of the Wicked Witch of the East that curled under Dorothy's house which fell from the sky, when Glinda the Good Witch of the North removed the Wicked Witch's ruby slippers" (ibid. 3). By comparing himself to the Wicked Witch of *The Wizard of Oz*, Fries identifies himself as

---

6 Later episodes introduce Dr. Milgram who suggests orthopedic shoes when Fries is still a child and Dr. Frankel whom he consults about his worsening back pain and who advises him to undergo a surgical procedure to have his anatomy altered and his leg stretched in length, which he declines.

evil/abnormal in a dichotomous assignment of values.[7] Dr. Mendotti's stare diminishes his strength, since in the popular story, the Wicked Witch is killed when Dorothy's house falls on her. What is left for her is to "curl" under the house and "recoil" her legs, a choice of words highlighting the apparently strange nature of Fries's feet.

Accordingly, the impaired body is associated with horror and tragedy in the medical setting, yet the experiencing I introduces a counterpoise when reminding himself that "in this situation, [he] must act as if [his] disability is the worst thing that could ever have happened" (ibid.) in order to comply with the doctor's point of view. The pressure to "act" not only illustrates that the relationship between the doctor and Fries is flawed – Fries remarks that "this examination, Dr. Mendotti's stare, are much more difficult to endure" than his impairment (ibid.) – but also emphasizes that their interaction is governed by unspoken rules he "must" follow. From Fries's perspective, the encounter is hence early on marked by force, coercion, and constraint and, as a consequence, it is clear that Fries has entered a social space with rigid hierarchies and fixed power relations. Garden, too, attributes great power to Dr. Mendotti in this particular scene and points to his discursive authority ("Disability" 70).

However, while Garden focuses on the technical language of medicine that is in fact negligible because there is no term for Fries's impairment and the doctor's utterances have been unprofessional at best so far, another aspect of discursive power is much more significant in the exchange, namely the silence imposed on the experiencing I, as well as the narrating I's attempt to break with this silence when he maintains: "'With the right shoes I walk just fine,' I *want* to tell him. [...] 'I'm okay as I am,' I do *not* say" (*History* 4; italics mine). A similar passage is included in Lorde's *The Cancer Journals* (cf. Chapter 4.3) when Lorde recounts the incident in her surgeon's office and the nurse's order to hide her mastectomy with a makeshift prosthesis so as not to lower "the morale at the office" (60), since she then writes that she "could hardly believe [her] ears! [She] was too outraged to speak then" (ibid.). Frank argues that the adverb "then" is crucial in this statement, for although the experiencing I may not have had the power to respond, the voice of the narrating I in the story now does and in voicing her outrage, "fulfills her responsibility" toward herself and other women (*Wounded* 132). In contrast to Lorde, however, it is not merely in remembering the exchange that Fries rewrites it by incorporating his own – though silent voice – and attempting to establish agency, but the struggle to

---

7 Fries's comparison to Lyman Frank Baum's novel is also revealing for its connection of his orthopedic shoes to the ruby slippers that have magical powers, an issue that I will return to below.

break with the discursive power of the doctor takes place in the immediacy of the scene, as illustrated by the present tense.

Yet as much as Fries "want[s]" to contradict the doctor's opinion that his impairment constitutes the ultimate tragedy, Dr. Mendotti's authority over the concept of disability and, by extension, Fries's identity is too strong. On the one hand, Garden is therefore right when she argues that the doctor's perspective challenges the narrative of the disabled person ("Disability" 70) because in this situation, Fries cannot assert a more positive stance in front of the doctor. On the contrary, the scene even casts doubt when Fries then begins to have misgivings and asks himself: "But am I okay?" (*History* 4) and notes that on leaving the examination room, his limp is more pronounced than usual (ibid. 6). On the other hand, the fact that the reader learns about Fries's objections in the narrative cannot be ignored and the two sentences introduce tension and potential conflict into the conversation. Moreover, the encounter challenges the hierarchy of the objective over the subjective perspective in the medical setting. The objective stance that commonly rests with the doctor is not only unmasked as unprofessional but also proves to be irrational and emotional compared to Fries's argumentative and reasoned subjective voice. The beginning of *The History* therefore erodes the doctor's authority and consequently challenges the medical model of disability.

In Chapter 3.1 I have argued that the medical model is today commonly considered dated and Disability Studies as an academic discipline and activist endeavor has made considerable efforts to stress the shortcomings of the medical model and elucidate the social construction of disability, i.e. the so-called 'social model.' Throughout Fries's work, it becomes clear that he is a strong proponent of the social model, yet the project of *The History* considerably goes beyond illustrating how society disables individuals. The social model is of immense importance as it has helped disabled people to forge a more or less coherent collective minority identity that relies on similarities and contrasts to other individuals and has significantly contributed to a more appropriate analysis of social interaction, larger power structures, and issues of (mis-)representation. Despite these successes, the social model has come under attack by a number of critics in the field of Disability Studies who call for a "more inclusive, more stable" analysis, more suited to the political and social needs of disabled individuals (Bickenbach 1180). Philosopher Jerome Bickenbach, for instance, finds fault with the social model and its conception of disabled people as a coherent minority group, maintaining that the group envisioned by the model is far too heterogeneous to share common experiences, most importantly due to the fact that people's impairments vary greatly. Along similar lines, he identifies issues within the Disability Movement itself and expounds the problems of the fact that many of its leaders may hardly be seen as representative of the general population of people with disabilities because many of the former are "highly educated, white middle-class males with late onset physical disabilities and minimal medical needs" (1180f.).

Bickenbach neglects another critical issue, though, namely the problem that in an attempt to create a coherent minority group, the social model purposefully shifts the focus away from the individual's impaired body and the corporeality of physical impairment. Pointing to lacking accommodations, the inaccessibility of buildings and public transport, and restrictions in access to education, adequate care, or the job market, the social model recognizes issues of dignity, yet the analysis of Fries's memoir elucidates that a sense of human worth is first and foremost linked to the perception of one's body. This is not only evident in his first demeaning encounter with Dr. Mendotti, but the remaining pages of the vignette expound the apparent impossibility of framing the impaired body in positive terms in more detail. Throughout these passages, Fries employs the symbol of the clock and the motif of temporality to situate his impaired body in the context of Darwin's theory and thus sketch the contested terrain in which impairment is perceived. Consequently, Fries's narrative deflects attention from the social model and its beginning necessitates an acknowledgement of the body.

As he waits for Dr. Mendotti to return to the examination room, his eyes fall on the clock on the wall, the "institutional clock" that reminds him of the clock in his classroom of the Brooklyn primary school and conjures up a memory:

"once again I am eight years old, staring at the P.S. 200 clock, its thin black second hand making its sixty-second round over and over again. In front of my third grade classroom, Mrs. Krimsky, my silver-haired teacher, is telling my class about Charles Darwin, his theory of evolution, the survival of the fittest. At her mention of this phrase, sharp to my skin as a surgeon's knife, I instinctively reach beneath my desk and clutch my legs, protectively lifting them so my shoe-clad feet rest against the edge of my chair." (*History* 2)

Fries is relegated into his childhood, not only due to the paternalistic and abasing attitude of the physician, who later tells him that he should go to see the doctors in Hartford who "'work with children like [him]'" (ibid. 4), but more so because the notion of the "survival of the fittest" surfaces as a conceptual trope in both situations to threaten Fries's conception of his own identity as a disabled person. The "institutional clock" connects present and past, as well as the examination room and Fries's primary school classroom. Like the doctor's office that stages a dehumanizing encounter, the innocent setting of a primary school, originally intended to nurture his developing identity, spurs the view that his body is faulty and unfit: The notion of the "survival of the fittest," which receives particular emphasis in the climactic sentence construction, even has a physical effect on Fries. Like the scalpel that has been raised to his skin many times in an attempt to correct the anatomical make-up of his legs and feet, the phrase is scary, arouses shame, and serves as a painful reminder of what is "normal" and normative.

Moreover, this passage reiterates Fries's wish to "recoil" his legs, hide and protect his feet, a concern that his first memoir *Body, Remember*, too, echoes when Fries refers to this significant event:

> "Around this time, in school, I first learned about Darwin's *The Origin of Species* and his theory of the survival of the fittest. As my teacher spoke I kept reaching down to touch my legs, as if to make sure they were still there. I began to feel that everyone in the room must be looking at me – with these legs I was not fit enough to survive." (*Body* 216)

In neither of the passages, the context of the phrase or its meaning is elaborated so that Darwin's theory and particularly the concept of "survival of the fittest" appears to stand alone, floating isolated from context and consequently open to any form of (mis-)interpretation. As such, both passages reflect the cursory public discourse on evolution and Darwinism. It should be noted that neither passage offers even the slightest hint that the teacher or Fries's fellow students link the lesson with Fries's body. Instead, Fries appears to have already internalized the misinterpretation of Darwin's theory that reduces his existence to a flaw in nature and renders his survival doubtful. "What am I afraid of? Other children's stares? Amputation?" (*History* 2), he asks in an attempt to identify the cause of the fear the teacher's lesson instilled in him and the very idea of the "survival of the fittest" is so diffuse that it precludes Fries from grasping its apparent momentousness, since possible consequences range from him becoming a social outcast to severe physical pain and the alteration of his body.

"Panic-stricken, I wonder as I grow older how will I be able to walk, let alone realize my childhood dreams of becoming a basketball player, a foreign diplomat, a United States senator. Forget about dreams, with these deformed legs and feet. How will I survive?" Fries similarly wonders (ibid.). The teacher's lesson apparently urges him to abandon these dreams of accomplishing something extraordinary, aspirations quite common to young children that would connect him to others of his own age. In light of the "survival of the fittest," the question ceases to focus on how he may fulfill these dreams and revolves instead around mere survival. As a consequence, impairment is portrayed as a fate that not only robs Fries of his boyhood dreams and isolates him from others but as a flaw that makes him unfit for life.

It is striking that this passage is the only scene from Fries's childhood in The History that he does not render in past, but in present tense, which attests to the haunting presence of the experience and his doubts about the future, and temporality in this context constitutes an abiding motif. In his inclusive classroom, as quoted above, Fries remembers "staring" at the clock on the wall (ibid.). "[O]ver and over again," the second handle turns round the clock, signifying the time that is not simply passing but rushing past and, in connection with Mrs. Krimsky's lesson, implying that time is running out. Later, the sight of the clock takes Fries back into the present and the doctor's examination room, where he realizes that "this clock does not tell the correct time" (ibid. 3). The frame of reference is not a watch attesting that it is now "later than one PM" but the knowledge that it was already one o'clock by the time he left Northampton for the doctor's office (ibid.), a comparison eliciting the existence of parallel worlds, a world inside the examination room and a world outside, each tuned to their times. Tellingly, the doctor's clock runs slow and symbolizes Dr. Mendotti's outdated perspective on disability that prompts him to voice the hushed – because illegal – offer for "medication" in case his disability becomes too unbearable and Fries wishes to commit suicide (ibid. 5). Fries, in contrast, has "outlived" this timeframe and his own perception of time suggests that, contrary to the fear that his time is running out, he continues living and exists past this time. While the physician cannot envision a future in Fries's life, the very reason for his visit is ensuring his future by safeguarding Social Security payments and health care.

In a similar vein, the gloomy and oppressive setting of the doctor's office stands in stark contrast to the world outside that "seems much brighter than [he] remembered it an hour ago" (ibid. 6). Yet even though the perception of the outside as particularly bright speaks to the impression that Fries leaves the examination room rather invigorated than powerless, the doctor's words and the image of the clock, i.e. his conception of disability and the idea of survival, continue to haunt him. As he drives away, he hears Dr. Mendotti echoing "You can walk on those?" and tries to resist the physician's disbelief that portrays Fries's everyday routines as verging on miracles:

"Through some act of God – not to mention doctors, shoe-makers, persevering parents, and some innate drive of my own – I am able to stand here with the assistance of a cane and twenty-year-old orthopedic shoes. In this suburban world of office parks and strip malls, I am sure that if I look up I will see cherubic angels, hear them trumpeting the proof of the miracle of my being alive at all. But I don't see angels. I don't hear trumpets." (ibid.)

By enumerating all the other people he attributes his ability to walk to – doctors, shoemakers, his parents, and, most of all, his own perseverance – Fries ridicules the idea that there was "some act of God" involved, a phrase too diffuse and intangible to shed light on his situation. Instead, the ending of the sentence highlights his cane and the "twenty-year-old orthopedic shoes," his two palpable aids. Exaggerating the hostility of the suburban environment that requires him to bridge extensive distances across office parks and between shops, Fries asserts that trumpeting cherubs would probably attest to the miracle that he is not only capable of walking, but is "alive at all." However, he holds that there are neither angels visible nor trumpets audible. These two matter-of-fact statements stand out from the rest of the passage not only due to their tone, but also due to their brevity. The previous long and elaborate sentences used to conjure the image of a miracle are refuted by the concise observation that the actual "proof[s] of the miracle" are lacking, and that there is indeed no miracle.

So in lieu of angelic trumpets, the initial line of the poem "Pied Beauty" by the English poet Gerald Manley Hopkins reverberates in Fries's mind. Written in 1877, the poem is a hymn to God's creation and its variety, since the speaker demands that

"Glory be to God for dappled things –
For skies of couple-colour as a brinded cow;
For rose-moles all in stipple upon trout that swim;
Fresh-firecoal chestnut-falls; finches' wings;
Landscape plotted and pieced – fold, fallow, and plough;
And áll trádes, their gear and tackle and trim.

All things counter, original, spare, strange;
Whatever is fickle, freckled (who knows how?)
With swift, slow; sweet, sour; adazzle, dim;
He fathers-forth whose beauty is past change:
Praise him." (137)

The poem begins by praising all the "dappled" things God has created, ranging from the sky to various animals, including the "finches' wings," and points to their particular appearances, before focusing on human practices, such as ploughing, and, in the final line of the first stanza, on "all trades." Nature, as well as human uses of it, are consequently traced to God's power and will, a worldview that stands in stark contrast to Darwin's theory of evolution, alluded to by the reference to finches. Contrary to Darwin, who used the example of the various finches on the Galápagos Islands to draft an argument on the geographical distribution of species and their adaptations in the *Origin*, Hopkins's poem suggests that any form of appearance, however curious it may be, is to be attributed to God. This is ultimately elucidated by the second stanza that asserts that every unique thing, even things that appear rarely and are against the norm, strange, and unique, have been brought into existence by God.

However, I do not read Fries's reference to Hopkins's poem as intertext as a reconciliation with religion in light of his inability to believe in a divine miracle. Religion does not figure anywhere in the material and secular life narrative and instead of joining the speaker of the poem in voicing his gratitude, he notes that he is "thankful for Hopkin's poem celebrating *all things counter, original, spare, strange*" (ibid. 6; italics in original), and thereby clearly shifts the focus of the poem's interpretation. As a quote, "all things counter, original, spare, strange," like other quotes in the text, are italicized but the italics here also attribute particular significance to these words – to the odd, weird, and extraordinary – and the narrating I interprets the poem as a celebration of variation, diversity, and bodily difference. Nevertheless, the poem does not just provide temporary solace for the inhumane and demoralizing encounter in the doctor's office, but has larger implications for the memoir and the writer's perspective on his impairment.

Revealingly, Fries asserts that his "childhood questions of survival," the very dramatic concerns the vignette has introduced earlier, "are answered by Hopkin's questions: how do each of us become *swift, slow; sweet, sour; adazzle, dim?*" and moves on to add "[d]isabled, nondisabled" to the speaker's list of opposites in the second stanza (ibid. 7). First of all, his response to the poem makes clear that the question posed about impairment is no longer one of mere survival, but has turned to making sense of the impaired body. This process of making sense decidedly differs from medical explanatory models and is also effectively removed from the context of deviance and pathology, because the question posed is "how each of us" has come to inhabit such different bodies and display such different characteristics. It is therefore an inclusive and all-encompassing question that reformulates impairment as a variation integral to the human condition. Moreover, by adding "[d]isabled, nondisabled," Fries disrupts the order of the dichotomous adjectives and their interpretation as positive/negative contrasts, transforming all of the characteristics mentioned into possible varieties, free of value. With this proposition, the first vignette of the memoir ends on an utterly positive note, having moved the interpretation of impairment from a tragedy to the notion of variation that in this context is not only a neutral observation, but a difference worthy of celebration. Paradoxically, though, this "answer" presents itself as yet another question and hence, instead of providing a definitive answer, first of all initiates a quest, similar to the one in Siri Hustvedt's memoir, since Fries notes that he is "just beginning to understand what survival of the fittest actually means" (ibid.). In the chapters to follow, he takes readers along on this journey and expounds how exactly impairment might be reconceptualized as 'variation,' a term borrowed from Darwin's evolutionary theory.

The first chapter of the memoir thus discloses the problems of both the medical and the social model of disability which do not provide adequate frameworks for reading the impaired body and points to an alternative reading which forms the basis for the creative argument he crafts throughout the memoir. As such, the first vignette parallels the opening of Darwin's *On the Origin of Species* in which Darwin outlines the principles of his theory of evolution by appealing to common sense and a record of what has long been known; this chapter then provides a stable framework for the introduction of Darwin's terminology and the concepts of his approach (cf. also Wallace 31). Similar structural parallels permeate the memoir and below, I aim to show how the narrating I inscribes new meaning onto the impaired body, harnessing both content and structure in the reappropriation of Darwin's theory of evolution.

7.2 REWRITING THE (HI)STORY OF THE IMPAIRED BODY IN FRIES'S MEMOIR

The History of My Shoes is unique for its plot. Defying a linear and sequential form, it is comprised of brief episodes alternating between Fries's present, past, and the future he anticipates, as well as the 19th century in which Charles Darwin recorded his voyage on board the *Beagle* and formulated his hypotheses on the origin of species. To the casual reader, the book may thus appear as a fragmented excerpt from Darwin's biography and a brief survey of natural history, but the relationship between evolutionary theory and Fries's autobiographical account is more complex than a distinction between a third-person perspective and a subjective experience may grasp. When *The History* and *The Origin* are read side by side, it becomes clear that Fries does not genuinely recount Darwin's theory but renders it through the eyes of a writer and Disability Studies scholar. Objective theory and personal experience come into a creative interplay to suit argumentative purposes and the following analyses will illustrate that Fries takes deliberate freedom with Darwin's groundwork in evolutionary biology when constructing the narrative of his impaired body. His argument does not only rest on the information he has chosen to include in his narrative but is deeply embedded in and receives great power from the structure of his book.

In my reading, I depart from Disability Studies scholar Stephen Kuusisto's argument that *The History* should not be read as a disability memoir, but rather as "a post-Victorian narrative about Darwin's strange legacy in our world of real bodies" ("History" n. pag.). While I strongly endorse his emphasis on the corporeality and the lived experience of the body that clashes with socially constructed ideas, as well as the fact that Darwin's theories continue to resonate in our minds, a reading of Fries's book strongly benefits from its contextualization as a disability life narrative, since it is then that the full potential of both its structure and content may be apprehended. After all, the narrative is a deeply personal story of living as a disabled person and evinces that "Darwin's strange legacy" is intricately intertwined with the ways in which disability is perceived, so that the two readings by no means need to exclude each other but work together to make explicit the political and cultural forces entangled with Fries's story. I therefore aim to reconcile these two readings and explore how the personal and the political operate in his memoir.

In this respect, Fries's own trip to the Galápagos Islands serves as a frame for the narrative, beginning with the couples' arrival[8] in the prologue and ending with their departure and return to the United States in the last chapter "Infinite Time and Space"[9] and thus reflects the common memoir trope of the journey as both travel and intellectual sojourn. "Travel produces a sense of newness so important for writing; and movement alone, it seems, is friendly to ideas," Sally Cline and Carole Angier hold, linking travelling to the emergence of new thoughts (83). Similarly, in *The Origin*, Darwin begins:

"When on board H.M.S. Beagle, as naturalist, I was much struck with certain facts in the distribution of the organic beings inhabiting South America, and in the geological relations of the present to the past inhabitants of that continent. These facts, as will be seen in the latter chapters of this volume, seemed to throw some light on the origin of species – that mystery of mysteries, as it has been called by one of our greatest philosophers. On my return home, it occurred to me, in 1837, that something might perhaps be made out on this question by patiently accumulating and reflecting on all sorts of facts which could possibly have any bearing on it." (1)

For Darwin, the journey provided the impetus for the development of his theory of evolution. As Carroll points out, he did not discover the principle of natural selection while traveling, but the journey allowed for observations in biogeography and paleontology that prompted him to investigate the data and samples he collected (*Reading* 227f.). Engels, too, stresses the significance of the *Beagle* voyage and purports that it has greatly influenced Darwin's life as a scientist ("Person" 18). Similarly, Fries's own travels alongside Darwin's journey form crucial moments in

---

8   Fries's text is one example of recent literary engagements with Darwin and his journey. In a very similar manner, the protagonist of Cathleen Schine's novel *The Evolution of Jane* (1998) retraces Darwin's voyage to the Galápagos Islands in order to explore her own past and *The Evolution of Bruno Littlemore* (2011) by Benjamin Hale draws, Virginia Richter observes, "extensively on Darwinian patterns" (147).

9   Like the other narratives discussed in this study, Fries's memoir, too, lacks a definite ending and the traditional sense of closure, as the title of the final vignette illustrates. Despite the fact that the book ends with Fries's return to the U.S., this brief chapter crafts a productive moment of friction between structure and content, as the ending points to the ongoing and never-ending process of evolution, echoing Darwin's concluding remarks at the end of *The Origin* that "[t]here is grandeur in this view of life […] and that, whilst this planet has gone cycling on according to the fixed law of gravity, from so simple a beginning endless forms most beautiful and most wonderful have been, and are being evolved" (560).

The History. Removed from Western culture, for instance during his travels in Thailand, or subjected to an entirely new vantage point on his rafting trip on the Colorado River, Fries develops a different perspective on his own impairment. Particularly his travels to the Galápagos Islands are a way of "re-observing" established knowledge. In this vein, travel writing may well be understood as a medium of research (cf. Carroll, *Reading* 206f.).

Yet although Carroll's concept adequately characterizes both Darwin's and Fries's journeys and the writing and ideas they instigated, it should be stressed that in *The History*, the significance of traveling, of literally leaving the beaten track, cannot be reduced to an intellectual quest. The physical journey and the materiality of the hardship associated with traveling rough terrain are equally significant in the context of disability memoirs. The previous chapters have expounded a number of plot structures, imageries, and themes common to the traditional rhetoric of illness and disability life narratives and the memoirs discussed here serve to problematize narratives of triumph and success during the course of which writers allegedly overcome their ailments and impairments. Such narratives are not only common to illness memoirs, but figure equally prominently in the discourse on disability, as I have outlined above (cf. Chapter 2.3). Here, narratives of triumph typically present disabled narrators or characters as so-called 'super crips.'

The term 'super crip' has been coined by disability activists[10] to denote "a person with a disability who lives out the popular representation of disability as adversity to be overcome" (Barton, "Textual" 185). For Linton, overcoming one's disability implies that strength or willpower has helped a person to either move beyond the limits of their disabilities or arise above common social expectations for people with disabilities. Yet as she deftly reminds readers, "it is physically impossible to *overcome* a disability," so what is in fact overcome in these cases is according to her the stigma associated with disability (*Claiming* 17). Their stories depict disability as a "depressing" condition to be transcended (Couser, *Signifying* 33f.) and disabled individuals may be portrayed mastering extraordinary physical achievements, such as climbing a mountain or winning a race,[11] achievements that,

---

10 Some sources attribute the term to sociologist Rebecca Chopp, while others see its first usage in the autobiographical essay "The Mountain" by the disabled and queer writer and activist Eli Clare, a text that Fries also references. Clare asserts that super crip narratives "reinforce the superiority of the nondisabled body and mind. They turn individual disabled people, who are simply leading their lives, into symbols of inspiration" (3).

11 The stereotype of the 'super crip' is particularly common in the representation of athletes (cf. e.g. Keith Gilbert's and Otto Schantz's edited volume *Paralympic Games: Empowerment or Side Show?* Maidenhead: Meyer and Meyer, 2008) and has also been well researched in analyses of visual culture (cf. e.g. Gerard Goggin and Christopher Newell's

as Wendell observes, are noteworthy even for individuals without a disability ("Toward" 271). Moreover, super crips may also be represented as leading their lives in such a manner that they will be allowed to pass and others will not consider them disabled (cf. Barton, "Textual" 185; cf. Chapter 6.3). Disabled people portrayed in this manner "become symbols of heroic control against all odds" and by conforming to able-bodied life, give the false impression that the body may be controlled (Wendell, "Toward" 271). Contemporary pop culture is rife with stereotypical representations of super crips, "heroes and heroines, valiantly struggling to achieve normalcy" (Barton, "Textual" 185). The formulaic ending of these stories is utterly positive, though, as Couser holds, unlikely, and is therefore not representative of the experiences of most persons with disabilities. Although these stories free the narrator from the stigma of his/her impairment, the story upholds the status quo, he argues, by retaining the stigma for other individuals who may not be as exceptional as the super crip (*Signifying* 33f.). Moreover, super crip narratives delineate and thereby implicitly reinforce a rigid image of normalcy and posit ability as the ideal that disabled persons must strive to attain.

Ultimately, these narratives do not dissolve the binary between "us" and "them," but rather work to increase the rift between abled and disabled identity, because the ordinary actions of disabled individuals, such as traveling, are viewed as extraordinary accomplishments. When disabled persons become symbols for resilience or perseverance, their status is abstracted and removed from the lived experience of disability, which precludes their recognition as individuals and the possibility for full and equal participation in society. In addition, the experience rendered in super crip stories is one narrated through an outside, ableist, perspective and hence significantly contorts the experience of disability. Indeed, Fries's life narrative may be read as a text that writes against the notion of the super crip, not only due to the fact that Fries's first-person perspective in the story of course ensures his agency in the construction of his identity. In attempting to dissolve the dichotomy between ability and disability, *The History* and most notably the passages of the memoir rendering Fries's travels deconstruct this popular narrative.

On more than one occasion during his travels, Fries explicitly references the idea of overcoming one's disability and, like Linton, turns critical encounters into teachable moments for the reader. When he maintains that, "[l]ike Eli Clare who loves the mountains with a 'deep down rumble' in his bones, I love to travel. And like Eli Clare and many other disabled people, I, too, carry the myth of the super-

---

essay "Fame and Disability: Christopher Reeve, Super Crips, and Infamous Celebrity." *M/C Journal* 7.5 (2004)). For an alternative theoretical and activist framework, see Robert McRuer's materialist critique in *Crip Theory: Cultural Signs of Queerness and Disability* (New York: New York UP, 2006).

crip" (*History* 152), he not only responds to the stereotype of the super crip, but by comparing himself to Clare and "many other disabled people," Fries stresses that the travels that take up a good portion of the book are not unparalleled events but instead quite ordinary. Another episode from his rafting trip on the Colorado is certainly the most explicit with regard to his resistance against the super crip motif. When another group of hikers passes Fries, a woman stops to offer her admiration: "We're just so impressed" (ibid. 161). His spontaneous reply is so surprisingly hostile he has difficulty relating to it: "'Don't be impressed,' I hear myself say. 'Read my books'" (ibid.). Interestingly, Fries refers to his books to counter the woman's dubious sense of admiration, presenting his first-person accounts as an alternative narrative. Finally, these scenes illustrate that even though the memoir revolves around Fries's ability as much as around his impairment, it neither transcends disability nor attempts to compensate for mobility or skills lacking. Repeatedly, he thus renders his fears in preparing for example the demanding rafting trip, or his preoccupation with the question of asking for help or receiving assistance from strangers during his travels (e.g. ibid. 69, 147, 155, 163).[12]

However, the memoir's rejection of the super crip narrative during Fries's travels presents only one way of amending the interpretation of the impaired body. Through the spatial proximity of Darwin and Fries that the journey to the Galápagos Islands enables, the account of Darwin's exploration and his theory becomes a framework for the story. Kuusisto purports that Fries, much like Darwin, embarks on a journey because he seeks to re-examine traditionally accepted concepts ("History" n. pag.). Attempting to see nature through Darwin's curious eyes, Fries revises his own perspective on the human body and on its evolution and aberration. The memoir reflects this not only on the plane of content, but also on the level of

---

12 The words 'help' and 'assistance' occur about as many times in chapters about Fries's life as they do in the chapters recounting the formation of Darwin's theory, thus establishing dependence as another theme that connects the two men. While Fries is at times dependent on the assistance of others, Darwin was dependent on the research of other scientists and on the financial resources in his family: "But I still feel uncomfortable not only needing help but also asking for it. Often the feelings of fear and shame are even worse after I get assistance. It seems easier somehow when I'm paying for someone to do something for me. Even though I paid for this trip, I know the guides are volunteers. I want to trust their assistance, as well as the mere offer of it, more than I do. Darwin's journey toward the theory of evolution itself was an act of reciprocity. His social situation, his finances, his family and friends, led to his collecting success, as well as to the publication of this theory. He used his family members in his experiments, and was assisted by neighbors. To arrive at the ideas at the core of On the Origin of Species, Darwin depended on the theories of others, such as Malthus, Lyell, and Wallace" (ibid. 163).

form, since neither Fries's nor Darwin's travels are traced linearly, but surface time and again in the episodic narration, structuring both his thoughts and the narrative. The structure of the book therefore lends itself to a reading guided by associations, connections, and juxtapositions that undermine what Lambeth calls "ableist hegemony" (n. pag.) and a narrative of continuous progress that dominates much of the writing on disability.

Instead, readers are invited to discover new connections between events and ideas and uncover alternative cause-and-effect relationships. The book therefore playfully, yet self-consciously transgresses the constraints traditionally associated with narrativizing impairment. In "A Little World within Itself," for instance, Fries recounts Darwin's arrival on the Galápagos Islands in 1835 where he encounters a vast number of animals previously unknown to him and unique to the islands, among them the marine iguana of Isabela Island. The marine iguana, Darwin notes, can only move "stupidly and sluggishly" on land; in the water, however, it swims "with perfect ease and quickness" (*History* 19). On James Island, in contrast, he spots the land iguana and begins to compare the two species of the same family in size, shape, and habit (ibid. 20). This way, the structure of the book introduces its thematic focus, namely that the idea of variation is not limited to the animal kingdom, because the subsequent vignette, "Bodies of Water," is linked to Darwin's observations through the proximity of the images used (cf. also Lambeth n. pag.) that call for an association: While Darwin compares the two iguana species, Fries recalls an episode at the local YMCA pool where he observes a male swimmer alone in the water and beholds his powerful body and movements, before sliding into the water himself, noting that "[s]wimming, back stretched, no pressure on [his] legs, the water neutralizing weight" is much easier than walking (ibid. 21).

Throughout *The History*, similar links between chapters may be detected which connect aspects of Darwin's life and theory to Fries's story. Following "What Wallace Found," the brief narrative about a baby orangutan Wallace took from the jungle and attempted to bottle-feed yet did not succeed so that the orangutan died (42), the vignette "My Salamanders" chronicles Fries's childhood trip upstate during which he collects salamanders and builds them a habitat in Tupperware containers, only to later find that they all have died removed from their natural environment (ibid. 44). "Under the Form of the Baboon" on Darwin's approach to sexual selection is followed by "Natural Affections," a vignette in which Fries narrates his initial sexual experiences with men (ibid. 105f.). "The Accumulation of Little Things" ending with Darwin's death in 1882 and his burial in Westminster Abbey (ibid. 120) immediately precedes the vignette "Shoes in a White Cardboard Box" (ibid. 121ff.) in which Fries desperately tries to walk in the new shoes made for him despite the pain they cause but eventually gives in, polishes his old shoes and discards the others: "I put the new pair in the white cardboard box, stash it in my bedroom closet, on top of the LPs I no longer use" (ibid. 122). Finally, "A Gap in the Wir-ing" on his partner Ian's attention deficit disorder where Fries notes that "Ian is late" (134) uses the association of time and lateness to connect to the subsequent chapter about Wallace titled "A Man in a Hurry" (135ff.). These associative links between chapters reinforce the inseparability of Fries's life and Darwin's approach and thus underscore the writer's identification with the subjects of Darwin's research (cf. also Lambeth n. pag.).

Moreover, as Beer already observes in the analysis of the structure of Darwin's book, these transitions illustrate that rather than recording a linear development, the narrative rests on the idea of variability and arises from moments of observation (59). Fries's memoir thus decidedly counters traditional ways of storying disability. When he writes in the chapter "The Origins of Desire"[13] that "culture demands explanations about most disabilities" (*History* 113), he demonstrates that impairment necessitates a story, or, put differently: "A person *became* deaf, *became* blind, *was born* blind, *became* a quadriplegic" (ibid. 114; italics in original). Not only does this demand a sequential narrative (cf. ibid.), but the emerging story will provide explanations of cause and effect that burden the disabled individual. Far from opposing the composition of stories about disability – after all he has made his career out of it – Fries does, however, criticize the emplotment of physical impairment. Told from multiple and individual perspectives, such stories seize the objective and neutral and transform it depending on the angle of vision. Consequently, the stories respond to the demand for explanations and thereby continue to posit impairment as aberrant, unnatural, and abnormal. Hence stories function as the primary means to uphold what Fries terms "[t]he dialectic of normalcy – for someone to be normal, someone had to be not normal" (*History* 114). "[N]ormal" and "not normal," purposefully not in inverted commas, stand as absolute opposites that neither allow blurriness nor negotiation. Impairment then ceases to constitute a physical fact and "becomes a story with a hero or a victim" (ibid.), i.e. a story inevitably confined to established frames and one that betrays lived experience.

In contrast, Fries urges his readers to stop demanding a story and let impairment "pass" without an explanation and thus accept it as difference. A watershed moment in *The History* occurs during Ian's and Fries's hike on the Galápagos Islands when their guide Javier takes them to see the Galápagos penguins. Living among the penguins, Fries observes, are colonies of blue-footed boobies, marine birds that are

---

13 The chapter, clearly an allusion to Darwin's *Origin of Species*, reflects on homosexuality, both in the context of Fries's life and in general terms. Fries cites the biologist Bruce Bagemihl whose findings reveal that heterosexual sex in humans and animals is mostly without reproductive intent and thus not different from homosexual sex. – "Except for the culture that labels it so," hence declaring homosexuality an aberration that demands explanation, similar, as Fries asserts, to disability (*History* 113).

noted for their striking blue feet (cf. 192). "'Why are their feet blue?'" Fries turns to Javier, who replies "'No reason'" (ibid.). Javier's refusal to tell a story, and thereby fashion a narrative from the causes and effects that have led to the birds' curious pigmentation is compelling. Rather than denoting ignorance or disinterest, Javier's shrugging "No reason" epitomizes biological variation and its contingency and coincidence. In its brevity and matter-of-fact tone, the answer cannot be challenged and, what is more, deflects the men's attention from the birds' extraordinary difference.

Lambeth holds that the birds are depicted as extensions of the writer's own physical difference and identity (n. pag.), since Javier's answer, Fries reflects, "echo[es] the answer I have given countless times to people who have asked about my feet" (*History* 192). In the context of Fries's search for explanations about the history of his own body, the scene provides comic relief by juxtaposing Fries and the blue-footed birds. But this juxtaposition is also crucial for another reason because it is in this scene that Fries most directly relates his own impairment to natural variation, thereby stripping it of stigma and the need for thorough explanation, or, as Nair argues: "[t]here are no real aberrations in nature" (n. pag.). This vignette thus reinforces the connection between Fries and the subjects of Darwin's research and, what is more, powerfully foregrounds 'variation' in his account of the impaired body.

The notion of variation offers a concise answer to Fries's question of how individuals turn out "*swift, slow; sweet, sour; adazzle, dim*" (ibid. 7; italics in original), seemingly ends the quest, and dramatically changes the tone of the account of his body, providing a stark contrast to his earlier bitterness and pain. "My mother never found a reason for my impairment. Neither have I. But she was, somehow, at some point, able to let it go," Fries recalls midway through the narrative (ibid. 93). The syntax of the first sentence highlights the importance of a reason for Fries's bodily difference, a reason that both mother and son have once sought to find. This reason or explanation is at the core of this passage, first stated directly and then resonating in the following sentences, since, even if it is not always voiced, it always provides the impetus for the quest and is never absent from the discussion about impairment and identity. However, through its parallel structure, his statement illustrates that he, unlike his mother, has until then not been able to "let it go," put the question to rest, and make peace with his impairment. Therefore the passage has a bitter and unhappy ring and in this respect, the recognition that there truly is no reason other than 'variation' – opposed to an assumed reason Fries is still desperate to find – creates immense relief, absolves him of the need to search further, and fosters a lasting sense of well-being.

Over the course of the narrative it therefore becomes clear that physical disability is more than "a useful organizing category for a motley collection of odd bodies" (Scully 57). In her essay on phenomenology and disability, bioethics scholar

Jackie Leach Scully probes disability as "a genuine ontological category" and proposes to read impairment not merely as a "*general* fact of embodiment" (ibid.; italics in original). Rather, she advises scholars to turn to the "*specifics*" of the impaired body to understand disability and its place in theory (ibid.; italics in original). It is through the impaired body – the specifics of Fries's embodiment – that his reappropriation of Darwin's theory gains shape. On the basis of Merleau-Ponty's *Phenomenology of Perception*, Scully begins to carve out a phenomenology of disability, arguing that a different embodiment will effect "higher order cognition" (60), i.e. one's ability to analyze or evaluate and the capacity to create something new. Since Scully's essay focuses on the implications of this idea for ethical considerations about disability, her conclusion is that a different form of embodiment will naturally bring forth a different way of thinking about ethics (ibid.). Similarly, for Fries, the "specifics" of his body have a profound impact on how he views his place in the world and conceives of the implications of the "survival of the fittest."

Along these lines, we may read his focus on the negative aspects of Darwin's evolutionary theory as triggered by his embodiment, by a profound fear of its consequences that might render his existence illegitimate. His memoir then complements the perspectives on the body touched upon in this study. Like for instance in Sacks's *A Leg to Stand On* (Chapter 5), embodiment significantly influences knowledge about the corporeality of the body. However, in Fries's life narrative, the focus is not so much on knowledge about what the body and, in extension, the self, can or fails to do, but on knowledge about the body's apparent incapacity in relation to its environment. Through what sociologist Kay Inckle terms a 'position of embodiment,' Fries reflects on the ways in which he as a disabled person is marginalized (389) and legitimizes his status as a disabled individual.

When he voices his bitterness over the fact that, for a long time, he could not put the question of his disability to rest, his narrative evinces how deeply embodiment as a lived experience also intersects with emotions and questions of the self (cf. ibid.). If disability "*is* an identity," Scully asks, "can it ever be anything other than a spoilt one […] that we are morally obliged to restore to normality if we can, or prevent from happening if we can't?" (57). Turning to the reappropriation of Darwin's theory, Fries is capable of lifting the stigma from his identity. The use of his body and bodily experience initiate the comparison between his own life and Darwin's theory and address the ethical issues Scully raises.

7.3 Variation and Contingency: Deconstructing Dis/Ability

Throughout the narrative, 'variation' is therefore expounded in greater detail as a crucial aspect of Fries's creative re-appropriation of evolutionary theory. First of all, the concept of variation is considerably extended to not only include modified traits and features passed on through reproduction[14] but to also refer to Fries's impairment. In *The Origin*, an impairment like Fries's deformed legs or his partner Ian's ADD would not be termed a variation, but would rather be conceived in terms of "monstrosity," "some considerable deviation of structure, generally injurious, or not useful to the species" (42) and would as such carry no weight for evolution. Additionally, variations are originally considered in the context of a species' development and in Darwin's evolutionary theory, variations are hereditary because they are based on mutation and recombination (cf. Huxley 250), even though scientists would only later reveal the principles of genetics underlying his theory. Fries, of course, has not inherited his impairment, nor will he pass it on to his prodigy. In the memoir, he therefore focuses on the idea of variation in the context of his and others' current state and weaves it, as the following analyses will illustrate, into the framework of evolution and human development to elucidate both the contingency of the impaired body and the necessity of disability in our society.

Throughout the narrative Fries makes utterly clear that both ability and impairment are context dependent, i.e. dependent on time, place, as well as on culture and society. For instance, "The Beehive," a chapter early in the narrative, relates Fries's and Ian's challenging climb to the Beehive summit on Mount Desert Island. In contrast to Ian, who has trouble "fit[ting] his size thirteen feet where they need to be to keep his six-foot one-inch body steady," Fries is able to fit his smaller feet into the steps of the ladders that bridge the gaps in height between the paths on the mountain (*History* 10). On this trip, it is Fries who is in fact more able than his able-bodied partner whose 'regular' size and 'big' feet cause him to frequently slip and lose control on the steep climb (cf. also ibid. 163). The account of this trip elucidates that it is the environment which determines whether a trait or physical characteristic is impairing. Ian's physical status which would be considered 'normal' or 'average' in many other contexts presents an impairment in this particular place, to

---

14 For Darwin, variations are "spontaneous" and "accidental" (e.g. 52, 205, 424). These characterizations, though, Darwin is careful to elaborate, do not entail that variations do not follow rules. Rather, Engels argues, "accidental" implies that variations have not been planned but merely turn out to be advantageous during the course of natural selection, which leads her to the conclusion that for Darwin, there does not exist a benevolent plan, or in fact, any predestined plan at all ("Person" 29; cf. also Beatty 148).

the extent that it keeps him from climbing any further. Fries's body, in contrast, appears to fit the conditions on the mountain perfectly.

Another telling example Fries offers is the childhood memory of sharing a trundle bed with his older brother. Before the two boys would fall asleep, his brother would tease him about his height, respectively his shortness. "'I'm not short, [...] everyone else is tall,'" Fries answers back (ibid. 115). Shortness or 'normal' size, the answer indicates, is always conceived in relation to something or someone else. The experience of sharing a bed merges past and present and allows Fries to ponder on his love relationship to Ian that he describes as harmonious, mutual, and understanding – it is Ian whom the book is dedicated to. Here, height it not an issue and Fries can accept "The Imperfections of Beauty," as the vignette is titled. His experience in the present reveals that beauty does not constitute a standard or even perfect ideal, but inevitably comprises imperfections. His shortness is then merely conceived as a minor flaw that does by no means diminish beauty and therefore fosters a positive identity construction. "Here in bed it feels as if the playing field has been literally leveled," Fries continues (ibid. 117) and expresses a concern frequently voiced by Disability Rights activists who call for minimum standard regulations which will ensure that disabled individuals have equal opportunities of accessing and participating in society. With the two partners lying side by side, size ceases to be a well-defined category.

In these scenes, Fries's rendering of his relationship to Ian repeatedly blurs the boundaries between ability and disability, most effectively in the chapters in which Fries references his partner's attention deficit disorder. "Throughout his life, Ian has tended toward lateness, has had difficulty completing projects, is constantly losing things like his keys and wallet," he remarks pointing out the troubles his partner's disorder causes (ibid. 126). In several subsequent chapters, he is thus prompted to reflect on Ian's ADD that at times places constraints on their lives, but most of all has begun to threaten Ian's graduate studies and his position as a fellow and thus appears to pose an utter disadvantage (cf. ibid. 133). On the one hand, he notes that a number of researchers have identified ADD as a "'modern disease' – as the inevitable byproduct of a culture addicted to speed: cell phones, beepers, overnight mail, powerful computer chips, hard-driving rock music, TV shows with images spliced together at hundredth-of-a-second intervals" (ibid. 129). The enumeration illustrates that both the recent technological progress and the influence of media and technology are overwhelming. While the beginning of the list with its short items is in line with the speed that cell phone communication and express mail promise, the subsequent items run counter to the fast pace as more attributes are necessary to properly characterize them. In other words, the mind's capacity to grasp these modern comforts is misaligned with the rush in which they sweep users away, thus demonstrating the collapse that is then indeed "inevitable." ADD is therefore presented as a problem conditioned by social and cultural contexts.

On the other hand, Fries introduces so-called 'Darwin medicine' as a counterstance. Researchers from this subfield of medicine which assumes an evolutionary perspective on the body and its diseases argue that our genetic make-up needs to be viewed in a more nuanced way with respect to apparently faulty or harmful genes: "many of the genes that predispose us to mental disorders may have fitness benefits as well" (ibid. 130f.). 'Fitness,' a term that in the context of evolutionary theory denotes the degree to which organisms have been able to adapt to their environment and can ultimately reproduce successfully, serves here to disentangle the link between aberrant genes and pathology. As a result, Fries redresses the notion of pathology – and to that effect normalcy – and refutes the belief that the genetic material of the body may be pathological per se. Instead, his reference to Darwinian medicine exposes that the body is inextricably linked to the context in which an organism lives because, according to Darwinian medicine, an organism's physical traits ensure its adaptation to its environment. Only with changes in the environment, previously advantageous traits may prove to be of disadvantage (Paul 257).

Eventually Fries turns to the early stages in human evolution and considers the environment in which humans lived then, the hunter-gatherer society radically different from today's technocratic age. "People with ADD are the leftover hunters," he claims (*History* 132). The characteristics attributed to people with ADD today, such as visual thinking, the constant monitoring of their environment, as well as their ability to react quickly and spontaneously change their strategy, Fries holds, would have immensely benefitted hunters (ibid.). As relicts from a past society, however, these individuals are maladapted to today's living conditions that demand different traits. In a similar vein, Sara Newman highlights that physical disability does not have a universal meaning but is based on a community's understanding of their members' roles in it. Accordingly, normality and ability are outlined by social constraints (8). Fries likewise refuses to locate the problem in individuals, but goes on to criticize the institutions that shape society: If schools were structured to allow such character traits, ADD would neither be viewed as conspicuous nor would there be a need to medicalize such behavior (*History* 132).

In a different environment, the jungles of Indonesia, Ian's disorder indeed proves to be an advantage, since it is only because "Ian's brain is firing on all cylinders, full of color, sound, light, and movement" and only through his eyes that Fries can finally spot a black monkey, the animal he has traveled "halfway across the world to see" (ibid. 139). The latter statement evinces that spotting the endangered monkeys in their natural habitat is an outstanding moment which, Fries's narration of the scene suggests, has only been made possible by Ian's disorder. As a consequence, his partner's ADD is depicted as utterly necessary in this situation. Exemplary for other vignettes, this scene revises traditional notions of disability and establishes that impairment is "fluid [...], necessary and universal" (Lambeth n. pag.). When Fries concludes that in this situation, "the hunter helps the starling"

(*History* 139), he alludes to their respective identifications – Ian as a "leftover" hunter and Fries as the weak and pleading starling they have witnessed before in an incubator – yet other vignettes make clear that their roles do alternate, for example when Fries is careful to allow the couple enough time before leaving the house to accommodate Ian's constant lateness (ibid. 126).

As I have pointed out above, Darwin did not intend his theory of evolution to apply to human beings, but makes clear that his observations are restricted to the realms of flora, fauna, and geology. It is only with a glimpse on the prospects of the future that Darwin draws attention to human life in the last paragraphs of his *Origin* and expresses the hope that his hypotheses may one day be applied to human evolution (559). Thus the most obvious form of resignification Fries undertakes is paralleling Darwin's theory with the story of his own life, thereby making explicit the connection of evolution and human life Darwin consciously avoided. According to Naomi Beck, the omission of any reference to human beings in *The Origin* was a strategic move. Well aware that believers in special creation[15] would take issue with his theory, Darwin excluded propositions for the evolutionary development of humans (Beck 195). First and foremost, Fries's *History* therefore turns against special creation and suggests that variations, fitness or unfitness are neither God's making nor part of a grant plan or design. That alone, it should be noted, does not bestow agency on human beings, since in Darwin's theory, Nature, personified and capitalized, emerges as the force that metaphorically selects (81ff.), much like Dr. Mendotti who deems Fries's body unfit. However, agency does arise in the course of a complex engagement with another fundamental idea of *The Origin* – the 'struggle for life' – that enables Fries to carve out a place for his seemingly unfit self in the theory of evolution as well as in society.

Of course, he is not the first to apply Darwinian ideas to human development. Although many Darwin scholars have stressed that the original theory of evolution did neither intend nor encourage the atrocities committed in the name of social Darwinism (cf. e.g. Engels, "Erkenntnis" 329; Engels, "Person" 11), the "survival of the fittest" is for Fries inextricably linked to social Darwinism. The term 'social Darwinism' was coined in Europe in the 1880s and spread to the United States in the early 20th century, where it quickly became fashionable (cf. Hofstadter, *Social*

---

15 Special Creationism is a literal reading of the Book of Genesis and conflicts with Darwin's theory of evolution because it postulates that God created the universe, the planet Earth, animals, plants, and human beings in the course of six days (Scott 60). The fitness of any organism is therefore seen the result of creation and, by extension, God's will (ibid. 82). Special creationism was the primary theory of evolution before *The Origin* (ibid. 178) and continues to attract attention and spur religious debates, for example over the status of the theory of evolution in American high school classrooms (ibid. 106).

xviii; Beck 195),[16] owing to its strong resonance, or, as historian Richard Hofstadter argues, to its being "suited to the American scene" ("Vogue" 389). According to him, social Darwinism was alluring because of its reassuring ring as a theory of progress based on science and its comprehensive scope "uniting under one generalization everything in nature from protozoa to politics" (ibid.). Only variations "fitted to the needs of civilized life" were deemed advantageous in the struggle, making human perfection not just possible, but ultimately also inevitable (ibid. 393).

In this context, impairment has come to be perceived as a threat to the progress of society (Barnes and Mercer 31) and notwithstanding the fact that social Darwinism significantly affected many areas of social life, its effect on the social construction and representation of disability is most striking. Inescapably, the rise of social Darwinism and the eugenics movement coincided with a radical shift in the representation and public visibility of disabled people, as social scientist Robert Bogdan convincingly argues.[17] According to him, social Darwinism and its "vicious" appli-

---

16 For a comprehensive overview of Social Darwinism in the United States, cf. Richard Hofstadter's *Social Darwinism in American Thought*. Originally published in 1944, it remains the most profound analysis of the causes that contributed to the quick rise and unprecedented popularity of (social) Darwinism in twentieth century American culture that did not only prompt American scientists to accept Darwin's principles, but move on to contribute to evolutionary science and apply it to outside the field of biology (cf. 5). Hofstadter's reading of social Darwinism is deeply intertwined with economics and conservatism, suggesting that the understanding of "survival of the fittest" in the context of social life would spur the idea of continuous improvement when "the best competitors in a competitive situation would win" (ibid. 6). In "Darwinism in the United States, 1859-1930," Mark Largent adds that the link between Darwinism and eugenics in the U.S. arises from the fact that many early twentieth century geneticists and biologists supported the movement (233).

17 Bogdan's work focusses primarily on the freak show, which is known to have a crucial impact on the representation of "extraordinary" bodies – most of which we would today call impaired – and from the middle of the nineteenth century to the early twentieth century, freak shows, carnivals, and traveling circuses dominated popular middle class entertainment. As its history and the traditional practices of representing the disabled body clearly go beyond the scope of this study, cf. the studies of Robert Bogdan, esp. *Freakshows: Presenting Human Oddities for Amusement and Profit* (Chicago: U of Chicago P, 1988), *Staging Stigma: A Critical Examination of the American Freak Show* by Michael M. Chemers (New York: Palgrave, 2008), John Springhall's *The Genesis of Mass Culture: Show Business Live in America, 1840-1940*. (New York: Palgrave, 2008), the volume *Freakery: Cultural Spectacles of the Extraordinary Body*, edited by Rosemarie Garland Thomson (New York: New York UP, 1996), as well as her study *Extraordinary Bo-*

cation in eugenics dramatically altered the ways in which nondisabled people perceived impairment and postulated that disabled individuals posed a threat to modern society which had thus far supported and protected its weak members, thereby impeding the "struggle for existence." Proponents of social Darwinism feared that if no actions were taken, "[t]he weak, the imperfect, the social, mental, and physical misfits […] would, if left unchecked, breed at such a rate as to outnumber the better breeding stock" and hence pass on their inferiority to the coming generations (*Freakshows* 62). Moreover, eugenicists devised links between intellectual and physical impairments and a plethora of social ills, such as unemployment, vagrancy, crime, or prostitution (Barnes and Mercer 32). Consequently, disabled people, formerly visible in society, particularly in the context of the spectacles of freak shows and carnivals, became victims to incarcerations and forced sterilizations in the name of 'social hygiene' (ibid.). As this practice of "negative eugenics" illustrates, the extraordinary body was not only removed from the public sphere, but the conception of human variation radically changed (cf. Bogdan, *Freakshows* 62).

Fries's memoir is aptly situated at the intersections of a reverberation of social Darwinism that attaches new stigma to the impaired body and the exploration and research which has gradually undermined the myths and stories fashioned for the representation of the extraordinary body at the turn of the century before impairment was stripped of its wonder and medicalized in the early twentieth century. The table of contents, for instance, is titled "List of Exhibits." Like a lengthy exhibition catalogue not unlike the lists of species brought back from expeditions, it lists the vignettes on three pages that introduce both Darwin and the animals he encountered, as well as the episodes from Fries's own life. Not only does the list present a kind of inventory, a neat orderly structure of the knowledge and experiences that have been gathered, but through the arrangement of his own life narrative into a "List of Exhibits," Fries himself becomes at once a sample specimen and a researcher and collector. Consequently, the list powerfully visualizes the tension at the heart of Fries's identity construction for it merges the object-body that is being gazed/stared at with the probing, subjective, and embodied stance.

At times this double role is hard to bear, as is illustrated by the scene in which Fries and his partner visit a reintroduction center for rescued endangered birds on

---

dies: Figuring Physical Disability in American Culture and Literature (New York: Columbia UP, 1997), and Rachel Adams's *Sideshow U.S.A.: Freaks and the American Cultural Imagination* (Chicago: U of Chicago P, 2001). The serious problems inherent in the exhibition of so-called 'freaks,' notwithstanding, many of these scholars have pointed out that freak shows firmly situated the extraordinary body in the realm of the everyday and fostered a view on disability marked by wonder and curiosity, as opposed to pathology, fear, and repulsion.

the islands. Part of the center is a section in which baby birds are raised to increase their chance of survival. On their guide's prompt to look inside one of the boxes, Fries sees "the tiniest bird" (*History* 50). Yet curiosity turns to terror as "the embryo-like creature opens its beak, pleading," and waiting to be fed (ibid.). The description of the bird as "embryo-like" is climactic compared to the "tiniest bird" Fries perceives on first glimpse and highlights the helplessness and the fact that its life is premature and unfit, were it not for the compassion of others. This is particularly emphasized by the verb phrase "pleading," the ultimate observation Fries makes and the note on which he ends his description of the bird before he immediately leaves the building.

Witnessing the young bird's helplessness is hence rendered as an intense experience for Fries and triggers a haunting association: "'Incubator,' is all I can say to [Ian]. This one word is enough. Ian knows that, because I was born a month premature, I spent the first four weeks of my life in an incubator. The doctors were not sure whether I would live" (ibid.). The experience is so intense that he is at the loss for all but one word. "Incubator" is the only word he can speak out aloud to Ian and that initiates his reaction and strong identification with the weak animals because it unites their dependency on others and technology, as well as the idea of a life that is neither ready, nor fit. However, while this encounter is first portrayed as unbearable, a memory of terror that the narrating I cannot possibly revisit, but only construct, the ending of the vignette contrasts this. Although Fries does not speak to his travel companions, his state is not a state of shock or numbness, since his mind is racing and revolves around his reaction to "the small embryo-like starling who opened its mouth to us as if its life depended on our decision whether to give what it needs to survive" (ibid. 51). Both the box and the feeding hands of others ensure the bird's survival and ultimately circumvent the Darwinian idea of a 'struggle for existence' and the social Darwinist assumption that if organisms "are not sufficiently complete to live, they die, and it is best they should die" (Spencer quoted in Hofstadter, "Vogue" 394). As Engels holds, the so-called 'struggle for existence' does not entail an actual struggle or fight, but rather denotes the mechanisms of natural selection ("Person" 27). For Darwin, natural selection depends on three factors, namely the competition between individuals of the same species and between different species, as well as an individual's struggle with its living conditions (73ff.).

Like the scene in the starling rescue center, the vignette titled "A Cane with No Story," in which Fries uses his cane to momentarily annul the principles of natural selection, becomes a parable for dependence and support. While Fries and Ian are hiking on Santa Cruz Island, they search for the land iguana, one of the species Darwin discovered on his journey. When they eventually spot the animal under a cactus plant, their guide tells them that it is waiting there for a cactus flower to drop so that it can eat it, which prompts Fries to "imagine herds of goats, grazing from cactus to cactus, devouring every flower before it has a change to fall" (*History*

188). He envisions the struggle for life, as the iguana, the weaker animal, is deprived of its food by the much bigger, stronger, and faster goats that outnumber the reptile and easily eat the flowers it subsists on, leaving the iguana to starve. Instantaneously, however, Fries moves to help the animal and, using his cane, "brushes against the flower, dislodges it. The flower falls to the ground. The iguana sees it – or hears it – fall into the brush. Two slow steps forward and the iguana is munching on the flower" (ibid. 188f.). The discourse time in this passage is extended considerably over the story time through the use of brief sentences which detail every motion slowly to illustrate the momentousness of Fries's defiance of the repeated order not to feed any of the animals they encounter on the islands.

7.4 "Everything an Adaptation": Alternative Ways of Coping with Impairment

It is only after this day that Fries's cane, previously a "Cane with No Story," "is beginning to have a story" as his adaptive device that saved the iguana from starvation (ibid. 189). The two passages from his travels therefore shift the focus from the "severe competition" all organisms face (Darwin 64) to dependence, compassion, help, and community. Beyond that, the men's encounter with the iguana on the Galápagos Islands attributes positive connotations to the cane, the experiencing I's second adaptation (apart from his shoes) to the hike on such uneasy terrain. Throughout the book, the use of adaptive devices plays on and revises the biological notion of 'adaptation.'

In Darwin's theory, adaptation is linked to the generational development of organisms, where variations and modifications of inherited structures have rendered them fitter and thus more successful in the process of natural selection (Carroll, *Reading* 203; Junker 45). As a result, adaptation is intricately intertwined with the environmental conditions in which organisms live and their relations to other organisms (Carroll, *Reading* 204). Yet while adaptation only figures as a process of natural selection and therefore receives little emphasis in the context of Darwin's entire *Origin*, Fries turns the idea into a central argument of his book, most of all by foregrounding his orthopedic shoes that have allowed his body to adapt to the environment. 'Adaptation' is hence removed from its original context to encompass not only alterations to the physical body to increase its fitness, but, in equal measure also adaptive devices and technologies that help the body to adjust to its living conditions. The latter aspect reveals that adaptations are universal, a thought that Linton, commenting on *The History* in a blog entry, finds particularly worthy of praise as an alternative critical perspective on disability ("Adaptation" n. pag.) and Fries's revision of the term further aids in destabilizing the firm divide between ability and disability.

In the prologue, Fries announces that he has arrived on the Galápagos Islands, the very place where Darwin's expedition began in 1835. If setting foot on the islands was a crucial moment for Darwin, whose "questions […] about what he saw around him would change not only the course of his life but the course of what we understand about life itself," tracing the naturalist's footsteps is no less crucial for Fries. "How did I get there?" he ponders and raises the question that provides the frame for his life narrative (*History* xvi). In the literal sense, the prologue suggests, Fries arrived there on his custom-made brown leather shoes in which the right sole has been raised three inches and shows an almost forty-five degree slope to the inner edge of his foot in order to accommodate the anatomy of this legs (cf. ibid.). For a long time, these shoes have come to signify only his disability, constantly reminding him of "the different way [he] walk[s]" (ibid.). However, Fries now acknowledges that they also signify ability, when he thinks about the various places his shoes have allowed him to travel to (cf. ibid. xvi). Letting him explore far-off places in Indonesia and Thailand, as well as on the Galápagos Islands and the canyons on the Colorado River, they "conjure unseen worlds" (ibid. xvii).

In contrast to the prostheses Audre Lorde so powerfully defies in *The Cancer Journals* (cf. Chapter 4.3), Fries's orthopedic shoes carry thoroughly positive connotations, precisely because the focus in this case is on function: they have tremendously increased his mobility and thus early on granted him access to many things that other disabled children were denied, such as a mainstreamed education. When Fries therefore speaks of their potential to "conjure" the unseen and unknown, he attributes mystical and magical qualities to his shoes, a strategy that resonates throughout the narrative, from childhood to adult age, turning the shoes – when they do fit his feet – into a synecdoche for well-being and a positive conception of the impaired body.

Since the regular sneakers his parents purchase for him in bulk continue to wear out too quickly, Dr. Milgram, Fries's physician at the time, cryptically commands the family to "'go to Eneslow'" (ibid. 15). Since neither Eneslow's full name, nor his profession is initially revealed, the shoemaker his physician has "conjured," exudes an aura of mystery, magic, and a form of power that cannot be fully grasped (ibid. 16). Similarly, on meeting Eneslow, Fries describes him as a "white-haired, distracted wizard," fashioning an enchanting image of the shoemaker and his made-to-order shoes (ibid.). Receiving his first pair is thus a special occasion, not only because he finally owns shoes that fit him, but also because of their representative "wing-tipped ornament gracing the toes, decorative like the balustrade at the top of Eneslow's staircase" (ibid.). The shoes reflect, as the simile implies, the decorative and noble interior of the shoemaker's shop and their ornaments likewise decorate Fries's feet.

Despite their portrayal as "decorative" and "festive," it is not solely the extraordinary the experiencing I links to his new shoes, since he remarks feeling "both normal *and* special" (ibid. 17; italics in original). Ultimately the shoes Eneslow crafts for the young Fries help to blur the boundaries between ability and disability and similarly, Fries's descriptions of both his shoes and the shoemakers he encounters stand in stark contrast to the title of the chapter – "Utilitarian Shoes." Although their purpose may be first and foremost utilitarian in that they enable Fries to walk, his repeated allusions to the fairy tale *Cinderella* make clear that the shoes transform his status and identity. Even if they do not grant him entrance to "the prince's ball," they do grant him access to a mainstreamed education (ibid.), a particular privilege usually not available to disabled children in the 1960s and 1970s before the Individuals with Disabilities Education Act was passed in 1975 (cf. also Chapter 6.2).[18] On several occasions, Fries recounts feeling "like Cinderella" (ibid. 17) and this simile as well as other explicit comparisons to the fairy tale suggest that the shoes profoundly impact the way in which he perceives his impaired body and the role of adaptive devices.

While the orthopedic shoes are at times portrayed as extraordinary and special adaptations, they are frequently also associated with assurance and familiarity. As Fries's body continues to grow, the shoes made by Eneslow wear out soon and cease to fit the changing anatomy of his legs. Ultimately, Dr. Milgram asks the family to consult a new shoemaker, Jerry Miller, whose logo on the card, Fries notes, almost looks like a finger print (ibid. cf. 30). Like his memory of Eneslow, Fries's recollection of Jerry Miller carries connotations of mystery. Yet in the case of Miller, mystery gives way to safety and familiarity when the shoemaker begins plastering the mould from which he will model a new pair of shoes: "My tired feet felt warm and comfortable, safe in the plaster [...]. My muscles relaxed as if my feet were in a hot bath after a long day's hike" (ibid. 31). Here, too, a simile is used to convey an utterly positive feeling and it is significant to note the trust, safety, and intimacy Fries links to the shoemaker and the process of crafting his new pair of shoes. Under the mould, he is able to relax in way unimaginable in the biomedical contexts in which he encountered the surgeons who scarred his legs and feet in their

---

18 Fries refers to the Disability Rights Movement on several occasions and stresses the hardships of disabled life before the appropriate legislation was passed. The Individuals with Disabilities Education Act (IDEA) fundamentally improved the educational situation of children with disabilities who were previously denied public education or attended segregated schools, because it guarantees disabled children "a free appropriate public education [...] in the least restrictive environment" (Individuals with Disabilities Education Act). For further information, consult e.g. the online resources on IDEA supplied by the U.S. Department of Education (http://idea.ed.gov).

attempts to normalize his anatomy, which reinforces the narrating I's determined avoidance of the settings of institutional medicine in which his body is sought to be corrected and repaired. The orthopedic shoes, in contrast, are fitted to his impaired body and accommodate its anatomy without changing it.

In a similar vein, the narrating I's memories of Frank, the cobbler, are equally positive. When he is ten years old, his parents allow him to accompany them to Frank who regularly repairs his shoes. Fries recalls finding himself in a dark shop with a counter that reminds him of "the drawbridge we passed on the way to visit my maternal grandparents in Far Rockaway every other Sunday" (*History* 30). Likewise, the black machine Frank's assistant is working on is evocative of Fries's "other, Orthodox Jewish grandmother" whom he remembers sitting in front of her old sewing machine. Even though Fries has never entered the shop before, he is enveloped in a sense of familiarity, belonging, and routine. Moreover, the shop smells "safe, like home," yet Fries is careful to point out that it is not the "homeyness associated with heavy curtains of upholstered chairs, but the masculine solidity of a bookshelf-lined study or a firm hug from my father" (ibid.). The kind of safety and homeliness Fries thus connects to the shop is not one that is overwhelming or smothering, but one characterized by comfort and acceptance. Intrinsically connected to Frank's shop, the shoes, too, come to signify comfort and acceptance.

Over time, however, the leather shoes Frank regularly repairs are not the only shoes Fries necessitates and the passage in which Ian accompanies him while shopping for the aqua booties he needs for the rafting trip elaborates on the meaning of adaptation. Having never worn store-bought shoes, Fries does not know which size might fit his feet but Ian carefully selects booties in size six and as he kneels before his partner to put the bootie on his foot, Fries "cannot help imagining Prince Charming. But if he is Prince Charming, then I am Cinderella, still embarrassed at fleeing the ball. No slippers, glass or otherwise, will slip easily onto my feet" (ibid. 148). On the one hand, the allusion allows the deeply affectionate relationship between the two men to surface, since, in the fairy tale, this moment leads to the lovers' happily ever-after. On the other hand, unlike in the fairy tale, Fries painfully notes that no shoe will fit on his feet and perceives his body in negative terms. Moreover, the comparison to Cinderella carries connotations of illegitimacy because her true status is concealed at the prince's ball to which she is only granted access in disguise when she can pass as one of the wealthy young women. To his great surprise, though, the size Ian has chosen fits and Fries marvels at the joy of wearing store-bought, even if special-sized, shoes which will enable him to go on the rafting trip.

While on the trip, he realizes that the shoes and aqua booties he wears are not the only adaptation made to a life on the river. "Almost everything on the shore is an adaptation," he observes, from the portable flooring, the makeshift kitchen and the outdoor toilets, the pump to purify their drinking water and their light for the night, to the boats they travel in (ibid. 159f.). Later, back in his own house, he notices that adaptations to contemporary life style are all around him there as well: "When I turn the toaster on [...] I realize that this appliance that I have taken for granted is not a given but it is an adaptation for the way we live now. So is the refrigerator, the stove, even the table and chairs [...]. Everything in my entire house – the entire house itself – everything as it is, but everything an adaptation" (ibid. 167). Appliances and objects that greatly facilitate our lives and to some extent even help to ensure our survival, he realizes, are not natural, but have entered all our lives as adaptations "for the way we live now" so that we may deal with the inhospitable conditions of our environment. In the final sentence of the quote, the repetition of the word "everything" and its place in the parallel sentence structure is revealing, for it foregrounds adaptations as all-encompassing and integral parts of everyday life, which nevertheless are – and the final position in the sentence highlights its significance – only adaptations.

As a result, the passages make evident that adaptations are not restricted to the context of impairment or a body that is faulty or lacking and needs support, enhancement, and hence depends on adaptations. Broadening the scope of the idea of adaptation and making its constant usage applicable and vital to all members of society, thereby defamiliarizing readers with their everyday lives, the memoir demystifies the difference commonly attributed to adaptations required by disabled individuals. Moreover, this strategy helps to corroborate the argument devised in earlier passages of the memoir, namely that impairment is to be understood in terms of variation and therefore needs to be stripped of the stigma attached to it. Fries's use of the term adaptation illustrates that survival is no longer merely dependent on the 'fit' body alone, but individuals may adapt to their environment in many other ways. Like during Fries's travels, when the principles of evolutionary theory are unhinged through help and community, the ability to craft adaptations suited to our needs overrides the 'struggle for existence' and its progress toward perfection by preparing the grounds for the acceptance of difference, variations, and deviance.

This notwithstanding, the orthopedic shoes are not always a source of well-being and of a positive and hopeful self-perception. Since corporeality is foregrounded in the life narrative, the text also documents the sorrow and exhaustion the experiencing I is confronted with when his pain increases and the shoes, now aged and torn in places, cease to provide a viable form of adaptation. In the vignette "Shoes on Fire," Fries recounts that while his shoes are being repaired at the shop once more, he is "lethargic, depressed": "I remain in bed until two in the afternoon, mourning the loss of the mobility I've had for thirty-seven years" (*History* 98). The narration in this scene entirely lacks transitional words that may bring coherence into the experience of pain and the staccato of the sentences in this passage portrays Fries's deep sense of isolation that is also underlined by the anaphora "I," which, used to begin almost every sentence, provides further evidence of the experiencing

I's isolation and aloofness from community caused by physical pain and the absence of his adaptive shoes. This makes clear that for Fries, his shoes are inextricably tied to his embodied position in the world and their absence is deeply disruptive.

One of the final chapters entitled "Shoes and the Calvaria Tree" begins by explaining how the calvaria tree, a species once endemic to Mauritius spread its seeds through fruits that the dodos ate but could not digest and therefore distributed all across the island. Yet once the dodos died out, their seeds withered in the fruits and "what once had been adaptive now was maladaptive" (ibid. 170). Instantaneously establishing a connection between the tree and his shoes through a flashback into his childhood when the family was able to retrieve his shoes again from the repair at Frank's shop, the statement holds equally true for Fries's shoes which now no longer correctly fit his feet and thus diminish his own 'fitness' that is literally dependent on fitting shoes.

These moments break with the positive and affirming outlook on variation and the belief that Fries's impaired body may transcend evolutionary principles, because doubts about his own body begin to surface. At the beginning of the narrative, when confronted with the decision whether or not to undergo surgery, the narrating I thus raises the question if his body has come to its limits and its capacity for movement and ability was exhausted: "had the time come when my asymmetrical body, with or without properly fitted shoes, had reached the apex of what it could do, of where it could take me?" (ibid. 5). Assuming a distance from "it," the experiencing I locates the shortcomings in his body, fears that his mobility is only temporary, and dreads the future. To be sure, questions about the contingency of the impaired body and its capacity for movement remain, yet at the end of this travels – at the end of the narrative – the memoirist notes that the question has "shift[ed]" and is now no longer the closed question whether or not he may continue to travel, but now centers on the instrumental dimension: "How might I continue to be able to take trips as physically demanding as this one?" (ibid. 186). At the end of the memoir, Fries looks back on the decision on the surgery, concluding that he "thought [his] evolution had come to an end" (ibid. 181) and the verb "thought" evinces that this opinion has now changed. The solution, the memoir shows, is presented by further adaptations that can accommodate the shifting shape of his body.

"Disability, perhaps more than other forms of alterity, demands a reckoning with the messiness of bodily variegation," Garland-Thomson argues ("Feminist" 283). While the social model of disability has been indispensable for the destigmatization of disability, she holds that "it also threatens to obscure the material and historical effects of those differences and to destabilize the very social categories we analyze and, in many cases, claim as significant in our own and others' lives," to the effect that the particularities of impairment and its embodied experience are not recognized (ibid. 282). As a result, the memoir counters the idea that impairment essentially signifies bodily insufficiency (cf. ibid. 283). Garland-Thomson demands that in order to do justice to the disabled experience, "embodied difference [...] should be claimed, but without casting the difference as lack" (ibid.). The analysis of the memoir has illustrated that although Fries claims his disability and impaired body, the focus is not on difference but rather on commonality, an aspect that introduces a significant shift into current debates on disability and the social model.

Indeed, the concept of impairment that surfaces in Fries's book is one that fills the emerging so-called 'universal model,' a skeletal theoretical approach to diversity and variation, with the flesh of corporeal experiences of searching for a common ground. The mentioning of compassion, help, and community at the starling rescue center and in the encounter with the iguana, as well as the elaborate discussion of adaptation as universal devices underline this and make commonality and interdependence possible. Wendell remarks that dependence on others' and their help, as it is portrayed in the book, may appear humiliating in a society in which independence is paramount ("Toward" 273). In this respect, Fries's life narrative is certainly "un-American," as it does not praise independence at all costs but in manifold ways cherishes community and thus sets out to rethink contemporary society.

On returning home from his travels, Fries receives a welcome package from a disabled friend and fellow writer containing a "T-shirt with four drawings of the evolution from ape to human, the most evolved human sitting in a wheelchair. Underneath is written: 'Adapt or perish – C. Darwin'"[19] (*History* 200). The T-shirt ironically subverts the Darwinian struggle for life and the narrow conception of fitness the memoir reads into Darwin's theory by putting forward the broader conception of adaptation Fries has devised toward the end of his memoir and depicting the use of the wheelchair not as an impaired body's turn for the worse, but as another, even higher stage in the development of its shape. In Darwin's theory, there is "no inbuilt trend forcing species to evolve in a certain direction," historian Peter Bowler maintains (13) and the print highlights this, while at the same time exposing Fries's rather partial reading of evolutionary theory.

"I suggest that there is more than 'one' Darwin," writes Virginia Richter in "Displacing Humans, Reconfiguring Darwin in Contemporary Culture and Theory" and points to the "richness, indeterminacy and even contradictoriness" of his writing (151). Similarly, Bowler locates "layers of interpretation and misinterpretation" in the reception of Darwin's theories and of his persona (2). Darwin has long served as a symbol for religious and ideological points of view, he continues (4), and Richter suggests that "[w]hich Darwin we need, and which Darwin we like, is highly

---

19 Although the statement is frequently attributed to Darwin, it is actually a quote from H.G. Wells's final brief book *Mind at the End of Its Tether* (1945) in which humanity is replaced by another species.

dependent on our various strategic position-takings and intellectual commitments" (152). In their introduction to the volume *Reflecting on Darwin*, Monika Pietrzak-Franger and Eckart Voigts note how the popular and scholarly reception of Darwin's scientific persona and his theory has evolved, how his work has been rewritten and appropriated in a number of ways (5f.). Their focus lies on the post-millennial trends in interpretation, particularly the reception of Darwin's theory and persona beyond the bicentenary celebrations in 2009. More recently, they argue, long held (mis)conceptions about his work are being reconsidered (2).

At the center of these revisionary readings is the evolutionary theory expounded in the *Origin*. Whereas numerous previous readings have echoed the fear of ruthless nature, a variety of more positive interpretations have emerged which acknowledge the contingency of natural selection as "a positive, dynamic force" (Richter 149). Levine, in *Darwin Loves You: Natural Selection and the Re-Enchantment of the World* detects "a kinder, gentler Darwin" in *The Origin* who celebrates the interdependence of the ecosystem he encountered (202). This is also elaborated in Angelique Richardson's essay which reads Darwin's and Francis Galton's publications and correspondence side by side to convincingly demonstrate that Darwin's work contains a strong critique of Galton's eugenic thought, particularly in his later *Descent of Man*, where Darwin reminds readers that neglecting the weak members of society would only be "for a brief contingent benefit, with a certain and present evil" (quoted in Richardson 25ff.). To a certain extent, *The History* does disclose this sense of interdependence and altruism, but the memoir cannot fully move beyond the – both covert and quite explicit – idea that help and assistance, though sometimes vital, as in the case of the iguana, the sterling, or Fries himself as a baby, are somehow illicit and illegitimate. Ingrained in the narrative appears to be a hierarchy, a subliminal sense of normativity, even as the memoir ostensibly rewrites it in such a creative manner and takes great care to blur the lines of dis/ability and to inscribe more positive connotations on the impaired body.

In *The History*, natural selection in the Darwinian sense is often tied to the painful undertones of eugenics which also reverberate elsewhere in Fries's writing: In *Body, Remember*, Fries recounts a visit to the National Holocaust Museum where he strongly identifies with the disabled depicted in the hospital at Hartheim, the site of the Nazi's T-4 program and observes the visitors' reactions to the exhibit. "How similar their reactions are to those whose stares and fears I have met on the streets of many places in countries all over the world," he notes (209). His statement evinces that for him (and readers must not forget that he simultaneously speaks from a queer and Jewish standpoint), disability and eugenics are inextricably historically linked. This link is one Fries also detects in/projects onto others, which attests to a pervasiveness of eugenic thought or, put more moderately but no less socially and culturally significant, a fear of difference and imperfection. On a meta-level, *The History* and Fries's reading of the evolutionary theory he reappropriates highlights the contradictory feelings Darwin's vision of evolution elicits and its great affective potential (cf. Bowler 1). The memoir thus exposes what Kuusisto calls "Darwin's strange legacy" ("History" n. pag.) but a perhaps even more important task it may perform is sensitizing readers to the significance of interdependence and altruism and the role adaptations play for an individual's sense of well-being.

The print on the T-shirt lifts the stigma attached to the use of a wheelchair, and, much like the narrative itself, from the impaired body, fashioning a hopeful perspective for the narrating I's uncertain future and, at the same time, taking a critical stand on the representation and perception of impairment:

"But now, after walking with only my cane in Thailand's temples, after kayaking shoeless among the limestone islands of Phang Nga Bay, after searching with Ian for black monkeys in the Balinese jungle, after being Aqua Bootied along the Colorado, after Tom's molding and adjustment of my new black shoes, plus the addition of the GapKids padded slippers to use at home, I realize that because my body keeps changing there is no one perfect pair of shoes. In fact, I no longer have only one pair of shoes. As my body has changed, I now have different kinds of shoes I can use in different situations. I also realize that eventually I will need to find other ways to take pressure off my body. Eventually, I will get a wheelchair, another 'pair of shoes' that will help me answer my ongoing question." (*History* 199f.)

The temporary answer Fries devises to his question is much more positive and hopeful than the fear and despair resonating in earlier pages have allowed readers to hope. Although the prospect of recurring and increasing un-wellness is foreshadowed here and therefore robs the memoir of full closure, the book's strong emphasis on emotional closure and well-being is manifested here. Fore Wendell, more knowledge about the qualitative experience of living with an impairment, it of utmost importance because it will reform our understanding of disability ("Toward" 271). In offering solace to his readers, both able-bodied and disabled, Fries's memoir does indeed invite them to "give up our idealizations and relax our desire for control of the body" (ibid.).

8. Rewriting the Diagnostic Narrative:
Siri Hustvedt's *The Shaking Woman or A History of My Nerves*

When Siri Hustvedt's illness memoir was published in 2010, it was met by many reviewers with utter surprise. Noting that despite the essays she has published and the lectures she holds, Hustvedt is commonly perceived as a novelist, literary critics voiced their astonishment over the fact that *The Shaking Woman or A History of My Nerves* is rather a piece of academic work than a personal memoir (Beyer 111). In an attempt to categorize her work, scholars have been tempted to create neologisms like "intellectual neuropsychoautobiography" (Švrljuga 222). Željka Švrljuga's term certainly adverts to the meticulous research involved in the production of the narrative, just like Gygax draws attention to the long list of endnotes which document Hustvedt's academic venture ("Theoretically" 180). In fact critic Brigitte Neumann quotes Hustvedt in an interview where she states that roughly 10 percent of the book deal with her personal story, while 90 percent address theoretical questions (n. pag.). On the formal level, this holds certainly true, as Hustvedt's work raises – more than it answers – profound and general questions about the self, character and personality, the mind and the brain.

The writer's emotional involvement, Jarmila Mildorf claims, is suspended in favor of a style that is more akin to popular scientific writing, thus lending it a sense of detachment[1] and turning the book into a veritable "tour-de-force" through scientific concepts and discourses (3f.). The narrative is grounded in thorough research in neuroscience, psychology, psychoanalysis, and philosophy of mind and accommodates Hustvedt's proclaimed interest in the cognitive sciences: She has been a

---

1 In her insightful essay, Mildorf looks at the doctor-patient encounters in the memoir, which serve as a frame for the narrative and for Hustvedt's search (4). Literary strategies, among them irony, caricature, and parody, Mildorf argues, enable Hustvedt to gain distance and, simultaneously, "subject medical discourse to Hustvedt's own (artistic) narrative" (1f.).

member of several discussion groups in the fields of neurology and psychiatry at The New York Psychoanalytic Institute, Columbia University, and Rockefeller University, holds lectures, teaches writing classes for psychiatric patients, and contributed to an online blog of *The New York Times* where she discussed migraine (Neumann n. pag.). It is therefore not surprising that reviews of the book feature numerous passages that, though benevolently written, make evident that the book is rarely received as a memoir, for instance when critic Susanne Beyer describes the story as "honest," yet at the same time "exhausting" on part of the reader, suitable only to be read the way books are read in the academic setting by using highlighters, taking notes on the margins, and writing excerpts (112). Critic Lynda Albertyn even comes to the conclusion that the story "may be too technical and 'medical' for lay readers" (59).

In other words, *The Shaking Woman* effectively subverts expectations about the form and perspective of a memoir in general and an illness memoir in particular and thus points to the emerging alternative "political" consciousness and theoretical "treatment" in illness memoirs. The neuroscientific and philosophical discourses Hustvedt utters serve a specific purpose, namely to scrutinize the construction of disease, illness, and health. In the course of the story, it therefore becomes clear that the focus is not merely on the question of which disease lies beneath Hustvedt's shaking, but rather on the experience of illness and on the ways in which illness affects life, self-image, and identity (cf. DasGupta and Hurst, "Gendered" 2).

By drawing on interpersonal relationships and the experiential quality of illness, the concept of self Hustvedt proposes throughout the course of the narrative creates a powerful counter-stance to recent attempts to conceptualize self and identity in the reductionist terms of neuroscience, such as Fernando Vidal's 'cerebral subject,' Nikolas Rose's 'neurochemical self,' and Joseph LeDoux's 'synaptic self.'[2] In man-

---

2 In "The Neurochemical Self and its Anomalies," Nikolas Rose scrutinizes, in a Foucaultian fashion, the gaze of psychopharmacology and psychiatry, and notes that "diseases of the will," such as alcoholism, have come to be seen as "diseases of the brain" (407). Such somatization, or, to be more precise, the conceptualization of the self in neurochemical terms, "flatten[s] out" the opposition between the mind and the brain, "between organs and conduct" (408f.). Neuroscientist Joseph LeDoux's concept of the 'synaptic self' proposes that "we are our synapses" (7; my translation). In other words, the self emerges through the interconnections between neurons, for these interconnections enable the flow and storage of information and therefore affect all processes in the brain (10). This approach, LeDoux stresses, is not supposed to substitute psychological, social, moral, and aesthetic theories of the self; instead, in his book, he sets out to explain these theories employing his synaptic model (10f.). In a similar vein, historian and philosopher of science Fernando Vidal has coined the notion of the 'cerebral subject' to read person-

ifold ways, *The Shaking Woman* is hence a successor to the life narratives by Audre Lorde and Oliver Sacks that I have analyzed in Chapters 4 and 5, as well as to countless other illness narratives published in the 1980s. Hustvedt's text shares the strong defiance of closure that has become evident in *The Cancer Journals* through the motifs of temporality and contingency. Even though her condition is by far less dramatic and life-threatening than Lorde's breast cancer, Hustvedt, too, becomes a member of the remission society and uses her new-found status to effectively undermine the firm divide between health and illness, as well as to promote an alternative vision of healing in opposition to the biomedical cure.

Like Oliver Sacks's *A Leg to Stand On*, *The Shaking Woman* treats a seemingly neurological symptomatology and revisits and reworks the case history to incorporate both objective and subjective knowledge, science and art. However, in contrast to Sacks's life narrative and in line with other contemporary memoirs of well-being, Hustvedt's book does not grant an active voice to medical practitioners, but introduces, as I will illustrate, the objective stance through the narrating I's voice, thus significantly extending Sacks's project of merging perspectives in the story of illness to gain deeper insight. In this vein, Hustvedt decidedly turns away from the biomedical discourse. Whereas Sacks's memoir sets out to reconceptualize neurological practice and the patient's role in it in order to arrive at a more adequate story of illness and healing, Hustvedt's narrative is situated at a meta-level, the level of discourse. As the narrating I challenges neuro-scientific, psychological, and philosophical discourses about disease, self, mind, and body, her story is removed from the biomedical realm and the diagnostic narrative devised there. Although medical terminology permeates the book, it does not mark Hustvedt's 'narrative surrender' but rather a narrative insurgency (cf. Chapter 3.2). I will therefore argue that Hustvedt employs a rhetoric of contingency to not only destabilize established notions of disease and health, but to also transcend the dichotomy between the writer and the scientist, literature and science. A close reading of the life narrative then reveals that the diagnostic narrative readers and critics were sure would await them in the memoir is supplanted by a 'therapeutic narrative' that situates healing and well-being outside professional medicine and neuroscience.

---

hood as 'brainhood.' In many ways, Vidal's work rests on LeDoux's and Rose's notion of the self, but significantly extends their theories by studying the 'cerebral subject' in the context of modernity and discourses on individuality and agency (cf. "Brainhood: Anthropological Figure of Modernity." *History of the Human Sciences* 22.1 (2009): 5-36; Also see the now completed research project "The Cerebral Subject: Brain, Self, and Body in Contemporary Culture" at the Max Planck Institute for the History of Science and its publication *Neurocultures: Glimpses into an Expanding Universe*. Eds. Francisco Ortega and Fernando Vidal. Bern: Peter Lang, 2011).

Published ten years after the end of the 'Decade of the Brain' President George Bush proclaimed in 1990 to incite research on "one of the most magnificent – and mysterious – wonders of creation" (n. pag.), *The Shaking Woman* is substantial evidence that neuroscience continues to fascinate both researchers and the general public. Journalist and psychopharmacologist Felix Hasler reports that numerous conferences in the field of neuroscience have already proposed the beginning of a 'Century of the Brain' attributing significance to the brain in similar ways in which genes have dominated biological discourses in the twentieth century (28f.). Next to the emergence of a plethora of fields and scientific theories with the prefix "neuro-," neuroscience has also changed the literary landscape in the United States and brought forth new approaches to literary texts.[3] In his essay "Will Neuroscience Kill

---

3 During the last 25 years, Fludernik and Olson contend, cognition has become a crucial point of inquiry in narrative studies and may even rise to the most significant concern in narratological studies (8). Narratives are read as a "mode of mental access" that allows theorists to study the mind, along with processes of perception and cognition (ibid. 3). The emerging narratology has been coined 'cognitive narratology' and needs to be seen as a subdomain of postclassical narratology. It encompasses research building on the work of classical structuralist critics by using concepts and methods that narratologists like Barthes, Genette, and Todorov did not have at their disposal at the time they were formulating their theories. The relationship between minds and narratives may be studied in terms of both construction and interpretation of texts, such as the ways in which the story is produced by the narrator and the processes through which readers may comprehend the storyworlds and the cognitive states and dispositions of the characters in the narrative. For an introduction to cognitive narratology, see David Herman's edited volume *Narrative Theory and the Cognitive Sciences* (Stanford: CSLI Publ., 2003), as well as his essay on "Cognitive Narratology" in *The Living Handbook of Narratology*, Jürgen Schläger's and Gesa Stedman's volume *The Literary Mind* (Tübingen: Narr, 2008.), Irving Massey's *The Neural Imagination: Aesthetic and Neuroscientific Approaches to the Arts* (Austin: U of Texas P, 2009), Mary Crane's and Alan Richardson's "Literary Studies and Cognitive Science: Toward a New Interdisciplinarity" (*Mosaic: A Journal for the Interdisciplinary Study of Literature* 32.2 (1999): 123-41), Monika Fludernik's "Narratology in the Twenty-First Century: The Cognitive Approach to Narrative" (*PMLA* 125.4 (2010): 924-30), and, for a critical perspective, Marie-Lauren Ryan's "Narratology and Cognitive Science: A Problematic Relation" (*Style* 44.4 (2010): 469-95). Recently, novel approaches to the study of autobiography have also emerged that transfer the concepts of Antonio Damasio's 'autobiographical self' and 'core self' to autobiographical subjects. Cf. especially Paul John Eakin's *Living Autobiographically: How We Create Identity in Narrative* (Ithaca: Cornell UP, 2008), as well as Jason Tougaw's "Brain Memoirs, Neu-

the Novel?" writer and editor Austin Allen even speaks of a watershed moment in American culture as "neurologically abnormal characters" and the languages of cognitive and neuroscience have begun to enter literary works of art (n. pag.). In her analysis of fictional texts in "Brain Plots," Gesa Stedman, too, comments on the recent tendency to incorporate neurological illness, medical jargon, and the terminology from the cognitive sciences in contemporary stories, as well as a return to modes of representation that invoke the workings of the mind and feature dreams, nightmares, and memories (113). Hustvedt's narrative, though of course not fictional, reveals similar characteristics.

The book begins on the day Hustvedt returns to the St. Olaf college campus, where her deceased father taught as a professor, in order to deliver a speech in his honor. As soon as she begins her talk, she starts to shake uncontrollably and can only stop when her speech comes to an end. Throughout the book, the narrating I returns to this day to observe it from different perspectives, as well as turns to other incidents and illnesses in Hustvedt's life to explore the question of who the shaking woman, the "shuddering stranger," is and what role she takes up in her life (*Shaking* 7). In her account, memories and dreams are, as is characteristic of 'brain plots,' interwoven with expert knowledge and quotations from other sources (cf. Stedman 122), in this case seminal works and recent advances in the fields of psychology, psychoanalysis, neuroscience, and philosophy of mind.

Above I have referred to Frank's notion of illness as a loss of orientation that required a different way of thinking (cf. ibid. 1). In fashioning a narrative for herself and the shaking woman, Hustvedt creates a new "map," albeit not a linear one that traces the progress of diagnosis, treatment, and cure and guides her to a definitive end-point. Rather, the plot of the book is an exploratory one, mapping the fields and perspectives involved in her idea of the shaking woman, for Hustvedt states: "The search for the shaking woman takes me round and round […]. I have to see her from every angle" (*Shaking* 73). Her journey thus becomes one that revolves around conceptual notions, rather than a spiritual quest, which ultimately transforms Frank's notion of "thinking differently." Whereas traditional quest memoirs frequently strive to find an alternative way to think about the individual affected by illness and how this person can go on living in the face of illness and the potential interruptions that this will hold (cf. Chapter 2.3), the endeavor in *The Shaking Woman* is to disclose the constructed nature of disease and health and the fuzzy boundaries that indeed eventually cease to separate these concepts.

By choosing to read the narrative along these lines, I do not mean to neglect the transformation of self and identity that Hustvedt sketches and the crucial role that

---

roscience, and the Self: A Review Article" (*Literature and Medicine* 30.1 (2012): 171-92).

intersubjectivity plays in grasping the meaning of her shaking. Rather, I wish to highlight that her narrative likewise transforms the ways in which science, theory, and knowledge are perceived, which entails a shift in perspective and direction. Frank's idea of "thinking differently" is governed by patients learning about their illnesses by "hearing themselves tell their stories, absorbing other's reactions, and experiencing their stories being shared" (*Wounded* 1), thereby turning their gaze inward and allowing their sense of self to be altered through their interaction with what lies outside. In this context, individuals and institutions beyond the patient's immediate experience affect how subjects choose to frame their experience over time. "[N]ot all stories are equal," Frank rightfully claims, and as the patient's story circulates, different voices and perspectives will assume power over the representation of illness and the construction of identity (ibid. 5). Hustvedt's book, in contrast, extends Frank's notion of the postmodern illness experience in that Hustvedt not only speaks for herself instead of having medicine speak for her (cf. ibid. 13) but that in the act of speaking, she openly challenges scientific, medical, and social premises, therefore claiming both experience and voice for herself.

8.1 THE PERSONAL MEETS THE SCIENTIFIC: THE 'BRAIN MEMOIR'

In her full-length study of Hustvedt's fictional writing, Christine Marks notes that the literary criticism on Hustvedt's oeuvre has been astonishingly sparse and little attention has been devoted to how medical and neurological discourses are employed in Hustvedt's reconceptualization of identity in the twenty-first century (*Relationality* 15). While her study provides an intriguing perspective on illness, as well as on the cultural, neurological, and medical discourses that permeate the characters' illness experiences, it can naturally not account for Hustvedt's non-fictional narrative that stands out due to the wealth and depth of discourses Hustvedt embeds into her story. However, *The Shaking Woman* and its conceptualization of the relationship between mind and body – or rather, mind and brain – do not constitute a singular and isolated instance of literary approaches to neuroscientific questions; rather, her book needs to be seen as one of the most prominent examples in the currently emerging genre Jason Tougaw terms 'brain memoirs' ("Brain Memoirs" 172).

These works do not only study a single self, but turn to investigations of selfhood on broader terms when their authors question the meaning of selfhood, as well as the emergence and development of the self (Tougaw, "Autobiography" 1). For Tougaw, the defining characteristic of this emerging genre is the use of neurology, neuroscience, and cognitive science in the texts in order to "help tell the story" (ibid. 13). He therefore sees the growing number of literary texts as a way to "translate" the third-person perspective of neuroscience into the subjective first-person stance and thus convey the qualitative dimension of neurological illness:

"[W]hile brain researchers like Damasio, Gerald Edelman, Jaak Panksepp, and Mark Solms are developing methods for integrating the examination of subjective experience into brain research and theory, a growing number of memoirists – many of them responding directly to the explosion in brain research in the last two decades – are experimenting with language and narrative forms that translate their private, first-person experience for readers." ("Autobiography" 14)

This observation certainly postulates a fundamental aspect but Tougaw's explanation does not grasp the full complexity of the purpose of neuroscientific discourses in these narratives. Surely philosophical questions of qualia and their application to literary works of art may help scholars to pinpoint the notions of subjectivity conveyed in these texts in critical and conceptual terms.[4] Beyond that, the direct response of these memoirs to seminal works in brain research needs to be stressed, as it is here that science and literature, as well as their perspectives clash and their encounter is mediated. In this respect, brain memoirs also work against the assumption that literary form and practice or the narrating subject may be reduced to science.

Although Tougaw views the writer primarily as an organism whose life is subject to physiological, cultural, familial, and circumstantial accidents ("Brain Memoirs" 173),[5] his definition does not lapse into determinism, since he stresses the role

---

[4] The subjective dimension of narratives is arguably the reason why audiences become immersed in these stories. On the issue of qualia in narratives, cf. especially David Herman's *Basic Elements of Narrative* in which he establishes qualia as a characteristic feature "prototypical for [...] narratives" (138): "Narrative representations convey the experience of living through storyworlds-in-flux, highlighting the pressure of events on real or imagined consciousnesses affected by the occurrences at issue. Thus – with one important proviso – it can be argued that narrative is centrally concerned with qualia, a term used by philosophers of mind to refer to the sense of 'what it is like' for someone or something to have a particular experience. The proviso is that recent research on narrative bears importantly on debates concerning the nature of consciousness itself." (ibid. 137; italics in original). In a similar vein, Fludernik in *Towards a 'Natural' Narratology* defines experientiality as the key criterion for the presence of narratives.

[5] In this context, it may also be interesting to study narratives that probe risk in the family and narrate hereditary illness, such as Alice Wexler's *Mapping Fate: A Memoir of Family, Risk, and Genetic Research* (1996) (cf. Chapter 1 and fn19 below).

of agency that writers craft in their memoirs: Brain memoirs bespeak a nuanced sense of agency, which allows the writers to cope with the accidental events beyond their control (ibid.). Yet he stresses that brain memoirs also contribute significantly to culture in further ways. Like other illness and disability memoirs, these first-hand accounts of neurological illness and impairment may serve as a source for information for both researchers and clinical practitioners, but also as solace to readers who share the writers' condition or their suffering, as well as to their caregivers. More than that, though, they spur philosophical debates surrounding the mind-body problem (cf. ibid.). As Tougaw points out in "Brain Memoirs, Neuroscience, and the Self," the integration of philosophical and abstract questions on the nature of the human mind and their connection to the body, the self, as well as the world are at the core of these narratives and intertwined with concrete physical experiences (172).

Tougaw's concept of the brain memoir thus seems to be an inherently academic genre, as participating in these debates requires insight into current neuroscientific and philosophical discourses. It is therefore no coincidence that a large number of the memoirs he mentions in his review article have been written by individuals with a career in the medical profession (Mark Vonnegut: *Just Like Someone with Mental Illness only More So: A Memoir*), psychology (Lauren Slater: *Lying*; Kay Redfield Jamison: *An Unquiet Mind: A Memoir of Moods and Madness*), neuro-anatomy (Jill Bolte Taylor: *My Stroke of Insight*), higher education (Temple Grandin: *Thinking in Pictures: My Life with Autism*) or by writers who as journalists substantially engage in public discourses, so that 'brain memoirs' may well be seen as overlapping with the genre of the academic memoir. As I have explored above, the genre of life writing lends itself particularly well to the connection between qualitative experiences and "deep theoretical questions" (Davis, "Introduction" 161; cf. Chapter 2.2). Moreover, as I have explored in greater detail above, academic accounts, even as they take on decidedly personal or "un-scholarly" forms and voices, bring to the fore issues that are not only individual, but at the same time also institutional, thus exposing how their writers' lives are shaped by institutions (Quinn-Brauner 2). While scholarship on the academic autobiography has as of yet limited the notion of institutions to the actual educational systems and networks of secondary and higher education, these arguments may well be expanded to view theoretical discourses and conventions as exercising similar power over individuals and inciting very similar ideological and epistemological struggles.

Brain memoirs, according to Tougaw, do not only demonstrate their writers' suffering in times of illness, but also their fascination with the "push-pull between their selves and their brains" ("Brain Memoirs" 172). Early in her narrative, Hustvedt explains that her fascination for psychoanalysis and neuroscience originated from the desire to understand the migraines she had been suffering from since her childhood but intensified during her research for her novel *Sorrows of an*

American. To "be" Erik, the protagonist of *Sorrows*, she begins studying pharmacology and mental disorders, attends lectures and becomes a member of a discussion group on neuropsychoanalysis (*Shaking* 5f.). Though not having undergone medical training and possessing applied professional expertise, one may certainly grant Hustvedt the status of an expert and literary critics attest her "dual proficiencies" in the scientific discourses (Deshauer 673), which in turn enables her to adopt a professional, third-person perspective on her illness.

Such a third-person perspective surfaces early on in the book, for instance when Hustvedt explains her year-long research on and her dedication to questions about the mind and the brain and assumes a generalizing perspective, stating: "Intellectual curiosity about one's own illness is certainly born of a desire for mastery" (*Shaking* 6). Her declaration, formulated in the passive voice so that any observer or active subject may be omitted, demonstrates an objective and detached vantage point. Additionally, the use of noun phrases lends a more formal tone to her statement and thereby also authority. Interestingly, she instantly and within the same chain of thoughts turns to a more personal voice when she states: "If I couldn't cure myself, perhaps I could at least begin to understand myself" (ibid.). In contrast to the previous statement, this thought is phrased in the active voice, thus foregrounding the "I," herself, as the active and acting subject. The determination and certainty of the first sentence here gives way to uncertainty, tentativeness, but also possibility as expressed through the use of the subjunctives "could" and "couldn't," as well as by the adverb "perhaps."

On first reading, Hustvedt's utterances reiterate the commonly deployed dichotomy between the third- and the first-person perspective that has also initially been at work in Sacks's memoir (cf. Chapter 5.2): The third-person point of view is characterized by distance, objectivity, and authority, whereas the first-person stance is involved, subjective, and less determined. On the other hand, however, Hustvedt plays on the value-laden distinction between the two perspectives. In her statements, it is no longer solely the objective perspective that is associated with knowledge. Knowledge is instead also alluded to in the subjective utterance through the verb "understand." Furthermore, it is the first-person stance that expresses possibility and prospect, that may put the detached voice of the objective statement into practice. What is more, the two perspectives supplement each other, as they revolve around the same thought. Not only do these two statements thus stress the tight relationship between the abstract and the concrete, as well as the first- and third-person perspective that is symptomatic for both her writing and the genre of brain memoirs, but it also foregrounds the purpose of an intellectual approach to any kind of illness experience and Hustvedt's own shaking in particular, namely "mastery" and "understanding."

What should strike readers is the fact that so early in the narrative, the idea of "cure" is supplanted by "understanding," since Hustvedt makes clear that in lieu of a cure for her condition, she seeks insight and knowledge.[6] This reveals a mindset removed from the biomedical conception of disease as an anomaly that needs to be repaired or mended (cf. Chapter 3.1). In this vein, it foreshadows a more flexible notion of health that is not absolute, but that may tolerate some disruption. "Mastery" does therefore not refer to a medical management of her affliction or to overcoming it, but ultimately to an intellectual avenue to grasp her shaking fits. Along these lines, the biological, and particularly the etiological questions about her disease move into the background and give way to questions about the discursiveness of her condition. By attributing equal importance to knowledge about her disease and to the belief systems that govern the interpretation of her condition, Hustvedt consequently points to the constructed nature of disease.[7]

It is precisely this intellectual approach to illness that has repeatedly been misread by reviewers and literary critics. Focusing on Hustvedt's role as a writer which seems to have been altered by the publication of *The Shaking Woman*,[8] Neumann

---

6   In her essay, Mildorf also analyzes Hustvedt's imaginary session with a psychoanalyst after which Hustvedt suggests she "would be cured" (*Shaking* 21) with a focus on its fictionality and the ways in which the narrating I reappropriates psychoanalytical discourse. As a consequence, she argues, Hustvedt undermines both the discourse of psychoanalytic therapy and its underlying concepts and beliefs (8).

7   Throughout her fictional and non-fictional writing, Hustvedt returns to the ideas of social construction and the biological grounding of behavior and Thiemann argues that "[e]vidence of Hustvedt's conflicting views on construction and essentialism" may be discerned in her texts (372f.).

8   I strongly disagree when these critics purport that Hustvedt's autobiographical work represents a sudden and harsh break in her oeuvre. In fact, I rather suggest reading *The Shaking Woman* as a continuation of Hustvedt's preoccupation with neuroscientific discourses and questions of self and other. These questions do not only figure prominently in the narration of psychiatrist Erik Davidsen, the protagonist of *The Sorrows of an American* (2008), but also in *What I Loved* (2003), where Violet and Bill Wechsler's aesthetic explorations of hysteria and eating disorders trigger notions of self and other – themes that surface again in her most recent novel *The Blazing World* (2014), as well as in her 2012 novel *Summer without Men*, in which the narrator Mia Fredrickson attempts to define her self after her husband, a fundamental part of her identity, has left her. For a thorough comparison of the themes in the former two fictional works, see Christine Marks's study *"I Am Because You Are": Relationality in the Works of Siri Hustvedt*. Similarly, much of her nonfictional writing is oriented on these themes. "Extracts from a Story of the Wounded Self," for instance takes the epileptic seizure of a stranger in the street as a starting point for the exploration of Hustvedt's migraines (and inspiration for her first no-

alleges that Hustvedt's move to introduce herself to the world as the shaking woman presents in itself a venture, as Hustvedt is known as a successful writer and "part of an admired couple" (n. pag.; my translation). In a similar vein, other articles engage in an outright gender-biased discussion: In her review, Beyer pointedly remarks that Hustvedt publicly transforms from a "female idol to a disturbed woman who devotes herself fervently and frantically to elusive material" (111f.; my translation). Placing heavy emphasis on the idea of madness, Beyer voices an essentialist supposition here and intertwines femininity with irrationality, unreasonableness, and emotions. Moreover, her review denies Hustvedt's endeavor to "master" her condition by associating science with the idea of the "elusive" and thereby implying that the scientific and intellectual material she concerns herself with is incomprehensible.

Reviewer Rachel Cooke takes a similar line, noting that "[i]n our culture, telling the world that you, a woman, suffer from migraine or other mysterious and difficult-to-treat disorders is still tantamount to telling the world you are mad: unstable, unreliable, moaning, self-obsessed" (1). She calls Hustvedt "brave" for sharing the story of her mysterious and unresolved illness, while simultaneously reading Hustvedt's intellectual approach to her own experiences as a defense strategy to appearing 'mad' (ibid.), thus stigmatizing her condition. Her review imputes the dichotomy between the objectivity, reason, and the alleged truthfulness and neutrality of science and the not merely subjective, but, worse, "unstable," "unreliable," even "moaning" and "self-obsessed" voice of the first-person to Hustvedt's account of her illness and hence reflects the high status that the scientific and intellectual take in society. These two perspectives, Cooke's review suggests, are incompatible and instead compete with one another.

While these critics do of course acknowledge the significance of gender in the context of Hustvedt's shaking, such essentialist readings of the memoir are neither productive nor truly recognize the text as a literary work of art. *The Shaking Woman* makes effective use of the flexibility of the memoir genre that I have outlined in Chapter 2.1 and in the following I aim to show that in the narrative, scientific discourses are not uttered neutrally in order to make Hustvedt appear rational in the face of her mysterious illness; rather, her approach as such to these discourses is deliberative and balanced. In doing so, Hustvedt transcends the very dichotomy these reviews insinuate, namely that between the writer and the scientist, between literature and science. Hence the interpretational focus should shift from an emphasis on the "intellectual" strategy that counters the alleged irrationality of femininity and illness to the consequences that the merging of the intellectual and the experiential

---

vel *The Blindfold*) and ponders what it means to "be one's self" when "interruptions, explosions, lapses, and inconsistencies" are equally part of the self (205).

has for Hustvedt's arising conception of her self and well-being as she may "begin to understand [her]self" (*Shaking* 6). "With understanding comes agency," Tougaw concludes and points to the fact that the wish to understand oneself and one's illness through the study of medicine, neurology or philosophy is a frequent concern of writers in brain memoirs ("Autobiography" 19). By extension, it is not only the study of the general terms of selfhood and illness that allows writers like Hustvedt to grasp their illness experience, but also the act of narrating it.

This issue is already reflected in the title of the narrative. Here, 'history' does not refer as much to the mere discovery, collection, and presentation of facts or events, as to the process of narration. The *Oxford English Dictionary* defines 'history' – particularly in book titles – first and foremost as a "written narrative constituting a continuous chronological record of important or public events [...] or [a] person's life" (n. pag.). Admittedly, Hustvedt's account is not chronological, but features many flashbacks to significant events of her childhood and the instances of her shakings over the course of the preceding years and frequently includes rapid shifts in tone and perspective, yet nevertheless fulfills the criterion of a history as being a "systematic account" (ibid.). In this vein, Mildorf, who reads the life narrative as a quest for knowledge, notes that the subtitle of the book already insinuates that the unfolding story will be one of self-exploration (2), an idea that is also expounded by Anna Thiemann who takes into account the cover designs of the Henry Holt and Sceptre editions of the memoir whose soft colors anticipate a deeply private text (377).

The second part of the subtitle, too, deserves attention because anthropologist of psychiatry Laurence Kirmayer notes that "nerves" are a "common idiom of distress" that is used to comment on both social and personal issues. Especially in the clinical setting, he highlights, "nerves" as a metaphor move the diagnosis to contested terrain, implying that the patient is to some extent involved in the cause of the disease ("Broken" 159). The conflict that Kirmayer's observation implies and that is certainly heightened by the fact that a nervous disease may not have organic, visible causes and is subject to greater stigma than other diseases, is reinforced in Hustvedt's book, since *The Shaking Woman* reveals that the relationship between 'illness' and 'disease' is, as Eisenberg argues, not necessarily a congruous one-to-one relationship (11). Evidently, disease may also exist without illness, i.e. without symptoms that make the patient aware of the condition or prompt feelings of unwellness (Schramme 24). In Hustvedt's memoir, though, the opposite is the case, because the experiencing I clearly feels ill, although no discernable disease appears to be present, despite the fact that her research uncovers numerous possible etiological frameworks.

In connection to this, the term 'history' also allows for the reference to a patient's medical history recorded by the doctor during the course of the examination in order to arrive at a diagnosis and provide adequate treatment options. As the definition in the *Oxford English Dictionary* makes clear, symptoms and signs are accounted for or related by the patient (n. pag.). This form of medical writing thus hints at the different perspectives involved in the perception and experience of illness: the doctor's objective third-person stance on the one hand which enables him to select from the subjective first-person account of the patient on the other hand. In Sacks's memoir, first- and third-person perspectives merge to provide a more insightful account of the experience through the form of the clinical tale. The dichotomy between disease and illness, as I have shown in Chapter 5, is neutralized, not least due to Sacks's role as doctor and patient. In a similar vein, Hustvedt's book avails itself of some of the conventions of a neurological case history, yet significantly revises and reappropriates its narrative conventions to dissociate her condition from the diagnostic plot that would eventually lead to treatment and possibly a cure.

Furthermore, Kathryn Hunter also points to the idea of knowledge inherent in the medical 'history.' Despite the fact that the term 'history' seems to imply epistemological authority, she notes that "what has occurred before the clinical encounter cannot be altogether reliably known" ("Making" 70). First of all, her thought alludes to the idea that the case history can never be entirely objective (cf. ibid.) but, more importantly, it also posits knowledge as a contested subject that complicates the creation of a story about the disease and the diagnosis of its causes. It is this contestation, the narrating I's unease about authoritative knowledge, that surfaces when the book is read as an alternative version of the traditional neurological case history.

8.2 BEYOND DIAGNOSIS: THE CASE OF *THE SHAKING WOMAN*

Strikingly reminiscent of the titles of other neurological case studies, such as A. R. Luria's *The Man with a Shattered World* or Oliver Sacks's "The Man Who Mistook His Wife for a Hat" and "The Disembodied Lady," *The Shaking Woman* may on first reading be aligned with a tradition of neurological writing that shifts the focus of the clinical gaze away from the physiological elements of the disease and instead centers on the individual affected by illness. In these stories, as the reading of *A Leg to Stand On* has also shown, auto/biography and case history are intertwined. Hawkins illustrates that this does not only serve the ethical concern to overcome a depersonalized view of the patient but a philosophical one as well by merging the corporeal and the experiential that are too frequently separated from each other, despite the fact that the disease cannot be split from the person suffering from it (cf. "A. R." 2). The subjective and qualitative experience of an illness is therefore crucial in these narratives⁹ and is merged with the medical practitioner's objective view on disease.

It should be noted though, that in the story of the shaking woman, doctors are absent to a large extent and are hardly granted a voice in Hustvedt's search for a diagnosis, an issue that also speaks to the postmodern illness experience, in which the truth about illness ceases to rest in the doctor's scientific, objectivist, and heroic stance (cf. Morris, "How" 8; cf. also Frank, *Wounded* 13). Consequently, the analysis of *The Shaking Woman* also departs from the common critical engagement with case studies that has centered on the perception and construction of the doctor-patient relationship and the different roles the case study holds for them (cf. Hunter "Remaking" 170) and instead raises further epistemological questions because it is Hustvedt herself who introduces the third-person perspective to her subjective illness experience through extensive references to academic and scientific frameworks. Despite the fact that the third-person perspective thus permeates her story, her use of first-person narration is significant, since it grants her agency. Furthermore, Hustvedt's story demonstrates, like Luria's *Man with a Shattered World*, the profound impact that writing and narrativizing has for the individual's sense of self: like Luria's patient Zazetsky, who "'finds' himself through his writing" (cf. Hawkins, "A. R." 12), the creation of a narrative also helps Hustvedt to perceive herself as a whole and coherent self and is in this respect rather therapeutic than diagnostic.

---

9 In his foreword to his collection of curious neurological stories *The Man Who Mistook His Wife for a Hat*, Sacks comments on the traditional case history that describes the course of a disease, from its onset to either healing or fatal resolution. Yet, as he aptly remarks, the mere depiction of the natural course of a disease is not capable of grasping the experience of the individual suffering from this disease. The traditional case history, Sacks concludes, lacks a subject – a fact that the common cursory phrase uttered in each introduction cannot hide (ixf.). By refusing to grant the patient the status of a speaking subject and reducing him/her to the biological qualities of the disease, the traditional case history thus turns the patient into a voiceless object under the physician's gaze. The "suffering, afflicted, fighting, human subject" is what Sacks instead seeks to locate at the heart of a new form of case history, one that extends the mere depiction of the natural disease to a narrative or tale: "only then do we have a 'who' as well as a 'what,' a real person, a patient, in relation to disease – in relation to the physical" (ibid.). Sacks thus tends to romanticize the case story of the nineteenth century, yet Tougaw maintains that the "human subject at their centers" were often viewed along the lines of cultural assumptions about class, gender, the body, and sanity that in fact led to an objectification of these subjects (*Strange Cases* 210).

Parallel to the medical case history, in which physicians begin by working backward from the current symptom to what they believe to be responsible cause (cf. Hunter, "Remaking" 163), Hustvedt's narrative is initiated by the first onset of her shaking fit and propelled by her search for the shaking woman, a diagnosis and explanation. Like the case history, Hustvedt strives to construct what Hunter in her discussion of the case study terms a "probable narrative" – however preliminary – from signs and clinical evidence (ibid. 163). These structural parallels have prompted critics to see the story of the shaking woman as a representation congruent with the conventional case history. Jörg Magenau, for instance, purports that in this story, Hustvedt transforms from a writer to a scientist, resorting to the objective jargon of scientific discourses in order to distance herself from her illness (n. pag.). On the one hand, this is certainly true, as the notion of the case study does indeed provide the opportunity to create distance and assume an outside perspective on the disease and the figure of the shaking woman. On the other hand, I do not agree when the story of the shaking woman is read as a case history in the conventional sense, a story devoid of anything personal and literary and a narrative that, as Hurwitz claims, assumes distance on the formal level as well, by omitting the patient's response and employing a syntactic structure that renders individuals afflicted with illness passive, and events, such as their treatment courses, agentless (cf. Hurwitz 230, 237). On the contrary, I fully agree with Marks who maintains that rather than approaching writing from a scientific point of view and applying the scientific methods she encounters, Hustvedt confronts science with the eyes of a writer. As a consequence, she refuses to take neuroscientific findings at their face-value and instead locates them in a larger social context (*Relationality* 212). Scientific and medical data thus become a crucial part of Hustvedt's rhetorical strategy that aims at mediating knowledge.

This is indeed a fundamental concern that her story and the case history share, as the narrative of the case history has come to be accepted as a legitimate tool for generating medical knowledge (cf. Hunter, "Remaking" 169). In a similar vein, Smith and Watson define the case study as "a life narrative that is gathered into a dossier in order to make a diagnosis and identification of a disease of disorder" (264). Hence the conventional medical case history, as Hunter notes, neither corresponds to the patient's story, nor intends to do so ("Remaking" 164). In an earlier article titled "Making a Case," Hunter expounds this by explaining that in the clinical encounter, it is customary to transform the patient's subjective experience of illness to a report that lists the clinical facts from the perspective of the doctor, thereby transforming the patient's *story* into a *case* (70). As a result, medicine turns patients into objects and knowledge (cf. Tougaw, *Strange Cases* 2).

Hustvedt, however, refuses to be turned into medicine's object, just as well as she refuses fixed and stable knowledge at the end of her story. By narrativizing not only her own experiences, but also the scientific findings she is confronted with during her search, Hustvedt turns the "case" of the shaking woman into her own story, recovering her self by retrieving the shaking woman from medical and scientific discourses. In this process, she shows that the (re-)location of scientific data in their sociocultural context significantly affects their reading. In this vein, *The Shaking Woman* thus constitutes an attempt to weave art and science together, demonstrating that, as Hawkins argues, both case history and biography inevitably entail interpretations in order to arrive at a coherent and intelligible story ("A. R." 2).

Against this background, Hawkins's considerations of biography and case history as "contextual" stories needs be refined. While Hawkins purports that both types of narratives "seek to understand an individual human being in the context of some other reality – in the case history the internal reality of anatomy and physiology, in a biography the external reality of family structure, cultural trends, and historical events" (ibid.), it should be noted that neither the "internal reality" or the "external reality" are stable and absolute. Both "realities," physiology and cultural trends, are in fact contingent and are themselves dependent on context. Consequently, the third-person perspective in the case study is neither fully reliable, nor authoritative, but assumes the role of what Hunter aptly terms an "investigative narrator" ("Remaking" 173).

Such an idea of investigative narration is also mirrored in the use of contemporary forms of the case history. Today, Tougaw argues, the case story is returning to medical discourses with new vigor, as medical professionals are probing the ways in which the patients' subjective experiences may be intertwined with scientific theories and medical practices (*Strange Cases* 1). Yet the critical analysis of case studies is no longer restricted to the field of medicine; in literary studies, too, the concept of the case history proves insightful for the interpretation of literary works of art. Reviewing contemporary case studies, critic Laura Miller reaches the interesting, though not original conclusion that case studies constitute "that unsung genre inhabiting the borderland between art and science" (n. pag.). Already in his seminal *Studies on Hysteria*, Freud writes: "It still strikes me myself as strange that the case histories I write should read like short stories and that, as one might say, they lack the serious stamp of science" (160). Nevertheless, he cherishes them for their strong connection between the suffering of the patient and the disease pattern and its symptoms (161).

Švrljuga points out that it is precisely this approach to illness and suffering that provides important insights. Medicine, attempting to give scientific explanations and claiming knowledge, always assumes an outside perspective, while disorders, particularly in the case of hysteria, the disease that Hustvedt feels drawn to, need to consider the body, something Švrljuga terms "'knowledge' from within" (20). Likewise, Hustvedt herself comments on the relationship between science and storytelling and the neglect of the latter in contemporary psychiatry:

"The DSM does not tell stories. [...] There is a companion *DSM-Casebook*, but notably, these narratives about real doctors and patients are gathered in their own volume, separate from the diagnostic tome. The fact is that all patients have stories and those stories are necessarily part of the meaning of their illnesses. This may be even more true for psychiatric patients, whose stories are often so enmeshed with the sickness that one can't be untangled from the other." (*Shaking* 36)

General theories cannot account for the subjective experience of the individual suffering from a particular disease. In various scenes throughout the book, Hustvedt therefore approaches the conventional case histories she has encountered while reviewing relevant medical literature with criticism.

The case of the patient V.A. published in a *Brain* study is representative. The authors of the article describe V.A. as a "fifty-one-year old, right handed woman, divorced, whose son died from heart disease a year prior to the study. Heaviness, weakness, and loss of dexterity of right limbs after her new companion suffered myocardial infarction while wrongly suspected of abusing a teenager. No sensory complaints" (*Shaking* 79f.). Hustvedt's own reading of the case story strikingly opens with the words "Poor V.A." (ibid. 80). In the following, she first of all returns a feeling of empathy to the anonymous case of V.A., when she addresses the reader directly by demanding "[i]magine the grief of losing a child to heart problems" (ibid.). More than that, Hustvedt goes on to create a narrative of V.A.'s illness that in her account helps to set straight the cause of the patient's symptoms. She points out that the patient has not only lost her son due to heart problems, but has also "[fallen] in love with a man who has a *heart* attack after being *falsely* accused of what appears to be the violence against or sexual molestation of some young person" (ibid.; italics in original). The words "heart" and "falsely" are in her narrative stripped of the neutral tone of the case history and give meaning to the patient's illness experience. Reading the authors' description of her case closely, she notes that the conjunction "while" in the case history denotes an enduring process of investigation that has led the couple to suffer which she illustrates with the bleak and oppressive metaphor of "a lowering black cloud they woke up to every morning and went to bed with every night" (ibid.). Hustvedt thus locates the emergence of the symptoms in what she presumes may have constituted the life reality of the patient and accordingly shifts the focus to V.A.'s subjective and lived experience. When she therefore arrives at the conclusion that the patient has "suffered too many blows involving hearts: her heart and the hearts of beloved others" (ibid.), she may not have reached deep medical insight, nor may she propose a way to cure V.A., as the authors of her case history do. However, Hustvedt has clearly shown the reader a direct answer to the problem that she has raised earlier, when she posed the question of whether narrative and illness may actually be separated: "Wasn't that narrative part of the sickness itself?" (ibid. 37). She shows instead that illness is intricately intertwined with a person's life story.

If a narrative is part of illness itself, it follows that narrative may help to give meaning to the experience of illness and also to come to terms with illness. Hence Tougaw notes that individuals affected by illness have to develop a narrative form that can encompass the consequences of pathological symptoms that alter a person's identity and support the complex questions arising in this context ("Brain Memoirs" 183). The relationship between brain/mind and self is not simply altered by illness, but continues to shift as patients react and respond to their conditions – most prominently by writing about them (ibid.). The subversion of the traditional case study is, however, not only a part of Hustvedt's narrative when she speaks about other patients, but also accounts for the emerging story of the shaking woman. The rhetoric of the case study does then finally not achieve distance from the shaking woman. Returning to Švrljuga's observation quoted above, it should first of all be noted that the form of the case study enables Hustvedt to draw on knowledge *about*, as well as knowledge *of* her illness and therefore allows these two potentially competing sets of knowledge to merge (cf. 59).

The idea of knowledge, however, is not only at the center of the case study, but also allows Hustvedt to transform the quest narrative as introduced by Arthur Frank as a spiritual journey to use suffering to gain something from the experience (*Wounded* 115) and that way endow illness with a sense of purpose (ibid. 117; cf. Chapter 2.3). A vast number of personal narratives that have been published about illness, as well as Frank's concept of illness as a journey or quest give the impression that the quest narrative is frequently a story in which selfhood remains to some extent compromised: enlightenment figures as the only way in which illness can be grasped as something other than suffering. Catherine Garrett therefore raises an important issue when she characterizes quest stories as comprising not only an individual's personal life narrative, but likewise sociological, philosophical, and religious (and cultural, one should add) narratives that function as 'stories' about suffering. These stories, Garrett asserts, are "about whole groups of people and how they suffer and are changed by their suffering" (147). In the context of illness memoirs, it is indeed of crucial significance to recognize the importance of such meta-narratives about suffering, yet Garrett's view of these stories as ways of giving shape and pattern to individuals' stories (cf. ibid.) should not be accepted free from value judgments. While they of course provide orientation for both writers and readers of illness memoirs and root stories firmly in social and cultural contexts, meta-narratives also establish a significant constraint when it comes to the ways in which suffering can be interpreted. "Quest stories tell of searching for alternative ways of being ill," Frank asserts (*Wounded* 117) but the conventional quest narrative operates within a framework that the individual cannot, or rather, does neither question nor change.[10]

Since the quest in *The Shaking Woman* is less spiritual than epistemological, the story does not adapt explanations to the social, cultural, and theoretical framework of illness and suffering, but instead sets out to re-conceptualize the framework that such narratives provide for personal accounts. Below, I will show how Hustvedt defies the idea of fixed and stable theories and scientific evidence by refusing to see conclusions as absolute, presenting and engaging in a critical dialogue with scholarly evidence, as well as by pointing to the limits of knowledge. On a personal level, her strategy helps to account for her unique experiences of shaking; on a broader scale, however, it also devises a theoretical statement of its own. As Hustvedt's narrative demonstrates, illness may then enable the memoirist to probe established knowledge.

8.3 "A WOMAN IS SHAKING:" HYSTERIA AND THE DISCOURSE OF DISEASE

The narrative opens with an epigraph citing the first part of a poem by Emily Dickinson that bespeaks two fundamental concerns:

"I felt a cleaving in my mind
As if my brain had split;
I tried to match it, seam by seam,
But could not make them fit."

---

10 As this study shows, a number of narratives refuse to connect illness to a sense of enlightenment. Consider, also for example, the ending of Aleksandar Hemon's autobiographical story "The Aquarium," a narrative about the illness and subsequent death of his infant daughter Isabel published in The New Yorker in June 2011: "One of the most despicable religious fallacies is that suffering is ennobling – that it is a step on the path to some kind of enlightenment or salvation. Isabel's suffering and death did nothing for her, or us, or the world. We learned no lessons worth learning; we acquired no experience that could benefit anyone. And Isabel most certainly did not earn ascension to a better place, as there was no place better for her than at home with her family. Without Isabel, Teri and I were left with oceans of love we could no longer dispense; we found ourselves with an excess of time that we used to devote to her; we had to live in a void that could be filled only by Isabel. Her indelible absence is now an organ in our bodies, whose sole function is a continuous secretion of sorrow."

The poem in which the speaker experiences a mental breakdown first of all raises the question of how the mind and the brain are related to each other. When the speaker feels a violent split in his/her mind, it is immediately compared to a split in the brain through a simile, thus connecting the rupture of the mental capacity to that of the physical.[11] In an allusion to a seamstress, the speaker attempts to sew the split mind back together, yet is unable to do so, since she cannot make the "seams" "fit" – mind and brain are not congruent anymore and are ultimately conceived of as two separate entities in this poem. Secondly, the poem foreshadows the lack of control on the side of the speaker, much like Hustvedt herself is at a loss when it comes to explaining and overcoming the shaking fits.

She then begins her story by recounting the first onset of her shaking, the event that eventually initiates her research. When she is asked to speak in honor of her deceased father at the college campus where he taught, she feels confident at first. However, when she begins her speech, she starts to shake violently "from the neck down":

"My arms flapped. My knees knocked. I shook as if I were having a seizure. Weirdly, my voice wasn't affected. It didn't change at all. Astounded by what was happening to me and terrified that I would fall over, I managed to keep my balance and continue, despite the fact that the cards in my hands were flying back and forth in front of me. When the speech ended, the shaking stopped. I looked down at my legs. They had turned a deep red with a bluish cast." (*Shaking* 3)

When Hustvedt concludes the account of her first shaking fit, she refers to it as a "mysterious bodily transformation" (ibid.), a profound change that has occurred with the first onset of the shaking. This "bodily transformation" is indeed so strange that it may only be grasped in indirect terms through the use of a simile:[12] In lieu of

---

11 In the context of today's advances in neurosurgery, audiences may, however, be tempted to further associations. The speaker's split brain prompts references to the neurosurgical intervention in epilepsy patients, during which their corpus callosum, the part of the brain that connects the left and right hemispheres, is separated in order to cure their fits, leaving these patients with two separate brain hemispheres – a "split brain." For a long time, researchers hypothesized that only one hemisphere (the left, as this is the one with greater language capacity) recognizes the self, yet studies with split brain patients have shown that both hemispheres are capable of recognizing and distinguishing the self from the other (Iacoboni, *Woher* 153f.).

12 Another revealing simile is also employed when Hustvedt's mother, who is part of the audience, later on tells her that the incident made her feel "as if she were looking at an electrocution" (*Shaking* 4). Thiemann reads this simile as the evocation of Sylvia Plath's

a name or explanation for her tremors, she compares them to "having a seizure," thereby moving the incident into established and uncontested medical, or rather, neurological terrain. From the beginning on, her narrative therefore suggests that the shaking should be understood as a disease, rather than an emotional response to the setting and circumstances of the talk.

In her account of the incident, Hustvedt identifies two simultaneous processes that appear to be causally connected, yet are rendered as two separate strands of action. On the one hand, her shaking is imagined as a violent, physical process, which affects her limbs to such a great extent that she fears she may lose her balance and fall off the stage. On the other hand, Hustvedt is detached from what is happening to her: She judges the shaking as "weird," compares it to a seizure and recounts that she felt both "astounded" and "terrified" as she was observing herself. This is also reflected in the syntax of the representation of the scene marked by brief and simple main clauses with parallel and anaphoric structures that describe her shaking body and, in stark contrast, a long and complex sentence comprising clauses with a participial construction and an adverb clause concerned with her thoughts and actions during the incident. These syntactic variations portray the irregularity that may be associated with the experiencing I's capacity to speak through her shaking. Moreover, in this brief passage it becomes clear that for Hustvedt, the shaking represents a split between her body, which she is no longer capable of controlling, and her cognitive capacities, which have remained intact during the incident. It is the latter that she increasingly turns to throughout the story when she defines her self along the lines of narration, albeit narration understood as a conscious, willed process.

Uttered on numerous occasions throughout the course of the story, the neck becomes the epitome and "perfect image" (*Shaking* 129) of this rupture, for instance when Hustvedt states that "[f]rom the chin up, I was my familiar self. From the neck down, I was a shuddering stranger" (ibid. 7). While her "familiar self" is perceived in terms of her cognitive capacities and originates in the chin – the body part

---

1963 *The Bell Jar* in which the narrator-protagonist is eventually cured of her "mental illness" (Esther Greenwood cannot see herself becoming confined to the socially accepted roles of wife and mother and strives to become a writer) through an electroshock therapy that is compared with Communist Ethel Rosenberg's electrocution (376). The idea of electrocution, despite its connotations of violence, punishment, and death, also allows for another revealing association, namely that of electricity and electric signals passing through the body. This is further underlined when Hustvedt remembers a similar incident in the past and states that "[i]t appeared that some unknown force had suddenly taken over my body and decided that I needed a good, sustained jolting. Once before, during the summer of 1982, I'd felt as if some superior power picked me up and tossed me about as if I were a doll" (*Shaking* 4).

that she sees when she faces herself in the mirror, the part that is known – the shaking woman has taken possession of her body and begins in her neck, the part of her body she cannot direct her gaze to. Depicted as a strange figure lurking in her back, the shaking woman thus receives threatening connotations.

"Isn't the neck the place where the head ends and body begins?" Hustvedt furthermore asks (ibid. 129). Yet more than that, the neck also contains the spinal cord extending from the brain to connect the neuronal circuits that control the rest of the body, a connection that is apparently flawed. This is elucidated by the dream Hustvedt recounts in which she learns that she is fatally ill with inoperable cancer and becomes "intensely aware of the tumors under the skin at [her] throat and around [her] neck" (*Shaking* 128). The use of cancer and its tumors as a metaphor expresses the fear and dread the narrating I links to her condition but it furthermore emphasizes that she conceives of the shaking as something alien that intrudes into her self.[13]

It is this flawed connection and the shaking woman's strangeness that is at the root of Hustvedt's struggle to integrate her into her "familiar self." Fonseca therefore argues that the narrative of the shaking woman forms the link between body and mind (2f.). Even though the narrative does not deliver a stable definition of the self, Hustvedt acknowledges that writing is a fundamental aspect, as it can heal the split between the body – the shaking woman – and the mind – the control Hustvedt feels she holds (cf. ibid. 5). In Chapter 5.1, I have characterized storytelling as an embodied practice that merges cognitive with physical capacities. Narrating here is not only a crucial strategy that helps Hustvedt to perceive the flawed connection between mind and body; it also allows her, in Fonseca's words, "to become aware of herself as a whole" (2f.). According to Tougaw, brain memoirs do not take selfhood for granted, but instead conceptualize it as a performative process. Selfhood, he maintains, is created and performed in the works by the interplay of mind, body, brain, and culture ("Brain Memoirs" 174).

If "[e]very sickness has an alien quality, a feeling of invasion and loss of control that is evident in the language we use about it" (*Shaking* 6), then Hustvedt's haunting sense of invasion and her lack of control crystallize in her representation of the shaking woman as the 'other.' In the following, two complementary perspectives serve to elucidate the otherness of the "shuddering stranger:" first, the relationship between illness and self that highlights Hustvedt's feeling of invasion and, second, the construction of the shaking woman as a mythical figure along the lines of the

---

13 Interestingly, in her dream, it is not merely the neck that is affected by the adverse attack, but also her throat, the part of the body where speech is articulated and where stories are voiced. The shaking woman, the dream illustrates, may also prove to be a threat to Hustvedt's capacity to tell stories.

'hysterical woman.' Initially, Hustvedt struggles to define the status of the shaking woman and her relationship to her own identity, for example when she notes that "[t]he shaking woman felt like me and not like me at the same time" (ibid. 7). While the ambiguity in this statement illustrates that she has trouble grasping both her identity and the nature of her illness, it is first of all noteworthy that she continuously speaks about her illness in terms of "the shaking woman," a discrete and self-contained entity. Her detachment from the shaking woman culminates in statements, such as "[a] woman is shaking" (ibid. 13), in which the use of the indefinite article suggests indeterminacy, detachment, as well as the unknown.

Hustvedt's initial idea of her shaking is strikingly different from the way in which she conceives her migraines as her identity. When an early shaking fit eventually results in a migraine that leaves her severely affected for almost a year (cf. ibid. 4), she is forced to consult a specialist: "My doctor gave it a name – *vascular migraine syndrome* – but why I had become a vomiting, miserable, flattened, frightened ENORMOUS headache, a Humpty Dumpty after his fall, no one could say" (ibid. 5; italics and capitalization in original). Hustvedt's experience with her diagnosis illustrates the connection between illness and self. Although she first refers to her illness as "it," marking it as a distinct entity, it also becomes clear that she considers the migraine something inextricably tied to her identity when she characterizes herself as "a vomiting, flattened, frightened ENORMOUS headache." This recognition, as well as the allusion to the nursery-rhyme character Humpty Dumpty, though, evince that illness in this case is not merely a part readily accepted into one's identity, but has caused the previous version of the self – a fragile entity – to be shattered beyond repair, so that it is entirely overwhelmed by illness.

Yet in the case of the shaking woman, Hustvedt does not grant her any authority that would allow illness to take over her self. The ensuing struggle with the shaking woman is one that first of all leads to the disruption of the self. Hustvedt's conception of the shaking woman as the "copy" against whom she, the "original," is waging war (*Shaking* 48) reiterates the separation and the dichotomy of mind and body that I have pointed out earlier and that also permeates Oliver Sacks's account of his illness. Referring to subsequent tremors, Hustvedt observes that "it takes great control *not* to be distracted by a violent convulsion of your own body" (ibid. 39; italics in original). Again, she associates her cognitive capacities with her self that struggles to maintain control, while attributing the distraction and shaking to her body. "Did I [...] have a kind of double consciousness – a shuddering person and a cool one?" (ibid. 27), she asks. Repeatedly, she takes up the notion of the double to describe her relationship to the shaking woman, who is "a Mr. Hyde to my Dr. Jekyll" (ibid. 47). Like the doppelgänger in *Dr. Jekyll and Mr. Hyde*, Hustvedt suspects the shaking woman will "torment and sabotage" her (ibid.). Comparing the shaking woman to the doppelgänger figure familiar from numerous literary works of art, she turns her into her evil twin, a dark side of her identity or, in short, 'the other.'

Hustvedt's continuous search for the shaking woman[14] then takes her through the history of neurology and psychoanalysis and begins with a reconceptualization of the meaning of medical diagnosis, which is illustrated in this passage worth quoting at length here:

"Nature, God, and the devil could wrack your body, and medical experts struggled to distinguish among causes. How could you separate an act of nature from a divine intervention or a demonic possession? Saint Teresa of Avila's paroxysmal agonies and blackouts, her visions and transports were mystical flights towards God, but the girls in Salem who writhed and shook were the victims of witches. [...] If my tremulous episode had occurred during the witch madness in Salem, the consequences might have been dire. Surely I would have looked like a woman possessed. But, more important, had I been steeped in the religious beliefs of the age, as I most likely would have been, the weird sensation that some external power had entered my body to cause the shudder probably would have been enough to convince me that I had indeed been hexed.

In New York City in 2006 no sane doctor would have sent me to an exorcist, and yet confusion about diagnosis is common. The frames for viewing convulsive illness may have changed, but understanding what had happened to me would not be a simple matter. I could go to a neurologist to see if I had come down with epilepsy [...]. [...] I knew that a careful neurologist would do an EEG, an electroencephalogram. I'd have to sit with gooey electrodes clamped to my scalp for quite a while, and my guess is that the doctor would find nothing. Of course, many people suffer from seizures that are not detected by standard tests, so the physician would have to do more tests. Unless I kept shaking, a diagnosis might not be forthcoming. I could float in the limbo of an unknown affliction." (*Shaking* 8f.)

Hustvedt's statement is a prime example of what Morris so fittingly describes as "the erratic landscape [...] where health and illness come in contact with cultural forces" ("How" 9), or, in other words, where the construction of disease is exposed. The historical instances illustrated here contextualize the diagnoses of similar shaking fits and are indicative of the fact that any diagnosis and explanation are dependent on the frame of reference through which they are perceived. Consequently, her explanation elucidates that medical knowledge is neither objective – "pure facts" – nor exists in a vacuum, but is instead, as Morris puts it, "historically situated and culturally inflected" and thus subject to political and social currents (ibid. 7). Different social climates have thus caused the reading of the disease to shift from "di-

---

14 Next to her search for the shaking woman, a second plotline may be identified in *The Shaking Woman*, namely Hustvedt's memory of her father whose memoir she was writing at the time. Memories of him, as well as dreams surface on various occasions, an issue that I will discuss in the next section of this chapter.

vine intervention" to "demonic possession," a dichotomous categorization that implicated dramatic consequences. Juxtaposing contact with divine forces and diabolical influence and illustrating how the same symptoms may be read as either end of the binary scale, her statement invites the interpretation that the framework for viewing these symptoms has been adapted arbitrarily in accordance with the respective social and cultural climate: "if you give it another name, it appears to be another *thing*" (*Shaking* 75; italics in original).

Hustvedt makes clear that these climates also bear direct effect on the perception of the afflicted individual when she contends that, had she been immersed in the religious belief of the seventeenth century as it would have been appropriate for her, she, too, would have believed in her own demonic possession. Her line of argumentation hence ultimately discloses that the ways in which individuals experience their illnesses are powerfully shaped by the culture in which they live (cf. also Morris, "How" 8). As a consequence, her statement demonstrates that it is not only disease that is socially and culturally constructed, but that the experience of illness, too, is constructed as culture and society give shape to how patients make sense of and come to terms with their illnesses. The stories told about illness significantly draw from and, in turn, contribute to the construction of the experience, so Hustvedt's move to defamiliarize her readership with the story of her potential diagnosis is strategic.

She phrases her anticipation as "com[ing] down with epilepsy," which is a phrase that may well be used in the context of a flu or cold, diseases of little severity that may be caught through contact with the environment. Her unusual and ironic phrasing disrupts the reader's understanding. Like the flu, it appears rather enervating instead, a feeling that is also underlined by her description of the examination procedure as irritating and bothersome, where she will have to endure "gooey electrodes" stuck to the bare skin of her head. Mildorf argues that particularly Hustvedt's account of the examination, the "gooey electrodes clamped to [her] scalp for quite a while," and, I should add, Hustvedt's characterization of her lack of diagnosis as "limbo," foretell the irony in tone that permeates the narrative in many scenes (6).

In her essay, Mildorf furthermore calls attention to the tense in the latter half of the text passage maintaining that despite the fact that the narrating I's concern that the medical practitioner "would find nothing" sounds strikingly prophetic, readers need to bear in mind that "by the time of writing, the doctor's lack of tangible results was no longer a 'guess' but a fact," which inevitably complicates the reading of Hustvedt's skepticism of the medical establishment in this scene (ibid.). The question of whether the experiencing I was already skeptical or whether it is only in hindsight that the narrating I voices such strong skepticism may be impossible for readers to discern. Yet what is crucial in this passage is the fact that Hustvedt voices her frustration over the lack of a diagnosis so decidedly. Both her frustration and the emphasis of an intelligible explanation for her tremors are evidence of the momentousness and the significance commonly attributed to a medical diagnosis to frame disease and any kind of illness experience. Her suspicion is, after all, that even new diagnostic tools will not reveal a valid diagnosis and she will "float in the limbo of an unknown affliction." The tone of this statement and the hyperbole "limbo" allows for a sense of ambiguity that shifts its reading from sincere fear to a comment on the meaning of medical diagnosis and the categorization of diseases through language: Apparently, a firm diagnosis would be needed to avoid the "limbo" of the unknown and the lack of control, direction, and agency that the verb "floating" entails. The question implicitly posed, however, is whether categorization and language itself are indeed an adequate means to grasp the experience of illness (cf. DasGupta and Hurst, "Narrative" 19).

Throughout the narrative, Hustvedt ponders on the meaning of categories and the categorization of conditions. Admitting that we need categories in order to make sense of the world and direct the focus that will enable scientific discovery and progress, she does not criticize categorization per se, yet rather directs her criticism towards the ways in which she sees these categories frequently used – as fixed frameworks, letting "little air in or out" and thus restricting science (*Shaking* 79). By professing that meanings may well be personal (ibid. 137), she returns the notion of subjectivity to science, much like the clinical tales of Sacks and Luria attempt to do. After all, "[w]hat is seen depends on the perspective of the seer" (ibid. 145). On numerous occasions, she therefore points to the significance of perspective in dealing with categories, as one's vantage point determines how to frame and "*read*" a condition and its symptoms (ibid. 69; italics in original). It is through the use of statements such as these that Hustvedt embraces the subjective perspective and decidedly positions herself not as a scientist, but as an artist. In contrast to the objective perspective, where the observer disappears from the discourse through the use of the passive voice to promote a sense of omniscience and the general, her point of view is personal and the "I" as the observing and commentating voice never disappears from her text. Particularly the choice and typographical emphasis of the verb "read" is crucial in this context, for it first of all compares Hustvedt's approach to that of a literary studies scholar who sets out to analyze and interpret, i.e. extract meaning from the text, and, secondly, it illustrates that conditions and symptoms are not given, but are always already part of a narrative that may be perceived and interpreted in various ways (cf. also Marks, "Ill Self" 80).

Likewise, perspective determines what is considered and what is dismissed (*Shaking* 69), a reason why her search for the shaking woman moves in circular ways, reconsidering the event again and again through various vantage points, as not to miss a significant detail. In her essay "Borderlands: First, Second, and Third Person Adventures in Crossing Disciplines," Hustvedt meditates on questions of perspective, particularly of first- and third-person points of view, and takes note of the fact that these are located in strictly separate spheres: While the first-person perspective is usually aligned with the artist, the third-person stance rests with the scientist. She recalls that artistic 'truth' is frequently referred to as "squishy," whereas scientific 'truth' is assigned characteristics, such as "hard, tough, verifiable, and rigorous," which causes incongruence between the perspectives since "[o]ur taxonomies, our categories, our truths vary" (111). Yet Hustvedt neither allows the third-person perspective to take over authority nor bows to the value assignment and deep chasm between the points of view, since she notes that the objective vantage point is "often muddled by dubious epistemological assumptions" (ibid.) and therefore just as "squishy" as the artist's stance. This is because every discipline follows its own set of "[r]ules for knowing – how we can know and what we can know" (ibid.); hence the ways in which individuals may gain knowledge in a certain discipline are governed by strict conventions, just as much as these conventions aid in the artificial construction and constraint of a discipline, which is reflected in Hustvedt's description of a discipline as an "edifice" (ibid. 112). Moving in circles around the shaking woman, Hustvedt is then able to consider all information that may be relevant for her understanding of her condition without being constrained by disciplinary boundaries and conventions.

For her it ultimately becomes clear that stable categorizations do not suffice to identify the shaking woman and explain Hustvedt's condition because she claims that her "pathology lays somewhere else, beneath or to the side of language" (ibid. 20). It is then that hysteria as a potential explanation for her shaking "announced itself" in an epiphany (ibid. 9) and thus appears as self-evident to her – a notion that should strike the reader, but one that also corresponds to Hustvedt's impression that the shaking woman cannot be fully grasped by language and strict scientific delineation and definition, but is rather someone who pushes from the subconscious to the surface. The epiphany is therefore reflective of hysteria as a medical and conceptual framework and recalls Hustvedt's earlier association with Teresa de Avila.

In *Hystories: Hysterical Epidemics and Modern Culture*, Elaine Showalter notes that whereas physicians and psychiatrists have discarded hysteria as a valid diagnosis, the disease still looms large in the humanities: It has "moved from the clinic to the library, from the case study to the novel, from bodies to books" and critics study hysteria particularly with respect to questions of language, narrative, and representation (6f.). Over a large portion of the narrative, Hustvedt attempts to explain her shaking through references to hysteria or what is nowadays termed 'conversion disorder' and devotes numerous pages to its history and diagnosis. Švrljuga argues that Hustvedt would have very much liked to embrace the diagnosis of hysteria if it provided more understanding of the causes for her tremors (222). Although hysteria may indeed provide temporary solace and serve as an explanation for her shaking on the surface level, in the narrative, it fulfills further important functions for Hustvedt's conceptualization of her self. Rather than in its literal and medical sense, hysteria should therefore be analyzed with respect to the social and cultural connotations it entails in general and its effects on Hustvedt's creation of a self in particular.

In this context, Fonseca notes that the hysterical woman is a permanent character in Hustvedt's story (2). Sacks claims that the archetypes of classical fables, such as the victim, the hero, and the warrior, may well be transferred to the context of the neurological case story, where they are often combined to describe the patient (*The Man Who* xi). Similarly, the archetype at work in *The Shaking Woman*, namely the hysterical woman, carries connotations of the victim and the defiant and unruly antagonist. The archetype of the hysterical woman is in this respect more than Hustvedt's means to assume distance from the disease and create a kind of detachment that allows her to objectively analyze her illness experience. Hysteria opens a discourse of doubt – first of all in the very nature of the disease and its causes, and secondly, in medical categorizations at large. Moreover, the concept of hysteria is intertwined with the idea of narrative. As Roy Porter notes, there is no single and coherent narrative that can retrace its history. Instead, he stresses, there can only exist "scatters of occurrences, histories of hysteria" (226). Like the narrative of hysteria, Hustvedt's narrative of her self is broken and resembles scatters of reoccurring shaking fits resisting coherent storytelling.

Hysteria is commonly referred to as the "signature disease" of women in the nineteenth century, yet may be traced back as early as Hippocrates's *On the Disease of Women*, which purports that the woman's wandering uterus ("hystera" in Greek) is responsible for the affliction and thus associated the disease with women (Showalter 15). Even as the factors causing the disease changed throughout history from the possession by evil spirits in the Middle Ages to excessive emotions in the mid-eighteenth century, hysteria continued to be regarded as a disease primarily afflicting women, the "nervous sex" (Marks, *Relationality* 126; Showalter 15),[15] so that Hustvedt's question "[a] woman is shaking. But why?" (*Shaking* 13) may also be read with an emphasis on gender. That Hustvedt is not oblivious of the gendered connotations of the disease becomes obvious when she states that

"[i]t is safe to say that if any one of the doctors mentioned above [Galen, Antonius Guainerius, Thomas Willis] had witnessed my convulsive speech, he might have diagnosed me with

---

15 Hustvedt notes that Jean-Martin Charcot, one of the most famous doctors treating hysteric patients did also identify men suffering from the disease (*Shaking* 22). Particularly with respect to shell-shock patients in the aftermath of the First World War, the diagnosis received relevance before it was abandoned in the clinical context. Hysteria in male patients is more extensively treated in the chapter "Hysterical Men" of Elaine Showalter's *Hystories: Hysterical Epidemics and Modern Culture*.

hysteria. My higher functions weren't interrupted; I remembered everything about my fit; and, of course, I was a woman with a potentially vaporous or disturbed uterus." (ibid. 11)

Her ironic comment clearly criticizes the gender bias of the diagnosis.[16] In the nineteenth century, Victorian virtues restricted women of the upper and middle classes to the domestic sphere and the dependence on their husbands. In this context, hysteria is frequently read as a response to these societal restraints and thus explicitly illustrates how the forces of culture operate on the individual (cf. Marks, *Relationality* 133). While in the nineteenth century, these restrictions and forces were firmly rooted in society, even in the context of the twenty-first century, hysteria can be read metaphorically in a similar vein when scientific discourses set the parameters that guide the understanding of a particular disease. The memoir reveals that whereas such an explanation sounds utterly ridiculous in contemporary times, this was long thought to be a valid explanation for the cause of hysteria. Hustvedt makes it clear that until the eighteenth century, hysteria was defined as a disease associated solely with the body "and the people suffering from it weren't considered insane" (*Shaking* 11).

Porter maintains that the diagnosis of hysteria inevitably leads to doubt, since professionals are still at odds when it comes to the question whether hysteria constitutes an actual disease – perhaps even one that is still not fully understood – or whether the diagnosis may even serve as a "cover-up for medical ignorance" ("Body" 226). In *Hysteria: The Biography*, sociologist Andrew Scull, too, illustrates how the cultural concept of hysteria has changed throughout the centuries, pointing to the ambiguities and contradictions involved in the understanding of the disease: "Was hysteria 'real' or fictitious, somatic or psychopathological? Might it constitute an unspoken idiom of protest, a symbolic voice for the silenced sex, who were forbidden to verbalize their discontents and so created a language of the body?" (7). Similarly, Marks notes that throughout its history, hysteria has repeatedly been pushed to either side of the mind/body-dichotomy when physicians attributed its emergence to either emotional shock or organic causes (*Relationality* 143). Hustvedt even drives this to the extreme by referring to a *New York Times* ar-

---

16 The issue of gender in *The Shaking Woman* is thoroughly explored in Anna Thiemann's comparative essay: "Shaking Patterns of Diagnosis: Siri Hustvedt and Charlotte Perkins Gilman." Thiemann identifies several intertextual references in the memoir, yet regards Charlotte Perkins Gilman's "The Yellow Wallpaper" as "the strongest and most obvious" intertextual link in the life narrative (376). In her close reading of both texts, she studies how Hustvedt borrows from and transforms the canonical text through her detached perspective, which she reads as a deliberate aesthetic strategy to counter Gilbert and Gubar's so-called 'mistress-plot' and, as a result, the victim status of women writers (382).

ticle titled "Is Hysteria Real? Brain Images Say Yes" (*Shaking* 33). Convinced by the colorful fMRI-images, the author of the article sets out to rescue the concept of hysteria from the realm of literary analyses, where it may have been useful at a time when it was "surely out of place in the serious reaches of contemporary science" (quoted in *Shaking* 33). Not only does this statement invoke a deep divide between art and science, but it also clearly demonstrates that the meaning of a disease changes once the categories through which it may be examined shift: The article attempts to frame hysteria in material, physical terms and the images produced by the fMRI are employed as convincing evidence since they illustrate activity in the brain during convulsive fits.

However, Hustvedt is not as convinced as the journalist when she reminds her readers that even though the brain scan images are highly valuable in neuroscientific research, they cannot provide an explanation for the neuronal changes they show, i.e. their function is merely descriptive: "They demonstrate that there are neuroanatomical correlates to a hysterical paralysis or blindness – an organic change – but how that happens can't be discovered from an fMRI; nor do those images tell doctors how to treat their conversion patients" (*Shaking* 34). Her statement illustrates that concerning patient-care, no progress has been made by the fMRI study and experts have not been able to gain new knowledge about the disease, thus relativizing the insights the article highlights and stressing the lack of knowledge that still does persist. Apart from granting the brain scan images the power to visualize neuronal processes, in other words, make them "real" for the public eye, she exposes these brain scan images as an unquestioned hype. What is more, her observation meditates on the relationship between scientific data and storytelling, highlighting that the impression that the raw data stripped of stories and literary art seem to convey objectivity cannot hold, since they require interpretation (cf. Hunter, "Remaking" 165), i.e. a form of narrativization. Using them to confirm the existence of hysteria, as the journalist Hustvedt cites apparently does, is then finally not pure objectivism, but the imposition of a new narrative, bent to a specific aim.

In the same manner in which Hustvedt has criticized the categorization of shaking in history, her examination of the current conception of hysteria and its apparent diagnostic means runs along very similar lines when she observes that "[t]he philosophical ideas that lie beneath calling one thing by one name and another by another often remain unexamined, and they may be determined more by intellectual fashions than by rigorous thought" (*Shaking* 188). The parallel syntax in this cautionary statement juxtaposes "intellectual fashions" and "rigorous thought" and thereby contrasts careful research and thorough argumentation with the superficiality and temporality of emerging and vanishing fashions.

The very definition of hysteria therefore remains ambiguous and Hustvedt notes that the contemporary notion of conversion disorder is listed in the *DSM* as a so-called 'somatoform disorder,' mental disorders that exhibit "disturbances of the body and physical sensations" (ibid. 11), an observation that illustrates her criticism as a new name has been created to alter the framework through which hysteria is to be read. These attempts to categorize hysteria in terms of either a mental or physical illness eventually lead to what Hustvedt metaphorically calls "psyche/soma trap" (ibid. 15) – eventually, attempts to locate the disease at either side of the mind/body dichotomy are futile, because they are soon made obsolete by new means of diagnosis and by "intellectual fashions." Hysteria defies a stable categorization, this becomes clear in Hustvedt's account of its history, and Porter argues that the reason for the sphinxlike nature of hysteria throughout its history is that the relationship between mind and body has been in itself enigmatic ("Body" 235). Hence the disease is also emblematic of Hustvedt's notion that there is no clear-cut distinction between mental and physical diseases, which becomes evident in her doubt in Hebb's law[17] when she defiantly asks: "Can I say that the shaking woman is a repeatedly activated pattern of firing neurons and stress hormones released in an involuntary response, which is then dampened as I keep my cool, continue to talk, convinced that I am not really in any danger? Is that all there is to the story?" (*Shaking* 116).

8.4 *THE SHAKING WOMAN* AS THERAPEUTIC NARRATIVE

In a similar vein, Hustvedt comments on a quotation from Nobel laureate Francis Crick's *The Astonishing Hypothesis* that maintains "You, your joys and your sorrows, your memories and your ambitions, your sense of personal identity and free will are, in fact, no more than the behavior of a vast assembly of nerve cells and their associated molecules" (quoted in *Shaking* 116). Like in other parts of the narrative, where Hustvedt accepts the materialist foundations of the self, she does not refute this statement per se, yet contends that there is still "something wrong" with the way it has been formulated (ibid.). This "something," rather than an issue that she can directly explain, appears to be intuitive, though not without reason, for it is in a reasoned comparison that she attempts to scrutinize her impression that "something [is] wrong": "Would anyone deny that Tolstoy's 'The Death of Ivan Ilych' is paper and ink or that Giorgione's *The Tempest* is canvas and paint?" (ibid. 116f.). While it is of course true to speak of Tolstoy's story as "paper and ink" or of Giorgione's painting as "canvas and paint," these statements are too simplistic and thus miss the key to understanding what these works of art are or why they are significant. Moreover, it is interesting that Hustvedt has selected works of art for her

---

17 "Neurons that fire together, wire together" (*Shaking* 116), implying that repeated actions form habits.

comparisons. Not only does she see art on the same level with science, evening out the supposed hierarchy between them, but, more importantly, she stresses that reductionist and materialist approaches fall short of a piece of art. By inviting a comparative reading of Crick's assertion about human nature and her question about the works of art, Hustvedt thus ultimately voices strong criticism against scientific and philosophical reductionism. Like the seams that cannot be fit in Emily Dickinson's poem in the epigraph to her story, her comparison makes it obvious that scientific data and experience do not fit neatly together in such a reductionist argument, either. In her account, science is incapable of grasping lived experience in its entirety, since she likewise asks whether she is "wrong in feeling that 'a vast assembly of nerve cells' is an inadequate description of *me* and that those words fail to answer the question, What happened to me?" (*Shaking* 117; italics in original).

Undoubtedly, her question is a rhetorical one. Hustvedt does not believe that a neuronal process is all there is to her story, although she never doubts its materialist foundations. "Meaning is something we find and make," she purports (ibid. 131) and hence assumes the authority to forge her own theory of the self that strongly stresses the in-between-spaces. The story of the shaking woman is also the story of her father's death and her memories of him: Hustvedt entangles the accounts of her shaking fits with memories of dreaming that she felt the line through her nose that supplied her father with oxygen during his last days, that she felt his lame leg and she, in fact, *was* her father in her dream, thus merging her perspective with that of her father (*Shaking* 125). Although she remarks that there is no "consensus that dreams *mean* anything" (ibid. 130; italics in original), and cites different theories in favor and against the interpretation of dreams at length, she does take a stand by interpreting her dream as the connection of her illness to her father's presence.

Similarly, she reconsiders her first shaking fit, remembering how she felt close to her father as she carefully selected which words to say, words that "fell somewhere between us – not his, not quite mine, somewhere in the middle" (ibid. 125). Moreover, she even recounts how she had the impression that she was hearing her father's voice (ibid. 3). By repeatedly shifting her focus to her relationship to her father, "who is the ghost somehow involved in [her] shaking" (ibid. 19), Hustvedt not only stresses intersubjectivity as one of the key principles of her conceptualization of self, but also the importance of 'knowledge from within,' even if this knowledge is limited. At the same time, her notion of intersubjectivity alludes to the limitations of science, since "[w]hat happens between two people [...] isn't easily quantified or measured" (ibid. 123). It is at this point in the story that Hustvedt utters strong criticism against "the scientific fetish for brain functions" that treats emotional and affective responses as though they happened in an "isolated, bodiless organ" (ibid. 89).

Hustvedt finds fault with the fact that numerous scientists and philosophers conceptualize the human mind in terms of a computer or a machine: "For one thing, machines aren't emotional, and without affective values," she argues (ibid.), disproving the scientific and philosophical theory with her own lived experience. Her second point of criticism is even stronger and points back to the notion of intersubjectivity when she states that

"[s]ubjectivity is not the story of a stable, absolute 'I' that marches through life making one conscious decision after another. It is not a disembodied brain machine, either, genetically preprogrammed to act in specified and predictable ways. […] Furthermore, our subjectivity is not closed but open to the outside world." (ibid.)

In these statements, Hustvedt expounds her own theory of the relationship between mind, brain, and body. We are embodied beings, she holds, attributing importance to both mental capacities and physical matter. However, she stresses that the brain does not solely define our existence; instead, she argues, we "always live in relation to that perceived external world as corporeal beings" and are "inhabited, occupied, plural" (ibid. 90).

Despite the fact that Hustvedt so empathically turns against a neuro-scientific explanation for her tremors and her relationship to the world around her, her own conceptual approach to the self and its relations to others bears striking resemblance to so-called mirror neuron systems. Mirror neurons, first detected in the brains of macaque monkeys, and then traced in the human brain, constitute a groundbreaking discovery in neuroscience and the understanding of the mind and brain, because they offer, for the first time in history, a neurophysiological explanation for processes of social interaction (Iacoboni, *Woher* 13, 271). To be more precise, mirror neuron activity establishes mental and emotional connections between individuals (ibid. 12). For instance, by allowing us to not only decode the facial expressions and gestures of someone in pain but to also feel their pain, mirror neurons form a pre-reflective and automatic basis for empathy and intersubjectivity, establish shared meaning between two people and constitute a "vehicle" of interdependency (ibid., 273, 276, 279; "Problem" 131). Beyond that, mirror neurons also have a significant impact on the development of an individual's self-consciousness because behavioral scientist Marco Iacoboni maintains that the self and the other "co-constitute" each other, in other words that a sense of self only emerges in the interaction with other people (*Woher* 143).

Nevertheless, Hustvedt's theory of an "occupied" being should not be read as a denial of agency or free will. In fact, her explanation stresses that subjectivity always entails intersubjectivity and establishing clear-cut borders between the 'I' and the 'you' is impossible, since "others are *of* us" (*History* 90). As a consequence, this also means that there is no distinct boundary between self and other, but in her conceptualization, the two merge. She illustrates her point by stating that "I am reflected in your eyes" (ibid. 91), or, in other words: I see myself through you, through the other. In this respect it becomes clear why not only her father but also the numerous patients of the case studies Hustvedt cites, and, finally, the shaking woman as well, play a crucial role for her conceptualization of her identity. When she recognizes for example that "the fictitious Mexican" in a case study, Lizzy, the woman in her writing class at the hospital, and she herself share something, she establishes a connection that goes beyond the superficial "grieving problem" the experiencing I identifies early in the narrative (ibid. 27). When encountering these real and fictitious men and women, she also encounters the various perspectives that may help to clarify who the shaking woman is and add further angles of vision to her story.

The merging of self and other is also relevant in the context of hysteria. Marks highlights that for the hysteric person, "everything is outward-directed and other-determined" (*Relationality* 134). The individual is hence entirely subjected to the control by outside forces and has no power to define their self. Ultimately, the self as a discrete and self-contained identity does not exist. Hysteria may then serve as a rhetorical strategy uttered outside institutional structures (Greene 189) and the bodily voice of the repressed and silenced. It is striking that both aspects, a powerful force and a repressed voice, can be observed in Hustvedt's account of the shaking woman, when she notes that "[t]he strangeness of a duality in myself remains, a powerful sense of 'I' and an uncontrollable other. The shaking woman is certainly not anyone with a name. She is a speechless alien who appears only during my speeches" (*Shaking* 47).

This also becomes evident when Hustvedt recounts another incident of her tremors months later while she is holding a presentation on literature:

"I walked up unto the stage and the moment I uttered the first word, it happened again. I was shaking in front of hundreds of people. I gripped the podium, but my arms, torso, and legs were shuddering so badly that there was no disguising it. I had managed to push through the first paragraph when I heard someone in a front row say, 'She's shaking' and then another person, 'I think she's having a seizure.' Pressing my hands hard onto the sides of the wooden podium in front of me as the mortifying spasms continued, I told the audience to bear with me, that I was actually going to discuss the shaking a little later in the talk." (ibid. 29)

In this scene, the shaking woman figures as the mere object that is objectively spoken about. The repeated use of "I" uttered as an anaphora in several subsequent sentences highlights the speaking, acting subject and establishes a strong opposition to the "it" that is again trying to push through to the surface yet may only cause the experiencing I's body to shudder. The shaking woman is not permitted to speak here but becomes instead a mere topic in the course of her speech, an object of her gaze, which again reinforces the shaking woman's 'otherness.'

Similarly, an acquaintance later tells Hustvedt that "it had been like watching a doctor and a patient in the same body" (ibid. 30). This observation not only implies that two perspectives meet, the subjective and the objective, but that the doctor's removed outside perspective remains authoritative. Accordingly, the shaking is overridden by the third-person voice and the rupture of the self cannot be merged: "Indeed, I had been two people that day – a reasonable orator and a woman in the middle of a personal quake," Hustvedt recalls (ibid.), repeatedly reinforcing the hierarchy that is inherent in her relationship to the shaking woman. The quotation here evinces that in her attempt to maintain control she, too, engages in the process of turning the shaking woman into 'the other,' an object tainted with the very stigma of hysteria. Like Charcot, she exposes the shaking woman in front of her audience and provides the framework in which they are supposed to understand her shaking. Likewise, the narrating I distances her process of narrating from the shaking woman: "The shaking woman is not the narrating woman. The narrating, interpreting woman continued on while the other shook. The narrator was a fluent generator of sentences and explanations. It is she who is writing now" (ibid. 54). Later, she remarks that the shaking woman "cuts [her] into two" and causes her to feel disrupted and divided (ibid. 165). She stresses the fact that her "narrating first-person subject" is opposed to her "recalcitrant body," pointing out that she understands herself by means of her inner voice. Language is thus crucial to her sense of self (ibid.).

Interestingly, the process of writing, of composing a narrative, does in fact bring the two identities together. Marks describes the significatory power of the hysteric's body as the "language of [the] unconscious" (Marks, "Hysteria" 3). In how far the unconscious or repressed memories are actually involved in Hustvedt's shaking, is not for the reader to evaluate. When Hustvedt dreams of dying, she later interprets her dreams as one "about [her] relation to another death" – that of her father – which she "seem[s] to be carrying around with [her] every day like a disease" (*Shaking* 137). What is more, the unconscious plays a major role in finally merging the "reasonable orator" and the shaking woman. This takes place first of all in the dream, the realm of the subconscious: "I may be wrong, but I feel I've never been as close to the shaking woman as in that dream," Hustvedt admits (ibid.).

In a similar vein, automatic writing becomes a strategy to merge the two aspects of Hustvedt's identity and to blur the boundaries between her "narrating [...] conscious, telling self" and the "shaking [...] flashback self" (ibid. 52). In the context of her work on the psychiatric ward, she introduces the principle of Joe Brainard's book *I Remember*, a detailed account of the author's memories, each beginning with the statement "I remember." "Writing the words *I remember* engages both motor and cognitive action," she explains (ibid. 63; italics in original). According to Laura Di Summa-Knoop, Hustvedt acknowledges here that writing one's self and one's life is not purely based on intention and choice but just as well depends on the mechanisms underlying cognition and language expression (156f.), thereby intertwining artistic practice and the corporeal, the mental and the physical.

Today, such a method of automatic writing is often viewed along the same lines as hysteria: outdated and "colored in sepia" (*Shaking* 71), yet Hustvedt is very critical of this: "We suffer from the hubris of the present: with our misguided notion of perpetual progress, we believe that we are always moving forward and getting better and smarter" (ibid.). Instead, she cherishes the power of automatic writing, since it gives her the feeling that she has been "taken over" and "the sentences come as if [she] hadn't willed them, as if they were manufactured by another being" (ibid. 72). For Hustvedt, automatic writing constitutes a comfortable lack of control and an occasion on which she gladly surrenders. She thus becomes the shaking woman when she is writing, as Tougaw observes: "she draws on what's unconscious to craft a sense of control – or agency – through writing" ("Brain Memoirs" 189). What is important in this context is that even though "much is generated unconsciously" when she writes (*Shaking* 88), Hustvedt stresses that the phrase "I remember" "assumes ownership of what is to come" (ibid. 64). It is hence through automatic writing that she is able to accomplish what she failed to do when she attempted to suppress or explain the shaking in public and berated herself with the words "Own this, This is you. Own it!" and reconcile the split self that becomes evident in her use of the second person (ibid. 40).

According to Tougaw, writing elucidates the dynamic exchange between the intentional and the peripheral ("Brain Memoirs" 189). The result is often a chain of associations. Such a chain guides Hustvedt's search for the shaking woman throughout the entire book, for instance when she moves from her exploration of the phrase "I remember" to different notions of subjectivity or when she uses automatic writing herself to generate childhood memories of her father's college campus, the site where the shaking first occurred, in order to add the perspectives of place, locus, and memory to her story (*Shaking* 88ff., 98f.). In Oliver Sacks's case, the spontaneous flow of music was responsible for merging the cognitive and the physical and restoring both agency and memories in the injured story-teller. Similar forces are at work in *The Shaking Woman* and one may therefore attribute the same qualities to her process of writing as I have attributed to music above.

The case of a patient talking about his mother's suicide, but not grasping its horrible and tragic dimensions, serves as a parable for Hustvedt's own narrative conclusion. After undergoing psychotherapy, the patient is reported to "sense a change, a new configuration of his consciousness that includes both knowing and feeling" (*Shaking* 197). He is then able to retell the story and, "in an act of creative memory," claims the story of the loss as his own (ibid. 198). This moment of individual (narrative) agency does not exclude the neuroscientific discourse, though, because Hustvedt immediately adds that "there are neuronal changes in his brain accordingly, in the limbic emotional systems and the pre-frontal executive areas" (ibid.). However, she does not allow these objective observations to override personal qualitative experience, since she ultimately explains: "There are times when we all resist claiming what should be ours; it is alien, and we do not want to take it into the stories we spin about ourselves" (ibid.). Not only does she restore the patient's agency at the end of his case story, but she also provides a more inclusive explanation by uttering the first person plural. Rather than offering merely "local and personal" insights, as Tougaw argues, Hustvedt does attempt to make more general claims ("Brain Memoirs" 176).

Throughout her narrative, Hustvedt has viewed neuroscientific reductionism with a critical eye. By extending the neuroscientific explanation, she shows that such stories do not take place inside "an isolated, bodiless organ" (*Shaking* 89) and allows for the two explanations to co-exist. Even though she finally consciously shies away from definitive answers, both for the causes of her shaking and to the plethora of questions that she has raised along her way, she stresses the importance of storytelling for the self:

"Clearly, a self is much larger than the internal narrator. Around and beneath the island of that self-conscious story-teller is a vast sea of unconsciousness, of what we don't know, will never know, or have forgotten. There is much in us that we don't control or will, but that doesn't mean that making a narrative for ourselves is unimportant." (ibid. 198)

Hustvedt hence readily embraces the fact that even after her search, she is still left with many issues that she cannot explain. Even narrative coherence cannot overcome a sense of ambiguity and when she describes ambiguity as not fitting "into the pigeonhole, the neat box, the window frame, the encyclopedia" (ibid.), it is not only her uncertainty that she describes, but it is also the nature of the shaking woman.

Mediating science, medicine and experience, Tougaw observes, eventually allows for an "organic acceptance that we do not know much about the relationship between the brain and the self," and the writer's opportunity to teach scientists "a lesson in humility" ("Brain Memoirs" 179). Rather than leaving readers with a sense of mastery, Hustvedt's narrative emphasizes the uncertainty that she has encountered in her dealing with theories and discourses (cf. also Gygax, "Life Writing" 298). The ambiguity she refers to here should not be read negatively as a failed effort to arrive at clear-cut definitions, but instead is inherently subversive, as Gygax points out when she argues that such a form of uncertainty undermines the conventional notion of theory (ibid.).

In a similar fashion, Hustvedt reports

"I can't tell what it is or if it is anything at all. I chase it with words even though it won't be captured and, every once in a while, I imagine I have come close to it. In May of 2006, I stood outside under a cloudless blue sky and started to speak about my father, who had been dead for over two years. As soon as I opened my mouth, I began to shake violently. I shook that day and then I shook again on other days. I am the shaking woman." (*Shaking* 199)

In the final paragraph, her story ultimately comes full circle when she retells the beginning of the book; now, however, she is able to add a conclusion and a closing statement that indicate that her search has come to an end: It ends with her acknowledgement that the shaking woman is in fact her. Rewriting the paragraph that has initiated her quest when she recounted the first incident of her shaking, Hustvedt now seems to have reached a sense of reconciliation and claims the shaking woman as her identity. The paratactic structure of the final sentences foregrounds the "I" in her narration and the short main clauses, particularly in the second half of the quote, have a strong and determined ring. However, despite the fact that the paragraph forms a brief story of her shaking, notions of cause and effect remain elusive. "Exactly what a self is remains controversial," Hustvedt acknowledges, when she uses the term herself to describe how the shaking woman has transformed from "a detested double" to "an admittedly handicapped part" of her self (ibid. 190).

In light of these final sentences, several reviewers have remarked that the ending is "slightly frustrating" or even "unoriginal," since Hustvedt does not reach a definitive diagnosis that explains the cause of her shaking (Albertyn 59; Magenau n. pag.; my translation).[18] The question that needs to be posed is of course for whom this constitutes a dissatisfying and unnerving ending. These critical reviews bespeak the pervasiveness of the restitution and triumph narrative. While triumphant narratives re-inscribe the boundary between health and illness (cf. Chapter 2.3), the ending of Hustvedt's narrative refuses such a clear-cut distinction by withholding a diagnosis, and in fact, any need for further medical probing.[19] For readers

---

18 Chloe Atkins's *My Imaginary Illness: A Journey into Uncertainty and Prejudice in Medical Diagnosis* provides another revealing literary account of the problem of diagnosis. A scholar of social and legal theory, Atkins writes with a critical eye to the medical system and the categories of evidence-based medicine that do not allow "statistical outliers" (*Imaginary* 145), an issue that is particularly at stake in her own memoir, since she never receives an official diagnosis for ailments, although they are at times life-threatening. Like Hustvedt, she makes the case that "[d]iagnostic categories also flex and are adapted as research and clinical experience reveal new information and knowledge about various ailments" and points to the idea that diseases may be amorphous and thus hard to categorize (ibid. 147f.). Her account has been published in the Cornell University Press series "How Patients Think," a series of books which the editors hope will "give patients a voice and create much needed dialogue" between individuals suffering from illness and medical professionals (ix). The book closes with a critical commentary by Brian D. Hodges, M.D., and thus establishes a structural frame that may be studied in more detail.

19 Historian Alice Wexler's *Mapping Fate: A Memoir of Family, Risk, and Genetic Research* ends on a very similar note, as Wexler, who has throughout the book looked at

who have internalized the triumph narrative, the defiance of closure, clarity and certainty, as well as the denial of explanations through language and categorization may certainly be unnerving. By refraining from a diagnosis and thus suspending the structural and formal elements that would provide the narrative with epiphany and closure, *The Shaking Woman* effectively breaks with the conventions of the triumph narrative. In addition, Garden notes that diagnosis with its strong focus on scientific knowledge and authority frequently fails to consider the patient's idea of health and healing ("Telling" 127), thus imposing an authoritative and artificial frame to constrain a narrative that has worked to subvert these frameworks. Why and how exactly the shaking woman is involved in Hustvedt's self, Tougaw notes, remains vague ("Brain Memoirs" 180), yet for Hustvedt, this ending is a decidedly powerful one, since she has accepted her "condition" – diagnosed or not – and turned it into her identity.

The ending thus also frames a statement that she makes earlier when reading the psychoanalyst Winnicott and stating: "I understand him to mean that health can tolerate some disintegration. At one time or another all of us go to pieces and it isn't necessarily a bad thing. That state of disunity may allow a flexible and open creativity that is part of a healthy being" (*Shaking* 80f.). The narrative stresses the close proximity of health and illness and, more than that, attaches rather positive connotations to the "state of disunity" as it will allow her, and is indeed necessary, to create strategies to forge unity, such as writing.

Returning to the discourse of hysteria, the so-called 'talking cure' comes to mind, a term that in its variation as 'writing cure' is frequently uttered in the context of contemporary illness narratives. Showalter maintains that hysterical patients were not capable of telling their entire, "smooth and exact" story but that their condition forced them to leave out, rearrange or distort repressed information (84). Only if this information was remembered and incorporated into a coherent story, the patients would be considered cured (ibid.). Of course readers would romanticize Hustvedt's story by viewing it solely in this frame of reference, as she does suggest that her shaking may have developed into a chronic ailment (*Shaking* 189). Nevertheless, Hustvedt, too, stresses the importance of the 'talking cure' since it grants the subject a voice that "reown[s] the experience" (ibid. 61).

As Herndl aptly notes, telling a story alone does not constitute a cure, since the individual affected by hysteria is still caught within the same constraints, definitions and representations ("Writing" 66). Consequently, the new narrative the subject

---

both her family's and the cultural history of Huntington's Disease, declines to take the genetic test that may reveal her predisposition for the disease, thereby foregoing a comic resolution and highlighting the ambiguity of her health status (for an analysis of the memoir, see e.g. Couser's "Un(Common)").

creates needs to go beyond these constraints. By critically engaging with scientific and philosophical discourses, Hustvedt has done exactly this. The narrative that she confronts her readers with has helped her to "reown" the experiences of her shaking by analyzing them from different perspectives, yet always as a speaking subject that defends her qualitative experiences against objective points of view. This is also emphasized when Hustvedt declares

"let us say that hidden somewhere in my brain, undetected by the MRI, there is a *lesion* that could be designated as the *cause* for shaking. I still don't believe I would have started shuddering if I had not been speaking about my father, or standing on that old ground of memory or if I hadn't been facing family friends I had known since childhood." (*Shaking* 187; italics in original)

In the end, it becomes evident that a diagnostic narrative does not suffice to grasp the nature of the shaking woman and the manifold ways in which the shaking has not only interrupted but also conjoined aspects of Hustvedt's life. What is needed, in contrast, is a 'therapeutic narrative.' Hunter utters this term in her discussion of case histories arguing that these stories may be therapeutic in twofold ways: by attending to the meaning that illness has in the patient's life and hence resetting the focus of therapy, particularly in case of patients suffering from chronic illness, and, secondly, by creating a narrative that bears witness to these questions ("Remaking" 175), an act that Hustvedt realizes for herself. Instead of portraying illness as something that needs to be overcome, ideally as quickly as possible so that one can carry on living, *The Shaking Woman* is ultimately a book that decidedly argues for a shift from 'cure' to 'healing.'

In "How to Speak Postmodern," Morris envisions such a shift by claiming that healing must be possible, even if a cure cannot be found. In doing so, he undermines the discourse of biomedicine with its focus on cure, asserting that the idea of healing is not merely a "discordant note" in this discourse, but has subversive potential (12). Like Hustvedt's narrative, his concept of healing stresses the recovery of interpersonal relationships and the connection between self and other (cf. ibid. 13). Similarly, Catherine Garrett's *Gut Feelings* intertwines her personal experiences with theoretical reflections on illness and healing. Although her perspective on healing is more spiritual than theoretical, some of her ideas may be applied to a broader context. Early in the book she posits healing as an alternative to cure and characterizes it as a "full life" in contrast to cure that may still leave scars or other traces perpetuating her suffering (8). In his concept, the attribution of values is note-worthy: whereas healing carries positive connotations, the promise of fulfillment and happiness, cure is still conceptualized as something close to suffering, sometimes even responsible for it, an issue that may rest in the fact that for Garrett, healing is not only removed from the medical context but – precisely because of that – is also possible even when an illness persists as chronic.

Moreover, healing is imagined as a personal endeavor, for Garrett states that it is something that she must bring about by herself (39). In her ideas it becomes evident that healing both encourages and necessitates agency.[20] In this respect, striving for healing transcends the passive state of patienthood that would require the individual to await a means of cure or to undergo treatment. On the contrary, "[h]ealing […] involves much more than coping," Garrett holds and instead describes it as a transformation process affecting the entire individual as she continues to spur that process, leading to "a kind of peace" that comes with "a growing understanding" (8). Consequently, healing is conceived of as personal growth, not merely a reaction or an arrangement to living with illness and suffering. It is crucial to understand that Garrett's notion of healing does not transcend the physical reality of illness; instead, the "growing understanding" that she postulates allow for a tight relationship between illness and healing. Eventually though, the ending of Hustvedt's narrative, even if it is not entirely happy, points to resolution and self-acceptance (cf. also Garden, "Telling" 124). Despite its vast amount of hard scientific facts and academic references the memoir turns back to the experience of illness, for Hustvedt's crucial recognition is that the shaking woman is becoming more familiar, literally "moving out of the third person and into the first" (*Shaking* 190).

---

20 While this is a powerful and enabling ending for Hustvedt, this may arguably be interpreted in more negative terms as well when it is read in terms of individual responsibility. In *Smile or Die: How Positive Thinking Fooled America and the World*, Ehrenreich is utterly critical of what she calls the "tyranny of positive thinking" (42), a strong ideological force she expounds also with regard to illness and healing in the chapter "Smile or Die: The Bright Side of Cancer." Here, she deconstructs the proposition that "attitude" is a decisive factor for successful treatment (33ff.), before tracing the history of positive thinking on later pages of her book. For her, positive thinking is the "constant interior labor of self-examination" (89), and, considering that if one constantly monitors one's self, a form of "work" that continuously creates distance between the self that needs to be worked on and the person committed to working on that self (91).

9. Conclusion

In this book I have explored what I take to constitute a significant subgenre of illness and disability memoirs, the memoir of well-being. The case studies have demonstrated that these memoirs employ a number of recurring motifs, themes, and plot structures to challenge the traditional notion of health, as well as the authority of cultural and scientific discourses to account for their writers' experiences. Memoirs of well-being, this study illustrates, destabilize the divide between health and illness/disability as the memoirists come to terms with their conditions, may heal and attain well-being, even in the face of chronic and persisting afflictions.

On the content level alone, these memoirs are remarkable for their privilege of well-being and healing over 'health' in the conventional sense. Far too little attention has so far been devoted to this shift in content, despite the fact that it presents such an urgent matter in the twenty-first century when a growing number of individuals identify as living with impairments or chronic conditions and campaigns call for patients to participate actively in managing their health (Moss and Teghtsoonian 3). "The future is one in which chronic illnesses and end-of-life conditions faced by aging populations will play an ever-greater role," predict Arthur Kleinman and Rachel Hall-Clifford and see the growing community of people with chronic conditions united "in desires for improved prevention, treatment, and care" (247). However, as this study has revealed, the memoirists in remission consciously and confidently abandon the realm of biomedicine, its language, treatment regimens, as well as its protocols for gaining and circulating knowledge.

In doing so, they challenge the foundations of the biomedical system and strongly contest the role of medicine in framing un-wellness and 'health' in contemporary culture and society. Since WWII, medicine as a "politico-economic institutional sector and a sociocultural 'good'" has grown tremendously and accordingly, the scope of clinical interventions has considerably extended, so that a variety of aspects of social life, such as death, alcoholism, child birth, or attention deficit disorder have come within the purview of medicine and are constructed as medical problems (Clarke et al. 161ff.). In the twenty-first century, these processes of medicalization are, Adele Clarke et al. argue, complicated through the rapid increase of manifold techno-scientific changes, among them molecular biology, transplant medicine or genome research, as well as the new protocols and practices they give shape to. "[M]edicalization," they conclude, "is intensifying, but in new and complex, usually technoscientifically enmeshed ways" (ibid. 162).

As a result, medical jurisdiction is no longer limited to aberrant bodies or behaviors, but is extended to health itself, so that health as a commodity assumes a vital role: "Managing" one's health properly becomes a primary pursuit, realized through access to knowledge, prevention, risk assessment, self-surveillance and by means of self-help or biomedical goods or services (ibid.). In turn, Clarke et al. note, new forms of embodiment and identity emerge (ibid.) and one only needs to go as far as the App Store to find a plethora of "body trackers" – pedometers, pulse or heart beat monitors, calorie counters, menstrual and ovulation calendars – which allow users instant access to data about their bodies. Along with exercise apps, online weight-loss coaching and mindfulness seminars, they demonstrate the pervasiveness of 'health' in U.S. culture and society. "[H]ealth becomes an individual goal, a social and moral responsibility, and a site for routine biomedical intervention" (ibid. 171) but memoirs of well-being actively resist the mandate imposed on the memoirists and thus take a political stand, as my close readings have illustrated.

The narratives reveal striking formal, structural, and aesthetic choices which underline their contestation of medical, scientific, and cultural discourses, as well as their refusal to comply with conventional modes of storying illness and disability. At the heart of this book are therefore the five "case studies" and their close readings. Though grouped in temporal order, these representative analyses do not sketch a continuous progress, the evolution of the subgenre into a certain direction. Rather, the structure of my thesis aims to elucidate the continuity in these texts from the era of politicized patienthood in the 1980s well into the early years of the twenty-first century, a time in which the idea of politicized *patienthood* inarguably requires reconsideration. The texts attest that, while disease and impairment, particularly when they assume long-term and chronic forms, are increasingly removed from the biomedical realm and experienced actively in a myriad of other ways than merely as a 'patient,' illness and disability remain highly politically charged conditions. As a result, they generate stories of *politicized selves* and lives in remission.

Several strands link the individual chapters to form the key characteristics of memoirs of well-being which effectively subvert the traditional triumph and restitution narrative in both content and form and blur the boundaries between health and states of un-wellness: (1) the memoirists' opposition to "cure" – the biomedical quick fix – and, directly related to this, (2) their efforts to draft a sense of healing and well-being beyond the dichotomous definition of 'health,' (3) the stories' preoccupation with community, (4) the writers' turn to their bodies, embodiment, and knowledge emerging from the body and, in turn, (5) their critical and creative engagement with scientific knowledge and discourses, as well as (6) a strong sense of temporality, contingency, and thus (7) their purposeful lack of closure. These features provide an extensive inventory and generic template from which the examples studied here have drawn. As in any genre, the ways in which these conventions are employed and combined varies but a text's compliance with a number of the features listed here signals its inclusion in the new subgenre.

Audre Lorde's *The Cancer Journals*, I have shown in Chapter 4, is chiefly invested in deconstructing the notion of health commonly employed in writing about breast cancer through the reconceptualization of reconstruction in the context of recovery and healing. I have focused on selected scenes in which Lorde uses outrageous encounters with doctors, nurses, and other representatives of the health care system to write back at the medical establishment. The category of 'angry pathography,' however, cannot exhaust the project of her memoir which is aimed at writing back at both American society and its view on the Black, female, queer and disabled body and the prosthetic narrative of breast cancer, which seeks to cover up unsightly mastectomy scars by means of prosthesis and the terrifying experience of cancer through the 'triumph narrative.' As a form of 'ampu-narration,' the memoir defies the normalizing quick fix of prosthesis and instead lays bare the post-mastectomy body, a body that is not the "pitted battlefield of some major catastrophic war" but all "soft brown skin" (*Cancer* 45) and thus envisions the theme of the memoir that mastectomy is not disfiguring and that it is possible for women to feel at ease with their post-surgical bodies. As opposed to prostheses and reconstructive surgery, which Jain refers to as "'objective' recovery" to which "subjective recovery" is only secondary ("Prosthetic" 48), the memoir fundamentally shifts the focus to women's subjective recovery, the process of healing, and the emerging feeling of well-being.

The conflict between an objective and a subjective recovery also takes center stage in Oliver Sacks's *A Leg to Stand On*. Here, Sacks subverts the triumphant narrative of the surgical cure by focusing on his qualitative feelings after waking up from the procedure that was intended to reconnect the injured muscles and nerve tissues in his leg yet leaves him feeling utterly disconnected, both from his leg and from his physical being more generally. His deep distrust of the biomedical cure is all the more highlighted through the fact that he is a medical professional himself. Healing and well-being, I have demonstrated in Chapter 5, are eventually achieved not through biomedicine but through music which unites the mental and corporeal aspects of Sacks's self.

Simi Linton's *My Body Politic* and Kenny Fries's *The History of My Shoes and the Evolution of Darwin's Theory* both disclose another form of countering triumphant narration. Linton's memoir, analyzed in Chapter 6, rewrites the conventional progress narrative by disabling health and focusing instead on the legislation that has improved her own life, as well as the lives of others around her. Her narrative of social and political progress is both a product of her time and intricately linked to community and sexuality, two themes commonly neglected in the discourse on disability which receive great weight in the story and significantly contribute to her sense of well-being. *My Body Politic* therefore needs to be read as a counter-narrative to the dominant biomedical, political, and cultural discourses on disability and difference. Fries's life narrative, on the other hand, which I have explored in Chapter 7, undermines the popular super-crip narrative and supplants it with a story that dissolves the line between ability and disability, the normal and the pathological by positing impairment as a variation and diverting the reader's gaze from the prospect of perfection and extraordinary accomplishment to the pleasures of the benefits of disability.

In *The Shaking Woman or A History of My Nerves*, Siri Hustvedt arrives at the conclusion that she cannot transcend her mysterious and unresolved illness and finds well-being in its embrace. Her recognition "I am the shaking woman" (*Shaking* 199) is emblematic for identity in memoirs of well-being because like Hustvedt, many writers take on a new, distinct, and self-aware identity: Lorde becomes the "post-mastectomy woman" (*Cancer* 7) and Linton self-consciously begins to speak about herself as a "disabled woman" (*Body* 118). While these terms renounce cure and link illness and impairment inseparably to their writers' lives and identities, their narratives inscribe their existences with a strong sense of well-being.

Furthermore, in challenging the triumphant plot lines of many earlier illness and disability narratives that end with the memoirists having their health restored or overcoming the constraints of their impairments and thus produce individual and individualizing narratives, memoirs of well-being turn to community. This turn is most explicit in Lorde's and Linton's memoirs which both express a strong sense of the communal. Lorde's narrative invokes the presence of other women by speaking for them and voicing the concern that her pain should be of use for other women. As she lacks suitable role models to guide her through the experience (conventional support networks, I have illustrated, do not allow room for her Black lesbian identity), she resignifies the figure of the Amazon warrior, thus immersing herself into an alternative imagined community in which she may attain agency, overcome the silence surrounding breast cancer at her time and, at the same time, create a lasting image that resonates in literary and academic texts well into the twenty-first century. Linton, too, finds herself at a loss for role models, yet rather because she initially subscribes to stereotypical views of disability. A key scene I have discussed, the "yoghurt affair," enables her to conceive of disability in other terms than passivity and isolation. Subsequently, other disabled individuals come to serve as *roll* models and in their community, Linton is gradually able to redefine 'disability' along more positive lines and craft a sense of identity that links her to her able-bodied self, the activist, the "robust" woman, the woman whose body affords her pleasure.

These two memoirs show that community is not only a significant and decisive aspect of healing and leading a life in remission, but that community also powerfully emerges through the autobiographical text. In this vein, Torrell is absolutely right in refuting Mitchell's and Snyder's concerns[1] that the autobiographical text with its presumably singular voice may spoil the linkage between the personal and the political (323). Quite to the contrary, it is capable of strengthening the close connection between both the personal and the political and the personal and the academic by delineating an exemplary life story in close connection to cultural politics and disability legislation. In both stories, other voices echo. They either become audible through the voice of the narrating I – one speaking for many – or when the narrating I joins their chorus and her voice is authenticated and authorized by others. The texts at hand therefore form instances, fragments (but by no means fragmented voices) of a larger community that may sometimes be imagined but is oftentimes real and stalwart. Illness and disability not only cease to be linked to isolation but these experiences also assume great momentousness. Perhaps more than other illness and disability memoirs, memoirs of well-being then "enact and encourage self-disclosure" (Couser, "Disability Life Writing" 2). The remission society, they ultimately make clear, is more encompassing than we might initially believe and by taking their well-being into their own hands, the members demand that their presence among us is not merely acknowledged, as Couser argues (ibid.), but also cherished.

In a number of the "case studies," embodiment figures prominently. In *The Cancer Journals*, Lorde claims and celebrates "a body that the dominant public treats as distorted, disabled, disfigured" (Knopf-Newman 116). Although her narrative does not extensively dwell on the separation between mind and body during the experience of illness, her refusal of prosthesis as a means of repairing the body, while neglecting the psychological effects of breast cancer and mastectomy foreshadows the critique of biomedicine and its view on the body as a machine. This is articulated more elaborately in Sacks's book in which the separation of mind and body initially dominates after his operation. For Sacks, the process of rehabilitation needs to restore his body, but also the unity of his mind and body, for his narrative reveals that both are intricately interwoven through the embodied condition of the self. The surgeon's words – "'You've torn a tendon. We reconnect it.'" (*Leg* 30) – hence take on a different meaning and are later cited as "'You'd been disconnected. We reconnected you. That's all'" (ibid. 95). For Sacks, healing needs to go beyond the anatomical sense and encompass something "much vaster […] – the sense in which E. M. Forster says 'Only connect'" (ibid.). The passage from Forster's novel

---

1   See their introduction to the edited volume *The Body and Physical Difference: Discourses of Disability* (Ann Arbor: U of Michigan P, 1997. 1-34) for a thorough discussion.

Howards End Sacks alludes to here, is worth considering because it can be read as a conclusion to Sacks's narrative and may indeed be conceived as a mantra in the story: "Only connect! That was the whole of the sermon. Only connect the prose and the passion, and both will be exalted, and human love will be seen at its height. Live in fragments no longer" (198). In the literal sense, connection needs to be established in the anatomy of the injured body and likewise in the process of storytelling, so that "the whole story" can be told. In this vein, the memoir problematizes the relationship between Sacks as a patient and his doctors who are unwilling to devote serious attention to his seemingly idiosyncratic feelings. From these insights, Sacks's vision of a neurology of identity emerges, a concept that entails yet another connection, that of subjectivity and objectivity.

Similarly, subjectivity and objectivity are at the center of Hustvedt's memoir and the narrative continues Sacks's preoccupation with the first- and third-person perspective by revisiting and revising the form of the case study and merging subjective experiences – referred to as "knowledge from within" (Švrljuga 20) – with objective knowledge from outside in form of a wide variety of scientific, philosophical, and psychological theories. Like *A Leg to Stand On*, *The Shaking Woman* subverts the separation of these two perspectives and forms of knowledge. Consequently, Hustvedt's memoir considerably extends Sacks's project of bringing science and art into a fruitful dialogue. Indeed, in both memoirs, the hierarchy of objective and subjective knowledge is suspended: Sacks's memoir unsettles the authority of third-person knowledge when he privileges qualitative knowledge about the body by not only devoting considerable story-time to recounting what the post-surgical leg feels like – or rather does not feel like – but also by attributing great emphasis to the significance of subjective knowledge in neurological practice. The patient's experiences and knowledge, his memoir suggests, may advance neurology and its diagnostic and therapeutic inventory. Hustvedt's memoir, on the other hand, significantly expands this view by questioning third-person knowledge and its alleged objectivity from her perspective, calling readers to reconsider the stability, authority, and neutrality of knowledge.

The condition of illness and embodied, subjective knowledge about it, these memoirs evince, fundamentally influences how their writers face and participate in the discourses that frame their conditions and traditionally endow them with meaning. In disability memoirs, this naturally assumes great relevance as well: Linton's memoir, for instance, inserts the sexualized body and bodily pleasure into the discourse on disability and Fries's *The History* sets out to rewrite the history of his impaired body. On several occasions in the memoir, Fries intertwines observations of nature with his own body and its history. Yet while Lambeth reads these connections as proof that his body and his shoes are governed by the same laws as the evolution (n. pag.), my reading has exhibited that Darwin's theory is reappropriated to recognize the sense of well-being that, in connection to the impaired body, is personal, as well as political and theoretical. The creative engagement with evolutionary theory, limited as Fries's reading of it may be, helps to rewrite the role of the impaired body and abandon the fear of the 'survival of the fittest' that has haunted the memoirist since childhood. It is integral to his sense of well-being and a positive body politics but also to the larger argument *The History* outlines. The memoir helps to shift the focus from difference to commonality, an aspect that introduces a significant shift into current debates on disability, difference, and inclusion.

Writing about the 'new disability memoir,' Couser argues that contemporary texts resignify what he terms "anomalous" embodiment ("Disability Life Writing" 9) and memoirs of well-being lend themselves to a very similar reading. More than that, though, they elucidate that the body needs to be regarded as a significant, although hitherto often neglected source of knowledge. In many of the examples, knowledge plays a decisive role in bringing into focus the memoirists' representations of cure, recovery, and healing, and, more importantly, their reluctance to align their stories with traditional notions of health. However, rather than introducing knowledgeable authorities into their texts to deliver lasting explanations, they mediate well-being against the backdrop of uncertainty. Temporality and contingency thus receive great relevance. In contrast to Couser's argument that a book-length illness narrative must strive for emotional and narrative closure (*Recovering* 40), Lorde's account of her breast cancer experience does not conceal the fact that temporality and contingency will continue to be decisive factors in her life and that conclusions may therefore be tentative and provisional only. Neither narrative nor emotional closure can be achieved as long as women struggle, which is why she hopes her successors will expand on her project and make use of her pain.

Similarly Hustvedt embraces the contingency of her illness. Garden states that "[e]xperiences of illness are not conclusive" (127) and Jurecic, too, claims that any definite conclusion in both fictional and non-fictional narratives about illness ultimately misrepresents life in the risk society and the indeterminacy that this entails (38). But the indeterminacy that Hustvedt stresses with the ending of her memoir is also crucial for another reason. I have shown that her explorations of hysteria reveal that any explanation of cause-and-effect can at best be temporal and contextual. In this vein, any explanation she may offer her readers at the ending of her story would first of all betray this principle and, secondly, be soon outdated. Unsettling what on first reading appears to constitute stable knowledge and accepting not only the contingency of her condition but also discursive ambiguities then enables her to formulate a positive identity politics: She claims the shaking woman for herself and the sense of well-being that the ending offers – despite its lack of explanations and closure – is made possible when the contingency and temporality of knowledge are accepted. Accordingly, health as a stable and absolute state is overwritten by a notion of well-being that may tolerate some "pathology."

Uncertainty therefore assumes a crucial role in memoirs of well-being. While none of the texts studied here may alleviate its threatening and gloomy connotations, many of the "case studies" may put uncertainty, contingency and temporality to prolific use by speaking through the unspeakable and filling the gaps and ambiguities of prognoses and medical knowledge. Especially in Hustvedt's memoir, the uncertainty and contextual contingency of knowledge is where science and literature intersect. Denying her narrative the closure that a diagnosis would bring, Hustvedt's narrating I takes a stand against the authority of the biomedical discourse that particularly the diagnosis with its implications for treatment represents (cf. Moss and Teghtsoonian 10).

In several of the memoirs, I have touched upon the idea of a dialogue – Sacks's imagined and actual dialogue with Dr. Swan, Hustvedt's "dialogue" with a great number of scholars or Linton's memoir which stages a communicative encounter between herself as a representative of the disability community and her (nondisabled) readership. In all of these cases, the memoirists address dominant discourses with their subjective and qualitative experiences. On a broader level, memoirs of well-being then serve a dialogic function between science and theory on the one hand and the life-realities of members of the remission society on the other hand. Their analysis makes a vital contribution to the discussions of knowledge currently led in American Studies, particularly to the ongoing conversations about the relationship between life writing and the life sciences.[2] Inserting their own experiences and their (bodily) knowledge into the discourse, the memoirists challenge the monopoly of biomedicine to determine and define the "healthy" life. In Chapter 1, I have explained my choice of naming their texts 'memoirs of well-being' not only with the WHO definition of 'health' as "a state of complete physical, mental and social well-being and not merely the absence of disease or infirmity" but also with the criticism this definition has subsequently met since it has frequently been read as undermining medical professionals' interpretative authority. When they are read as a dialogue and an occasion for knowledge exchange, however, the texts also have something to offer to the life sciences.

Autobiographical narratives may, as Banerjee maintains in her analysis of Rachel Adams's recent memoir *Raising Henry: A Memoir of Motherhood, Disability, and Discovery* (2013) and Jason Kingsley's and Mitchell Levitz's collaborative 2007 autobiography *Count Us In: Growing Up with Down Syndrome*, supply bio-

---

2   Cf., for instance the DFG research training groups "Presence and Tacit Knowledge" (2012) and "Life Sciences, Life Writing: Boundary Experiences of Human Life between Biomedical Explanation and Lived Experience" (2014) or the topic of the 2015 annual conference of the German Association for American Studies, "Knowledge Landscapes North America."

medical discourses, prognoses and predictions with "the meaning of lived experience," making life writing more than "a mere footnote or a supplement to the life sciences" ("Writing" 2). Banerjee begins from the claim that the life sciences and life writing are not independent from one another, but in fact mutually constitutive. Accordingly, she argues, the perspective developed in autobiographical texts may counter and refute the power of the life sciences to interpret the body, illness, and disability (ibid. 1). Her paper reads the diagnosis of Down syndrome through the lens of lived experience yet carefully distances her argument from the view that biomedicine only "coloniz[es] our life-worlds" so that, in turn, the only recourse autobiographical narratives may take is to "write back" at the biomedical discourse (ibid. 6). Instead, she turns to questions about the production of knowledge and the place of authorities in these processes by asking "who defines human life? Who is to say which life is worth living? And on whose certainty may this prediction be premised" (ibid.)?

The texts studied here vividly illustrate this by taking scientific knowledge to its limits and moving beyond the narrow confines of diagnoses and predictability. After all, in contrast to science, literary texts do not need to resolve ambiguities and uncertainties but may openly address them. Ultimately, they evince the presence of *knowledges* and grapple with the authority that the use of the plural implies. Clarke et al. suggest that the sources from which knowledge about health may stem have not only increased but also diversified in recent years and list numerous sources other than medical professionals, such as patient advocacy groups which democratize the production of knowledge and people's access to it (177). Memoirs of well-being spell this out by no longer strictly separating 'expert' and 'lay' knowledges (cf. also ibid.). On the one hand, their focus on embodied knowledge adds a qualitative, material reality to the biomedical discourse that the scientific arguments lack (Banerjee, "Writing" 6) and may thus translate the abstract into concrete terms. Against the background of statistical quantifications which override individual identities with, for instance, the general and anonymous 'high risk' or 'Syndrome X sufferers' status (cf. Clarke et al. 162), memoirs of well-being perform an utterly important function in preserving the presence of the individual experience, while at the same time highlighting community and the politicized experience of illness and disability and thus clearly move beyond group allegiances on the basis of medical categories only.

On the other hand, biomedical definitions and theoretical explanatory schemes, as this study has elucidated, may not necessarily correspond to the subjective experience of illness and disability (cf. also Stone 208). The texts under analysis here unsettle the hegemonic assumption that ill and disabled individuals "do not have the authority to know and care for their bodies" and instead need to be subjected to medical surveillance (Stone 206). In authorizing themselves as experts on their bodies, the memoirists subvert the belief that their knowledge has, as Moss and

Teghtsoonian suspect, a less privileged status (11). The writers' expert status is legitimized in the chorus of voices, in which some of them speak, and, more than that, emergent and rapidly expanding disciplines such as the Medical Humanities or practices like Rita Charon's visions of a Narrative Medicine acknowledge the new expertise these texts generate. Memoirs of well-being thus serve a crucial function in the interdiscursive "co-production of knowledge" (cf. Banerjee, "Writing" 7).

They begin to flesh out the 'cripepistemology' several critics in Disability Studies are currently advocating and substantiate the question of "who [may] 'know' about 'disability'" (Johnson and McRuer 130). In itself a theory "from below," originally emerging not through academic writing, but informal chatter and social networks (ibid.), cripepistemology brings the question of knowledge into the foreground. It calls for the relocation of knowledge in the disability community (ibid. 133), although Lisa Johnson and Robert McRuer remind readers that knowledge about disability should not be exclusively held by disabled individuals only, thus lapsing into another epistemological and authoritative extreme, but needs to be articulated in a dialogue between disabled and able-bodied people (141).

An important factor in this is undoubtedly the memoirists' expert status – as intellectuals, academics and activists – to begin with, which arguably underlines the processes to self-authorization at work in their stories. Unlike traditional illness narratives which, as Sayantani DasGupta and Marsha Hurst expound, mend the disruptions that illness causes ("Gendered" 1), memoirs of well-being not only claim disruptions but render them in such a manner that they cease to constitute mere disruptions to be bridged, both in life and in writing. Quite to the contrary, continuity figures as a vital undercurrent in all of the memoirs studied here and well-being is in many cases explicitly tied to the reconstruction or realignment of the illness and disability experience with their writers' interests and academic or professional pursuits. In Lorde's case, for instance, writing decidedly links her experience with breast cancer to her activist work and her ampu-narration also exposes what she sees as the real causes of breast cancer, both socio-political and environmental.

Similarly, Linton's memoir establishes, as I have emphasized in my reading of *My Body Politic*, continuity in her activist work through the frame of narrative and the use of temporality to connect her disabled self to her previous activist work. Revolving around what Ellen Barton calls the disabled individual's "achievement" of a disability identity, "a fused personal and political awareness," the memoir bespeaks the declared aim of most Disability Studies scholars ("Disability" 95) and therefore creates seamless links to Linton's and others' work in the field. The development and showcasing of a positive disability identity, Barton elaborates, has become the preferred narrative in the discipline as well as in the movement, turning into a new dominant narrative of disability (ibid. 96). While this is definitely a welcome development, Barton also calls attention to the fact that this counter-narrative may not be representative of the stories told by many other disabled people (ibid.).

Transferred to Linton's memoir, Barton's criticism is directed at both her privileged position – which Linton is very well aware of (cf. also Torrell 334), yet may equally well refer to the nature of her impairment which does, after all, not impede her independent life-style, travels, teaching, and finally her political activism. Individuals not committed to the cause, however, are invisible and silent in the narrative. This is not to criticize the voices Linton has chosen to include in her story, but I agree when Barton comes to the conclusion that such a narrative does not only impact disabled people, but society as well ("Disability" 96), which is an important thought in relation to the 'new' disability memoir's rise in popularity. Although it has not suspended deep-seated preconceptions of disability as tragedy, it has become a very powerful counter-narrative and a fashionable mode of storying disability, particularly in activist and intellectual circles. Against this background, the significance of the ending of *My Body Politic* cannot be emphasized enough, for while the memoir features a number of disruptive moments that point to shortcomings in the current legislation and the prejudices disabled individuals are frequently exposed to, the ending moves these issues into sharp focus and accentuates that the counter-narrative does not provide closure but rather calls for continuous activism and the continuation of Linton's work.

Similarly, as Fries's journey comes to a close, the question reverberates in his mind: "how might I continue to be able to take physically demanding trips like this?" (199) and the frailty of the impaired body that has surfaced numerous times throughout the book now looms large. Nonetheless, the book ends on a strong and powerful note as the narrating I remarks: "The meaning of what it means to be human is wide open. Who decides riding a motorcycle is cool whereas riding a wheelchair is not? Who decides drinking through a straw is sexy but breathing through a respirator is not? Who decides using a personal computer is natural but using a Braille 'n Speak, a variation of a PC, is not?" (180). These questions are of course rhetorical, aimed at challenging what we perceive as "cool," "sexy," or even "natural," and the climactic order of the adjectives makes clear that what is at stake are our assumptions about normalcy. Fries's questions hence call for the collective challenge of the 'normal' and for a revision of society and the roles of impairment and adaptive devices in it and thus connect the ending of the memoir to activism and scholarship.

In Sacks's book, yet another form of reconnection surfaces when the physician-writer not only attains bodily "wholeness" but can powerfully merge his perspective as the recovering patient with that of the medical professional. For Hull, healing greatly depends on the patient's capacity to reconnect with his or her identity in the altered circumstances of illness (112). In this light, Sacks's return to his profession and to his neurological writing, his reconnection with the world of professional medicine, needs to be seen as a significant aspect of the healing process as well and

I have critically discussed the authority he draws from his experience as a patient, as well as its potential benefits for neurological practice.

Finally, Hustvedt's memoir also makes it possible to discern a strong sense of continuity with regard to knowledge and aides in the construction of her literary and scientific persona. Though concerned with healing, the book is not invested in catharsis and reconstruction as much as for instance Lorde's text but serves significant strategic purposes by aligning her story with her academic commitment and the many theoretical ideas with permeate her oeuvre. In contrast to the concerns expressed in the critical reviews I have briefly discussed, the publication rather lends her greater authority than diminishes it.

Two significant concerns need to be addressed at this point. My research corpus has been limited to established and intellectual authors. In how far self-published texts, blogs or oral histories engage with knowledge(s) at the present moment, remains to be seen. Certainly, these texts will voice other problems that have largely been silent in the texts under analysis here, such as health insurance or the lack thereof and resulting financial troubles that might inhibit well-being. The second question that certainly needs to be posed is Atlas's "Can it last?" (n. pag.) Atlas's skepticism is first of all targeted at the memoir boom and what he calls "the danger of burn-out," yet he acknowledges that "the form could turn out to be surprisingly robust" – with both scholars' and publishers' interests showing no signs of ebbing (ibid.). Likewise, his question may be directed at the popularity of personal criticism. However, with Nancy Miller I maintain that personal criticism like the kind brought forth in memoirs of well-being is not merely "an academic fashion" quickly losing its provocative charge (284), but that the interconnection of the theoretical and autobiographical has the potential to raise crucial questions about the nature of critical authority and the ways in which theory is produced in the academy (ibid. 282; cf. also Popkin, "Academic" 195). Memoirs of well-being then underline the significance of the autobiographical impulse for the creation of theory. Whether or how the notions of well-being the books illustrate may enter disciplinary knowledge and rework traditional definitions remains to be seen, but the publication of their stories counters the memoirists' exclusion from the discourses on their conditions.

With regard to the latter issue, the texts discussed here also incite questions of accessibility and accommodation which significantly go beyond the disabling architectural choices some of the memoirs lament, as they pertain to the accessibility of knowledge and the written word. Not all of the primary texts discussed here are offered as in alternative formats[3] and may thus be made more easily available to read-

---

3 *The Cancer Journals*, *The Shaking Woman*, and *A Leg to Stand On* are available for download as Kindle-versions, yet it should be noted that e-book formats, particularly Amazon's Kindle, are not automatically accessible for blind readers or users with im-

ers with disabilities. A discussion on the Disability Studies listserv has taken up these concerns, criticizing also the ways in which knowledge, as well as literary and cultural criticism in the discipline is circulated. Pointing to the high price of secondary literature, John Clark observes that "people with disabilities are consistently poorer and less employed than are able-bodied people" and accordingly finds fault with the fact that criticism and knowledge about the disability community, as well as books advocating or speaking for people with disabilities are reserved for the privileged who may both afford to pay the high price and can access the studies. Ultimately, we as scholars need to lower the thresholds to our work. In the long run, our choices about where and how to make knowledge accessible will effect lasting changes.

Moreover, this book has been selective in its scope and has presented representative examples rather than an exhaustive overview of the many titles that may fall into the subgenre. The corpus might therefore be extended to cover a wider array of media, for instance graphic memoirs and multimodal (digital or online) narratives. A fascinating starting point, for instance, may be the campaign "HospitalGlam – Taking the shame out of being in treatment one selfie at a time" initiated by the Los Angeles-based disabled artist Karolyn Gehrig in December 2014. Featuring the hashtag #HospitalGlam on social media sites, such as Twitter, Instagram, and Tumbler, Gehrig has begun to share 'selfies' from waiting areas, examination rooms, and hospital beds while undergoing treatment for her connective tissue disorder in order to counter her invisibility: "'[E]very time I got sicker I'd disappear from my commitments and then feel shy about explaining where I'd been when I knew there was absolutely nothing wrong with pursuing treatment for my disabling chronic illnesses,'" she explains her motivation to share photos of herself during these moments (quoted in Bahadur n. pag.). Her posts reappropriate the selfie as a popular form of recording perfection, beauty, and the joy of the everyday and its vanity to produce carefully composed and compelling images of the imperfect body as Gehrig strikes poses reminiscent of models in art and fashion photography. At the same time, her posts invite fellow patients to circulate their photos and the movement is picking up significant momentum, followers, and "likes" after reports in *The Huffington Post* and *The Guardian* in late January 2015, so that it may at this point well be understood as a collective visual online narrative that runs counter to

---

paired vision. Oliver Sacks's *A Leg to Stand On* is also available in audiobook format, which is certainly due to its successful sales and the large publishing house Touchstone, an imprint of Simon & Schuster. Ironically, *My Body Politic* and *The History of My Shoes*, the books most closely associated with the disability community, are not yet accessible in alternative formats and only Linton's memoir is scheduled to be published as an e-book version in 2015.

the sense of imperfection conventionally associated with being disabled and/or chronically ill and particularly foregrounds emotional well-being.

Finally, memoirs of well-being may become a productive medium to foster the social participation of chronically ill and disabled individuals beyond the 'inclusionism' Mitchell and Snyder lament in their study on *The Biopolitics of Disability* or the efforts of inclusion they have criticized elsewhere for "making estranged bodies better fit normative expectations" (Mitchell, Snyder and Ware 298). Ingrained in inclusionism, they argue, is the desire for the 'normal' (ibid.), much like the desire for health remains a pervasive social and cultural force. In turning away from 'health' and normalcy, as well as from conventional – normalizing – restitution narratives, memoirs of well-being then realize the "productive potential of failing normalization" (ibid. 299). As Couser notes, they "constitute a form of social participation and can encourage participation on the part of others" ("Disability Life Writing" 3). The memoirs analyzed here all point to the necessity of rethinking illness, disability, and 'health' and simultaneously offer ways of conceptualizing well-being. Looking and writing beyond a diagnosis, engaging with unpredictability and uncertainty, the narratives introduce new (embodied and subjective) knowledge into the discourse. The memoirists make utterly clear that neither illness nor disability constitute devastating tragedies and therefore undermine the stigma associated with these conditions (cf. ibid.). Beyond that, the texts are invested in a "personal revaluation," yet this study has shown that they *do* more than only responding to previous misrepresentations (ibid. 6). They generate a new narrative for the remission society which enables readers to engage with bodily difference and we may well read this narrative along the lines of Mitchell's, Snyder's and Ware's vision of inclusion: For them, inclusion is "neither a discourse of 'specialness'" wherein able-bodied people begin to "value disabled people as 'human', too," nor based on an understanding of physical disability as "extraordinary" and the disabled body as equipped with compensatory qualities. Finally, inclusion is not an "opportunity for political correctness wherein all bodies are valued for 'diversity' in a relativistic equation of multicultural differences" (297). Instead, inclusion resists "culturally rehabilitating disabled people's experiences" and honors difference (ibid. 298f.). In this light, the personal that memoirs of well-being narrate is at once political and theoretical, turning the memoirists into more than "wounded storytellers."

Bibliography

A Litany for Survival: The Life and Work of Audre Lorde. Dir. Ada G. Griffin and Michelle Parkerson. PBS, 1995. DVD.

Accad, Evelyne. *The Wounded Breast: Intimate Journeys through Cancer.* Melbourne: Spinifex, 2001. Print.

Adams, Lorraine. "Almost Famous: The Rise of the Nobody Memoir." *Washington Monthly.* April 2002. Web. 11 Dec. 2014.

Adams, Rachel. "All Tomorrow's Parties." *Avidly/Los Angeles Review of Books.* 29 Oct. 2014. Web. 30 Oct. 2014.

—. *Raising Henry: A Memoir of Motherhood, Disability, and Discovery.* New Haven/London: Yale UP, 2013 Print.

—. *Sideshow U.S.A.: Freaks and the American Cultural Imagination.* Chicago: U of Chicago P, 2001. Print.

Alcoff, Linda Martin. *Visible Identities, Race, Gender, and the Self,* New York: Oxford UP, 2006. Print.

Alexander, Elizabeth. "'Coming out Blackened and Whole': Fragmentation and Reintegration in Audre Lorde's *Zami* and *The Cancer Journals.*" *American Literary History* 6.4 (1994): 695-715. Print.

Al-Zubi, Hasan. "Autopathography and Audre Lorde's *The Cancer Journals* as a Narrative of Illness: Revising the Script of Disease." *Dirasat: Human Social Sciences* 34 (2007): 857-70. Print.

Agazzi, Evandro. "Illness as Lived Experience and as the Object of Medicine." *Life Interpretation and the Sense of Illness within the Human Condition: Medicine and Philosophy in a Dialogue.* Eds. Anna-Teresa Tymieniecka and Evandro Agazzi. Dordrecht: Kluwer Academic, 2001. 3-15. Print.

Ahlzén, Rolf. "Illness as Unhomelike Being-in-the-World? Phenomenology and Medical Practice." *Medical Health Care and Philosophy* 14 (2011): 323-31. Print.

Albertyn, Lynda. "The Shaking Woman or a History of My Nerves." *Journal of Child and Adolescent Mental Health* 23.1 (2011): 59-60. Print.

Allen, Austin. "Will Neuroscience Kill the Novel?" 20 Nov. 2012. Web. 12 Dec. 2012.

Americans with Disabilities Act of 1990 as Amended, 1990. Web.

Aronowitz, Robert A. *Making Sense of Illness: Science, Society, and Disease.* Cambridge: Cambridge UP, 1998. Print.

Atkins, Chloe. *My Imaginary Illness: A Journey into Uncertainty and Prejudice in Medical Diagnosis.* Ithaca: Cornell UP, 2010.

Atlas, James. "Confessing for Voyeurs: The Age of The Literary Memoir Is Now." *The New York Times Magazine.* 12 May 1996. Web. 20 Oct. 2014.

Audi, Robert. "Embodiment." *The Cambridge Dictionary of Philosophy.* 2nd ed. Ed. Robert Audi. Cambridge: Cambridge UP, 2006. 258. Print.

Aull, Felice and Bradley Lewis. "Medical Intellectuals: Resisting Medical Orientalism." *Journal of Medical Humanities* 25.2 (2004): 87-108. Print.

"Autobiography." *Oxford English Dictionary.* 2014. Web. 24 Mar. 2014.

Avrahami, Einat. *The Invading Body: Reading Illness Autobiographies.* Charlottesville: U of Virginia P, 2007. Print.

Baena, Rosalía. "Disability Memoirs in the Academic World: Mary Felstiner's *Out of Joint* and Simi Linton's *My Body Politic.*" *Interdisciplinary Literary Studies* 15.1 (2013): 124-40. Print.

Baglieri, Susan and Arthur Shapiro. *Disability Studies and the Inclusive Classroom: Critical Practices for Creating Less Restrictive Attitudes.* New York: Routledge, 2012. Print.

Bahadur, Nina. "#HospitalGlam Is How Artist Karolyn Gehrig Shows That Chronic Illness Doesn't Stop You From Being Glamorous." *Huffington Post.* 14 Jan. 2015. Web. 21 Jan. 2015.

Ball, Charlene. "Old Magic and New Fury: The Theaphany of Afrekete in Audre Lorde's 'Tar Beach'." *NWSA Journal* 13.1 (2001): 61-85. Web.

Banerjee, Mita. "Writing the Citizen: Growing Up with Down Syndrome in *Raising Henry* and *Count Us In.*" Workshop: Autobiography and the Production of Knowledge, Münster (Germany). 11-12 March 2015. Unpublished Manuscript.

Banerjee, Mita et al. "Panel on Life Science and Life Writing." *American Lives.* Ed. Alfred Hornung. Heidelberg: Winter, 2013. 537-60. Print.

Barnes, Colin, and Geof Mercer. *Disability.* Malden: Blackwell Publishers, 2003. Print.

Barnes, Sharon L. "Marvelous Arithmetics: Prosthesis, Speech, and Death in the Late Work of Audre Lorde." *Women's Studies* 37 (2008): 769-89. Print.

Bartlett, Jennifer. *Autobiography/Anti-Autobiography.* Palmyra: Theenk Books, 2014. Print.

—. "Interview with Jennifer Bartlett." *Wordgathering: A Journal of Disability Poetry* 5.2 (2011). Web.

Barton, Ellen. "Disability Narratives of the Law: Narratives and Counter-Narratives." *Narrative* 15.1 (2007): 95-112. Print.

—. "Textual Practices of Erasure: Representations of Disability and the Founding of the United Way." in: *Embodied Rhetorics: Disability in Language and Culture*. Eds. James C. Wilson and Cynthia Lewiecki-Wilson. Carbondale: Southern Illinois UP, 2001. 169-99. Print.

Beam, Jeffery. "Kenny Fries (1960 -)." *Contemporary Gay American Poets and Playwrights: An A-to-Z Guide*. Ed. Emmanuel S. Nelson. Westport: Greenwood Press, 2003. 171-77. Print.

Beatty, John. "Chance and Design." *The Cambridge Encyclopedia of Darwin and Evolutionary Thought*. Ed. Michael Ruse. Cambridge: Cambridge UP, 2013. 146-51. Print.

Beck, Naomi. "Social Darwinism." *The Cambridge Encyclopedia of Darwin and Evolutionary Thought*. Ed. Michael Ruse. Cambridge: Cambridge UP, 2013. 195-201. Print.

Becker, Gay. "Phenomenology of Health and Illness." *Encyclopedia of Medical Anthropology: Health and Illness in the World's Cultures*. Vol. I: Topics. New York et al.: Kluwer Academic, 2004. 125-36. Print.

Beer, Gillian. *Darwin's Plots: Evolutionary Narrative in Darwin, George Eliot and Nineteenth-century Fiction*. 3rd ed. Cambridge: Cambridge UP, 2009. Print.

Bell, Catherine. *Ritual: Perspectives and Dimensions*. New York: Oxford UP, 1997. Print.

Belling, Catherine. "The Death of the Narrator." *Narrative Research in Health and Illness*. Eds. Bruce A. Hurwitz, Trisha Greenhalgh, and Vieda Skultans. Malden: Blackwell, 2004. 146-55. Print.

Benstock, Shari (ed.). *The Private Self: Theory and Practice of Women's Autobiographical Writings*. Chapel Hill: U of North Carolina P, 1988. Print.

Berger, James. "Falling Towers and Postmodern Wild Children: Oliver Sacks, Don DeLillo, and Turns against Language." *PMLA* 120.2 (2005): 341-61. Print.

Bérubé, Michael. "Foreword." *Claiming Disability: Knowledge and Identity*. Simi Linton. New York: New York UP, 1998. vii-xi. Print.

—. *Life as We Know it: A Father, a Family, and an Exceptional Child*. New York: Vintage, 1998. Print.

Beyer, Susanne. "Die doppelte Frau." *Spiegel* 2 (2010): 110-14. Print.

Bickenbach, Jerome E., et al. "Models of Disablement, Universalism and the International Classification of Impairments, Disabilities and Handicaps." *Social Science & Medicine* 48 (1999): 1173-87. Print.

Birkle, Carmen. "Communicating Disease: An Introduction." *Communicating Disease: Cultural Representations of American Medicine*. Eds. Carmen Birkle and Johanna Heil. Heidelberg: Winter, 2013. ix-xxxiv. Print.

"Body Politic." *Oxford English Dictionary*. 2014. Web. 10 Sept. 2014.

Bogdan, Robert. *Freakshows: Presenting Human Oddities for Amusement and Profit*. Chicago/London: U of Chicago P, 1988. Pint.

Bolaki, Stella. "Challenging Invisibility, Making Connections: Illness, Survival, and Black Struggles in Audre Lorde's Work." *Blackness and Disability: Critical Examinations and Cultural Interventions.* Ed. Christopher M. Bell. East Lansing/Münster: Michigan State UP/Lit Verlag, 2011. 47-74. Print.

—. "Re-Covering the Scarred Body: Textual and Photographic Narratives of Breast Cancer." *Mosaic* 44.2 (2011): 1-17. Print.

Boorse, Christian. "Gesundheit als theoretischer Begriff." *Krankheitstheorien.* 1st ed. Ed. Thomas Schramme. Berlin: Suhrkamp, 2012. 63-110. Print.

Boston Women's Health Book Collective. *Our Bodies, Ourselves.* New York: Simon & Schuster, 1973 Print.

Bowler, Peter. *Charles Darwin: The Man and His Influence.* 1990. Cambridge: Cambridge UP, 1996. Print.

Boyd, Brian. *On the Origin of Stories: Evolution, Cognition, and Fiction.* Cambridge: Bellknap, 2010. Print.

Brody, Howard. *Stories of Sickness.* New Haven: Yale UP, 1987. Print.

Brooks, Peter. *Reading for the Plot: Design and Intention in Narrative.* Cambridge: Harvard UP, 1988. Print.

Brown, Theresa L. "Storytelling and Trauma: Gender, Identity, and Testimony in a Contemporary Context." Dissertation. *University of Chicago*, 1994. Print.

Brownworth, Victoria A. (ed.). *Coming Out of Cancer: Writings from the Lesbian Cancer Epidemic.* Seattle: Seal Press, 2000. Print.

Brune, Jeffrey and Daniel Wilson. *Disability and Passing: Blurring the Lines of Identity.* Philadelphia: Temple UP, 2013. Print.

Budge, Alice. "The Doctor as Patient: Bioethical Dilemmas Reflected in Literary Narratives." *Literature and Medicine* 7 (1988): 132-37. Print.

Bury, Michael. "Chronic Illness as Biographical Disruption." *Sociology of Health and Illness* 4.2 (1982): 167-82. Print.

Bury, Mike and Lee F. Monaghan. "Chronic Illness." *Key Concepts in Medical Sociology.* 2nd ed. Eds. Jonathan Gabe and Lee F. Monaghan. London: Sage, 2013. 72-6. Print.

Bush, George W. "Presidential Proclamation 6158." 1990. Web. 8 May. 2013.

Buss, Helen M. *Repossessing the World: Reading Memoirs by Contemporary Women.* Toronto: Wilfrid Laurier UP, 2002. Print.

Caesar, Michael. *Dante: The Critical Heritage.* New York/London: Routledge, 1989. Print.

Canguilhem, Georges. *Das Normale und das Pathologische.* München: Hanser, 1974. Print.

Carel, Havi. *Illness: The Cry of the Flesh.* Durham: Acumen, 2008. Print.

Carroll, Joseph. *Literary Darwinism: Evolution, Human Nature, and Literature.* New York: Routledge, 2004. Print.

—. *Reading Human Nature: Literary Darwinism in Theory and Practice.* Albany: State U of New York P, 2011. Print.

Casamayou, Maureen H. *The Politics of Breast Cancer*. Washington: Georgetown UP, 2001. Print.

Case, Gretchen A. "Medical Scarring and the Performance of Memory." Dissertation. *University of California*, 2005. Print.

Cassuto, Leonard. "Oliver Sacks and the Medical Case Narrative." *Disability Studies: Enabling the Humanities*. Eds. Sharon L. Snyder, Brenda J. Brueggemann, and Rosemarie Garland-Thomson. New York: The Modern Language Association of America, 2002. 118-30. Print.

—. "Oliver Sacks: A Conversation with Leonard Cassuto." *The Barnes & Noble Review* 26 Oct. 2010. Web.

—. "The Uncanny Symphony of Oliver Sacks (Review)." *Chronicle of Higher Education* 2 Nov. 2007. Web.

Chandler, Marilyn R. "A Healing Art: Therapeutic Dimensions of Autobiography." *a/b Auto/Biography Studies* 5.1 (1989): 4-14. Print.

Charon, Rita. *Narrative Medicine: Honoring the Stories of Illness*. Oxford, New York: Oxford UP, 2006. Print.

Chemers, Michael M. *Staging Stigma: A Critical Examination of the American Freak Show*. New York: Palgrave, 2008. Print.

Cheu, Johnson F. "Disabling Cure in Twentieth-Century America: Disability, Identity, Literature and Culture." Dissertation. *Ohio State University*, 2003. Print.

Clare, Eli. "The Mountain." *Exile and Pride: Disability, Queerness, and Liberation*. Cambridge: South End Press, 1999. 1-13. Print.

Clark, John L. "Re: [DS-HUM] accessibility of DS Reader." E-mail. 24.12.2014

Clarke, Adele et al. "Biomedicalization: Technoscientific Transformations of Health, Illness, and U.S. Biomedicine." *American Sociological Review* 68.2 (2003): 161-94. Print.

Clarke, Hilary. "Introduction: Depression and Narrative." *Depression and Narrative: Telling the Dark*. Ed. Hilary Clarke. New York: State U of New York P, 2008. 1-12. Print.

Cline, Sally and Carole Angier. *The Arvon Book of Life Writing: Writing Biography, Autobiography and Memoir*. London: Methuen, 2010. Print.

Conner, Nancy. "Amazon Warriors." *Classical Mythology*. n.d. Web. 27 July 2014.

Conway, Kathlyn. *Illness and the Limits of Expression*. Ann Arbor: U of Michigan P, 2007. Print.

—. *Ordinary Life: A Memoir of Illness*. New York: W.H. Freeman and Company, 1997. Print.

Cook, Kay K. "Filling the Dark Spaces: Breast Cancer and Autobiography." *a/b Auto/Biography Studies* 16.1 (1991): 85-94. Print.

—. "Medical Identity: My DNA/Myself." *Getting a Life: Everyday Uses of Autobiography*. Eds. Sidonie Smith and Julia Watson. Minneapolis: U of Minnesota P, 1996. 63-85. Print.

Cooke, Rachel. "*The Shaking Woman* by Siri Hustvedt." 2010. Web. 28 Aug. 2012.

Cooper, Joanne E. "Shaping Meaning: Women's Diaries, Journals, and Letters – the Old and the New." *Women's Studies International Forum* 10.1 (1987): 95-9. Print.

Corker, Mairian. "Differences, Conflations and Foundations: The Limits to 'Accurate' Theoretical Representation of Disabled People's Experience?" *Disability & Society* 14.5 (1999): 627-42. Print.

Couser, Thomas G. "Conflicting Paradigms: The Rhetorics of Disability Memoir." *Embodied Rhetorics: Disability in Language and Culture.* Eds. James C. Wilson and Cynthia Lewiecki-Wilson. Carbondale: Southern Illinois UP, 2001. 78-91. Print.

—. "Disability, Life Narrative, and Representation." *PMLA* 120.2 (2005): 602-6. Print.

—. "Disability Life Writing and/as Social Participation." *Social Participation.* La Trobe University, Melbourne. November 2011. Keynote Vortrag.

—. "Genre Matters: Form, Force, and Filiation." *Life Writing* 2.2 (2005): 125-40. Print.

—. "Introduction: The Embodied Self." *a/b Auto/Biography Studies* 6.1 (1991): 1-7. Print.

—. "Introduction. (The Empire of the 'Normal': A Forum on Disability and Self-Representation)." *Amerian Quarterly* 52.2 (2000): 305-10. Print.

—. *Memoir: An Introduction.* Oxford, New York: Oxford UP, 2012. Print.

— *Recovering Bodies: Illness, Disability, and Life Writing.* Madison: U of Wisconsin P, 1997. Print.

—. "(Un)Common Conditions: Narratives of Illness and Disability." *Michigan Quarterly Review* 37.2 (1998). Web.

—. "Undoing Hardship: Life Writing and Disability Law." *Narrative* 15.1 (2007): 71-84. Print.

—. *Signifying Bodies: Disability in Contemporary Life Writing.* Ann Arbor: U of Michigan P, 2010. Print.

—. *Vulnerable Subjects: Ethics and Life Writing.* Ithaca: Cornell UP, 2004. Print.

Cousins, Norman. *Anatomy of an Illness as Perceived by the Patient.* New York: WW Norton, 1979. Print.

Crane, Mary T. and Alan Richardson. "Literary Studies and Cognitive Science: Toward a New Interdisciplinarity." *Mosaic: A Journal for the Interdisciplinary Study of Literature* 32.2 (1999): 123-41. Print.

Darwin, Charles. *The Origin of Species by Means of Natural Selection or The Preservation of Favoured Races in the Struggle for Life.* London: Oxford UP, 1956. Print.

DasGupta, Sayantani and Marsha Hurst. "The Gendered Nature of Illness." *Stories of Illness and Healing: Women Write Their Bodies.* Eds. Sayantani DasGupta and Marsha Hurst. Kent: Kent State UP, 2007. 1-7. Print.

—. "Narratives of Body and Self: The Experience of Illness." *Stories of Illness and Healing: Women Write Their Bodies*. Eds. Sayantani DasGupta and Marsha Hurst. Kent, Ohio: Kent State UP, 2007. 17-20. Print.

Dash, Mike. "Dahomey's Women Warriors." *Smithsonian*. 23 Sep. 2011. Web. 27 July 2014.

Davis, Lennard J. "Constructing Normalcy: The Bell Curve, the Novel, and the Invention of the Disabled Body in the Nineteenth Century." *The Disability Studies Reader*. Ed. Lennard J. Davis. New York: Routledge, 1997. 9-28. Print.

—. "Crips Strike Back: The Rise of Disability Studies." *American Literary History* 11.3 (1999): 500-12. Print.

—. *My Sense of Silence: Memoirs of a Childhood with Deafness*. Champaign: U of Illinois P, 2008. Print.

—. "The Rule of Normalcy: Politics and Disability in the USA [United States of Ability]." in: Disability, Divers-Ability and Legal Change. Eds. Melinda Jones and Lee Ann Basser Marks. The Hague: Kluwer, 1999. 35-47. Print.

Davis, Rocíco G. "Academic Autobiography and Transdisciplinary Crossings in Shirley Geok-lin Lim's *Among the White Moon Faces*." *Journal of American Studies* 43.3 (2009): 441-57. Print.

—."Introduction: Out of the University: Reading Academic Autobiographies." *Prose Studies: History, Theory, Criticism* 31.3 (2009): 159-65. Print.

Deegan, Mary Jo and Nancy Brooks (eds.). *Women and Disability: The Double Handicap. New Brunswick*: Transaction Books, 1985. Print.

Dennett, Daniel C. *Kinds of Minds: Towards an Understanding of Consciousness*. London: Weidenfeld & Nicolson, 1996. Print.

DeNora, Tia. *Music in Everyday Life*. Cambridge: Cambridge UP, 2000. Print.

Deshauer, Dorian. "A Well-Grounded Approach to the Mind-Body Problem: *The Shaking Woman or A History of My Nerves.*" *Canadian Medical Association Journal* 182.13 (2010): 673-74. Print.

DeShazer, Mary K. *Fractured Borders: Reading Women's Cancer Literature*. Ann Arbor: U of Michigan P, 2008. Print.

—. *Mammographies: The Cultural Discourses of Breast Cancer Narratives*. Ann Arbor: U of Michigan P, 2013. Print.

Diedrich, Lisa. *Treatments: Language, Politics, and the Culture of Illness*. Minneapolis: U of Minnesota P, 2007. Print.

—. "Treatments: Negotiating Bodies, Language, and Death in Illness Narratives." Dissertation. *Emory University*, 2001. Print.

Diekmann, Lara E. "Audre Lorde (1934-1992)." *Significant Contemporary American Feminists: A Biographical Sourcebook*. Ed. Jennifer Scanlon. Westport: Greenwood Press, 1999. 156-62. Print.

"Disability Rights and Independent Living Movement: Introduction." *Bancroft Library*. n.d. Web. 22 Jan. 2015.

Di Summa-Knoop, Laura T. "The Art of Telling about the Self: Memoirs in Literature and Film." Dissertation. *City University of New York*, 2013. Print.

Donaldson, Elizabeth. "The Corpus of the Madwoman: Toward a Feminist Disability Studies Theory of Embodiment and Mental Illness." *NWSA Journal* 14.3 (2002): 99-119. Print.

Eakin, Paul J. *How Our Lives Become Stories: Making Selves*. 1st ed. Ithaca: Cornell UP, 1999. Print.

—. *Living Autobiographically: How We Create Identity in Narrative*. Ithaca: Cornell UP, 2008. Print.

—. *Touching the World: Reference in Autobiography*. Princeton: Princeton UP, 1992. Print.

Ehrenreich, Barbara. *Smile or Die: How Positive Thinking Fooled America and the World*. London: Granta, 2010. Print.

—. "Welcome to Cancerland: A Mammogram Leads to a Cult of Pink Kitsch." *Harper's Magazine* (2001): 43-53. Print.

Eisenberg, Leon. "Disease and Illness: Distinctions between Professional and Popular Ideas of Sickness." *Culture, Medicine and Psychiatry* 1 (1977): 9-23. Print.

Eisenstein, Zillah. *Manmade Breast Cancers*. Ithaca/London: Cornell UP, 2001. Print.

Elliot, Amy. "Aesthetic Illness Narratives: Reconstructing Identity through the Performative in Writing, Photography and Dance-Theater while Living with a Life-threatening Illness." Dissertation. *New York University*, 1998. Print.

Emens, Elizabeth F. "Shape Stops Story." *Narrative* 15.1 (2007): 124-32. Print.

Engelberg, Miriam. *Cancer Made Me a Shallower Person: A Memoir in Comics*. New York: HarperCollins, 2006. Print.

Engelhardt, H. Tristram. "Die Begriffe ‚Gesundheit' und ‚Krankheit'." *Krankheitstheorien*. 1st ed. Ed. Thomas Schramme. Berlin: Suhrkamp, 2012. 41-62. Print.

Engels, Eve-Maria. "Charles Darwins evolutionäre Theorie der Erkenntnis- und Moralfähigkeit." *Charles Darwin und seine Wirkung*. Ed. Eve-Maria Engels. Frankfurt: Suhrkamp, 2009. 303-39. Print.

—."Charles Darwin: Person, Theorie, Rezeption. Zur Einführung." *Charles Darwin und seine Wirkung*. Ed. Eve-Maria Engels. Frankfurt: Suhrkamp, 2009. 9-57. Print.

Evans, Martyn. "Medicine and Music: Three Relations Considered." *Journal of Medical Humanities* 28 (2007): 135-48. Print.

Evans, Martyn and Ilora G. Finlay. "Introduction." *Medical Humanities*. Eds. Martyn Evans and Ilora G. Finlay. London: BMJ, 2001. 7-12. Print.

Fine, Michelle, and Adrienne Asch. *Women with Disabilities: Essays in Psychology, Culture, and Politics*. Philadelphia: Temple UP, 1988. Print.

Finger, Anne. *Elegy for a Disease: A Personal and Cultural History of Polio*. New York: St. Martin's Press, 2006. Print.

—. *Past Due: A Story of Disability, Pregnancy, and Birth*. London: The Women's Press, 1991. Print.
Fish, Stanley. "Interpreting the *Variorum*." *Critical Inquiry* 2.3 (1976): 465-85. Print.
Fleischer, Doris, and Frieda Zames. *The Disability Rights Movement: From Charity to Confrontation*. 2nd ed. Philadelphia: Temple UP, 2011. Print.
Fludernik, Monika. "Narratology in the Twenty-First Century: The Cognitive Approach to Narrative." *PMLA* 125.4 (2010): 924-30. Print.
—. *Towards a 'Natural' Narratology*. London: Routledge, 1996. Print.
Fludernik, Monika, and Greta Olson. "Introduction." *Current Trends in Narratology*. Ed. Greta Olson. Berlin: de Gruyter, 2011. 1-36. Print.
Fonseca, Renan R. "Writing Self-Disruption in *The Shaking Woman or A History of My Nerves* by Siri Hustvedt." 2012. Web. 1 Jan. 2013.
Forster, E.M. *Howards End*. Hazleton: Pennsylvania State University, 2007. pdf file.
Frank, Arthur W. *At the Will of the Body: Reflections on Illness*. Boston/New York: Houston Mifflin, 1991. Print.
—. "Reclaiming an Orphan Genre: The First-Person Narrative of Illness." *Literature and Medicine* 13.1 (1994): 1-21. Print.
—. "Tricksters and Truth Tellers: Narrating Illness in an Age of Authenticity and Appropriation." *Literature and Medicine* 28.2 (2009): 185-99. Web.
—. *The Wounded Storyteller: Body, Illness, and Ethics*. Chicago: U of Chicago P, 1995. Print.
Franke, Alexa. *Modelle von Gesundheit und Krankheit*. 3rd Ed. Bern: Huber, 2012. Print.
Franklin, Cynthia G. *Academic Lives: Memoir, Cultural Theory and the University Today*. Athens/London: U of Georgia P, 2009. Print.
Freadman, Richard. "Cure and Care: G. Thomas Couser and the Ethics of 'Pathography.'" *Philosophy and Literature* 35.2 (2011): 388-98. Print.
Freud, Sigmund and Josef Breuer. *Studies on Hysteria (1893-1895)*. 2nd ed. New York: Basic Books, 2000. Print.
Friedman, Susan. "Women's Autobiographical Selves: Theory and Practice." *The Private Self: Theory and Practice of Women's Autobiographical Writings*. Ed. Shari Benstock. Chapel Hill: U of North Carolina P, 1988. 72-82. Print.
Fries, Kenny. *Anesthesia*. Louisville: The Avocado Press, 1996. Print.
—. *Body, Remember: A Memoir*. 1997. Madison: Wisconsin UP, 2003. Print.
—. *Desert Walking*. Louisville: The Avocado Press, 2000. Print.
—. *The Healing Notebooks*. Berkeley: Open Books, 1990. Print.
—. *The History of My Shoes and the Evolution of Darwin's Theory*. New York: Carroll and Graf Publishers, 2007. Print.
Gallagher, Shaun. *How the Body Shapes the Mind*. Oxford: Clarendon P, 2005. Print.

Garden, Rebecca. "Disability and Narrative: New Directions for Medicine and the Medical Humanities." *Medical Humanities* 36 (2010): 70-4. Print.

—. "Telling Stories about Illness and Disability: The Limits and Lessons of Narrative." *Perspectives in Biology and Medicine* 53.1 (2010): 121-35. Print.

Gardner, Kirsten E. "Disruption and Cancer Narratives: From Awareness to Advocacy." *Literature and Medicine* 28.2 (2009): 333-50. Web.

Garland-Thomson, Rosemarie. *Extraordinary Bodies: Figuring Physical Disability in American Culture and Literature.* New York: Columbia UP, 1997. Print.

—. "Feminist Theory, the Body, and the Disabled Figure." *The Disability Studies Reader.* Ed. Lennard J. Davis. New York: Routledge, 1997. 279-92. Print.

—. (ed.). *Freakery: Cultural Spectacles of the Extraordinary Body.* New York: New York UP, 1996. Print.

—. "Integrating Disability, Transforming Feminist Theory." *Feminisms Redux: An Anthology of Literary Theory and Criticism.* Eds. Robyn Warhol-Down and Diane Price Herndl. New Brunswick: Rutgers UP, 2009. 487-513. Print.

—. "Shape Structures Story: Fresh and Feisty Stories about Disability." *Narrative* 15.1 (2007): 113-23. Print.

—. *Staring: How We Look.* Oxford: Oxford UP, 2009. Print.

Garrett, Catherine. *Gut Feelings: Chronic Illness and the Search for Healing.* Amsterdam/New York: Rodopi, 2005. Print.

Garrison, Kristen. "The Personal is Rhetorical: War, Protest, and Peace in Breast Cancer Narratives." *Disability Studies Quarterly* 27.4 (2007): Web.

Garro, Linda C., and Cheryl Mattingly. "Narrative as Construct and Construction." *Narrative and the Cultural Construction of Illness and Healing.* Eds. Cheryl Mattingly and Linda C. Garro. Berkeley: U of California P, 2000. 1-49. Print.

Gilbert, Keith, and Otto Schantz (eds.). *Paralympic Games: Empowerment or Side-Show?* Maidenhead: Meyer and Meyer, 2008. Print.

Gilman, Sander L. *Picturing Health and Illness: Images of Identity and Difference.* Baltimore: Johns Hopkins UP, 1995. Print.

Gilmore, Leigh. *The Limits of Autobiography: Trauma and Testimony.* 1st ed. Ithaca: Cornell UP, 2001. Print.

Goffman, Erving. *Stigma: Notes on the Management of Spoiled Identity.* 1963. New York: Simon & Schuster, 1991. Print.

Goggin, Gerard and Christopher Newell. "Fame and Disability: Christopher Reeve, Super Crips, and Infamous Celebrity." *M/C Journal* 7.5 (2004): Web.

Goodley, Dan. *Disability Studies: An Interdisciplinary Introduction.* Los Angeles: Sage, 2011. Print.

Goodwin, James. *Autobiography: The Self Made Text.* New York: Twayne Publishers, 1993. Print.

Gordon, Deborah. "Tenacious Assumptions in Western Medicine." *Biomedicine Examined.* Eds. Margaret M. Lock and Deborah Gordon. Dordrecht: Kluwer Academic Publishers, 1988. 19-56. Print.

Gottschall, Jonathan and David S. Wilson. *The Literary Animal: Evolution and the Nature of Narrative*. Evaston: Northwestern UP, 2005. Print.
Graham, Peter W. "Metapathography: Three Unruly Texts." *Literature and Medicine* 16.1 (1997): 70-87. Print.
Greaves, David. "The Nature and Role of Medical Humanities." *Medical Humanities*. Eds. Martyn Evans and Ilora G. Finlay. London: BMJ, 2001. 13-22. Print.
Greene, Logan D. *The Discourse of Hysteria: The Topoi of Humility, Physicality, and Authority in Women's Rhetoric*. Lewiston: Edwin Mellen P, 2009. Print.
Gubar, Susan. "Living With Cancer: Coming to Terms." *The New York Times* (Well Blog). 22 Jan. 2015. Web. 22 Jan 2015.
Gusdorf, Georges. "Conditions and Limits of Autobiography." in: *Autobiography: Essays Theoretical and Critical*. Ed. James Olney. Princeton: Princeton UP, 1980. 28-48. Print.
Gygax, Franziska. "Life Writing and Illness: Auto/Bio/Theory by Eve Sedgwick, Jackie Stacey, and Jill Bolte Taylor." *Prose Studies: History, Theory, Criticism* 31.3 (2009): 291-99. Print.
—. "Theoretically Ill: Autobiographer, Patient, Theorist." *The Writing Cure: Literature and Medicine in Context*. Eds. Alexandra Lembert-Heidenreich and Jarmila Mildorf. Münster: LIT, 2013. 173-90. Print.
Hammond, Michael, Jane Howarth and Russell Keat. *Understanding Phenomenology*. Oxford: Blackwell, 1991. Print.
Haller, Beth. *Representing Disability in an Ableist World: Essays on Mass Media*. Louisville: Advocado Press, 2010. Print.
Hasler, Felix. *Neuromythologie: Eine Streitschrift gegen die Deutungsmacht der Hirnforschung*. Bielefeld: transcript, 2012. Print.
Hawkins, Anne H. "A. R. Luria and the Art of Clinical Biography." *Literature and Medicine* 5 (1986): 1-15. Print.
—. "Oliver Sacks's *Awakenings*: Reshaping Clinical Discourse." *Configurations* 1.2 (1993): 229-45. Print.
—. *Reconstructing Illness: Studies in Pathography*. West Lafayette: Purdue UP, 1993. Print.
Heifferon, Barbara A. "Look Who's Not Talking: Recovering the Patient's Voice in the Clinique." Dissertation. *University of Arizona*, 1998. Print.
Hemon, Aleksandar. "The Aquarium." *The New Yorker*. 13 June 2011. Web. 5 March 2015.
Henderson, Bruce. "Visuality, Performativity, and 'Extraordinary Bodies': A Review Essay." *Text and Performance Quarterly* 30.4 (2010): 456-67. Print.
Henke, Suzette A. *Shattered Subjects: Trauma and Testimony in Women's Lifewriting*. 1st ed. New York: St. Martin's Press, 1998. Print.
Herman, David. *Basic Elements of Narrative*. Malden: Wiley-Blackwell, 2009. Print.

—. "Cognitive Narratology." *The Living Handbook of Narratology*, 2011. Web. 13 Dec. 2011.

—. (ed.). *Narrative Theory and the Cognitive Sciences*. Stanford: CSLI Publ., 2003. Print.

Herndl, Diane Price. "Disease versus Disability: The Medical Humanities and Disability Studies." *PMLA* 120.2 (2005): 593-98. Print.

—. "Our Breasts, Our Selves: Identity, Community, and Ethics in Cancer Autobiographies." *Signs* 32.1 (2006): 221-45. Print.

—. "Reconstructing the Posthuman Feminist Body Twenty Years after Audre Lorde's *Cancer Journals.*" *Feminisms Redux: An Anthology of Literary Theory and Criticism*. Eds. Robyn Warhol-Down and Diane Price Herndl. New Brunswick: Rutgers UP, 2009. 477-86. Print.

—. "The Writing Cure: Charlotte Perkins Gilman, Anna O., and 'Hysterical' Writing." *NWSA Journal* 1.1 (1988): 52-74. Web.

Hill, Laura. "*Invitation to Dance.*" 10 June 2013. Web. 18 Aug. 2014.

"History." *Oxford English Dictionary.* n.d. Web. 13 Dec. 2012.

"History of Disability Inclusion at UC Berkeley." *Independent Living USA*. n.d. Web. 22 Jan. 2015.

Hockenberry, John. *Moving Violations: War Zones, Wheelchairs, and Declarations of Independence*. New York: Hyperion. 1995. Print.

Hofstadter, Richard. *Social Darwinism in American Thought*. 1944. Boston: Beacon Press, 2006. Print.

—. "The Vogue of Spencer." *Darwin: Texts, Backgrounds, Contemporary Opinion, Critical Essays*. Ed. Philip Appleman. New York: Norton, 1970. 389-99. Print.

Hooper, Judy. "Beauty Tips for the Dead." in: *Minding the Body: Women Writers on Body and Soul*. Ed. Patricia Foster. New York: Anchor Books, 1994. 107-37. Print.

Hopkins, Gerard Manley. "Pied Beauty." 1877. *The Poems of Gerard Manley Hopkins: A Sourcebook*. Ed. Alice Jenkins. London/New York: Routledge, 2006. 137. Print.

Hoquet, Thierry. "The Evolution of the *Origin* (1859-1872)." *The Cambridge Encyclopedia of Darwin and Evolutionary Thought*. Ed. Michael Ruse. Cambridge: Cambridge UP, 2013. 158-64. Print.

Howarth, William. "Oliver Sacks: The Ecology of Writing Science." *Modern Language Studies* 20.4 (1990): 103-20. Web.

Hughes, Bill, and Kevin Paterson. "The Social Model of Disability and the Disappearing Body: Towards a Sociology of Impairment." *Disability & Society* 12.3 (1997): 325-40. Print.

Hull, Andrew J. "Fictional Father? Oliver Sacks and the Revalidation of Pathography." *Medical Humanities* 39.2 (2013): 105-14. Print.

Hunter, Kathryn M. "Making a Case." *Literature and Medicine* 7 (1988): 66-79. Print.

—. "Remaking the Case." *Literature and Medicine* 11.1 (1992): 163-79. Print.
Hunter, William. "Your Friendly Neighborhood Neurologist: Dr. Oliver Sacks and the Cultural View of Physicians." *Journal of Popular Culture* 28.4 (1995): 93-102. Print.
Hurwitz, Brian. "Form and Representation in Clinical Case Reports." *Literature and Medicine* 25.2 (2006): 216-40. Print.
Hustvedt, Siri. *The Blazing World*. New York: Simon & Schuster, 2014. Print.
—."Borderlands: First, Second, and Third Person Adventures in Crossing Disciplines." *American Lives*. Ed. Alfred Hornung. Heidelberg: Winter, 2013. 111-35. Print.
—. "Extracts from a Story of the Wounded Self." *A Plea for Eros*. New York: Henry Holt, 2006. 195-228. Print.
—. *The Shaking Woman or A History of My Nerves*. New York: Henry Holt, 2010. Print.
—. *Sorrows of an American*. New York: St. Martin's Press, 2008 . Print.
—. *The Summer Without Men*. New York: Picador, 2011. Print.
—. *What I Loved*. New York: Picador, 2003. Print.
Huxley, Julian. "Evolution: The Modern Synthesis." *Darwin: Texts, Backgrounds, Contemporary Opinion, Critical Essays*. Ed. Philip Appleman. New York: Norton, 1970. 244-65. Print.
Iacoboni, Marco. "The Problem of Other Minds is not a Problem: Mirror Neurons and Intersubjectivity." *Mirror Neuron Systems*. Ed. Jaime Pineda. New York: Springer, 2009. 121-33. Print.
—. *Woher wir wissen, was andere denken und fühlen. Die neue Wissenschaft der Spiegelneuronen*. Trans. Susanne Kuhlmann-Krieg. München: Deutsche Verlags-Anstalt, 2009. Print.
Illouz, Eva. *Die Errettung der Modernen Seele: Therapien, Gefühle und die Kultur der Selbsthilfe*. 1st ed. Frankfurt: Suhrkamp, 2009. Print.
Individuals with Disabilities Education Act. Part B, Sec. 611. 3 Dec. 2004. Web. 23 Sept. 2014.
Inckle, Kay. "A Lame Argument: Profoundly Disabled Embodiment as Critical Gender Politics." *Disability & Society* 29.3 (2014): 388-401. Print.
Johnson, Merri Lisa, and Robert McRuer. "Cripistemologies: Introduction." *Journal of Literary & Cultural Disability Studies* 8.2 (2014): 127-47. Print.
Johnston, Chris. "'Exhausted' Readers Shun Celebrity Memoirs as Autobiography Sales Fall." *The Guardian*. 20 Dec. 2014. Web. 5 Jan. 2015.
Junker, Thomas. "Charles Darwin und die Allmacht der Naturzüchtung." *Darwin und die Bioethik: Eve-Marie Engels zum 60. Geburtstag*. Ed. László Kovács. Freiburg: Alber, 2011. 43-54. Print.
Jurecic, Ann. *Illness as Narrative*. Pittsburgh: U of Pittsburgh P, 2012. Print.

Käser, Rudolf. "Metaphern der Krankheit: Krebs." *Lesbarkeit der Kultur: Literaturwissenschaft zwischen Kulturtechnik und Ethnographie*. Eds. Gerhard Neumann and Sigrid Weigel. München: W. Fink, 2000. 323-42. Print.

Katan, Tania. "*The Cancer Journals* by Audre Lorde (1980)." *50 Gay and Lesbian Books Everybody Must Read*. 1st ed. Ed. Richard Canning. New York: Alyson Books, 2009. 267-71. Print.

—. *My One-Night Stand with Cancer*. New York: Alyson Books, 2005. Print.

Keating, AnaLouise. "Myth Smashers, Myth Makers: (Re)Visionary Techniques in the Works of Paula Gunn Allen, Gloria Anzaldúa, and Audre Lorde." *Critical Essays: Gay and Lesbian Writers of Color*. Ed. Emmanuel S. Nelson. New York: Harrington Park Press, 1993. 73-95. Print.

—. *Women Reading Women Writing: Self-invention in Paula Gunn Allen, Gloria Anzaldúa, and Audre Lorde*. Philadelphia: Temple UP, 1996. Print.

Kedrowski, Karen and Marilyn S. Sarow. *Cancer Activism: Gender, Media, and Public Policy*. Chicago: U of Illinois P, 2007. Print.

Kerr, Lisa. "Always the Same Story: Familiar Narrative Structures in Oliver Sacks and Nancy Mairs." *Family Medicine* 42.2 (2010): 97-99. Print.

Khalid, Robina J. "Demilitarizing Disease: Ambivalent Warfare and Audre Lorde's *The Cancer Journals*." *African American Review* 42.3-4 (2008): 697-714. Print.

Kimmich, Allison. "Writing the Body: From Abject to Subject." *a/b Auto/Biography Studies* 13.2 (1998): 223-34. Print.

King, Samantha. *Pink Ribbons, Inc.: Breast Cancer and the Politics of Philanthropy*. Minneapolis: U of Minnesota P, 2006. Print.

Kirmayer, Laurence J. "Broken Narratives: Clinical Encounters and the Poetics of Illness Experience." *Narrative and the Cultural Construction of Illness and Healing*. Eds. Cheryl Mattingly and Linda C. Garro. Berkeley: U of California P, 2000. 153-80. Print.

—. "Mind and Body as Metaphors: Hidden Values in Biomedicine." *Biomedicine Examined*. Eds. Margaret M. Lock and Deborah Gordon. Dordrecht: Kluwer Academic Publishers, 1988. 57-94. Print.

Kleinman, Arthur. *The Illness Narratives: Suffering, Healing, and the Human Condition*. New York: Basic Books, 1988. Print.

Kleinman, Arthur and Rachel Hall-Clifford. "Afterword: Chronicity-Time, Space, and Culture." *Chronic Conditions, Fluid States Chronicity and the Anthropology of Illness*. Eds. Lenore and Carolyn Smith-Morris. New Brunswick: Rutgers UP, 2010. 247-51. Print.

Knopf-Newman, Marcy J. *Beyond Slash, Burn, and Poison: Transforming Breast Cancer Stories into Action*. New Brunswick: Rutgers UP, 2004. Print.

Kushner, Rose. *Breast Cancer: A Personal History and Investigative Report*. New York: Harcourt Brace Janovich, 1975. Print.

Kusnetz, Ella. "The Soul of Oliver Sacks." *The Massachusetts Review* 33.2 (1992): 175-98. Web.

Kuusisto, Stephen. "*The History of My Shoes*: Field Work with Body and Soul." 2007. Web. 20 Nov. 2013.
—. *Planet of the Blind*. London: faber and faber, 1998. Print.
Lambeth, Laurie C. "Fries, Kenny. *The History of My Shoes and the Evolution of Darwin's Theory*." *Disability Studies Quarterly* 28.2 (2008). Web.
Largent, Mark A. "Darwinism in the United States, 1859-1930." in: *The Cambridge Encyclopedia of Darwin and Evolutionary Thought*. Ed. Michael Ruse. Cambridge: Cambridge UP, 2013. 226-34. Print.
Larson, Thomas. *The Memoir and the Memoirist: Reading and Writing Personal Narrative*. Athens: Swallow P/Ohio UP, 2007. Print.
Lasser, Terese and William Kendall Clarke. *Reach to Recovery*. New York: Simon and Schuster, 1972. Print.
LeDoux, Joseph E. *Das Netz der Persönlichkeit: Wie unser Selbst entsteht*. Düsseldorf: de Gruyter, 2003. Print.
Lennon, Kathleen. "Feminist Perspectives on the Body." *Stanford Encyclopedia of Philosophy*. 28 Jun. 2010. Web. 10 Jan. 2015.
Lerner, Barron H. "*First, You Cry*, 25 Years Later." *Journal of Clinical Oncology* 19.11 (2001): 2967-69. Print.
—. *When Illness Goes Public: Celebrity Patients and how We Look at Medicine*. Baltimore: Johns Hopkins UP, 2006. Print.
Levine, George L. *Darwin Loves You: Natural Selection and the Re-Enchantment of the World*. Princeton, Princeton UP, 2006. Print.
—. *Darwin the Writer*. Oxford: Oxford UP, 2011. Print.
Lim, Shirley G.-l. "Academic and Other Memoirs: Memory, Poetry, and the Body." *Ethnic Life Writing and Histories: Genres, Performance, and Culture*. Eds. Rocíco G. Davis, Jaume Aurell, and Ana B. Delgado. Münster: Lit Verlag, 2007. 22-39. Print.
Linton, Simi. "Adaptation is in the Air." *Disability Culture Watch*. 28 June 2007. Web. 26 July 2013.
—. *Claiming Disability: Knowledge and Identity*. New York: New York UP, 1998. Print
—. "Disability Studies/Not Disability Studies." *Disability & Society* 13.4 (1998): 525-39. Print.
—. *My Body Politic: A Memoir*. Ann Arbor: U of Michigan P, 2006. Print.
—. "*My Body Politic: An Illustrated History*." n.d. Web. 18 Aug. 2014.
Linton, Simi and Christian von Tippelskirch. "*Invitation to Dance*." 11 June 2013. Web. 18 Aug. 2014.
Lochlann Jain, Sarah S. "Be Prepared." *Against Health*. Eds. Jonathan Metzl and Anna Kirkland. New York. New York UP, 2010. Print.
—. "Living in Prognosis: Toward and Elegiac Politics." *Representations* 98 (2007): 77-92. Print.

—. "The Prosthetic Imagination: Enabling and Disabling the Prosthesis Trope." *Science, Technology, & Human Values* 24.1 (1999): 31-54. Print.

Lock, Margaret M. and Deborah Gordon (eds.). *Biomedicine Examined*. Dordrecht: Kluwer Academic Publishers, 1988. Print.

Longmore, Paul K. "'Heaven's Special Child': The Making of Poster Children." *The Disability Studies Reader*. 4th ed. Ed. Lennard Davis. New York: Routledge: 2013. 34-41. Print.

—. *Why I Burned My Book, and Other Essays on Disability*. Philadelphia: Temple UP, 2003. Print.

Longmore, Paul K., and Lauri Umansky. "Introduction: Disability History: From the Margins to the Mainstream." *The New Disability History: American Perspectives*. Eds. Paul K. Longmore and Lauri Umansky. New York/London: New York UP, 2001. 1-29. Print.

Lorde, Audre. "A Burst of Light: Living with Cancer." *A Burst of Light*. Ithaca: Firebrand Books, 1988. 49-134. Print.

—. *The Cancer Journals*. 1980. San Francisco: Aunt Lute, 1997. Print.

—. "Uses of the Erotic: The Erotic as Power." *Sister Outsider: Essays and Speeches by Audre Lorde*. Berkley: Crossing Press, 1984. 53-9. Print.

—. *Zami: A New Spelling of My Name*. London: Sheba, 1982. Print.

Lorde, Audre and Adrienne Rich. "An Interview with Audre Lorde." in: *Revising the Word and the World: Essays in Feminist Literary Criticism*. Eds. VeVe A. Clark, Ruth-Ellen B. Joeres and Madelon Sprengnether. Chicago: U of Chicago P, 1993. 13-36. Print.

Loustaunau, Martha O. and Elisa J. Sobo. *The Cultural Context of Health, Illness, and Medicine*. Westport: Bergin & Garvey, 1997. Print.

Love, Susan. *Dr. Susan Love's Breast Book*. Reading: Addison-Wesley, 1991. Print

Luft, Sebastian and Soren Overgaard (eds.). *The Routledge Companion to Phenomenology*. London/New York: Routledge, 2012. Print.

Lupton, Deborah. *Medicine as Culture: Illness, Disease and the Body in Western Societies*. Repr. London: Sage, 1995. Print.

MacArthur, Janet. "Disrupting the Academic Self: Living with Lupus." *Unfitting Stories: Narrative Approaches to Disease, Disability, and Trauma*. Eds. Valerie Raoul, et al. Waterloo: Wilfrid Laurier UP, 2007. 171-79. Print.

MacLachlan, Malcolm. *Embodiment: Clinical, Critical and Cultural Perspectives*. Maidenhead: Open UP, 2004. Print.

Magenau, Jörg. "Kontrollverlust über den eigenen Körper." 2010. Web. 28 Aug. 2012.

Mairs, Nancy. "But First,." *Carnal Acts*. New York: HarperCollins, 1990. 1-18. Print.

—. "Carnal Acts." *Carnal Acts*. New York: HarperCollins, 1990. 81-96. Print.

—. "The Literature of Personal Disaster." *Voice Lessons*. Boston: Beacon Press, 1994. 123-35. Print.

—. *Waist-High in the World: A Life among the Nondisabled.* Boston: Beacon Press, 1996. Print.

Major, William. "Audre Lorde's *The Cancer Journals*: Autopathography as Resistance." *Mosaic: A Journal for the Interdisciplinary Study of Literature* 35.2 (2002): 39-56. Web.

Malhotra, Ravi and Morgan Rowe. *Exploring Disability Identity and Disability Rights through Narrative: Finding a Voice of Their Own.* London: Routledge, 2014. Print.

Marks, Christine. "Hysteria, Doctor-Patient Relationships, and Identity Boundaries in Siri Hustvedt's *What I Loved.*" *Gender Forum. An Internet Journal for Gender Studies* 25 (2009). Web. 13 Dec. 2012.

—. *"I Am Because You Are": Relationality in the Works of Siri Hustvedt.* Heidelberg: Winter, 2014. Print.

—. "The Ill Self, Memory, and Narrative Identity in Siri Hustvedt's Memoir *The Shaking Woman or a History of My Nerves.*" *Living American Studies.* Eds. Mita Banerjee, et al. Heidelberg: Winter, 2010. 75-94. Print.

Massey, Irving. *The Neural Imagination: Aesthetic and Neuroscientific Approaches to the Arts.* 1st ed. Austin: U of Texas P, 2009. Print.

Mattingly, Cheryl. *Healing Dramas and Clinical Plots: The Narrative Structure of Experience.* Cambridge: Cambridge UP, 1998. Print.

Mattlin, Ben. *Miracle Boy Grows Up: How the Disability Rights Revolution Saved My Sanity.* New York: Skyhorse, 2012. Print.

McBryde Johnson, Harriet. *Too Late to Die Young: Nearly True Tales from a Life.* New York: Picador, 2005. Print.

McEntyre, Marilyn C. "Hope in Hard Times: Moments of Epiphany in Illness Narratives." *The Gift of Story: Narrating Hope in a Postmodern World.* Eds. Emily Griesinger and Mark Eaton. Waco: Baylor UP, 2006. 229-45. Print.

McGinn, Colin. *Minds and Bodies: Philosophers and Their Ideas.* New York: Oxford UP, 1997. Print.

McRae, Murdo W. "Oliver Sacks's Neurology of Identity." *The Literature of Science: Perspectives on Popular Scientific Writing.* Ed. Murdo W. McRae. Athens: U of Georgia P, 1993. 97-110. Print.

McRuer, Robert. "Compulsory Able-Bodiedness and Queer/Disabled Existence." *The Disability Studies Reader.* 2nd ed. Ed. Lennard J. Davis. New York/London: Routledge, 2006. 88-99. Print.

—. *Crip Theory: Cultural Signs of Queerness and Disability.* New York: New York UP, 2006. Print.

Medved, Maria I. and Jens Brockmeier. "Talking about the Unthinkable: Neurotrauma and the 'Catastrophic Reaction'." *Health, Illness and Culture: Broken Narratives.* Eds. Lars-Christer Hyden and Jens Brockmeier. New York: Routledge, 2008. 54-72. Print.

—. "Weird Stories: Brain, Mind, and Self." *Beyond Narrative Coherence*. Eds. Matti Hyvärinen et al. Amsterdam: Benjamins, 2010. 17-32. Print.

Merleau-Ponty, Maurice. *Phenomenology of Perception*. 1945. London/New York: Routledge, 2002. Print.

Meyer-Abich, Klaus M. *Was es bedeutet, gesund zu sein: Philosophie der Medizin*. München: Hanser, 2010. Print.

Mihirad, Leigh. "Review: Linton, Simi. *My Body Politic: A Memoir*." *Library Journal* 131.1 (2006): 130. Print.

Mildorf, Jarmila. "Narrative Refashioning and Illness: Doctor-Patient Encounters in Siri Hustvedt's *The Shaking Woman*." Manuscript in review.

Miller, Carolyne. "Genre as Social Action." *Quarterly Journal of Speech* 70 (1984): 151-67. Print.

Miller, Laura. "The Last Word. Scheherazade in the Consulting Room." *New York Times*. 15 June 2003. Web. 11 Feb. 2013.

Miller, Nancy K. "Getting Personal: Autobiography as Cultural Criticism." *Autobiography: Critical Concepts in Literary and Cultural Studies. Vol. III*. Ed. Trev L. Broughton. London/New York: Routledge, 2007. 282-309. Print.

Mintz, Susannah B. "Dear (Embodied) Reader: Life Writing and Disability." *Prose Studies: History, Theory, Criticism* 26.1-2 (2003): 131-52. Print.

—. "Lyric Bodies: Poets on Disability and Masculinity." *PMLA* 127.2 (2012): 248-63.

—. *Unruly Bodies: Life Writing by Women with Disabilities*. Chapel Hill: U of North Carolina P, 2007. Print.

Mishler, Elliot G. "Viewpoint: Critical Perspectives on the Biomedical Model." *Social Contexts of Health, Illness, and Patient Care*. Eds. Elliot G. Mishler et al. Cambridge: Cambridge UP, 1981. 1-23. Print.

Mitchell, David T. "Body Solitaire: The Singular Subject of Disability Autobiography." *Amerian Quarterly* 52.2 (2000): 311-15. Print.

Mitchell, David T. and Sharon L. Snyder. "Introduction: Disability Studies and the Double Bind of Representation." *The Body and Physical Difference: Discourses of Disability*. Eds. David T. Mitchell and Sharon L. Snyder. Ann Arbor: U of Michigan P, 1997. 1-34. Print.

—. *Narrative Prosthesis: Disability and the Dependencies of Discourse*. Ann Arbor: U of Michigan P, 2000. Print.

Mitchell, David T., Sharon L. Snyder and Linda Ware. "'[Every] Child Left Behind': Curricular Cripistemologies and the Crip/Queer Art of Failure." *Journal of Literary & Cultural Disability Studies* 8.3 (2014): 295-313. Print.

Moran, Dermot and Timothy Mooney. *The Phenomenology Reader*. London/New York: Routledge, 2002. Print.

Morris, David B. "How to Speak Postmodern: Medicine, Illness, and Cultural Change." *The Hastings Center Report* 30.6 (2000): 7-16. Print.

—. *Krankheit und Kultur: Plädoyer für ein neues Körperverständnis*. München: Kunstmann, 2000. Print.
Morris, Margaret K. "Audre Lorde: Textual Authority and the Embodied Self." *Frontiers* 23.1 (2002). Web.
Moss, Pamela, and Katherine Teghtsoonian. "Power and Illness: Authority, Bodies, Context." *Contesting Illness: Processes and Practices*. Eds. Pamela Moss and Katherine Teghtsoonian. Toronto: U of Toronto P, 2008. 3-27. Print.
Murphy, Robert. *The Body Silent*. New York: Henry Holt, 1990.
Murray, Craig and B. Harrison. "The Meaning and Experience of Being a Stroke Survivor: An Interpretative Phenomenological Analysis." *Disability and Rehabilitation* 26.13 (2004): 808-16. Print.
Nagel, Thomas. "What Is It Like to Be a Bat?" *The Philosophical Review* 83.4 (1974): 435-50. Web.
Nair, Yasmin. "Kenny Fries' *The History of My Shoes and the Evolution of Darwin's Theory*." 29 Aug. 2007. Web. 26 July 2013.
Nario-Redmond, Michelle. "Simi Linton." *SAGE Reference: Women in Today's World*. n.d. Web. 27 Aug. 2014.
Nettleton, Sarah. *The Sociology of Health and Illness*. Reprint. Cambridge: Polity Press, 1999. Print.
Neuman, Shirley. "'An Appearance Walking in a Forest the Sexes Burn': Autobiography and the Construction of the Feminine Body." *Signature* 2 (1989): 1-26. Print.
Neumann, Brigitte. "Ich bin die zitternde Frau." 2010. Web. 28 Aug. 2012.
Newman, Andy. "Facing Their Scars, and Finding Beauty." *The New York Times*. 18 June 2006. Web. 9 Aug. 2014.
Newman, Sara. *Writing Disability: A Critical History*. Boulder: FirstForumPress, 2013. Print.
Nora, Pierre. *Essais d'ego-histoire*. Paris: Gallimard, 1987. Print.
O'Brien, Alyssa. "Theorizing Feminisms: Breast Cancer Narratives and Reconstructed 'Women.'" *Exclusions in Feminist Thought: Challenging the Boundaries of Womanhood*. Ed. Mary F. Brewer. Brighton/Portland: Sussex Academic P, 2002. 149-66. Print.
O'Brien, Ruth (ed.). *Voices from the Edge: Narratives about the Americans with Disabilities Act*. Oxford: Oxford UP, 2004. Print.
O'Hara, Susan. "The Disability Rights and Independent Living Movement." *Bene Legere: Newsletter of the Library Associates* 55 (2000). Web.
Olney, James. "Autobiography and the Cultural Moment: A Thematic, Historical, and Bibliographical Introduction." in: *Autobiography: Essays Theoretical and Critical*. Ed. James Olney. Princeton: Princeton UP, 1980. 3-27. Print.
Olson, James. *Bathsheba's Breast: Women, Cancer and History*. Baltimore: Johns Hopkins UP, 2002. Print.

Olson, Lester C. "On the Margins of Rhetoric: Audre Lorde Transforming Silence into Language and Action." *Quarterly Journal of Speech* 83.1 (1997): 49-70. Print.

Ortega, Francisco, and Fernando Vidal (eds.). *Neurocultures: Glimpses into an Expanding Universe*. Bern: Peter Lang, 2011

Parsons, Talcott. *The Social System: The Major Exposition of the Author's Conceptual Scheme for the Analysis of the Dynamics of the Social System*. 1951. Toronto: Collier-Macmillan, 1964. Print.

Paul, Sabine. "Zivilisationskrankheiten: Neue Lösungswege der Evolutionären Medizin." *Darwin und die Bioethik: Eve-Marie Engels zum 60. Geburtstag*. Ed. László Kovács. Freiburg: Alber, 2011. 255-69. Print.

Perreault, Jeanne. "'That the Pain Not Be Wasted': Audre Lorde and the Written Self." *a/b Auto/Biography Studies* 4.1 (1988): 1-16. Print.

—. *Writing Selves: Contemporary Feminist Autography*. Minneapolis: U of Minnesota P, 1995. Print.

Pickens, Theri A. "The Body Speaks: Interrogating the Material Body in Contemporary Arab American and African American Literature and Cultural Production." Dissertation. *University of California*, 2010. Print.

Piepmeier, Alison. "Saints, Sages, and Victims: Endorsement of and Resistance to Cultural Stereotypes in Memoirs by Parents of Children with Disabilities." *Disability Studies Quarterly* 32.1 (2012). Web.

Pietrzak-Franger, Monika, and Eckart Voigts. "Introduction: Cultural Reflections on Darwin and Their Historical Evolution." *Reflecting on Darwin*. Eds. Eckart Voigts, Barbara Schaff, and Monika Pietrzak-Franger. Farnham: Ashgate, 2014. 1-13. Print.

Pitts, Mary E. "Reflective Scientists and the Critique of Mechanistic Metaphor." *The Literature of Science: Perspectives on Popular Scientific Writing*. Ed. Murdo W. McRae. Athens: U of Georgia P, 1993. 249-72. Print.

Poirier, Suzanne. "Medical Education and the Embodied Physician." *Literature and Medicine* 25.2 (2006): 522-52. Print.

Pollock, Donald. "Physician Autobiography. Narrative and the Social History of Medicine." *Narrative and the Cultural Construction of Illness and Healing*. Eds. Cheryl Mattingly and Linda C. Garro. Berkeley: U of California P, 2000. 108-27. Print.

Popkin, Jeremy D. "Academic Autobiography." *Auto/Biography and Mediation*. Ed. Alfred Hornung. Heidelberg: Winter, 2010. 195-204. Print.

—. *History, Historians, and Autobiography*. Chicago: U of Chicago P, 2005. Print.

Porter, Roger J. "Figuration and Disfigurement: Herculine Barbin and the Autobiography of the Body." *Prose Studies: History, Theory, Criticism* 14.2 (1991): 122-36. Print.

Porter, Roy. "The Body and the Mind, the Doctor and the Patient: Negotiating Hysteria." *Hysteria beyond Freud*. Eds. Sander L. Gilman, et al. Berkeley: U of California P, 1993. 225-85. Print.

Potts, Laura K. "Publishing the Personal: Autobiographical Narratives of Breast Cancer and the Self." *Ideologies of Breast Cancer: Feminist Perspectives*. Ed. Laura K. Potts. Basingstoke: Macmillan Press, 2000. 98-127. Print.

Price, Reynolds. *A Whole New Life: An Illness and a Healing*. New York: Scribner, 2003. Print.

Quinn, Roseanne L. "Mastectomy, Misogyny, and Media: Toward an Inclusive Politics and Poetics of Breast Cancer." *Violence, Silence, and Anger: Women's Writing as Transgression*. Ed. Deirdre Lashgari. Charlottesville: U of Virginia P, 1995. 267-81. Print.

Quinn-Brauner, Mearah V. "Recovering the Conflicts: Memoirs of the Late-twentieth Century American Literary Academy." Dissertation. *University of Pennsylvania*, 2001. Print.

Rak, Julie. "Are Memoirs Autobiography? A Consideration of Genre and Public Identity." *Genre* 37.3-4 (2004): 305-26. Print.

—. *Boom! Manufacturing Memoir for the Popular Market*. Waterloo: Wilfrid Laurier UP, 2013. Print.

"Rehabilitation." *Oxford English Dictionary*. n.d. Web. 4 Sept. 2013.

Ricciardi, Gabriella. *Autobiographical Representation in Pier Paolo Pasolini and Audre Lorde*. Tübingen: Stauffenburg, 2001. Print.

Richardson, Angelique. "'I differ widely from you': Darwin, Galton and the Culture of Eugenics." *Reflecting on Darwin*. Eds. Eckart Voigts, Barbara Schaff, and Monika Pietrzak-Franger. Farnham: Ashgate, 2014. 17-40. Print.

Richardson, Tina. "Changing Landscapes: Mapping Breast Cancer as an Environmental Justice Issue in Audre Lorde's *The Cancer Journals*." *Restoring the Connection to the Natural World Essays on the African American Environmental Imagination*. Ed. Sylvia Mayer. Münster: Lit, 2003. 129-47. Print.

Richter, Virginia. "Displacing Humans, Reconfiguring Darwin in Contemporary Culture and Theory." *Reflecting on Darwin*. Eds. Eckart Voigts, Barbara Schaff, and Monika Pietrzak-Franger. Farnham: Ashgate, 2014. 147-164. Print.

Rimmon-Kenan, Shlomith. "The Story of 'I': Illness and Narrative Identity." *Narrative* 10.1 (2002): 9-27. Print.

Rollin, Betty. *First, You Cry*. New York: J.B. Lippincott, 1976. Print.

Romdenh-Romluc, Komarine. "Maurice Merleau-Ponty." *The Routledge Companion to Phenomenology*. Sebastian Luft and Soren Overgaard. London/New York: Routledge, 2012. 103-12. Print.

Rose, Nikolas. "The Neurochemical Self and its Anomalies." *Risk and Morality*. Eds. Richard Ericson and Aaron Doyle. Toronto: U of Toronto P, 2003. 407-37. Print.

Rosenberg, Charles. "Introduction: Framing Disease: Illness, Society, and History." *Framing Disease: Studies in Cultural History*. Eds. Charles Rosenberg and Janet Golden. New Brunswick: Rutgers UP: 1992. xiii-xxvi. Print.

Rosenfield, Israel. *The Strange, Familiar and Forgotten: An Anatomy of Consciousness*. New York: Alfred A. Knopf, 1992. Print.

Roulstone, Alan. "Book Review: *My Body Politic: A Memoir*, Simi Linton, 2006; *Out of Joint: A Public and Private Story of Arthritis*, Mary Felstiner, 2005." *Disability & Society* 21.7 (2006): 741-44. Print.

Rousseau, George S. *Nervous Acts: Essays on Literature, Culture and Sensibility*. Basingstoke: Palgrave Macmillan, 2004. Print.

Rousso, Harilyn. *Don't Call Me Inspirational: A Disabled Feminist Talks Back*. Philadelphia: Temple UP, 2013. Print.

Russell, Emily. *Reading Embodied Citizenship: Disability, Narrative, and the Body Politic*. New Brunswick: Rutgers UP, 2011. Print.

Ryan, Marie-Lauren. "Narratology and Cognitive Science: A Problematic Relation." *Style* 44.4 (2010): 469-95. Print.

Sacks, Oliver. *An Anthropologist on Mars*. New York: Knopf, 1995.

—. *Awakenings*. New York: Random House, 1999.

—. "The Bull on the Mountain." *The Norton Book of Personal Essays*. Ed. John Epstein. New York/London: Norton, 1997. 342-58. Print.

—. "Foreword to the 1987 Edition." *The Man with a Shattered World*. 1972. A. R. Luria. Cambridge: Harvard UP, 1987. Print.

—. *A Leg to Stand On*. London: Picador, 1984. Print.

—. "The Leg." *London Review of Books* 4.11 (1982): 3-5. Print.

—. *The Man Who Mistook His Wife for a Hat*. 1985. Basingstoke: Picador, 2011. Print.

—. "Neurology and the Soul." *The New York Times Review of Books* 22 Nov. 1990, 8. Print.

—. *Musicophilia: Tales of Music and the Brain*. Basingstoke: Picador, 2008. Print.

Schiffer, Eckhard. *Wie Gesundheit entsteht: Salutogenese: Schatzsuche statt Fehlerfahndung*. Weinheim: Beltz, 2006. Print.

Schläger, Jürgen, and Gesa Stedman, eds. *The Literary Mind*. Tübingen: Narr, 2008. Print.

Schleier, Curt. "Dr. Oliver Sacks Treats The Brain By Understanding The Heart." *Biography* 2.2 (1998). Web.

Schramme, Thomas. "Einleitung: Die Begriffe ‚Gesundheit' und ‚Krankheit' in der philosophischen Diskussion." *Krankheitstheorien*. 1st ed. Ed. Thomas Schramme. Berlin: Suhrkamp, 2012. 9-37. Print.

Scott, Eugenie C. *Evolution vs. Creationism: An Introduction*. Berkley: U of California P, 2004. Print.

Scull, Andrew. *Hysteria: The Biography*. Oxford: Oxford UP, 2009. Print.

Scully, Jackie Leach. "Disability and the Thinking Body." *Arguing About Disability: Philosophical Perspectives.* Eds. Kristjana Kristiansen, Simo Vehmas, and Tom Shakespeare. London/New York: Routledge, 2009. 56-73. Print.

Shakespeare, Tom. "Review Article: Disability Studies Today and Tomorrow." *Sociology of Health and Illness* 27.1 (2005): 138-48. Print.

Shakespeare, Thomas, and Nicholas Watson. "The Social Model of Disability: An Outdated Ideology?" *Research in Social Science and Disability* 2 (2001): 9-28. Print.

Shapiro, Kevin. "Mystic Chords: *Musicophilia: Tales of Music and the Brain.* (Review)." *Commentary* 124.5 (2007): 73-7. Print.

Showalter, Elaine. *Hystories: Hysterical Epidemics and Modern Culture.* New York: Columbia UP, 1997. Print.

Siebers, Tobin. *Disability Theory.* Ann Arbor: U of Michigan P, 2008. Print.

Silverberg, Cory. "A Review of: *My Body Politic: A Memoir.*" *Journal of Sex & Marital Therapy* 33.2 (2007): 188-90. Print.

Silvers, Anita. "Feminist Perspectives on Disability." *Stanford Encyclopedia of Philosophy.* 4 May 2009. Web. 10 Jan. 2015.

Singer, Linda. *Erotic Welfare: Sexual Theory and Politics in the Age of Epidemic.* Eds. Judith Butler and Maureen MacGrogan. New York/London: Routledge, 1993. Print.

Smith, Sidonie. *A Poetics of Women's Autobiography: Marginality and the Fictions of Self-Representation.* Bloomington: Indiana UP, 1987. Print.

Smith, Sidonie, and Julia Watson. *Reading Autobiography: A Guide for Interpreting Life Narratives.* 2nd ed. Minneapolis: U of Minnesota P, 2005. Print.

Snow, Charles P. *The Two Cultures and a Second Look.* Cambridge: Cambridge UP, 1965. Print.

Society for Disability Studies. "Mission and History." n.d. Web. 21 Aug. 2014.

Sontag, Susan. *Illness as Metaphor.* 1st print. New York: Farrar, Straus and Giroux, 1978. Print.

Spiro, Howard. "When Doctors Get Sick." *Annals of Internal Medicine* 128.2 (1998): 152-54. Print.

Springhall, John. *The Genesis of Mass Culture: Show Business Live in America, 1840-1940.* New York: Palgrave, 2008. Print.

Stacey, Jackie. *Teratologies: A Cultural Study of Cancer.* New York/London: Routledge, 1997. Print.

Stedman, Gesa. "Brain Plots. Neuroscience and the Contemporary Novel." *The Literary Mind.* Eds. Jürgen Schläger and Gesa Stedman. Tübingen: Narr, 2008. 113-24. Print.

Stoller, Paul. "Cancer Rites and the Remission Society." *Harvard Divinity Bulletin* 41.1-2 (2013). Web.

Stone, Jon, Perthen, Jo and Alan Carson. "'A Leg to Stand On' by Oliver Sacks: A Unique Autobiographical Account of Functional Paralysis." *Journal of Neurology, Neurosurgery and Psychiatry* 83 (2012): 864-67. Print.

Stone, Sharon Dale. "Resisting and Illness Label: Disability, Impairment, and Illness." *Contesting Illness: Processes and Practices*. Eds. Pamela Moss and Katherine Teghtsoonian. Toronto: U of Toronto P, 2008. 201-17. Print.

Storey, Robert. *Mimesis and the Human Animal: On the Biogenetic Foundations of Literary Representations*. Evaston: Northwestern UP, 1996. Print.

Svenaeus, Fredrik. "What is Phenomenology of Medicine? Embodiment, Illness, and Being-in-the-World." in: *Health, Illness, and Disease: Philosophical Essays*. Eds. Havi Carel and Rachel Cooper. Durham: Acumen, 2013. 97-111. Print.

Švrljuga, Željka. *Hysteria and Melancholy as Literary Style in the Works of Charlotte Perkins Gilman, Kate Chopin, Zelda Fitzgerald, and Djuna Barnes*. Lewiston: Edwin Mellen Press, 2011. Print.

Thatcher, Carter. "Body Count: Autobiographies by Women Living with Breast Cancer." *Journal of Popular Culture* 36.4 (2003): 653-68. Print.

Thiemann, Anna. "Shaking Patterns of Diagnosis: Siri Hustvedt and Charlotte Perkins Gilman." *Communicating Disease: Cultural Representations of American Medicine*. Eds. Carmen Birkle and Johanna Heil. Heidelberg: Winter, 2013. 365-86. Print.

Thomas, Carol. "How is Disability Understood? An Examination of Sociological Approaches." *Disability & Society* 19.6 (2004): 569-83. Print.

—. "Theorien der Behinderung: Schlüsselkonzepte, Themen und Personen." *Disability Studies: Ein Lesebuch*. Eds. Jan Weisser and Cornelia Renggli. Luzern: SZH/CSPS, 2004. 31-56. Print.

Torrell, Margaret R. "Plural Singularities: The Disability Community in Life-Writing Texts." *Journal of Literary & Cultural Disability Studies* 5.3 (2011): 321-38. Print.

Tougaw, Jason. "Autobiography of a Brain." 2012. Web. 11 Dec. 2012.

—. "Brain Memoirs, Neuroscience, and the Self: A Review Article." *Literature and Medicine* 30.1 (2012): 171-92. Print.

—. *Strange Cases: The Medical Case History and the British Novel*. New York: Routledge, 2006. Print.

Troxell, Jane. "Exposing the Scars: An Interview with Kenny Fries." *Lambda Book Report* 5 (1997): 6-7. Print.

Turner, Victor. *The Ritual Process: Structure and Anti-Structure*. Ithaca: Cornell UP, 1969. Print.

U.S. Census Bureau. "Americans with Disabilities: 2010." 25 July 2012. Web. 20 Dec. 2014.

Vidal, Fernando. "Brainhood: Anthropological Figure of Modernity." *History of the Human Sciences* 22.1 (2009): 5-36. Print.

Vignemont, Frédérique de. "Bodily Awareness." *Stanford Encyclopedia of Philosophy*. 2011. Web. 22 Feb. 2012.
Waites, Kathleen J. "Memoir." *Encyclopedia of Women's Autobiography. Vol. 2: K-Z*. Eds. Victoria Boynton and Jo Malin. Westport: Greenwood P, 2005. 379-81. Print.
Wallace, Jeff. "Introduction: Difficulty and Defamiliarisation – Language and Process in *The Origin of Species*." *Charles Darwin's* The Origin of Species: *New Interdisciplinary Essays*. Eds. David Amigoni and Jeff Wallace. Manchester: Manchester UP, 1995. 1-46. Print.
Wallace-Wells, David. "A Brain with a Heart." *New York Magazine*. 2012. Web. 3 Dec. 2012.
Wallis, Katherine E. "At Play in Her Clearing: Centering the Personal Experience of Physical Disability within Irigarayan Philosophy." M.A. Thesis. *University of Texas*, 2009. Print.
Waples, Emily. "Avatars, Authority: Embodied Experience in Autopathographics." *Configurations* 22.2 (2014): 153-81. Print.
Ward Brian, Schiller Jeannie, and Richard Goodman. "Multiple Chronic Conditions among US Adults: A 2012 Update." *Preventing Chronic Disease 11* (2014). Web.
Wasserstein, Alan G. "Toward a Romantic Science: The Work of Oliver Sacks." *Annals of Internal Medicine* 109.5 (1988): 440-44. Print.
Waxman, Barbara F. *To Live in the Center of the Moment: Literary Autobiographies of Aging*. Charlottesville: UP of Virginia, 1997. Print.
Wear, Delese and Lois L. Nixon. *Literary Anatomies: Women's Bodies and Health in Literature*. Albany: State U of New York P, 1994. Print.
Weber, Ingeborg. "'I Feel, Therefore I Can Be Free': Audre Lordes autobiographische Subjectkonstruktion im Spannungsfeld von Kultur und Körper." *Spannung: Studien zur englischsprachigen Literatur (Für Ulrich Suerbaum zum 75. Geburtstag)*. Eds. Raimund Borgmeier and Peter Wenzel. Trier: wvt, 2001. 240-51. Print.
Weitz, Rose. *The Sociology of Health, Illness, and Health Care: A Critical Approach*. Belmont: Wadsworth Pub, 1996. Print.
Wendell, Susan. *The Rejected Body: Feminist Philosophical Reflections on Disability*. New York: Routledge, 1996. Print.
—. "Toward a Feminist Theory of Disability." *The Disability Studies Reader*. Ed. Lennard J. Davis. New York: Routledge, 1997. 260-78. Print.
—. "Unhealthy Disabled: Treating Chronic Illnesses as Disabilities." *Hypatia* 16.4 (2001): 17-33. Print.
Wexler, Alice. *Mapping Fate: A Memoir of Family, Risk, and Genetic Research*. Berkeley: U of California P, 1996. Print.

Wilkerson, Abby. "Disability, Sex Radicalism, and Political Agency." *Feminist Disability Studies*. Ed. Kim Q. Hall. Bloomington: Indiana UP, 2011. 193-217. Print.

Wilson, James C., and Cynthia Lewiecki-Wilson. "Disability, Rhetoric, and the Body." *Embodied Rhetorics: Disability in Language and Culture*. Eds. James C. Wilson and Cynthia Lewiecki-Wilson. Carbondale: Southern Illinois UP, 2001. 1-24. Print.

Windisch, Monika. *Behinderung, Geschlecht, soziale Ungleichheit: Intersektionelle Perspektiven*. Bielefeld: transcript, 2014.

Whitlock, Gillian. "Disciplining the Child: Recent British Academic Memoir." *a/b: Auto/Biography Studies* 19.1-2 (2004): 46-58. Print.

Wood, David H. "'Fluster'd with flowing cups': Alcoholism, Humoralism, and the Prosthetic Narrative in *Othello*." *Disability Studies Quarterly* 29.4 (2009). Web.

Woods, Angela. "Beyond the Wounded Storyteller: Rethinking Illness, Narrativity, and Embodied Self-Experience." *Health, Illness, and Disease: Philosophical Essays*. Eds. Havi Carel and Rachel Cooper. Durham: Acumen, 2013. 113-28. Print.

World Health Organization. "WHO Definition of Health." 2003. Web. 7 Nov. 2014.

Wu, Cynthia. "Marked Bodies, Marked Time: Reclaiming the Warrior in Audre Lorde's *The Cancer Journals*." *a/b Auto/Biography Studies* 17.2 (2002): 245-61. Print.

Yagoda, Ben. *Memoir: A History*. New Haven: Riverhead Books, 2009. Print.

Zahavi, Dan. *Phänomenologie für Einsteiger*. Paderborn: Fink, 2007. Print.

Zola, Irving K. "Bringing Our Bodies and Ourselves Back In: Reflections on the Past, Present, and Future of 'Medical Sociology.'" *Journal of Health and Social Behavior* 32.1 (1991): 1-16. Print.